RADICAL PACIFISTS
IN ANTEBELLUM AMERICA

PETER BROCK

Augsburg College
Lindell Library
Minneapolis, MN 55454

PRINCETON UNIVERSITY PRESS
PRINCETON, NEW JERSEY
1968

Copyright © 1968 by Princeton University Press
ALL RIGHTS RESERVED
Printed in the United States of America
by Princeton University Press, Princeton, New Jersey
This book has been composed in Linotype Caledonia

This book is sold subject to the condition that it shall not, by way of trade, be lent, resold, hired out, or otherwise disposed of without the publisher's consent, in any form of binding or cover other than that in which it is published.

RADICAL PACIFISTS
IN ANTEBELLUM AMERICA

To Carmen

Preface

The present volume forms part of a more extensive book, *Pacifism in the United States: From the Colonial Era to the First World War* (Princeton University Press, 1968). Chapters 10-17 of this larger work are reprinted here in full as chapters 1-8. The present Prologue and Epilogue are drawn mainly from the larger work, too. The Appendix is reprinted, with the permission of the editor, from *Quaker History*, vol. 54, no. 2 (Autumn 1965).

PETER BROCK

Toronto, Ontario, Canada
1 July 1968

Contents

Preface	vii
Prologue	xi
1. Pioneers of the American Peace Movement: Dodge and Worcester	3
2. The American Peace Society: The First Decade	36
3. The Genesis of the Garrisonian Formula: No-Government and Nonresistance	77
4. The New England Non-Resistance Society	113
5. The Ideology of the New England Non-Resistance Society	139
6. The Moderate Pacifists and the League of Universal Brotherhood	170
7. The Ebbing of the Pacifist Impulse	221
8. The Civil War and the Antebellum Pacifists	240
Epilogue	264
Appendix: Quakers and the Antebellum Peace Movement	268
Bibliography	281
Index	293

Prologue

Pacifism in North America grew out of European roots. Its origins can be traced back to the nonresistant sects that arose in Europe in the period opened by the Protestant Reformation. But in the course of several centuries, after transplantation to the New World, it developed characteristics of its own. It acquired an autonomous existence, so that, although there continued to be interconnection between the peace sectaries of the two continents, pacifist thought and practice took on some of the coloring of its native American environment. It ceased to represent merely a reflection of, an overflow from, modes of thought and feeling that had matured in the Old World. Faced with fresh problems and with new demands on the part of a society that usually remained as firmly resistant as ever to the pacifist ethos, American pacifists—despite the traditionalism that was a major ingredient in the outlook of all the peace sectaries, at least—were eventually forced to rethink inherited positions and to devise new strategies and new arguments to meet situations that could not easily have been foreseen in their Old World environment.

This transformation happened within the first half century of the arrival on the American continent of the Quakers, the first group to implant there the lasting seed of a nonviolent ethic. In the first place, early American Quakers—the original immigrants would, of course, have regarded themselves rather as English or Scottish, Irish or Welsh, German or Dutch Quakers, according to the place of their origin—were required to exemplify their belief in nonviolence personally in ways that had seldom been practised back in the old country.

The first Quaker to arrive on the American continent reached these shores in 1656, barely half a decade after the crystallization under the leadership of George Fox (1624-1691) of a Quaker Society of Friends in Britain. For the Quakers, who now began to emigrate in increasing numbers, the environment they met was, indeed, in many ways quite new. For instance, an Indian on the warpath, inflamed to savagery by repeated acts of injustice and cruelty suffered at the hands of white settlers, was a novel phenomenon for those New England Quakers (the first, apparently, among Friends who had to cope with a situation of this kind) who were now caught up in the midst of interracial warfare. They, too, in the beginning had been persecuted, and then barely tolerated, by the Puritan regimes of Massachusetts and Connecticut; but they were of the same color and origin as the Indians' enemies and were liable, therefore, to become victims of their rage. Might they not, living as they did, dispersed among a non-Quaker white population, seek protection, if not in arms, at least in the fortified places provided by their fellow citizens?

A similar situation faced the isolated Quaker communities scattered throughout the islands of the British West Indies; only, in place of angry redskins, there were the equally menacing pirates or privateers of varied European extraction and, in the seat of white government, not pious Puritans, but blustering colonial officials and tough-minded planters. Dissociation from the power structure, so far as possible, and reliance on the reconciling force of the spirit as manifested in calm behavior—this, broadly, was the strategy Quakers employed in conflict situations.

Yet power and pacifism could not so easily be dissociated in all circumstances attending the Quaker plantation in America. First in the colony of Rhode Island (where the Quaker response was ambiguous) and then more emphatically in the Quaker commonwealth of Pennsylvania, founded in 1682 by William Penn (1644-1718), Friends attempted to mediate between reasons of state and the demands of the law of love. Just as American Indian warfare and the West Indian piracy posed problems for the practical implementation of a nonviolent way of life that had not been presented by the occasional highwayman or marauder in Britain, so the establishment of a Holy Experiment in government faced Friends with dilemmas scarcely dreamed of back in Britain, where even the Glorious Revolution of 1688 meant no relaxation in the will to exclude Quakers and other dissenters from any share of government. Quaker rule in Pennsylvania, therefore, constitutes a second area where, comparatively early, the Quaker peace testimony underwent subtle permutations in adapting itself to its American environment.

However, while the Quaker politicians of Pennsylvania (and Rhode Island) attempted, especially in the later phases of their rule, to pare down their Society's repudiation of war until it came to have scarcely any relevance on the political level, radicals within Pennsylvania Yearly Meeting, like John Woolman (1720-1772), strove to give their peace testimony new meaning by sensitizing Friends' minds to its implications and by making them aware of the full significance of a religious community dedicated to the path of nonviolence. At the very moment in 1756 when Quaker government petered out, Woolman and his associates were exploring new ways of making Quaker pacifism a more vital belief. Whether in their reexamination of the tax issue or in their struggle to free their Society from the taint of slaveholding (in which they rightly detected the hidden seeds of war) or in their first stumbling efforts to relate their views on war to inequalities in the social order, these Friends were pioneers. Their radicalism was a country radicalism, based mainly on the rural meetings of Pennsylvania and New Jersey rather than on the still influential city meetings of Philadelphia with their strongly ingrained politicism; the pacifist rigorism of the radicals, like many other of their sociopolitical beliefs, was homespun from the same cloth that produced the agrarian democracy of the early American republic.

In the Revolution, it is true, Quakers had obtained a reputation for "Toryism," for pro-British sympathies. And certainly, even in the country meetings, traditionalism of a kind long held sway as much as did social conservatism among the Quaker grandees of Philadelphia. The history of the Quaker peace testimony in America, indeed, presents, over the first two and a half centuries at least, the interplay of two major forces: inherited norms of social conduct alongside fresh approaches periodically undertaken.

If in early America Quaker rural radicalism and the urban Whig politics of Philadelphia Friends each served, though from opposing standpoints, to integrate the Society's peace testimony with American thought and society as these began gradually to take on shapes distinct from those of the mother country, the rural isolation and cultural ghetto, in which most Mennonites and Dunkers and other German-speaking nonresistant sects lived after their arrival in America from the last quarter of the seventeenth century onward, tended to freeze their thinking and practice on the issue of peace, as on other aspects of their creed, at the stage reached immediately prior to their departure for the New World. In one group, however—the Moravians—acculturation proceeded more rapidly and brought with it around the turn of the eighteenth century (if not earlier) the complete abandonment of their objections to military service. Still, the example of the Moravians is scarcely evidence that even a far-reaching integration of sect with society must inevitably entail the repudiation of a pacifist stance. It does show, though, that this is likely if no steps are taken to adapt items of the ancestral faith to meet the exigencies of a novel and changing environment.

The American frontier left its impact on the peace sectaries of this continent, changing their outlook on state and society. The changes were greatest when frontier conditions were experienced by groups migrating from the more cultivated societies of the eastern seaboard, where contact with the Old World was always fairly closely maintained, to the wilderness of the West. But the effect of this experience on the evolution of the peace testimony among the Quaker communities of the areas opened up by the westward migration differed radically from the response it brought out from the German-speaking nonresistant groups. These groups, on account of language, way of life, and rural habitat, had become largely closed societies. True, the evangelical and revival movements of the nineteenth century succeeded in breaking through in certain areas. But acculturation to American society on a wide scale was to come only in the twentieth century with the spread of urbanization to these communities. The contours of Mennonite and Dunker pacifism, therefore, were—at least externally—to remain much the same until the end of the nineteenth century. And this stability was almost as typical of their churches in the eastern states as of those in the Midwest.

The Society of Friends, on the other hand, owing to its use of the English language and the closer assimilation of its members to the American milieu (and for all its distinctive and rigorously upheld peculiarities of speech and dress, conduct and thought, and religious practice) was a more open community. The Society's adaptability led much more easily to the eventual infiltration of new modes of religious thought, not only in its old habitat but in the novel environment of the frontier areas. For this reason, too, the Society in the new communities received an inflow of fresh recruits, many of whom were unprepared to assimilate important aspects of Quaker belief, including its peace testimony. However, the full impact of this process did not appear fully until the present century.

The pacifism not only of the Quakers, Mennonites, and Dunkers but of various other smaller religious groups was a sectarian pacifism. Adherence to it was conditioned by acceptance of the other tenets of the sect; its outreach, therefore, was limited by the missionary potentiality of the sect. The German-speaking peace sects, even before their departure for North America, and the Quakers, too, within a half century or so of their arrival, ceased for some time to be effective proselytizing agencies; even the militant Shakers fairly soon contracted their activities to await the millennium within the confines of their little communities. Thus the impact on American society at large of a philosophy of nonviolence as formulated by these groups was necessarily limited. While the constitutional claims and practices of early eighteenth-century Pennsylvania Quakers found a ready response in wide circles of politically conscious Americans, the pacifism of the Society of Friends, since it was presented as an integral part of a sectarian ethic, had only a very limited influence, at least on contemporaries.

The conclusion of the War of 1812 and of the Napoleonic struggle in Europe saw the birth of a nonsectarian peace movement uniting—

somewhat uneasily, it is true—both nonpacifist workers in the cause of permanent and universal peace and believers in one form or another in a nonviolent approach in national and international affairs. Although with both wings of the movement the primary inspiration remained religious, the peace issue was detached from its association with the discipline and theology of any one sect. A parallel movement had developed in Britain (and, less effectively, on the European continent). But the American peace societies of the nineteenth century arose independently and, for all their ideological roots in the Old World and the continuous interchange of ideas and personalities between America and Europe, remained an integral part of the great American reform movement that ranged from millennialism and utopian communitarianism to a motley variety of humanitarian crusades.

The pages that follow tell the story of the pacifists, both the less and the more radical, who formed the most vigorous element within the wider antebellum peace movement. Sometimes they worked alongside, at other times they fiercely opposed, those peace workers who did not share their objections to all war. From the conflict of ideas, both within the peace movement and with opponents outside its ranks, modern American pacifism was born.

RADICAL PACIFISTS
IN ANTEBELLUM AMERICA

Chapter 1

Pioneers of the American Peace Movement: Dodge and Worcester

I

An organized peace movement on the American continent dates from the conclusion of the Napoleonic wars.[1] Before 1815 the pacifist position had been almost entirely confined to the peace sects: Quakers, Mennonites, Dunkers, and several smaller bodies. Outside these groups, it is true, an isolated individual in one of the other churches would very occasionally raise his voice in protest against all Christian participation in war; during the Revolutionary War, too, as shown in *Pacifism in the U.S.*, there have come to light cases involving conscientious objectors against militia service who had no affiliation with any of the pacifist sects. But it is not really until the early decades of the nineteenth century, a period of continuous war back in Europe, that we discover other pacifist stirrings alongside the peace testimony of the sects. Indeed, a growing number among the clergy, though still only a handful, had now begun to attack the institution of war in general terms on both Christian and humanitarian grounds; and to this censure was added, after the outbreak in 1812 of hostilities between the United States and Britain, a wave of political opposition to the war throughout the New England states, although it derived more from the injury the conflict threatened to the economic interests of the area than from a moral repugnance to the waging of war itself.

In the War of 1812 conscientious objection was still confined almost exclusively to the peace sects. However, the recorded cases of Baalis Bullard of Uxbridge (Mass.) and of Joshua P. Blanchard (1782-1868), who was later to become a veteran member of the peace movement, are not likely to have been the only ones involving men who did not share this sectarian background. Bullard (described in his obituary as "a real Puritan, inflexible in his adherence to what he deemed

---

[1] The most important studies of the subject are Merle E. Curti, *The American Peace Crusade*, and W. Freeman Galpin, *Pioneering for Peace*. See also Christina Phelps, *The Anglo-American Peace Movement in the Mid-Nineteenth Century*, passim; A.C.F. Beales, *The History of Peace*, passim; Alice Felt Tyler, *Freedom's Ferment*, pt. III, chap. 15; Frank Thistlethwaite, *America and the Atlantic Community: Anglo-American Aspects 1790-1850*, pp. 96-102.

right"),[2] whose decision to refuse military service stemmed "from his solitary study of the Gospel," petitioned the Massachusetts legislature for exemption "on the ground of conscientious scruples," and presumably it was given to him. He was later to become a deacon and a pillar of his local Congregational church.

More significant for the future than these isolated witnesses for peace was the conversion to pacifism in the latter years of the Napoleonic struggle of a prosperous New York merchant, David Low Dodge (1774-1852),[3] with whose activities the organized peace movement in America really begins. Dodge was a largely self-taught and self-made man, who had worked his way up from a humble Connecticut farmstead to considerable affluence as a result of his successful business activities. An elder of the Presbyterian church, rigidly Calvinist in his theology, and a respectable member of middle-class society, he was deeply imbued with the evangelical and philanthropic spirit of his time, and this spirit provided the main source from which his pacifism sprang. For many years, however, he had not questioned the conventional Christian acceptance of war, had exercised with the militia, and had been ready to carry firearms on his business journeys when an outbreak of highway robberies seemed to make this precaution necessary. An incident at an inn where he was spending the night, when he nearly shot the landlord in mistaking him for a robber, led him for the first time to question the compatibility of carrying arms with the profession of a Christian. "I pondered on the event," he writes, "and tried to realize what would have been my situation and feelings had I taken his life; but especially in what light God would have viewed the transaction? I then resolved, by the help of God, to examine the question by the light of revelation, as to the duty of Christians arming themselves with deadly weapons for self-defence."

Over the next three years Dodge studied the question more deeply, finding to his surprise that, whereas the letter and spirit of the gospels seemed to him to rule out armed defense and the prosecution of war by Christians, the theologians and moralists down through the centuries had almost unanimously upheld the right to use force in self-defense or for a just cause. The contradiction worried him. "I struggled hard to satisfy myself that defensive war, in extreme cases, might be tolerated by the Gospel; otherwise, the American revolution could

[2] *Advocate of Peace*, XII (1857), 382.
[3] The source for Dodge's life on which all subsequent accounts are based is his "Autobiography," printed in the *Memorial of Mr. David L. Dodge*. See also Edwin D. Mead, "David Low Dodge: Founder of the First Peace Society," *World Unity* (N.Y.), 1933, XI, no. 6, 365-72; XII, no. 1, 29-36.

4

not be justified."[4] He was puzzled, too, to find that, when he took his doubts to those friends whom he esteemed most highly, they all avoided discussion of the scriptural basis for an opinion on the subject and justified war primarily on grounds of expediency. "In this inquiring state of mind," he writes, "no one circumstance led me so much to doubt the soundness of the sentiments of my opponents as their general want of faith in the promises and providential protection of God; and when I laid aside my pistols, exchanging them for the protection of the Lord God of Hosts, I was no more tormented with the fear of robbers."

In 1808 came his final conversion to the full nonresistant position, the consequence of what appears to have been an almost mystical experience during a nearly fatal attack of spotted fever. The whole question became quite clear to him. "From this period, my war spirit appeared to be crucified and slain." He only regretted that hitherto he had failed to take a public stand against all war; he resolved, therefore, if he recovered, to devote himself henceforward to furthering the cause of peace.[5]

The result appeared the next year in the publication in New York of a small tract entitled *The Mediator's Kingdom not of this World but Spiritual, Heavenly and Divine*. This was Dodge's first literary effort; it appeared anonymously as the work of "an inquirer." The pamphlet made quite a stir at the time, and the first edition of 1,000 copies was sold out within a fortnight. "Three literary gentlemen" replied, also anonymously, to Dodge's arguments, and the latter published a brief answer to their objections. "These publications," writes Dodge, "gave the first impulse in America (if we except the uniform influence of the Friends) to inquiry into the lawfulness of war by Christians."[6]

In his pamphlet[7] Dodge uncompromisingly condemns defensive wars as well as personal self-defense: "that all kinds of war, revenge, and fighting were utterly prohibited under the gospel dispensation we think appears evident not only from the life of our glorious Mediator but from his express precepts." A host of texts from the New Testament, as well as the example of the early Christians, is summoned in support of the thesis that love and forgiveness and prayer can be the Christian's only answer to enmity and hatred. The horrors of the battlefield provoke him to inquire: "Who amongst our fellowmen would

---

[4] Later, Dodge testified (*Memorial*, pp. 90, 101), "my greatest impediment in advocating the doctrines of peace in the United States" lay in "the example of our fathers in the American Revolution."

[5] *Memorial*, pp. 77-81.   [6] *Ibid.*, p. 89.

[7] I have used Mead's edition of 1905, where it is printed on pp. 123-68, along with the later and longer *War Inconsistent with the Religion of Jesus Christ*.

receive the thrust of a sword as an act of kindness?" Existing governments which uphold warfare are pagan, "under Satan's dominion" (on principle, Dodge would neither vote nor hold office),[8] to be obeyed, certainly, but only insofar as they did not require any act—like fighting, for instance, which he dubs "spiritual whoredom" in a Christian—repugnant to a Christian's conscience.

This modest little pamphlet is, indeed, a pioneering work, yet it suffers from several defects. In the first place, the style, overloaded as it is with Biblical quotations and farfetched interpretations of prophetic passages along with its almost apocalyptic tone, makes the work difficult reading—at least for later generations. Secondly, the argument is mainly negative: Dodge nowhere alludes to any alternative to the violent method of resisting evil, beyond a somewhat naive reliance on God's protection. Indeed, it was to be several decades before any of the early pacifists were to come to grips with this problem.

His three critics had in their pamphlet charged Dodge with a willingness in fact, if not in intention, to hand over the law-abiding to the mercies of the wicked.[9] While stating his belief that "peaceable men are not more liable to be assaulted than the retaliating," Dodge in his reply relies mainly on the moral imperative: under the new dispensation, in contrast to the Mosaic, God has commanded Christians to forgive, not to destroy, their enemies. "Until it is proved, from the Scriptures, that destroying an enemy is consistent with forgiving him, we cannot admit the principle of war as a gospel doctrine.[10]

Dodge had refrained from answering his critics in the sarcastic and ironic tone they had employed against him. Courteous and charitable in all his dealings, this respectable New York citizen patiently explained that he had not taken up an unpopular position simply in order to be different; it had, in fact, been a trial for him to have to disagree with so many of his most respected friends, and only a strong sense of duty had driven him to persist in his course.[11] Some of these friends soon began to gain interest in his ideas,[12] and by 1812 the

[8] *Memorial*, p. vii. A twentieth-century Mennonite historian, Guy F. Hershberger, has called Dodge "a nonresistant biblicist who rejected the state and the social order of this world as fully as the nonresistant sects ever did" ("Some Religious Pacifists of the Nineteenth Century," MQR, X, no. 1 [Jan. 1936], 80).
[9] *The Duty of a Christian in a Trying Situation*, pp. 25, 26, 29, 30.
[10] Dodge, *Remarks upon an Anonymous Letter*, pp. 24, 31, 32, 36, 37.
[11] *Ibid.*, pp. 5, 6.
[12] An echo of Dodge's ideas is to be found in the letters written home from Bombay in India by the Rev. Gordon Hall (1784-1826), one of the first missionaries sent out to that country by the American Board of Commissioners for Foreign Missions. Hall, a New Englander by birth and education, writes: "As to war, you may mark me for a thorough Quaker. . . . I wish everybody could read Barclay,

project of forming a peace society in New York had taken shape in the minds of Dodge and these associates. The outbreak of hostilities with Britain, however, caused them to postpone its realization in order to avoid possible confusion of their movement with a purely political opposition to the war. Instead, his friends urged him to prepare a longer essay on the relationship of Christianity and war, which he completed by the end of the year.[13] The publication of his book, which he called *War Inconsistent with the Religion of Jesus Christ*, was held up by its author until the conclusion of the war in 1815 for the same reason that had caused the postponement of the projected peace society.

Dodge had been surprised that, in an age when so many good Christians had had their consciences aroused against institutions such as the slave trade or intemperance, they still remained silent, on the whole, concerning the much greater evil of war. The reason for this indifference, he concluded, lay in the propensity of human nature to accept without questioning time-hallowed institutions and customs—unless aroused by some vigorous and sudden challenge to the evils involved in their continuance.[14] His book was intended as just such a challenge.

His argument against giving any kind of sanction to war or violence is carried on here on several different planes. Fundamentally, of course, its core is religious, but economic and political factors, as well as general humanitarian considerations, are blended in to form a well-knit whole, with the Biblical text taking a subordinate place in the general pattern.

First, there is the economic case against war, as Dodge saw it. War entails both the destruction of property, thus damaging the material interests of the well-to-do classes, and the infliction of great hardship on the poor, who do most of the actual fighting and on whose shoulders finally the cost of war usually rests. "The calamities of war necessarily fall more on the poor than on the rich, because the poor of a country are generally a large majority of its inhabitants." But, even so, Dodge argued in anticipation of Norman Angell in the next century,

---

Clarkson, and Dodge, on this subject." Hall succeeded in converting two evangelically inclined young British officers to his views, and they thereupon resigned from the army. "You must leave the army, or do violence to your conscience," Hall had told them. The correspondence, dated August to October 1813, is reprinted in an 11-page pamphlet, *The Military Profession Unlawful for a Christian* from the 1834 Glasgow edition of Horatio Bardwell, *Memoir of Rev. Gordon Hall, A.M.* For the correspondence, see also the Andover 1834 edition, pp. 80-91.

[13] *Memorial*, p. 95.
[14] Dodge, *War Inconsistent with the Religion of Jesus Christ*, pp. 75-77.

no one really gains from war, not even the wealthy, because war is a waste of man's resources, of God's gifts. "Notwithstanding an avaricious individual or nation may occasionally in war acquire by plunder from their brethren a little wealth, yet they usually lose on the whole more than they gain." Think of the prosperity which would have come, if all the money expended on the destruction of war over the last two decades had gone into peaceful enterprises.[15] Curti has suggested that the losses Dodge's firm had incurred during this period as a result of the seizure of merchandise by the European belligerents led him to consider the economic as well as the strictly religious and moral arguments against war.[16] Such losses at least may have sharpened his pen.

War, in Dodge's view, is not merely economically unprofitable in the long run; it is unsound biologically, too. It kills off the young and healthy, the flower of the human race, who are attracted to enlist because of the false glamor of military life. "To be active in any measure which has a natural tendency to wantonly multiply widows and orphans in a land," pleads Dodge, "is the height of inhumanity as well as daring impiety," for Christian philanthropy must strive to provide for the widowed and fatherless and destitute. Moreover, in addition to corrupting the morals of those who enlist, war leads to a decline in morality in the population at large. Desecration of the Sabbath and spiritual pride, stealing and financial scandals, drunkenness and brawling and gambling, profanity and licentiousness are all concomitants of war. War, too, Dodge holds, is politically absurd, self-defeating, because it is incapable of securing what it sets out to achieve: protection against attack and personal liberty. Above all, military preparations conjure up counter-preparations. Each state wishes to be stronger than the others, an arms race ensues, and the resulting war tends to engulf nation after nation. Because of the hatreds engendered by war and the desire for revenge among the defeated, peace when it comes fails to break the accursed circle. Defense by means of arms proves an illusion. "The pretended distinction between offensive and defensive war," Dodge concludes, "is but a name." Likewise, war and militarism are destructive of civil liberty within a nation, while violent revolution to overthrow despotism usually leads to the imposition of a worse tyranny in its place (a fact which "ought well to be considered by every one of a revolutionary spirit"). History shows that warlike nations have usually lost their liberties. Civic free-

[15] *Ibid.*, pp. 8-11, 28-30.
[16] Curti, *American Peace Crusade*, p. 7.

dom flourishes only in time of peace.[17] The course of recent events in France provided ample proof of this point for the worthy New York merchant.

On the servile condition and moral depravity of that unhappy being, the enlisted man, Dodge also grows eloquent. He is ready to concede that some soldiers may be naturally kind and humane, but their occupation, he claims, forces them to inflict injury and pain on others, hardening their hearts and making them insensitive to human suffering, when Christianity enjoins love and forgiveness of injuries and tenderness toward others. They must risk the likelihood of dying in a state of sin for the sake of the things of this world, which should count for nothing in comparison with the glories of eternal bliss. The life of at least the private soldier, too, is a miserable one, especially in wartime. But this disadvantage is nothing compared to the bondage in which the conscience of the fighting man is kept by the governments of the world. He must always kill when ordered, so that, even if it were possible (which it is not, Dodge again reminds us) to distinguish between defensive wars and wars of aggression, it would still not be practicable for governments, democracies as well as despotisms, to allow the soldier to decide according to his conscience. For this indulgence would undermine military discipline and the country's fighting potential. Moreover, even if an individual soldier might be found here and there ready to risk being shot rather than execute an unjust command, such action would involve him in breaking his previous oath of obedience taken upon entry into the service—which is also a sin in the eyes of God. Thus, Dodge concludes:

> Soldiers actually resign up their consciences to their commanders, without reserving any right to obey only in such cases as they may judge not contrary to the laws of God. Were they at liberty to judge whether commands were morally right or not, before they yielded obedience, it would be totally impracticable for nations to prosecute war.[18]

Dodge, having dealt with the inhumanity of war and its folly, goes on to discuss its "criminality . . . when judged on the principles of the gospels." This charge, of course, constitutes the core of his objection to war and the use of armed force. But his previous utilitarian arguments, it is interesting to observe, are not kept in isolation; instead, they are fused with the purely religious objections to form an integral

---

[17] Dodge, *War Inconsistent* . . . , pp. 16-20, 23-28, 31-33, 36-42, 44-47.
[18] *Ibid.*, pp. 2-6, 14, 15, 42-44, 49-55.

whole. Since war is inhumane and "very unwise" even from a worldly point of view, how much more must it "be wrong for Christians to do anything to promote it, and right to do all in their power to prevent it." But there are, of course, particular reasons grounded in the scriptures why men of religion should renounce war. Here Dodge elaborates many of the arguments used in his pamphlet of 1809, dwelling now more on the spirit of the gospels than on the importance of any one text. Christ taught men to show mercy, to forgive enemies, to put up patiently with oppression, returning only good for evil and love for hatred. All these precepts are completely contrary to the prosecution of war: "the whole trade of war is returning evil for evil: this is a fundamental principle of the system of self-defence." Therefore, if Christ's injunctions were fulfilled in earnest, it would mean an end to the institution of war, which at best aims to accomplish good by evil means. "Christ taught his disciples the doctrines of peace, and commanded them to take up the cross and follow him; to live in peace and follow peace with all men."[19] Repeatedly, Dodge underlines the conclusion to be drawn from this argument, an inference before which many previous writers condemning war on humanitarian and Christian grounds—Erasmus, for instance—had stopped short: that Christians should take no part in war, should refuse to participate in it in any way.

Dodge had expressed his surprise, as we have seen, that so many good Christians who had been aroused to protest against the evils of the slave trade or of intemperance had failed to see the total incompatibility of war and the carrying of arms with the Christian message.[20] To help resolve their doubts he attempts toward the end of his book to answer possible objections that may have been aroused in the minds of his readers.

First come difficulties connected with personal nonresistance and the so-called right of self-defense. In fact, Dodge is careful to point out, this problem, however important it is in itself, has little relevance to the problem of war. "War between nations is a business of calculation and debate, affording so much time for reflection that men need not act from sudden and violent impulse." This might not be the case with an armed attack on one's person, such as was envisaged by the nonpacifist objector. Yet even in this case, in Dodge's view, we must not look to consequences and refuse on that account to follow the Christian way. God is ruler of the universe, and there cannot be two contradictory rules of conduct; both originate from the same source, so

[19] *Ibid.*, pp. 47-49, 56-75.   [20] *Ibid.*, pp. 75-77.

that natural law and the gospels can never conflict. Let the nonresistant trust in God's protection and in the power of love, such as had been exemplified in the history of the Society of Friends, and he would in all likelihood survive.[21]

Dodge goes on to wrestle with a second possible objection. Could not the lawfulness of war be grounded on the books of the Old Testament? Dodge concedes the lawfulness of the wars of Old Testament times, which were approved by God for the Jews under the old dispensation. (Indeed, what good Presbyterian of the early nineteenth century could fail to concede this!) Yet, although it is quite true, he writes, that

> the essence of religion is the same under the present as under the former dispensation, . . . the laws for external conduct under the two dispensations differ widely, and the practice of war involves much of the external conduct of men. It was never right for men to indulge unholy feelings in the act of war, but the external act was required as a means of executing the divine vengeance; the gospel does not command, but seems plainly to forbid, the external act of war. . . . It is perfectly plain that if God should positively command Christians to take the weapons of war and not only repel invasion but actually exterminate nations, it would be their duty to obey, and a refusal would be open rebellion against God. The Old Testament saints received such commands, but Christians have no such authority, which makes a material difference in the circumstances.[22]

The reasoning here seems to belong to an earlier age. More telling for us today is Dodge's further contention that both wars of aggression and slavery, already widely condemned by Christians of his time, might also be justified by an appeal to the Old Testament.

A third line of defense in the armory of his opponents lay in the overwhelming support given to war by the Christian churches down through the centuries. But this, says Dodge, is in fact no proof that they were not in error. Let us look to the gospels and to the example of the early church for the touchstone of conduct. This suggestion leads him, of course, into the familiar discussion of the New Testament texts on the subject. For the pacifism of the early church he draws upon the writings of the church fathers, as well upon Erasmus and the recent work of Thomas Clarkson.[23]

Finally, having disposed of the nonpacifist's objections based on

[21] *Ibid.*, pp. 24, 77-87.   [22] *Ibid.*, pp. 22, 87-99.
[23] *Ibid.*, pp. 99-102, 112, 113, 116-19.

the Old and the New Testaments, Dodge goes on to consider the relationship between the claims of the individual Christian conscience and those of the magistrate. It is not true, he urges, that nonresistance applies only in private life and not in national and international affairs. War and the use of force cannot in this way be brought in through the back door. The teachings of the gospels are universally valid, "so that whatever is morally wrong for every individual must be equally wrong for a collective body." A nation is not an abstraction: "a nation is only a large number of individuals united so as to act collectively as one person." Pacifism does not mean anarchy, the undermining of the authority of the magistrate. For, truly, the powers that be are ordained of God. They are, indeed, serving God—sometimes in spite of their wickedness; so that, for instance, if commanded to go to war, Christians must refuse and suffer the consequences.[24]

Dodge's book remained the most effective American statement of Christian pacifism for some decades, and much of it still remains relevant today. As has been pointed out, many sections are devoted to presenting what is, for all its outmoded theology, essentially a rationalist and humanitarian case against war. The tract is immensely more readable than his effort of 1809. The style is clear and pungent, the argument usually convincing and always buttressed with a wide array of facts, which henceforth became the stock-in-trade of antiwar writers. Above all, his sincerity and moral integrity and his concern for the welfare of his fellowmen shine clearly from its pages. His condemnation of all war was uncompromising. With this slim volume of Dodge's, pacifism takes its place among the reform movements of the age along with antislavery, penal reform, temperance, education, and the many other contemporary manifestations of the spirit of philanthropy.

The coming of peace in 1815 had opened the way for the publication of Dodge's plea for pacifism; the same year also saw the maturing of Dodge's second long delayed project—the creation of an instrument through which to propagate the doctrines of peace. In August 1815 the New York Peace Society came into being with Dodge as its first president. It was probably the first peace society in the world. The idea had been Dodge's (he tells us in his autobiography that he had no knowledge of the efforts along the same lines that were being made

[24] *Ibid.*, pp. 102-12. Among several unpublished works Dodge left at his death in 1852 was an essay on "The Relation of the Church to the World" (see *Memorial*, p. vii). The allegiance of the Christian, he pleads, is solely to Jesus Christ and not to any earthly government, "whose ultimate reliance is the sword." Perhaps he may have come later under the influence of Garrisonian "no-government" ideas.

simultaneously in Massachusetts and back in England), and the driving force behind the Society's work over the next decade and more was to be his, too. At the beginning it numbered between thirty and forty members, mostly solid New York citizens with a sprinkling of well-to-do Quakers and "respectable clergymen" in the city. Within a couple of years membership had doubled, but thereafter it began to decline. "Our object," writes Dodge, "was not to form a popular society," to pursue "a popular course." Instead, by means of discussion in small groups and the circulation of peace literature, the good word was to be disseminated gradually.[25] The small band was to act as a leaven within American society.

What was the program of this first modern peace society? Mead[26] and Curti[27] agree that it came out on a full-fledged nonresistant platform, that it specifically condemned defensive wars along with wars of aggression. Galpin, on the other hand, believes that, if not at first, at least by the time its constitution was published in 1818 its stand was more moderate.[28] Dodge himself writes in his autobiography: "Our articles of association were of the strict kind, against all carnal warfare, whether offensive or defensive, as being wholly opposed to the example of Christ, and the spirit and precepts of the gospel."[29] This was, admittedly, written some years later, but it is unlikely that Dodge's memory would have been completely astray on such an important issue. A careful reading of the Society's first annual report containing its constitution may help to elucidate the matter. There it is stated that the executive committee should be open only to persons "decided in the belief that war is inconsistent with Christianity and the true interests of mankind," only, that is, to Christian nonresistants of Dodge's own stamp. On the other hand, all persons "disposed to aid in the promotion of peace on earth and goodwill to men" (one may be surprised that this category appeared only to embrace three score of the citizens of the city of New York) might, on paying the necessary fee, become ordinary members of the Society.[30] Thus, it would seem that the controlling elements in the Society were all convinced pacifists but that it also attempted to enroll other sincere peace lovers behind its banners. That those among the rank and file who did

---

[25] *Memorial*, pp. 95, 99, 100.
[26] Introduction to *War Inconsistent* . . . , pp. xx-xxii.
[27] *American Peace Crusade*, p. 8.
[28] Galpin, *Pioneering for Peace*, p. 16. However, Galpin quotes a letter written by William Ladd in 1836 to Henry Wright, stating that the New York Peace Society took a stand against all war (p. 108).
[29] *Memorial*, p. 99.
[30] *Report of the New York Peace Society* . . . *1818*, p. 7.

not feel strong enough to accept the whole of the absolutist doctrine grew impatient with the line dictated by Dodge from above is made clear in the following passage in his autobiography:

> The lax doctrines advocated in [the *Friend of Peace*, edited by Noah Worcester: see below] decreased the zeal of some of our members. The investigation of the question upon secular principles turned away the thoughts of some of the members from the divine prohibition of war, to the mere question of its expediency and utility. Doubts began to arise whether, under the light of the gospel, its precepts were equally binding on nations as on individuals. On the other hand it was urged, that all under the light of the gospel were morally bound by its precepts; and if these are binding on every one individually, they must of course be binding on the whole community, or nation. It was further urged against the lax sentiments of the "Friend of Peace," which permitted in extreme cases defensive war, that the gospel made no such distinction, but on the contrary, its most pointed precepts were directly against the principles of defensive war with carnal weapons. So, if it was morally wrong for individuals to quarrel and fight, instead of returning good for evil, it was much more criminal for communities and nations to return evil for evil, and not strive to overcome evil with good.[31]

The membership of the little Society was eminently respectable, decidedly bourgeois, with its Wall Street brokers, merchants and businessmen, clergymen and philanthropic gentlemen active "in the most benevolent enterprises of that day." That Dodge was able to shape it so uncompromisingly in his radical mold is perhaps a tribute to his patent sincerity and the force of his personality. His high hopes at first that "these sentiments would become universal on the fulfilment of the prophecies concerning the prevalence of Christianity" were not to come about within the lifetime of the Society—or his own.[32] The report of 1818 remarks optimistically: "The number of decided friends of Peace upon the basis of Christian principles, and in opposition to all war, is by no means inconsiderable; and of those disposed to inquire into the subject, there are many in almost every town and village." But numbers in the Society did not increase, despite all the efforts of Dodge and his friends with their publication and circulation of tracts on peace, including Dodge's own *Observations on the Kingdom of Peace, under the Benign Reign of Messiah* (1816) in 1,000 copies and those of the Massachusetts and London Peace So-

[31] *Memorial*, p. 101. [32] *Ibid.*, p. 100.

cieties.³³ The resourceful Dodge is said to have packed boxes of the Society's literature along with his own merchandise to help spread the word of peace.³⁴ In 1828, after more than a decade of a somewhat vegetating existence, the New York group decided to fuse with the newly founded American Peace Society (see below), thus becoming merely one of its branches. Its impact on society at large had been minimal, its influence barely perceptible outside the confines of New York City, its membership restricted to a handful of the well-to-do, at whom its propaganda seems to have been mainly directed. Nonetheless, as Galpin writes, "the mere fact . . . that the body held together and kept the peace flag flying was vital and significant."³⁵

Within Dodge's circle of friends there arose several expositions of Christian pacifism that do not, perhaps, have quite the qualities that give special value to the city merchant's treatise on war and are now quite forgotten. But they still have considerable interest as pioneer works in the history of the peace movement.

We may mention first Dodge's own father-in-law, the Rev. Aaron Cleveland (1744-1815), of Norwich (Conn.), well known as an opponent of slavery. Early in the second decade of the century, out of some twenty evangelical clergymen with whom Dodge had been in correspondence—including that militant Calvinist, the Rev. Lyman Beecher—Cleveland alone had come round to Dodge's nonresistant

---

³³ Among the tracts circulated by the New York Peace Society at this time must have been Dodge's own *Observations on the Kingdom of Peace, under the Benign Reign of Messiah*, an 11-page reprint of an address given to the Society in 1816. In it (p. 9) Dodge prophesies: "We, my brethren, live in the last days, under the mediatorial reign of Messiah, when all these glorious events [i.e., the second coming of the Prince of Peace] are to be fulfilled." Another, and slightly less millennial, production of the same year emanating almost certainly from Dodge's circle was Eleazar Lord's *Thoughts on the Practical Advantages of those who hold the Doctrines of Peace, over those who vindicate War*. On p. 20, Lord, who may be described as a forerunner here of modern war resistance, tells his fellow radical pacifists: "Wars . . . will never cease, unless your sentiments and practice are generally complied with . . . it were absurd to hope for such an event, unless the spirit and principles, and practices of war, are first renounced by individuals. War will become unpopular, and fail of support, in proportion as the number of individuals, who embrace the doctrines and habits of peace, is enlarged." The same emphasis on personal renunciation of war is found in the Society's Tract Number III issued in 1818 with the title *The Question of War Reviewed*. Should a "sober," "humane," "conscientious" Christian wait until all have abjured the barbarity of war before doing so himself, the tract's anonymous author asks (p. 13)? "Even should war continue for ever to be perpetrated by the lowest and worst of the species, will that recommend it to such a man . . . ?" War, then, like drink, it is implied, is a sin that must be given up regardless of the consequences.

³⁴ Curti, *American Peace Crusade*, p. 9.

³⁵ *Pioneering for Peace*, p. 18. See also Curti, *American Peace Crusade*, pp. 30, 31, and *Peace or War*, pp. 36, 37.

position, though "for two years [he] disputed every inch of ground."[36] In March 1815, Cleveland preached two sermons on the text "Thou shalt not kill." The spirit and the reasoning are very similar to Dodge's. The Mosaic dispensation, which permitted war at God's behest, has been replaced by the new Christian gospel. Henceforth, the sixth commandment admitted of no exception; Cleveland speaks of "the anti-gospel law of self-preservation." Christ's teaching and practice, and that of the apostles and early church (how useful Clarkson was to be to pacifist-minded divines!), forbade taking life even in self-defense. And this prohibition held for communities and nations, not merely for individuals—more so perhaps, because who in practice could distinguish in the international arena between the attacker and the attacked?

All this was, of course, to become familiar stuff in later pacifist literature, but in 1815 it was novel, daring indeed for a Connecticut Congregationalist minister. Cleveland is perhaps a little more subtle than his son-in-law in his discussion of the limits of pacifism. Here, in fact, he brings to mind the arguments of the sixteenth-century Antitrinitarian, Faustus Socinus (whom he had certainly not read). He is ready, specifically, to give sanction to the coercive power of the state. Moreover, he approves the necessity of "confinements and constraints" on the wicked for the sake of the well-being of society, provided this does not entail the taking of life. Certainly, "the Christian principle of non-resistance" means a readiness for martyrdom such as the apostles and early church had shown. Therefore, even if attacked by an armed man intending to kill—the traditional test case of the anti-pacifist debater—the Christian nonresistant must refrain from taking, or threatening to take, life. "But should you maim him for the purpose of disarming him," Cleveland goes on, "this would not be rendering evil for evil.... Thus you may bind, or maim, or disarm an enemy, and at the same time, act not inconsistently with his best good." To kill a man is always wrong, even in the name of the law or in self-defense. But to kill in repelling an unprovoked attack by some individual or nation is less heinous a sin than to kill where no such excuse exists. But these were borderline cases of mainly theoretical interest. What was important for Cleveland, as for Dodge and most of the early peace advocates, was international war as it existed in practice in their own day, an evil that admitted of no excuse or palliation, a crime of utmost magnitude that was at the same time unfortunately accepted with resignation by the overwhelming majority of their

[36] *Memorial*, pp. 90-92. See also Devere Allen, *The Fight for Peace*, p. 8.

fellow Christians. "Surely, blood-shedding is the crying sin of the world," Cleveland exclaims. He goes on: "Christians by abetting wars, delay the millennium. . . . We may never expect the world to reform in matters of war and blood-shedding, so long as Christians hold swords, and countenance it in others."[37] Here lay the most important sphere of activity for the Christian pacifist.

Dodge and his new Peace Society had another keen supporter in the prominent New York minister, the Rev. Samuel Whelpley (1766-1817)—like Dodge, a devout Presbyterian. In 1815 Whelpley began a series of open letters to Governor Caleb Strong of Massachusetts, "showing war to be inconsistent with the laws of Christ and the good of mankind" (clearly an echo of the title of Dodge's pamphlet). These he later published in book form under the pseudonym "Philadelphus," dedicating the volume to Governor De Witt Clinton of New York. The treatise ran into several editions, being published as late as 1870 by the Peace Association of Friends in America. It is, indeed, an effective propaganda piece for the pacifist cause.

"The question has been agitated of late," Whelpley tells Governor Clinton, "whether Christians have a right to engage in war." He had himself been led to study the matter as a result of the impact of the recent series of bloody revolutions and wars in Europe. "I have been much gratified," he remarks optimistically, "to hear that several societies are already formed for the promotion of the principles of peace. The effects of union and concentration are well known and were never more necessary than in this grand concern. I trust that measures will not be delayed to let the remote and solitary friends of peace, in various parts of the country, know that the subject is under consideration, and that they do not stand alone."[38] In the course of his letters the author presents the results of his own investigations into the problem of war and the Christian. His conclusion, after consideration of the Biblical evidence and the witness of the early church, is a conviction of the complete incompatibility of war "in every form" and of capital punishment, too, with the profession of a Christian. As civilization and knowledge extend, the peace movement would grow. And he appeals to his fellow churchmen to speed the work on: "The change of times, of manners and customs, and of the established religion of nations, seems to lay Christians now under incomparably stronger obligations than ever before, to be pacific, and renounce war and resistance. Surely, if the primitive Christians did not fight, when they had

[37] Aaron Cleveland, *The Life of Man Inviolable by the Laws of Christ*, pp. 3-9, 19, 20, 22, 31, 32, 36-39.
[38] Samuel Whelpley, *Letters addressed to Caleb Strong*, pp. iii, 125.

no other way to save their lives, why should Christians resist and shed blood now, when their religion is established by law, and persecution has ceased through Christendom."[39] Perhaps Whelpley had forgotten here what he had written earlier about the early church falling away from its nonresistant principles, not on account of "her sufferings, but by her prosperity"[40]—or possibly he was just more optimistic, more imbued with current notions of human progress, than his fellow pacifist, the Rev. Cleveland, with his talk of the "dark and depraved world."[41]

The epistolary form used by Whelpley as a vehicle for his ideas deprives his work of the easy sequence into which the arguments in Dodge's treatise fit. It lacks the wealth of illustrative material drawn from the social and economic field that Dodge marshals behind his case against war. The theme of individual conscientious objection is kept in the background. Whelpley, however, is clearer than Dodge (who evidently had difficulty in imagining a government that would be truly Christian) in envisaging the consequences of the adoption of pacifism not only on the individual but also at the national level.

While not excluding the possibility that God might work miracles to protect from injury those following out Christ's example of love and nonresistance, Whelpley cites in support of his case the Quakers' policy of nonbelligerency, which had frequently permitted them to go peaceably about their business unharmed amidst the turmoil of war and rival armies. The results of personal nonviolence in the case of "an individual, refusing from principle to fight or take life on any account" he depicts as follows:

> Let that man go through the world, among all nations, both civilized and savage, and his person will be considered as sacred. This is a known fact, which no one will controvert. He may meet with ignorant savages, who will mistake him for a spy, or an enemy in disguise, and may take his life. But let them once understand that he is perfectly harmless, and they will not hurt him, but treat him with kindness. It must be allowed that they may sometimes lay hands on his property by stealth, or by violence, and may on that account take his life; but this is not common. A man known to be a son of peace, in China, India, Persia, Turkey, Tartary, and among the rudest savages of Africa and America, as well as through all Europe,

[39] *Ibid.*, pp. v, 10-25, 42, 56, 104-12, 122.
[40] *Ibid.*, p. iv.
[41] Cleveland, *The Life of Man Inviolable* . . . , p. 24.

is generally speaking, considered inviolable, both in his person and property.[42]

Not that Whelpley is overly concerned, it should be noted, about the defense of property. Elsewhere he points out the close connection between the pursuit of wealth and the way of violence. Wars (unless they are being waged for that chimera, so-called national honor) turn out more often than not to be sordid businesses of profit and monetary gain.[43] How rarely are they truly wars to protect the life and liberty of the state's citizens. "In fine, if there were no wars but such as are strictly defensive, and none were to kill, but such as have a right to do it on the principle of justice, there would be few wars, and few men would fall in battle."[44]

Never wage an "unjust" war, then, and, in Whelpley's view, one would have gone the better part of the way toward abolishing international war altogether. He does not, however, avoid the issue of what would result for a nation adopting a policy of unilateral disarmament. The common view—that such a nation "would be liable to insult, degradation, oppression and subjugation"—was plausible, certainly; yet it would not stand up, he believed, under close examination. For himself and his family he would opt—"all other circumstances being equal"—to live in a pacifist state rather than in one that was militarily strong and powerful.

Let us suppose, to take a concrete case, that Great Britain disarmed and announced to the world that she had abandoned the use of armed force. What, asks Whelpley, would happen to her? First of all, before embarking on such a course, the government would certainly have taken steps to rectify all outstanding grievances with other nations and thus have removed the main causes of a future war. But more important would be the vast moral influence that such a renunciation of force would exert throughout the civilized world. This, Whelpley believed, would suffice to ward off invasion. "The whole world would say, 'These people make no war: they even refuse to shed blood in their own defence; their dealings are just and honourable; they live in peace; they injure nobody; and shall we invade and seek to destroy them? God forbid!' . . . Should Great Britain declare for peace and non-resistance, it is not probable she would long remain alone, on that ground." True Christians, all the friends of peace, would rally round her. Governments would adopt international arbitration, would set up

[42] Whelpley, *Letters*, pp. iii, 30, 31, 89, 90, 121-23.
[43] *Ibid.*, pp. 117-21.   [44] *Ibid.*, pp. 76, 103.

a supernational tribunal to administer the law of nations, and would use this as a means of settling disputes instead of appealing to the arbitrament of war. Finally, even if in some rare instance a pacifist nation might be invaded by a power-lusting adversary and subjugated, had not this frequently been the fate of nations armed to the teeth? Putting on one side for the moment consideration of the Christian basis of pacifism, Whelpley draws up the balance sheet between a policy of unilateral disarmament and the pursuit of security through armaments. Over against the remote possibility (in his opinion) of invasion of a disarmed nation, we must mark up against war (the inevitable outcome, he thought, of preparation for war) the destruction of life in battle and among the civilian population, the moral wickedness accompanying all armed conflicts and their vast expense, and—not least—the aftermath of human suffering lasting many decades. "War is, therefore, incompatible with the best interests of nations." A nonresistant people would enjoy God's special protection and favor, since only a virtuous nation would be ready to take the first step in renouncing war in this radical way. On grounds of both expediency and Christianity, therefore, unilateral disarmament is the best policy.[45]

A third work on pacifism emanating from Dodge's group came from the pen of Adna Heaton (ca. 1786-1858), who was also a member of the Society of Friends. His *War and Christianity Contrasted*, published in 1816, was a plea to the Protestant churches to complete the Reformation by abandoning their support of war.[46] As a member of the New York Peace Society, Heaton had evidently seen the need, if the Society was to expand, of drawing upon the vast resources represented by church membership. The work is scarcely original—unless it be in the prominence given to Old Testament prophecies of the coming of Christ's kingdom as an argument for pacifism. It draws heavily on the previous writings of Clarkson and Dodge. At the same time, it is simply and clearly written and not excessively weighed down with Biblical citations, which figure so prominently in the writings of many of the early peace advocates. Judged by the membership roll of his Peace Society, however, Heaton's small book can have made little impression.

Among those drawn very largely by their reading of Dodge to espouse complete pacifism may probably also be numbered a young Baptist minister from New England, Daniel Chessman (1787-1839). Chessman's first doubts about the legitimacy of war were aroused in

[45] *Ibid.*, pp. 88-103.
[46] For Heaton's tract, see the article by Robert H. Morgan in *Friend*, vol. 114 (1940), no. 6, pp. 91-93.

1815, soon after the return of peace, when he came upon a small tract against war (very possibly Dodge's effort published around that time) which prompted him to begin a careful examination of the Bible to see what it really said on the question and to discuss the whole matter with his friends. "The more I read, and conversed, and reflected," he relates, "the more my doubts prevailed, the more my mind was shaken," until, finally, he started to put his thoughts down on paper in an effort to clarify his own beliefs. "The result was a complete conviction, that war in all its forms, is contrary to the gospel." "An Essay on Self Defence designed to show that War is inconsistent with Scripture and Reason," a work of some 20,000 words, was finished on 8 June 1816.[47] Its author's attempts to find a publisher were, however, unsuccessful—the time was still premature for the pacifist case to find an easy hearing in America—and so "the Chessman manuscript . . . browning at the edges, the ink fading on the passionate pages" remained undiscovered until a couple of decades ago.[48]

Chessman was quite an able writer, a man of some education—he held degrees from Brown University—and one, too, who obviously felt keenly on the subject of war. Not political considerations, he stressed, but deep religious conviction had led him to compose the essay. "I . . . feel it my duty," he wrote, "to avow my sentiments, and use all my influence to spread the light of the gospel of the Prince of Peace."

In his discussion of the New Testament basis of pacifism and in his pleading of the humanitarian case against war, Chessman has little to say that was not to be said with greater or less eloquence by the other publicists of the contemporary Anglo-American peace movement. On the other hand, he shows greater awareness than some among the latter of the fact that war is not simply the outcome of human sin but is a more complex phenomenon—the result, too, of social maladjustment. While believing that a truly peaceable nation would most likely be secure from attack. Chessman has a vague notion of the need to devise a nonviolent strategy of defense, although he puts forward no concrete proposals. Unlike Dodge, he does not consider that government is incompatible with nonresistance. He conceives of a noninjurious use of force in dealing with the "enemies" of the community. In this case, he sees no parallel between law enforcement and the bringing of serious offenders to justice and the unchristian arbitrament of war. The death penalty and harsh punishments are certainly wrong. But "for incorrigible offenders, confinement to

---

[47] The manuscript is now in the S.C.P.C. See esp. pp. 4-18, 26, 27, 73-76.
[48] See Devere Allen, "Daniel Chessman: An Unheard Voice for Peace." *Friend* (Phila.), 10 July 1952.

labor for a period, or for life, would effectually preserve the peace of society" in a pacifist state, provided it was understood that the prevention of crime, and not revenge, was the object.

In several passages Chessman deals with the position of the conscientious objector. He is opposed to any refusal to pay taxes on the grounds that "they may be appropriated to improper uses," that is, to the support of war. He believes, too, that a pacifist, if called upon to serve in a military capacity, might disengage himself, where possible, by the payment of a fine, "which is the same as a tax." But under no circumstances should a Christian objector agree to perform any kind of military service. In wartime, Chessman advises, "it might be prudent for Christians to retire as far as possible from the bustle of war" to avoid any temptation to abandon the way of nonviolence; for, although he advocated personal nonresistance in case of attack, he realized that there might be situations when it would be extremely difficult for a man, in the heat of the moment, to resist resort to armed defense.

II

While Dodge and his associates were preaching nonresistance down in New York, a second center of peace activities was forming in Boston around the person of the Unitarian minister, the Rev. Noah Worcester (1758-1837). Dodge and Worcester were, indeed, the real founders of the American peace movement, each at the beginning working independently without knowledge of the other's efforts and never wholly united on the means to be pursued toward their common goal of universal peace.

Worcester, like Dodge, had been raised on a small New England farm, and he spent most of his early life in his native New Hampshire. In his childhood he had listened to Quaker views on war, but, whatever fruit they may later have borne, they made little impression on the lad at the time. He had blithely enlisted in the Revolutionary army and felt little or no scruples at that time about participating in war. According to his own account (set down by him in 1822), his conversion to an antiwar stand came only gradually, in stages. The first impulse to serious reflection on the consistency of war with the Christian religion was given him by the minister of the country parish to which he came at the end of the Revolutionary War. The Rev. E. Estabrook, whose antiwar stand is cited briefly in chapter 6 of my larger work, *Pacifism in the United States*, was not the missionary type of pacifist, but he gave Worcester a book examining the arguments both for and against war from a Christian point of view that profoundly affected the young man. Though far from being a pacifist yet, Worcester says of himself: "I could no longer take pleasure in anything of a military nature." Ordained as a Congregational minister (Worcester was later to go over to Unitarianism) and soon Estabrook's successor, Worcester came more and more to feel that all war was a horrible business and that preparation for it, too, was incompatible with Christianity. He began to doubt the propriety of the military chaplain's office. But still, as he wrote later, "my ideas on the subject were dark, perplexed and confused. . . . I did not then understand that all wars are conducted in an offensive as well as defensive manner, nor that the spirit of war is repugnant to the spirit required by the gospel, and exemplified by the Prince of Peace."[49] When Dodge published his little peace tract in 1809 Worcester thought the New Yorker had gone too far in his uncompromising condemnation of all wars.[50] It was the War of 1812, he tells us, that "was the occasion of perfecting the revolution in my mind in regard to the lawfulness of war." He believed the war to be unnecessary for either side, to be "unjust." He preached in favor of peace and felt unable to offer up prayers in church for the success of the republic's arms, becoming, as the struggle progressed, increasingly convinced of the barbarous and unchristian nature of the whole war method as a means of settling disputes.

Out of this conviction of the wrongness of war arose a short treatise to which he gave the title *A Solemn Review of the Custom of War*. It appeared in print in Boston on Christmas Day 1814 just as the Treaty of Ghent bringing the war to an end was being signed in Europe. In the course of writing the little work, says Worcester,

> I became thoroughly convinced that war is the effect of delusion, totally repugnant to the Christian religion and wholly unnecessary except as it becomes necessary from delusion and the basest passions of human nature; that when it is waged for a redress of wrongs, its tendency is to multiply wrongs a hundredfold; and that in principle, the best we can make of it, is doing evil that good may come.[51]

Curti has described the *Solemn Review* as "an epoch-making classic in the history of peace literature." It was to be many times republished and has exerted a very considerable influence on the peace movement since Worcester's day. However, at the time, with the war

---

[49] Henry Ware, Jr., *Memoirs of the Reverend Noah Worcester*, pp. 60-63.
[50] *Memorial*, p. 89.
[51] Ware, *Memoirs of . . . Worcester*, pp. 64, 66, 67.

still on and no organized peace groups in existence to serve as sponsors, it had been impossible to find a publisher for it, and the author paid for its printing himself out of his very modest resources.[52]

Worcester's overriding theme in the pamphlet is the inhumanity and unchristian character of international war and the possibility of its abolition, which was as feasible, he argues, as had been the abolition of the slave trade by the British. He reviews in turn, and refutes, the arguments urged in favor of war: that it has been sanctioned by God through the Old Testament or that it is necessary to redress national wrongs, to defend national honor, and to resist aggression. The Messiah's kingdom, he replies, which has replaced the law of the old dispensation, should be a reign of peace. For the righting of grievances not war, which usually only aggravates the evil, but the formation of "a confederacy of nations" and of "a high court of equity to decide national controversies" is the answer. And as for the danger of aggression and of national humiliation, which it is alleged would result from "a spirit of forbearance on the part of a national government," Worcester points to the experience of two pacifist sects, the Quakers (especially Penn's experiment in Pennsylvania) and the Shakers (whom he must have known in his own New Hampshire), for proof that a policy of peace was most likely to evoke a like spirit in the other party.

War and preparation for war, then, must be "abolished," "banished," from the intercourse of civilized nations. For this end Worcester goes on to plead two further reasons. There is, in the first place, the difficulty in a quarrel between two or more governments of distinguishing which among them is truly the aggressor: a vital point, since wars of aggression by this date were pretty generally condemned among Christians. Secondly, the involvement in war of guilty along with the innocent, which is almost inevitable under modern conditions, makes it ineffective as a moral agent. In most cases, the people actually responsible for an evil national policy escape scot-free in war, while those who had nothing to do with the framing of policy suffer and die for the sins of the rulers. "A mode of revenge or redress which makes no distinction between the innocent and the guilty ought to be discountenanced by every friend to justice and humanity."[53]

Immediate action was necessary if war was ever to be abolished. As a first step, Worcester proposes the organization of peace societies throughout Christendom to put pressure on the governments to pur-

[52] Curti, *American Peace Crusade*, p. 10.
[53] Worcester, *A Solemn Review of the Custom of War* (1904 edn.), pp. 3, 4, 6-12, 14-16.

sue a conciliatory foreign policy and at the same time to spread peace literature among the peoples of the world. Education in peace had a vital role to play in this work and so did organized religion. Worcester pleads for ministers of religion and Bible and missionary societies to join in the crusade alongside the Quakers and Shakers and peace sects.[54]

Worcester, unlike Dodge, was always a gradualist in this question of war. He aimed, by the slow dissemination of the word of peace through societies and convinced individuals, to eliminate war from the civilized world. Dodge always had at the back of his mind—and we can see this train of thought between the lines of all that he wrote —a personal refusal by the Christian man of peace to have anything to do with the work of war. When he read the *Solemn Review*, he regretted what he considered Worcester's prevarication, regarding him as a man of merely half measures. But he adds of Worcester: "He took an intermediate course, as a matter of expediency, rather than his own private sentiments."[55] That, as Dodge hints here,[56] Worcester even as early as this was more radical in his peace views than most writers have thought seems to be true. His message was directed primarily at his fellow Christians; the inconsistency of armed conflict with the gospel teachings was at the heart of his objection to war. It is extremely probable that privately, in the recesses of his heart, he had already come to accept the radical position; at least, if not, he was on the brink of doing so. In his *Solemn Review* Worcester puts forward no plea for "defensive" wars, never urges that in some—however unlikely—circumstances the waging of war is compatible with Christianity. He simply does not come down on either side; he ignores the whole question of the relationship between the Christian witness and the state's demand of military service from the individual citizen. But he does speak glowingly of the peace testimonies of Quakers and Shakers and does not attempt to soften their absolutism. It is the institution of international war, however, that is the real enemy for him; there is no need to cloud the issue by considering the question of individual conscientious objection. The "custom of war" (one of his favorite phrases) must be brought into disrepute and finally eliminated altogether, with arbitration and a world court substituted as a means

[54] *Ibid.*, pp. 5, 18-20. [55] *Memorial*, pp. 89, 90.
[56] Dodge's associate, the Rev. Samuel Whelpley, writing in 1815 in his *Letters* (p. 9), also regards Worcester as then opposed to all war. Joshua Blanchard, on the other hand, who was associated with the Massachusetts Peace Society from 1816 on, writing much later implies that at the time of his joining the Society Worcester still balked at condemning defensive wars as unchristian. See his statement in S. E. Coues's "Peace Album," Harvard University Library, MS Am.635*.

of settling international disputes. This was the most pressing task as the war drew to a close, and the coming era of peace gave promise of the fulfillment of his hopes.

On 28 December 1815—almost exactly a year after the publication of his *Solemn Review*—Worcester, together with a few intimate friends, brought into existence the Massachusetts Peace Society at a meeting held in Boston.[57] The membership list of the new Society was eminently respectable, more august, indeed, than Dodge's New York Peace Society, for it included, in addition to an imposing array of ministers of religion and substantial Boston merchants, "the names of the governor, the lieutenant governor, two respectable judges, the president and several professors of Harvard University." Clearly, from the outset, it accepted persons who did not hold the full pacifist position. Indeed, at first, the nonpacifists easily predominated. Its object was simply to unite all those who wished to exclude the war method as both unchristian and inhumane from the community of civilized nations. As the constitution passed at the opening meeting and designed—as it said—"to embrace the friends of peace of every name, . . . men of different sentiments, both as to politics and religion" expressed it:

> We intend that this society shall be established on principles so broad, as to embrace the friends of peace who differ on this as well as on other subjects. We wish to promote the cause of peace by methods which all Christians must approve,—by exhibiting with all clearness and distinctness the pacific nature of the gospel and by turning the attention of the community to the nature, spirit and causes and effects of war. We hope that by the concurrence of the friends of peace in all nations, and by the gradual illumination of the Christian world, a pacific spirit may be communicated to governments,—and that, in this way, the occasions of war, and the belief of its necessity, will be constantly diminished, till it shall be regarded by all Christians with the same horror with which we now look back on the exploded and barbarous customs of former ages.[58]

There was nothing revolutionary or antipatriotic or subversive, therefore, about Worcester's Society; it was much less uncompromising in its stand than either the New York Peace Society or the London Peace Society set up in the following year. Its main work was to en-

[57] See esp. Curti, *American Peace Crusade*, pp. 11ff.; Galpin, *Pioneering for Peace*, pp. 25ff.
[58] *A Circular Letter from the Massachusetts Peace Society*, pp. 4, 11, 14-16.

lighten public opinion through tracts and articles on the moral iniquity, the economic waste, and the unchristian character of international war. It strove to influence those in high places.[59] It hoped to work through governments (even the Holy Alliance won the Society's praise until the Society became disillusioned with its reactionary policies). At first, the Society appeared to be making fairly good, if slow, progress. In 1818 it had about 1,000 members, including those in local branches outside Boston. But during the twenties numbers began to drop off; with only wavering support now from the branches, the parent Society began to wither. In 1828, like the New York Society, it merged with the newly founded American Peace Society.

It was, indeed, quite a diversified group that Worcester had gathered under the umbrella of his Peace Society. For, in addition to prominent figures in politics and law, education and the ministry, who gave the Society its respectability, there were also a few radicals in it who insisted on condemning all wars, defensive as well as aggressive, and on identifying Christianity with a Quakerlike pacifism. Worcester, as we have seen, was himself sympathetic to this viewpoint. Then there were such men as Joshua P. Blanchard who, despite his well-to-do Boston mercantile background, had consistently refused to serve in the militia and, as we have seen, had been a conscientious objector during the recent war. It may have been their influence that led the Society in 1816 to petition the state legislature against compulsory militia service for those conscientiously opposed to it. (The militia, it is true, was also none too popular in wide circles that had no connection with pacifism.) It asked for the exemption not only of Quaker objectors, "but of all that believe with them that war is inconsistent with Christianity," regardless of which church they belonged to.[60]

The Society was probably responsible, too (though not, perhaps, officially), for an interesting little pamphlet published two years later, which in dialogue form pleads the case for widening the exemption granted hitherto only to Quakers. "Other Christians may have consciences and rights," Mentor argues. What advantage can be derived

[59] But it did not meet with approval everywhere. Ex-President John Adams in 1816, on receiving an invitation from Worcester to become a member of the Society, wrote: "Experience has convinced me, that wars are as necessary, and as inevitable, in our system, as hurricanes, earthquakes and volcanoes. . . . Instead of discouraging a martial spirit, in my opinion it ought to be excited. We have not enough of it to defend us by sea or land. Universal and perpetual peace, appears to me, no more nor less than everlastingly passive obedience and nonresistance. The human flock would soon be fleeced and butchered by one or a few. I cannot therefore, Sir, be a subscriber or a member of your society." (Quoted in Allen, *The Fight for Peace*, pp. 208, 209.)

[60] Curti, *American Peace Crusade*, pp. 21, 30.

by the state from forcing men to serve against their consciences? Furthermore, he asks the skeptical Telemachus, supposing it "to be one article of your religious faith, that public war[61] is absolutely murderous, and perfectly repugnant to the precepts and the spirit of the Messiah, thru' whom you hope to be saved," in this case do you think it fair to be required to pay a fine—like a criminal—in exchange for exemption (as in peacetime was usually done in cases of conscience, instead of putting the objector in prison)? Is not this penalizing a man for doing what he considers right, for following his religious convictions; in fact, is it not an infraction of our constitutional rights? He points out to Telemachus that in their own state of Massachusetts fines and imprisonment had in fact been meted out to a number of young men for refusal to train with the militia; and Mentor reckoned the total number of persons throughout the country holding Quaker views on war to run into many thousands. Finally, of course, the doubting Telemachus is won over by his opponent's arguments in favor of granting complete exemption to objectors from the nonpacifist denominations.[62] The lawmakers of the commonwealth, however, remained unconvinced, and prosecutions for dereliction in regard to militia duties, as we shall see, cropped up from time to time well on into the century.

The same pattern we have observed in the case of the Massachusetts Peace Society, of including radical pacifist and conservative peace worker within one organization, can also be seen in a whole host of small (and mostly short-lived) peace groups that sprang up in various other parts of the country from Georgia in the South to Indiana in the West and Maine in the North, spilling over even into Upper Canada and Nova Scotia.[63] In several of these societies Quaker influence

[61] This term—"public war"—is frequently used by peace advocates like Worcester and Ladd to denote war between states, as distinct from civil war or, of course, self-defense or the use of armed force to maintain the law. Mentor seems to be pleading here for a right to refuse military service, not only for full Christian pacifists outside as well as inside the peace churches but also for men whose objection (naturally, on religious grounds, too) is to international war and not necessarily to all uses of armed force. Such objection is, in fact, what in the twentieth century would be called a political, a selective one. Mentor's plea was, therefore, in harmony with the policy of the Massachusetts Peace Society in not touching the question of personal nonresistance.

[62] *A Dialogue, between Telemachus and Mentor, on the Rights of Conscience, and Military Requisitions*, pp. 2-7, 10.

[63] In the first half of the nineteenth century, seemingly the only known instance from the area that was to become the Dominion of Canada of a person converting to a completely pacifist position (i.e., outside the three peace denominations: Quakers, Mennonites and Amish, and Brethren in Christ) is that involving the Rev. Nathaniel Paul, Baptist minister at Wilberforce Settlement in Upper Canada. His acceptance of pacifism stemmed from a lecture that he had heard given in

was strong—in the Warren County (Ohio) Society, for instance, which antedated Worcester's Society by a few weeks, or in Rhode Island where that doughty (and wealthy) Friend, Moses Brown, was the *spiritus movens*. The fifty or so societies that came into existence during this period appear to have contributed little, if anything, directly to the evolution of pacifist thought. But at least they helped lay the foundations for the development of radical pacifism in the thirties and forties by being the first to plant the seed of peace in the hearts of many a later nonresistant radical.

They proved, also, to be useful fields of activity for those who had already embraced pacifism before becoming connected with any peace society. Take, for instance, the case of the Rev. Henry Holcombe, D.D. (1760-1824), for many years pastor of the First Baptist Church in Philadelphia. The doctor as a young man had served as a soldier in the Revolutionary War. The War of 1812 prompted him to examine the problem of pacifism, but he had concluded then that, if all peaceful means of defending independence and liberty against aggression and tyranny failed, the use of armed force was not in fact contrary to the profession of the Christian.[64] Further reading and meditation, and some knowledge, perhaps, of the Quakers, Mennonites, and Dunkers of his own Pennsylvania, however, caused him to reverse his opinion. At the beginning of the 1820's, as a leading member of the Pennsylvania Peace Society, which he had been instrumental, along with some Quakers, in bringing into being at the end of 1822,[65] he preached radical pacifism from his pulpit and censured communicants in the church and his fellow ministers for giving support, whether active or passive, to the war system. He had no desire, he wrote, to

> ... diminish a particle from the merited eulogy bestowed on thousands for their patriotism and bravery in the revolutionary war. I, implicitly, like many others, held their sentiments, until, at the pressing instance of a learned friend, I was recently led to examine them

---

London in 1835 by the pacifist apostle, George Pilkington, late captain in the Royal Engineers. See Pilkington, *Testimonies of Ministers, of Various Denominations, showing the Unlawfulness to Christians of All Wars*, pp. 35, 36. The only other testimony printed by Pilkington from the New World was from the Quaker evangelical, Elisha Bates.

[64] Holcombe, *The First Fruits, in a Series of Letters*, pp. 135-44.

[65] In 1829, after Holcombe's death, the Pennsylvania Peace Society was responsible for issuing a radical pacifist organ, the *Advocate of Peace and Christian Patriot*. The journal had to close after a few months, however, for lack of funds. In its last issue (vol. I, nos. 10-12 [June 1829]) we find the following typical comment: "As to *defensive* war, it is altogether a vague and indeterminate term; each nation claims to justify itself under this specious pretence" (p. 75).

in the light of the gospel: the result was my cordial renunciation of the principles of war "in its fairest form," as by no means congenial with the religion of our common Lord. I now see, as war is respected, in a new light, his precepts, life, and whole ministry.[66]

It was not enough to renounce only offensive wars; for who in the Christian churches admits to supporting them? Condemnation of wars of aggression alone would leave the door open for the justification of every war that had ever taken place. "After, and above all, where does any inspired writer say, 'Thou shalt not kill,' *except in self-defence?* ... Is not, let me die, rather than kill my brother, the language of every consistent Christian?" Let those who think like him have the courage to come out into the open, to risk being dubbed "a maniac or a Quaker," or losing employment or customers, or offending friends and relatives. He called on all the churches in turn, from Roman Catholic to Congregationalist, to come forth boldly with a similar condemnation of all war as contrary to their Christian religion.[67] The summons of course—it was a century or more too early—remained without response.

Returning now to the dominant figure in the early peace movement —if such a phrase may be used of the mild and sweet-tempered Dr. Worcester—we can detect in the course of the decade following the end of the war a certain radicalization in his public utterances on the peace question. Later historians have usually considered that Worcester throughout his career sanctioned wars of defense in certain circumstances, or at least left the question open. Devere Allen, for instance, describes him as merely "a near-pacifist."[68] On the other hand, his contemporary, the famous Unitarian minister, William Ellery Channing (1780-1842), wrote of this last period in Worcester's life: "On the subject of war, Dr. Worcester adopted opinions which are thought by some to be extreme. He interpreted literally the precept, Resist not evil; and he believed that nations as well as individuals would find safety as well as 'fulfil righteousness' in yielding it literal obedience."[69] And who was in a better position to know the exact state of Worcester's

[66] Holcombe, *The Martial Christian's Manual,* p. 15.
[67] *Ibid.,* pp. 13-20.
[68] Allen, *The Fight for Peace,* pp. 365-69.
[69] Ware, *Memoirs of . . . Worcester,* p. 141. George Beckwith, Ladd's successor as secretary of the A.P.S. and, hence, third in line from Worcester, wrote later of the gradual evolution in the thinking of his two predecessors from a limited justification of some wars to belief in the incompatibility of all warfare with Christian principles. William Ladd himself, on the basis of conversations later with Worcester on the subject, dated the latter's conversion to the complete pacifist position to the mid-1820's. See his *Obstacles and Objections to the Cause of Permanent and Universal Peace,* pp. 4, 5.

thinking on the subject than Channing, who, though not himself a pacifist ("Brother Farley, sometimes we *must* fight!"),[70] was Worcester's close associate from the beginning in the work of the Massachusetts Peace Society? As his whole career would lead one to expect, Worcester never denied that men might be good Christians (many of them better Christians, he said, than himself) and yet believe in the necessity of what they considered purely defensive wars.[71] But an examination of the files of the *Friend of Peace*, the journal which Worcester edited between 1815 and 1828 under the pseudonym "Philo Pacificus" and for which he wrote most of the columns himself, confirms the impression that he had by this time reached the full pacifist position, although—not wishing to create dissension in the ranks of the peace movement—he was careful to avoid pressing his views on those who could not yet follow him so far along the road.

Take, for instance, the imaginary dialogue on the "Duty of Self-Preservation"[72] between "Beza" (the nonpacifist interested in the problem of peace) and "Erasmus" (the supporter of the work of the peace societies), which was published in the third volume of the *Friend of Peace*. It almost certainly comes from Worcester's own pen. Beza begins by asking Erasmus his opinion on the justifiability of defensive wars. He has been worried by the fact that the *Friend of Peace* has printed little or nothing in their favor. Erasmus answers that history cannot show a single example of such a war, that, moreover, the first to start a war is not necessarily the guiltier party. "Every public war," he goes on, "is on both sides a war of aggression.... Hence as wars are generally conducted, the pretended distinction between offensive and defensive war is worse than useless." To justify the latter is, in fact, to justify all wars; to condemn wars of aggression is tantamount to condemning all wars. International conflict should be treated in the same way as the practice of fighting duels. We do not ask who is the aggressor and who the aggrieved; instead, we forbid the practice altogether. In the end, of course, Beza is won over by Erasmus to "the principle that all wars and fightings are antichristian." Nations, like individuals, may do everything to protect themselves and their property from attack—everything, that is, consistent with Christian love and peaceableness, of which war is the complete antithesis. "The precepts of the gospel are the best laws of self-defence and self-preservation, both to individuals and nations." They cannot guarantee, it is true, any more than the war method, absolute immunity from at-

---

[70] Allen, *The Fight for Peace*, p. 368.
[71] Ware, *Memoirs of . . . Worcester*, pp. 68-70.
[72] *Friend of Peace*, III (1824), no. 6, 169-72.

tack and even loss of life. They are more likely, however, to bring security, and they are, besides, morally binding on the followers of Christ.

In 1828 Worcester retired from active work, though he was to live on, a respected figure, for another nine years. Worcester's withdrawal from the scene, which coincided with the creation of a united American Peace Society, gathering together into one fold the scattered peace groups up and down the country, marks the end of the first chapter in the history of the organized peace movement in America.

The movement which, as we have seen, had sprung up spontaneously around 1815 in more than one part of the world ("the world in 1815 had particular reason to be weary of war," writes Curti),[73] had in America grown only very slowly, especially if we compare its progress with the overoptimistic hopes of its leaders and with the exaggerated claims put forward in its publications. It made as yet little headway outside New England. The movement, especially the faith of the radical minority, was widely held to be unpatriotic, directed against the security of the state and the safety of its citizens.[74] Witness, as an illustration of this attitude, the use of pseudonyms by writers like Dodge or Whelpley or Worcester to put forward what they rightly feared would be unpopular views. Not that these men lacked courage or willingness to make sacrifices for the cause; their whole careers show that they were prepared to risk opprobrium and to give freely of their time and money to further what they considered right. But they were a mere handful (despite the weight given by a few dignitaries who supported the work of the Massachusetts Peace Society) pitted against the combined forces of tradition and inertia. They lacked men; they lacked money. They had only boundless enthusiasm and limitless optimism.

Most of these pioneer peace men, the rank and file as well as the leaders, were recruited from members of the larger churches. There were Unitarians, Presbyterians, Congregationalists, Baptists, and Methodists. Episcopalians and Roman Catholics were scarcely, if at all, represented. Officially, of course, the Protestant churches held aloof. Strangely enough, the Society of Friends in America, though their historic peace testimony was a constant inspiration for early pacifist writers—conservatives as well as radicals—contributed (see the

[73] *American Peace Crusade*, p. 4.
[74] The case for defensive war is argued, e.g., by the Rev. Sylvanus Haynes, a Baptist minister from upstate New York, in *A Brief Reply to the Friend of Peace, or A Concise Vindication of Defensive War*, published in 1824. Unlike the authors of some other similar efforts, Haynes is never vituperative in his arguments against the peace men, whose sincerity and goodwill he recognizes.

Appendix) very little directly to the work of the peace groups. A few Quakers, though none were among the most prominent peace leaders, joined the new societies, and some were active in their work. But there was little collaboration between the peace societies and any of the Quaker yearly or quarterly meetings. Dodge, according to Curti,[75] "had a peculiar prejudice against the Quakers"; in New England, on the other hand, many Friends were suspicious of Worcester's group because of its refusal to condemn all war.

The peace societies were predominantly middle-class in composition (though men like Dodge and Worcester had worked their way up from the humble farmhouse), with clergy and teachers and professional men most largely represented. It was at this class of persons that their tracts and pamphlets were primarily directed.[76]

As we read the pacifist literature of this period, we are frequently struck by the naive optimism and the oversimplifications, the kind of thing we meet in the works of the utopian socialists which began to appear around this time. But this is understandable. The pacifists' appeal was primarily, of course, to the scriptures interpreted in a fundamentalist, literalist spirit, as might be expected before the era of Biblical criticism. (The liberal Unitarian, Worcester, was an exception here.) The familiar distinction was made between the old Mosaic dispensation, when the Jews waged righteous wars at God's express command, and the new dispensation ushered in by Christ. Texts, naturally enough, were bandied about by all the writers: the Sermon on the Mount, as it must be with all pacifist exegetes, was the favorite. However, it was the gospel spirit, Christ's law of love that suffuses the whole New Testament, that they exalted rather than the letter of the text. The radicals concluded from the example of the first Christians, as portrayed in the pages of Clarkson's work on the early church, that the performance of military service is incompatible with the profession of a Christian. And nearly all peace writers agreed with the Rev. Whelpley[77] in castigating the professional soldier as little better than a murderer. Many of the pioneers were already elderly before they reached the full pacifist position, or else their clerical profession exempted them from military service. (The office of military chaplain, it should be noted, was regarded with nearly as much disfavor by the conservatives of the movement as by the radicals.) Some young men, however, were to be found outside the peace sects who refused, when called upon, to serve in militia or army.

[75] Curti, *American Peace Crusade*, pp. 16, 17.
[76] See Curti, *Peace or War*, pp. 13, 36, 37; Galpin, *Pioneering for Peace*, pp. 66-71, 210, 211.
[77] *Letters*, pp. 61-63.

The religious objections to war in the writings of these pioneers were buttressed by more secular arguments. Not only the cautious Worcester but the nonresistant Dodge attacked war for its inhumanity[78] and its economic waste; they held it up as an enemy of liberty and morality. Even those who conceded the theoretical possibility of a defensive war were prepared to admit its unlikelihood in practice. The absolute pacifists, on the other hand, were ready to demonstrate that, in fact, a ban on all wars but the "just" would be equivalent to the condemnation of warfare altogether. The radical Whelpley joined with the conservative Worcester in pleading for international arbitration and the establishment of a world court.

This concentration on the evils of war as an institution may explain in part the absence of any serious attempt on the part of the absolute pacifists of this period (with the exception of Whelpley) either to envisage the consequences of a nation adopting a policy of unilateral disarmament or to provide a nonviolent alternative to the war method. We are in most cases told to trust in God and to pray for his protection. If the abandonment of arms is the gospel method, it is binding on all Christians, who must follow it regardless of consequences. True, one could point to the experience of the Quakers, especially with the Indians in Pennsylvania or their story during the Irish rebellion of 1798 as told by Dr. Hancock, to show that pacifism was also a practical policy, that it had proved to be as secure as, perhaps even more secure than, the pursuit of armed might. But the main task of these writers, as they conceived it, was to measure war and the way of arms by the gospel standard, and by humane and civilized values, and to show by how much they fell short. Theirs were thin voices crying in the wilderness. Their aim was to rouse men to the monstrous evils of war and armed force, not to think through the consequences of their abandonment. In view of the thick crust of indifference and downright hostility they had to hew their way through, this latter task might be left to later generations.

From the outset, indeed, the peace movement was divided, as we have seen, over the limits of pacifism. Did it apply only to relations between states and to wars of aggression? Were defensive wars ("so-called," the radicals were careful to qualify) and armed police action consistent with the peace principles of a Christian? Might one plead a genuine conscientious objection to military service for "public war" and yet not oppose the use of arms in self-defense or for the enforcement of the law? How far must the radical pacifist go in refusing

[78] He also condemns it for its cruelty to the innocent animals, who are slaughtered in its battles. See his *War Inconsistent* . . . pp. 6-8.

to collaborate with a state, which depends upon the use of armed force and exacts the penalty of death from its malefactors? Was a pacifist state, indeed, possible at all? Again, must the radical pacifist be a nonresistant; were there even subtle differences of opinion within this last category? All these questions were raised during this early period, and answers attempted according to the beliefs of the different writers. They did not yet, however, threaten to split the movement, which, in any case, was only very loosely organized. Nonresistants and radical pacifists of various shades worked fairly harmoniously alongside the more conservative peace men: in Dodge's New York Peace Society under radical leadership, and with the conservatives in command in the Massachusetts Peace Society and the groups that had arisen under its inspiration. To turn men's minds toward the way of peace, to challenge age-old beliefs in military glory—these tasks were more than enough to occupy the meager forces of the peace societies in those early days. Soon, however, as the radicals grew in strength and influence within the movement and the divergencies in thinking became clearer, the time arrived for a more thorough examination of the principles underlying the practical activities of the peace societies.

Chapter 2

The American Peace Society: The First Decade

The foundation in 1828 of an American Peace Society uniting in some form of loose association the diverse groups which had been active over the last decade and a half marks a new stage in the development of the peace movement. It coincides, too, with a change in the leading figures that directed its work. Worcester retired in the same year, and Dodge had already made his important contribution by that date. The regional societies that they had founded now became merely sections of the national organization—national, however, mainly in name, for New England continued to be the center of the peace movement's activities for some decades to come. Growth, indeed, only came slowly; at the beginning, the new national Society had only about 300 members.[1]

It was on the stalwart former sea captain, William Ladd (1778-1841), that Worcester's mantle had fallen.[2] Ladd became the new Society's acting secretary and the editor of its journal, *Harbinger of Peace*, which started publication in May 1828. The son of a well-to-do merchant, Ladd had exhibited no interest in scholarly studies during his years at Harvard; instead, shortly after graduating, he had gone to sea for a number of years. Forced out of business by the War of 1812, he had settled in Maine on a large farm owned by his family. Ladd loved rural life and country pursuits, and the farm remained his headquarters even later during his hectic years as a peace propagandist. For many years merely lukewarm toward religion, around the year 1818 Ladd experienced within himself a renewal of religious feeling and became an active member of the Congregational church. His interest in peace dated only from the early 1820's when he read Worcester's *Solemn Review*, joined the Maine Peace Society, and became associated, too, with the larger Massachusetts Peace Society. Peace, therefore, was a latecomer among the good causes to which Ladd gave enthusiastic support. But temperance, Sunday schools, home and foreign missions, the welfare of seamen, as well as of the American Indians, and antislavery were in the end all to take second

---
[1] Curti, *American Peace Crusade*, p. 43.
[2] See John Hemmenway, *The Apostle of Peace: Memoir of William Ladd*; Curti, *American Peace Crusade*, pp. 34-36.

place behind the overriding demands of the peace movement. To it Ladd was soon devoting much of his time and energy, writing to the papers and traveling around giving lectures. The captain had a fluent pen and was an excellent speaker.[3] This work was to grow immensely after he took over the helm from Worcester. His influence on the peace movement, writes one of its earliest historians,[4] "was correlative to that of Noah Worcester. He gave it popularity among the people such as Worcester had won for it among thoughtful clergymen. He carried the doctrine among the mass which before had been confined to the study, or despised as the harmless heresy of a few retired minds." He was untiring in his devotion to the cause of peace; as the leading figure in the American Peace Society, he traveled constantly up and down New England and the middle states. "I would impress it on every friend of peace," he had written in 1827, "that he must act as though the peace of the world depended on him alone."[5]

Ladd would only reach the full pacifist position slowly and after much soul-searching; like Worcester, he always remained a moderate. "He was a conservative reformer," writes his successor as secretary of the Society, George Beckwith (1800-1870), who knew him well. Beckwith goes on: "Not William Penn himself was more thorough on peace, yet he preached no crusade against church or state, nor allowed himself to weaken the foundations of either. . . . He did not expect men to come, at a single leap, the whole length of any reform."[6] This sensible, kindly, and tolerant man, who was at the same time practical, not given much to abstract speculations, yet genuinely idealistic and deeply religious, is one of the most attractive figures in the early peace movement. As we watch him making gallant, though not always successful, attempts to curb his own hasty temper after his conversion to the cause of peace, or applying his gift for conciliation and his bluff good humor to a situation threatened by the strife of colleagues, we are struck by his transparent sincerity and his capacity for leading a movement that was already experiencing the growing pains of early manhood. That he was not successful in preventing it from splitting proved only that the underlying differences of approach had outgrown the possibility of keeping all the peace forces within one organization.

[3] According to Dr. Potter of Union College: "The students would hear him for hours, and never grow weary of his anecdotes and illustrations" (letter from Aaron Foster, 7 Feb. 1845, in S. E. Coues's "Peace Album," Harvard University Library, MS Am.635*).
[4] Frederick W. Holland, "The History of the Peace-Cause," B.P.L., MS *5577.98, p. 40.
[5] Quoted in Curti, American Peace Crusade, p. 36.
[6] George C. Beckwith, Eulogy on William Ladd, pp. 18, 19.

The American Peace Society had come into existence in New York on 8 May 1828. As might be expected from the fact that Worcester himself had drawn up its constitution, which was adopted with only small changes,[7] it continued the policies and principles of its predecessor, the Massachusetts Peace Society. It opposed, in Ladd's words, "the custom of war" as unchristian, "subversive of the liberty of mankind, and destructive to their happiness." Its object was to enlighten men's minds concerning war's iniquity and to bring about its eventual abolition. In respect to the troubled question of the legitimacy of so-called wars of defense, Ladd has this to say on the new Society's position in the first issue of its periodical:

> We do not, as a society, agitate the question, whether *defensive* war can be carried on on Christian principles. We receive into our communion all who seek the abolition of war, whether they hold to the lawfulness of defensive war, or condemn all war in every shape —whether they allow a latitude of construction to the injunctions of our Saviour, or take the exact and strict letter of them. We endeavour to avoid all "doubtful disputation," and to walk peaceably with all who will walk with us, whether they go further, or not so far, as the majority of the society.

Ladd adds, however (following Worcester's line of argument mentioned earlier), that the abolition of wars of aggression would, in fact, mean that an end would be put to war as a whole. "Tamerlane and Napoleon called their wars defensive; and all conquerors, from the one to the other, have done the same. *Such* defensive wars we condemn." The whole controversy, he implies, is a bit academic, irrelevant to the real task awaiting them.[8] But, in fact, as Ladd himself remarks in a later issue, the overwhelming majority in the movement were not pacifists.[9] It might include within its active membership men like Blanchard and Dodge and the Quakers, George Benson of Connecticut and Moses Brown of Rhode Island, but at the other extreme it also numbered in its ranks an array of military officers[10] and state officials.

At the outset, in his first issue, Ladd had opened the columns of the *Harbinger of Peace* to discussion of the limits of pacifism. Contributions to the subject would be welcome, he stated. In his capacity as editor, however, he would be strictly neutral between the two parties:

[7] Curti, *American Peace Crusade*, p. 43.
[8] *Harbinger of Peace*, I, no. 1 (May 1828), 6, 7, 17.
[9] *Ibid.*, I, no. 4 (Aug. 1828), 91.
[10] Galpin, *Pioneering for Peace*, p. 215.

the absolute pacifists and the protagonists of the admissibility of defensive wars. "We shall lay no such restraints on our correspondents," he goes on, "and will receive with pleasure, any well written essays on the great cause, should the writer take either side of the question for granted. We have no Procrustean measure by which to gauge our correspondents."[11]

The commonsense, middle-of-the-road attitude which comes out in these remarks is typical of Ladd. Mention a little later of "our own private views" leads one to ask what position Ladd himself had arrived at by this period. The sources do not provide a completely clear answer: at least we cannot exactly date the various stages in the evolution of his views on peace and war. From a perusal of Ladd's signed contributions to the *Harbinger of Peace* during the two years of its existence, as well as the unsigned editorials which presumably were his, also, it seems that he was not far from, if he had not already accepted completely, the full pacifist position. In April 1830, for instance, we find him writing: "We hesitate not to say that from the advent of our Saviour to the present day, there *never has been* a war, in which both sides have not broken his commands. Nor is it at all probable, that there ever will be a war, in which this will not be the case."[12] There is still the element of hesitation that we have noticed with Worcester at a similar stage in his development, an unwillingness to commit himself unreservedly to what many considered an extreme standpoint. But that he had gone far beyond the neutral position which he believed incumbent upon himself to take up officially on this question seems quite clear. Some of his pacifist friends, like Samuel J. May (1797-1871), who as Unitarian minister at Brooklyn (Conn.) was active in his local peace society in Windham County, thought Ladd far too cautious, too slow, too much concerned with the danger of alienating the conservative wing of the peace movement. "We differed only upon one point," writes young May, "the expediency of pressing the highest truth first. No non-resistant believed more sincerely than Mr. Ladd did, that the most strictly defensive war could not be justified upon Christian principles. But he forbore, as I thought too long to press the faith upon others—saying, 'it is never wise to drive a wedge butt-end foremost.' "[13]

From the early thirties on, at any rate, Ladd was openly stating his belief that no Christian should participate in war, that all warfare was —in the current expression—"unlawful for a Christian," and that it was

[11] *Harbinger of Peace*, I, no. 1, 21, 22.
[12] *Ibid.*, vol. II, no. 12. See also II, no. 10, 217, 218.
[13] Letter from Samuel J. May, 4 Jan. 1845, in Coues's "Peace Album."

wrong to take human life under any circumstances, even in self-defense or to protect others. "I am not afraid" in case of attack, he writes, "to trust to moral weapons and the providence of God, and to do as I suppose Christ or Stephen, or any of the apostles would have done in like circumstances, and leave the consequences to God."[14] He supported the stand of the conscientious objector to service in the state militia.[15] He continued, however, like Worcester, to speak in respectful terms of his fellow Christians, who believed in the necessity of sometimes using the sword, trusting that they might eventually be enlightened as to the full truth; and he was always careful to point out that this position was not *ipso facto* incompatible with opposition to every form of international war.[16] He strove, in fact, to keep the issues of "public war" and personal pacifism completely separate. It was the entanglement of these two questions that was soon to cause so much trouble within the peace movement.

The story of his gradual conversion to pacifism is set forth most vividly in an autobiographical passage from an article he contributed to the *Christian Mirror* in 1837. He wrote there as follows of the inner road he had traversed:

> When I first began to act in the cause, I saw only "men as trees walking." I saw in war an iron colossus stalking over the earth and trampling down the inhabitants, impoverishing the nations, the father of every crime. But I paid but little attention to the immortal souls which war was sweeping into eternity "with all their sins on their heads." Nor was I aware of the full extent of the law of love. I thought all which was expected of a follower of Christ was, that he would live peaceably with those who would live peaceably with him. Like the first temperance societies, which were established on the principle that it was right to drink a little, but not to drink too much; so I thought it right for Christians to fight a little, pro-

[14] Hemmenway, *The Apostle of Peace*, pp. 71, 72.
[15] "Are you past the age of boyhood?" he wrote in one article. "You may soon be called upon to decide, whether you will give your testimony in favour of the horrid and demoralizing custom of war, or not: for you may be called on to do militia duty. . . . On your decision may hang your eternal destiny. As you value your immortal soul, I conjure you to keep away from such scenes. *Now* is the time for *you* to decide. If you once submit, it will be difficult for you to refuse hereafter. Make up your mind, and plead the liberty of conscience guaranteed to you by the constitution, and to which you have as good a right as a Quaker, a Shaker, or a Moravian. You may suffer for it; but if you suffer for conscience sake, you will not lose your reward." (William Ladd, *Obstacles and Objections to the Cause of Permanent and Universal Peace considered by a Layman*, p. 37.)
[16] Hemmenway, *The Apostle of Peace*, pp. 13, 58, 59; *Advocate of Peace*, IV, no. 12 (Dec. 1842), 268.

vided they did not fight too much. It was more than seven years before I could so far divest myself of the prejudices of education, as to see clearly, that *all* war is absolutely forbidden in the Gospel. ... I cannot distinctly mark the time when my mind changed; ... I have read almost everything written on this subject, which I have ever heard of, and I have retreated before the light of truth, step by step, until I have at length, as I think, got on gospel ground.[17]

Ladd's public witness, then, was against the institution of international war; privately, however, he had reached the Quaker, indeed almost the full-blown nonresistant testimony against all use of armed force. His position was more radical than Worcester's had been; at the same time, all his influence was used in favor of moderation, of a united front of all shades of peace opinion against their common enemy—war between nations. And, indeed, one of Ladd's favorite peace concerns was the congress of nations: the projected establishment of an international parliament drawn from the representatives of all civilized governments with a tribunal attached for the peaceful arbitration of international disputes. The idea, which has a long history stretching back at least to the fifteenth century, if not to the ancient Greeks, was one which could be supported by those who asserted the right of national self-defense, not to speak of personal resistance to attack. Ladd, along with other publicists of the American peace movement, had been writing on behalf of the project from at least the beginning of the thirties; his work for this cause reached its climax in the publication in 1840 of his famous essay on a congress of nations. Providing "a cheap and sure mode of redress" in the case of national grievances and designed "to moderate the severity of war" should it nonetheless break out,[18] the congress, in Ladd's view, was a desirable step on the road toward a peaceful world. No sanctions were envisaged in Ladd's plan to enforce the decisions of congress or international

---

[17] Quoted in Hemmenway, *The Apostle of Peace*, p. 64. In 1826, for instance, we find him telling the selectmen of Exeter (N.H.): "I detest all war (for measures purely defensive I do not call war)" (*Christian Mirror*, 28 July 1826). His conversion to personal pacifism must have come sometime before the end of that decade or very shortly thereafter.

[18] William Ladd, *An Essay on a Congress of Nations for the Adjustment of International Disputes without Resort to Arms*, 1916 edn., pp. 17, 96. Ladd's essay was originally published in 1840, along with those of the five winners in the prize essay competition on the subject sponsored by the American Peace Society. Ladd's work was meant as a summary of the most significant points in the rejected essays, but, in fact, it constitutes an original contribution. See also Sylvester John Hemleben, *Plans for World Peace through Six Centuries*, pp. 104-13. See A.C.F. Beales, *The History of Peace*, pp. 56-64, for American and British support for a congress of nations during this period.

court, apart from the moral force of international opinion. On the other hand, the scheme fell short of complete pacifism. And, as critics have pointed out, it ignored both the question of national oppression and the problem of social injustice within the state—two subjects of acute interest to the nineteenth and twentieth centuries. Ladd's interest in the scheme does witness, however, to the catholicity of his concern for peace.

The first couple of years of the American Peace Society and of Ladd's leadership in the movement saw the growth—timid as yet and confined, as we have noted, to only a handful—of the radical pacifist position. Several members or associates of the Society, unfettered by the official responsibilities of a Ladd or perhaps not so fearful of offending the susceptibilities of their less enlightened brethren, now gave open expression in address or pamphlet to their views on the disputed questions of defensive wars and personal nonresistance. Indeed, as we have seen, Ladd himself had encouraged such discussion in the columns of the journal he was editing for the Society. Let us briefly take a look at some of these writings; though they contain little that had not been said before, they will help to show the stage which pacifist thought had reached at this time.

"Thus saith the Lord" is their keynote. Even though the Old Testament warfare was permissible under the Mosaic dispensation, Christ's law of love has precluded the waging of national wars since his coming. What he has laid down for the individual is binding also on the group, the nation. All this is familiar stuff. The Rev. Henry Grew, addressing the Hartford Peace Society in September 1828, impressed on his hearers that the war method was ruled out for Christians as a means by which to defend liberty or property (rank heresy this, in the America of the 1820's!) or to obtain redress for personal or national injuries. Even if we are invaded, we are not justified in killing enemy soldiers—unless, possibly (he leaves the contingency vague), as a last resort in case of an actual attempt on our lives. If we do not resist the invaders by force, Grew believes, they will not actually try to kill us. He reminds his listeners that renunciation of war does not mean opposition to government. "Surely a right to punish those who *do evil*, implies no right to inflict evil on thousands who *do well*."[19]

Two months after Grew's discourse, the Rev. Elijah Jones in his address on 5 November to the peace society in Ladd's own township of Minot in Maine, while acknowledging that "peace societies in this country have not generally denied the right of absolute self-defence, when actually invaded" and asserting his disinclination on this occasion

[19] Grew, *Address delivered before the Peace Society of Hartford*, pp. 8-11, 15.

to discuss the pros and cons of personal nonresistance, stated it as his own opinion, based on the experience of the past, that an unarmed people could survive. The Jews of old had been "God's executioners" in the wars they waged. "At his command they cut off nations whom he thought proper to destroy." But the gospel principle meant nonviolence: the early Christians had preferred death to service in the Roman army. In any case, he concluded, the civilized world must outlaw war as a method of settling international disputes. Although he admitted his idea of a nation modeling its foreign policy on Christian love might appear visionary, Jones was certain that international war could be abolished in the present.[20]

In 1829 a young Massachusetts clergyman, the Rev. Thomas T. Stone (1801-1895), produced a small volume of *Sermons on War*. In these sermons Stone runs over the usual arguments of the contemporary peace movement against war, based on scripture, morals, and practical utility. It might, he continues, seem "expedient" sometimes to wage war for the sake of "national preservation"—though on no other grounds. In all other instances, negotiations and concessions are preferable to a resort to war, even on the practical plane. Hinting at, though never explicitly owning to, a personal faith in nonresistance, Stone does, however, advocate national renunciation of the use of force, pleading that his own United States should provide an example here to the world by undertaking unilateral disarmament. This, he admits, would entail risk in the world as constituted in his day. But we must "act as Christians." We must adopt a peaceful stance if we wish others to take the way of peace. And he believed the other nations would ultimately follow in his own country's footsteps, if it disarmed completely.[21]

In the same year that Stone published his peace sermons, we find that ardent pacifist, Joshua Blanchard, addressing the Massachusetts Peace Society (now an affiliate of the American Peace Society) on the occasion of its thirteenth anniversary and expatiating on the nature of true patriotism. He looked forward, he said, to the day when the United States—"to which I owe my dearest political affection"— would abandon the use of arms, even for defense, and devote itself, instead, entirely to the pursuits of peace, "to the diffusion of its own comforts and improvements, and liberty, and religion, through a suffering and darkened world." "What brighter vision could Patriotism unfold?" The example of such disinterested concern for humanity

---

[20] Elijah Jones, *Address delivered at the Fifth Anniversary of the Peace Society of Minot*, pp. 3, 4, 8-11, 17-21.
[21] Thomas T. Stone, *Sermons on War*, pp. 85-87.

would be a surer bulwark against attack than all the country's armaments on land and sea. People might call this utopia, he added, but the gospels promise the coming of peace on earth, which it is the duty of Christian peoples to strive to bring about.[22]

More specific than Blanchard in his advocacy of the nonviolent way, and more radical than Grew or Stone in the matter of personal nonresistance, was the Rev. Samuel W. Whelpley, a namesake of the pacifist author of the *Letters to Caleb Strong* (see earlier). In 1830 we find him addressing a meeting of the Hartford County Peace Society on the question whether "in any case" a man has the right to take the life of his fellowman. His answer is a decided negative. He does not avoid (as Ladd, for instance, did) the term "nonresistance." "Our Saviour," he says, "expressly, constantly and very strongly inculcated the doctrine of passive obedience and non-resistance in opposition to the principle of retaliation and war." For the state to exact the death penalty was an unmitigated evil. Instead, he suggests that "perpetual confinement with hard labour" would be a more effective deterrent than death—and it would also give the criminal ample time for repentance.[23] Whelpley does not touch upon the question of the refusal of military service by the individual Christian convinced of the wrongness of war: he seems to presume that wars are waged on the voluntarist principle.

In the same year, however, another clergyman—this time, it is interesting to note, an Episcopalian, the Rev. Ezra B. Kellogg—asserted the duty of conscientious objection in forthright fashion in a sermon preached before the Windham County Peace Society. God must be obeyed rather than human governments in cases where the two conflicted, he told his audience. The question to be asked was: "Has God given Christians a right to fight and war?" If they believed (as he did) that this was expressly forbidden them, it was then the responsibility of each individual to see that he did not break God's law. Kellogg made good use of the researches of his fellow Anglican, Clarkson, into the attitude taken up by the primitive church in regard to war, quoting with approval the examples of early Christian conscientious objectors to service in the Roman army. He also cites the Quaker, Hancock, on the pacifist stand of the Society of Friends during the Irish rebellion of 1798 and the often quoted Pennsylvania experiment

---

[22] Blanchard, *Address delivered at the Thirteenth Anniversary of the Massachusetts Peace Society*, pp. 13-15.

[23] S. W. Whelpley, *An Address delivered before the Peace Society of Hartford County*, pp. 5-9, 12, 13.

in order to buttress his case against the participation of churchmen in war.[24]

Finally, let us consider the 28-page pamphlet written under the pseudonym of "Pacificus" and published in 1830 by the executive committee of the American Peace Society under the title *Appeal to American Christians on the Practice of War*. The little work deals mainly with a couple of subjects, which had become by now standard themes in the literature of the peace movement: the horrors and moral evils of war and military life in general and, secondly, "the Christian testimony against war" as reflected in the books of the New Testament and the history of the early church. It condemns the terrible record of Christianity in bringing war and desolation, the sword along with the Bible, to the heathen continents of Asia, Africa, and South America, and in its final pages it calls on the churches to unite in a condemnation of all war.[25] What is interesting about the pamphlet is not the general arguments, which are similar to those we have been discussing, but the fact that here a radical position is taken up in a publication issued officially in the name of the Society.

In its pages "Pacificus" contests in the strongest terms the permissibility of defensive wars for the followers of Christ.[26] He does not, it is true, go on to condemn, as Whelpley had done, the retention of capital punishment by the state. This question, in his view, is entirely separate from that of war between nations. "I can understand," he writes, "how the punishment of death for capital offences may be inflicted, as to promote rather than sacrifice the future happiness of the criminal."[27] On the positive side of his general argument, the author recommends the establishment of an international tribunal for settling disputes between governments. This, combined with a national policy of goodwill toward all the world's peoples, should suffice to assure peace to the country.

But what, it might be asked, if no government were yet ready to try this way? What should the peace-loving Christian citizen do in the meantime if his nation was involved in war? "Pacificus" replies: "The time was, (and it may again arrive, after so many ages of moral darkness), when the declaration, 'I am a Christian,' was equivalent to a renunciation of military service. . . . The course then which Christians may pursue, is an extremely obvious one. It may be self-denying and hazardous." He is ready to

[24] Kellogg, *War Contrary to the Gospel*, esp. pp. 24, 25, 27, 28.
[25] *Appeal*, pp. 26-28.
[26] *Ibid.*, p. 28. See Allen, *The Fight for Peace*, p. 380.
[27] *Appeal*, p. 19.

... admit the right of individuals, in circumstances where little time is left for reflection, and where no alternative is presented but that of killing or being killed, to follow the first impulse of nature and protect themselves at every expense, without justifying the practice even of defensive war. [However,] there is no such alternative, as the one supposed, presented to a nation, by its most insulting and ambitious enemies. A declaration of war is a subject of cool deliberation, and may usually be prevented by a comparatively trivial sacrifice. ... Do not, because Providence has placed you at a distance from the scene of blood, or your profession, or any other cause, protects you against the summons to arm and prepare yourself for actual combat, imagine that you have nothing to do with the subject of war. You may hereafter have a more painful connexion with its calamities than you now anticipate.[28]

While prepared for the sake of argument—as we have just seen—to concede to the individual the right of self-defense in the case of armed attack on his person, "Pacificus" hastens to explain that he himself is far from convinced of its permissibility. Against the use of arms for self-defense he urges three considerations. We must put our trust in God's protection alone. We should draw back before the awful prospect of sending a fellowman, the murderer, to his death unprepared and with the certainty of eternal damnation awaiting him on the other side (a curious argument, perhaps, to us today but one quite frequently urged by pacifist writers of the evangelical age). And, thirdly, should we shrink from the privilege of suffering martyrdom for obedience to Christ's commands?[29]

"Pacificus" was obviously an absolute pacifist, albeit a conservative one, and it is, therefore, a little surprising that his pamphlet came out under the official imprint of the American Peace Society at this time, when the nonpacifist element within the Society was still in control and Ladd in his *Harbinger of Peace* was pursuing a neutral line in the debate over defensive wars and personal nonresistance. We know from the *Christian Mirror* (3 February 1831) that the author was a New York clergyman and that his tract was distributed free by the Society. The circumstances of its appearance, therefore, and the voices in favor of absolute pacifism being raised from time to time in the Society's local branches indicate that a fresh wind was blowing in the Society's ranks.

The most sensational statement of the pacifist case, and from a most unexpected quarter, came in 1832. In that year a respected South

[28] *Ibid.*, pp. 22-24, 26.   [29] *Ibid.*, pp. 24, 25.

Carolina lawyer, Thomas S. Grimké (1786-1834),[30] was invited by the Connecticut Peace Society, an affiliate of the American Peace Society, to speak in New Haven at their first anniversary meeting on Sunday evening, 6 May. The state legislature was then in session, and, therefore, many of its members, together with state dignitaries, attended Grimké's *Address on the Truth, Dignity, Power and Beauty of the Principles of Peace, and on the Unchristian Character and Influence of War and the Warrior.* "For sheer audacity coupled with cogent pacifist apologetics," writes Devere Allen,[31] "its equal is almost non-existent. Dehydrate it by removing the sanctimonious verbiage and the rhetorical flourishes *au fait* of the period, and the effort is extraordinarily powerful."

Since his undergraduate days at Yale, Grimké had been distinguished for his evangelical piety (he was an Episcopalian) and for the excellence of his classical scholarship. He had had a successful career in law in his native South Carolina; a brilliant orator, he had sat in the state senate for four years. Like so many evangelicals of the period, he had striven to express his faith in works and had given enthusiastic support to a number of "causes," from Sunday schools to the defense of the rights of the Cherokee Indians. "One of the most famous rulers in the benevolent empire" is how a recent historian has described him.[32] Grimké had become interested in the subject of peace toward the end of the 1820's. It was then that he had begun to correspond with Ladd and Samuel J. May, and around 1830 he read—and was greatly influenced by—Hancock's account of the Irish Quakers during the rebellion of 1798 and, a little later, Jonathan Dymond's treatises on peace. He was to have copies of Hancock's book distributed in large numbers among Sunday school children in the South.[33] It was his known interest in peace that prompted the Connecticut group to invite the distinguished Southerner, and Yale graduate, to address their public meeting. His whole career, as well as his family background, was conservative (and he was himself a slaveowner of considerable affluence!); he had not so far openly displayed any particular sympathy with the radical peace position. It was not, in fact, until 1832,

---

[30] See the *Calumet*, vol. II, no. 5, Jan.-Feb. 1835; Catherine H. Birney, *The Grimké Sisters*, pp. 102, 103; Allen, *The Fight for Peace*, pp. 375-80.
[31] *The Fight for Peace*, p. 377.
[32] Gilbert Hobbs Barnes, *The Antislavery Impulse*, p. 153.
[33] "Do you want any of Hancock on Peace?" Grimké wrote to Ladd early in 1833. "I have already distributed upward of seventy or eighty of the precious seed, and I doubt not it has made many a one think who never thought before, and has made many a one acknowledge the true courage of the peace principle" (*Calumet*, I, no. 12 [March-April 1833], 364).

in the course of preparing his *Address*, that he became fully convinced of the incompatibility of war with Christianity and the obligation laid on the Christian to refuse war service.[34] This fact explains the sensation his *Address* made within peace circles, as well as with the general public.

The underlying message, which runs like a thread through the whole *Address*, is the contrast between "the law of violence" exemplified in war and "the law of love" exemplified in peace. It is the spiritual, the moral damage done by war rather than the physical destruction, the losses in lives and property, that is emphasized by Grimké. He does not spare even his beloved classics but condemns them for their dangerous cult of militarism, which inspired youth with a false sense of the glories of war. "Why," he asks, "should the children of a *Christian peaceful* people, be forever under the influence of men, so entirely *the reverse* of what *they* ought to be?" Ancient history's chief value (indeed, the value of all human history) was to show the futility and destructiveness of war. That "the mysterious providence of God" tolerated "the law of violence and retaliation" in Old Testament times, and even used it for his own ends in governing the world, must not lead us to glorify war in the same spirit as the classical historians, because Christ came to institute a new war, the war for peace.[35]

So far, perhaps, Grimké was not likely to have caused offense, at least to anyone ready to attend a meeting of a peace society. Sentiments little different from these had been heard for centuries from countless pulpits. It was the conclusions he was to draw that aroused a storm of criticism.

"War," he goes on to say, "in any shape, from any motive, and carried on in any mode, is utterly indefensible on Christian principles and utterly irreconcilable with a Christian spirit." "There was a time," he reminds his audience, "when the distinguishing mark of Christians was, that they would not bear arms. . . . O! that Christians had persevered in the primitive spirit, which regarded the character of a soldier as pagan, not Christian! O! that they had abided inflexibly by the rule, never to bear arms!" Instead, the Christian church had succumbed first to the martial spirit of the Roman Empire and then to the barbarism of the northern invaders, when its followers should have refused to take up arms to resist the barbarians and have suffered the consequences. They should have answered the call to service by saying: "We will love them that hate, and pray for such as persecute and oppress us. Thus

[34] *Calumet*, II, no. 5, Jan.-Feb. 1835, 136.
[35] Grimké, *Address*, pp. 3-6, 10, 26.

and thus only will we conquer our enemies, and convert the heathen to Christianity."[36]

Finally, Grimké brings up as a test case the American Revolution. Here, at least, for almost all Americans of his day, was an example of a war, the justice of which only enemies of liberty or the pusillanimous would deny. Yes, says Grimké, its aims were unimpeachable, but the means used were wholly wrong and unchristian. After exhausting all possible channels for negotiation, placing their case squarely before the British government and public, the Americans should have told them: "Our purpose is irrevocably taken: we will be free: we will have the precious rights of British freemen; but, never shall violence and bloodshed be our arms." Grimké was convinced (like Whelpley before him) that by pursuing a policy of nonviolent resistance against Britain, "in such an age and such a country, with such a government and such a religion," the American people (had they not, moreover, been endowed with a divine mission, did they not enjoy the special favor of God?) would have ultimately won through to freedom.[37]

Grimké's oration was greeted with shocked ridicule by the general public. It did not by any means win the approval, either, of the whole peace movement, small as it then was. The Connecticut Peace Society, which published the *Address* in pamphlet form, was careful to point out that Grimké alone was responsible for his sentiments on the American Revolution: "On this subject, various opinions exist in the minds of members of peace societies and of others eminent for talent and piety."[38] However, Ladd, while reserving the American Peace Society's neutral position in relation to the legitimacy of defensive wars, commented favorably in the Society's official journal on Grimké's presentation of the radical viewpoint. "To object to war," he writes, "is so contrary to the whole course of our education, that there is a very strong reluctance, in the mind, against thinking of it as unlawful. To one, however, who will take the pains to examine defensive war by the light of the Gospel, it will appear that the opposers of it have much better ground to stand upon than he at first imagined. The subject undergoes an entire change in the examination; and one is astonished at his former opinions."[39]

Other correspondents wrote in to controvert the views of the *Address*. One writer, for instance, while agreeing that nonviolent resistance was fine in theory, thought that in practice it would mean the subjection of civilized nations to ruthless barbarians. What of the fate

[36] *Ibid.*, pp. 29, 30. [37] *Ibid.*, pp. 42-48. [38] *Ibid.*, p. 42.
[39] *Calumet*, I, no. 8 (July-Aug. 1832), 232.

of the peaceful Peruvians at the hands of the Spaniards? Was not the most effective policy for peace to try to restrict warfare to the strictly defensive and to humanize its conduct when it became unavoidable? In reply Grimké urged the necessity of obedience to Christ's commands (his adversary agreed that this seemed to imply pacifism), of trust in God's protection (which the latter seemed to feel less certain about), and of a readiness, like that of the early Christians, to suffer martyrdom. As for the Peruvians, did not the warlike Aztecs of Mexico also suffer the same fate? And, in any event, the former were scarcely Quakers "without arms or fortifications or military instruments, but the reverse"; the parallel, therefore, did not apply.[40] The argument is interesting, since it is one that was frequently to crop up between pacifists and their opponents. The latter would often cite some instance of the subjugation or extermination of a people who, while not fully pacifist perhaps, were said to be peace-loving and nonresistant; the pacifist, like Grimké, would reply that, in fact, the case did not fit, since the moral force of a nation abandoning arms from conscientious scruples and relying on the power of reconciliation was absent.

Having on account of his *Address* stirred up plenty of opposition in New England both within and without peace circles, Grimké had then to face fresh trouble on his return to South Carolina when he attempted to measure up to his principles in his native state, which was at that time in a condition of acute political crisis. In 1832 a state convention duly elected at the call of the legislature had declared that recent commercial tariffs introduced by the federal administration were contrary to the Constitution and thereby null and void, and that, furthermore, the state had a right to secede from the Union rather than be forced to submit to measures which were deemed a deadly menace to Southern agriculture. President Andrew Jackson reacted strongly to this policy of "nullification" in its most extreme form, and for a time war seemed to threaten between South Carolina and the federal forces, until finally a compromise on the issue was reached. Meanwhile, Grimké, one of the most prominent citizens of the state, felt it incumbent upon himself to make his position perfectly clear in case the impending conflict should come to a head. "For myself," he addressed the people of South Carolina and their leader, John C. Calhoun, in an open letter,[41] "I trust, that I hold with an inflexible conviction the sentiment, that the character of the Warrior, in any point of view is UNCHRISTIAN, and

---

[40] *Ibid.*, I, no. 13 (May-June 1833), 402-8. See also Grimké, *Correspondence on the Principles of Peace, Manual Labor Schools,&.*, pp. 3-7. "Mine is the *Christian*, yours the *heathen* theory," he told one correspondent who disagreed with his nonresistant position.

[41] Grimké, *A Letter to the People of South Carolina*, p. 15.

in CIVIL contest, is absolutely and unchangeably ANTI-REPUBLICAN." Moreover, whatever the wrongs his beloved state might have suffered, fratricidal conflict should be avoided at all costs. Let "the law of love" be substituted for "the law of violence," "the law of the sword," he now told his own people, as he had told his New Haven audience a little earlier.

With civil war threatening, the state legislature had proceeded to raise the age limit for those liable for service in the state militia. Grimké, aged 47, came within its net—at least in theory, for it is scarcely probable that he would in fact have been called upon. The conscientious lawyer nevertheless felt obliged to petition the state senate for exemption—or perhaps he welcomed the opportunity to make a public protest in favor of Christian pacifism and against the political policy of "nullification." He pleaded his case solely on the grounds of religious objection to all war, a position he had reached—he states— only about a year previously as a result of a careful investigation of the New Testament. "For the sincerity of these opinions, your petitioner can only refer to the best testimony which man can offer to his fellowman, the uniform tenor of his public and private life." He believed he could truthfully say now that, unless he completely lost command over himself, he would never wittingly take a human life or even answer blow with blow. He was confident that "to grant his petition will be an act of magnanimity, and of justice to the rights of conscience: and can be no disadvantage to the public; as your petitioner knows of no other person in the State who is of the same opinion." This might, it is true, be regarded as "a strong argument to prove that he is in error; but is it not a still stronger one to establish the strength of his conviction and the sincerity of his scruples? . . . he thus exposes himself in the cause of conscience to . . . ridicule and contempt."

The petition[42] was rejected, Grimké's political opponents representing it to the legislators—it was reported—"as a violent and inflammatory production." Grimké's failure to gain exemption (which apparently did not have any practical ill consequences for him) was undoubtedly the result of political considerations, anger at his determined stand against the dominant majority's policy of "nullification," rather than by the religious pacifism which underlay his objection to military service. His house had been threatened with attack, and he became one of the most hated men in the state.[43]

[42] It is printed in full in the *Calumet*, I, no. 14 (July-Aug. 1833), 432, 433. See also vol. II, no. 6 (March-April 1835).

[43] For Grimké as a many-sided reformer in state politics, see William F. Freehling, *Prelude to Civil War*, pp. 180-82.

Within the somewhat narrow limits of the peace movement, Grimké's challenging stand on behalf of absolute pacifism made a big impact. As we have seen, there had already been some discussion of the problem in the columns of the American Peace Society's monthly organ, the *Harbinger of Peace,* and occasionally in the local societies, too. The debate continued in the Society's new journal, a bimonthly which appeared in succession to the *Harbinger* from 1831 on under the title *Calumet,* the name given to the symbolic peace pipe of the American Indians. Ladd was still in charge, although he did not act officially as editor now on account of the difficulties encountered in running a paper published in New York or Boston from his farm at Minot up in Maine. Soon a lively controversy inspired by Grimké's utterances was being waged in the pages of the *Calumet.*

Meanwhile, the peace groups of Connecticut, emboldened by Grimké's stand in his May *Address,* had temporarily become a center of the more radical pacifist opinion. The Windham Peace Society, in fact, had been responsible in the previous March for printing the first American edition of the famous pacifist tract by the English Quaker, Jonathan Dymond. It was published at Brooklyn (Conn.) in 1,000 copies under the title *On the Applicability of the Pacific Principles of the New Testament to the Conduct of States: and on the Limitations which those Principles impose on the Rights of Self-Defence.* We have seen what an influence its brief 19 pages was to have on the receptive mind of Thomas S. Grimké.

The Windham County Society during this period had as its corresponding secretary the young Unitarian pastor at Brooklyn, Samuel J. May, with whom we shall be concerned later in his role as a devoted Garrisonian abolitionist and nonresistant and as a close friend of the master. In 1832 we find the young minister already grappling with a problem that was to haunt him all his life: the dilemma of how to reconcile Christian nonviolence with the struggle for human freedom. In his review of the Society's activities over the past year, May had mourned the failure of Poland's recent fight against Tsarist oppression. "We deprecated that catastrophe as fervently as any could have done," he wrote, "although that ill-fated nation sought her deliverance by an appeal to arms. While the issue of her contest was undetermined, we cordially united in the wish that she might throw off the yoke of her oppressor." In retrospect, however, the main lesson of the Polish uprising appeared to May to illustrate the futility of a resort to arms in however just a cause. "War is not the means appointed by our heavenly Father for the redress of any of our grievances." And he lamented the fact that the Poles, for all the righteousness of their aims, had not realized this in time, "had not learnt the more excellent way of overcoming evil." On the whole, however, he assessed most positively the stirrings of liberty on the European continent, which had begun to shake the reactionary obscurantist forces that hitherto had almost everywhere been in control. The people were awakening—and this was all to the good in May's view, for the growth of self-awareness among the masses meant indirectly an increase of the sentiment for peace. "We therefore hail every indication of increasing knowledge among the people (however it may be attended by temporary commotions) as auspicious to the cause of peace." That cause, he believed, too, meant pacifism and the refusal of military service in the name of Christ.[44] Not all Christian pacifists, it is true, then or later, looked with such favor on the revolutionary political and social movements of their time. We need not be surprised, then, that May soon found himself on the left wing of the peace movement.

In November 1832 the Rev. Cyrus Yale (1786-1854) spoke—in a more conservative strain than May's remarks just quoted—to a meeting organized by the neighboring Hartford County Peace Society on the theme *War Unreasonable and Unscriptural*. His talk was confined mainly to a discussion of the religious and moral objections to the institution of international war, for, as he said,

> The society which I have the honor to address, stops not to settle the question of defensive war. At this point, the members agree to differ. To those who ask, what shall we do in case of invasion and rebellion? This society would simply say; let us do all we can to persuade other nations not to invade us—to persuade our own countrymen to "leave off contention before it be meddled with."[45]

When the address was printed, however, Yale added a few pages at the end[46] urging some nation—preferably his own United States—to try the experiment of abandoning reliance on the method of armed defense, in the expectation that its courage would find favor in God's sight and its example be followed gradually by the other governments of the world. "There must be a *beginning* somewhere," he wrote. It would entail risks, of course, but not more than the war method which he had shown to be wanting. He cites the examples of the un-

[44] May's remarks summarized here are found in extracts from the sixth annual report of the Windham County Peace Society, which was published as an appendix (pp. 13-16) to a pamphlet by the Rev. Richard P. Cleveland: *Abstract of an Address before the Peace Society of Windham County, at its Annual Meeting in Brooklyn, August 22, 1832*. Cleveland's address contains nothing of particular interest.
[45] Yale, *War Unreasonable and Unscriptural*, p. 1.
[46] *Ibid.*, pp. 17-24.

armed Quakers and Shakers, and he points out that the partitioning of Poland, for instance, was not inflicted on a nation that had renounced the use of arms. Was not the experiment of unilateral disarmament worth trying out at least once? "In case of failure, it will be easy to resume the sword."

Of interest, too, are the reasons urged by Yale for the United States to become the first country to adopt what he calls "the principle of entire abstinence from war." The country was, as he says, somewhat removed from the center of militarism in Europe, and its people were not yet inured to the continuous warfare to which the European nations had been subjected over the centuries. Moreover, it had more than enough territory to satisfy the needs of its population for a long time to come; it was unlikely, therefore, to have any inclination to embark on a war of conquest. It was prosperous; there was no lack of employment; there was no economic motive for the people to desire war. A democratic government, the absence of a power-lusting monarchy or aristocracy, was a further guarantee of peaceful intentions. (Yale does admit, though, that the country was perhaps more subject to internal dissension than some European lands.) Finally, on the moral side, he paints a picture of a nation more susceptible than others to philanthropic appeals, strong in the faith of Biblical Christianity, and ready in its youthful vigor to respond to new ideas. Thus we see even America's pacifists at that time sharing in some way in the general feeling of their country's manifest destiny—a destiny, as they saw it, to lead the peoples of the world into an era of universal peace.

In the following year, this time to celebrate the second anniversary of its founding, the Connecticut Peace Society invited a local clergyman, the Rev. Laurens P. Hickok (1798-1888), later to achieve some renown as a professor of philosophy, to address it. More circumspect than his predecessor Grimké, Hickok was careful to remind his audience that the Society itself did not presume to take sides on the question whether any wars were ever justified by Christian standards, that its members agreed to differ on this question, uniting in the desire to bring about the abolition of war and the establishment of universal peace. But he, too, in the course of his lecture declared himself personally a pacifist. "I have no hesitation," he said, "in declaring it as *my own* solemn conviction, that, even to the full extent of non-resistance in all cases of aggression, the danger would be far less than seems generally to be apprehended." He himself believed that the view common among the peace groups that renunciation of defense by arms must await the moment when all had agreed to disarm was an illusion.

regrettable in that many potential recruits to the movement were kept away on this account.[47]

In 1834 the Connecticut group even went so far as to publish as its Tract No. I a small pamphlet entitled *War Unchristian; or the Custom of War Compared with the Standard of Christian Duty*, which came out strongly against the whole concept of defensive wars and in favor of nonresistance. The distinction so often made by peace advocates between wars of aggression and just wars of defense was, it claimed, "specious," "a mere delusion," invented by the protagonists of militarism to obscure the issue. Until this fact is realized by the peace movement, it said, the movement will make no progress. The early Christians had preferred death to bearing arms for any cause. Every conflict ever fought, moreover, had been justified as a righteous war. Neutrality was not enough.

> It is frequently said by those who attempt to advocate the cause of peace, that they do not intend to say any thing on the subject of *defensive* war. Plainly, then, they had better be silent. For if this false distinction is to be kept up, and if what is called defensive war is justified, or even tolerated, then the cause of Peace has already triumphed; and there is probably not another convert to be made to it in Christendom. For it may be doubted whether any one can be found with the slightest knowledge of the Bible, who will pretend for a moment to justify what is generally called offensive war.[48]

The pacifist current within the movement was not by any means confined to Connecticut. Even as far west as Circleville, Ohio, for instance, we find the Rev. R. V. Rogers—an Episcopalian, too—putting the "argument from Scripture against defensive war" in a sermon to his congregation.[49] Many of the younger men, new recruits to the cause, were strongly influenced by the trend toward radicalism. Take as an example the case of the young banker, Amasa Walker (1798-1873), then in his early thirties.[50] Usually on the side of moderation, he was later to become a leading figure in the American Peace Society and a

---

[47] Hickok, *The Sources of Military Delusion*, pp. 8-10, 12.

[48] *War Unchristian*, pp. 5-10.

[49] Printed in the *Calumet*, vol. I, nos. 14-15 (July-Oct. 1833). Galpin (*Pioneering for Peace*, p. 98) mentions a synod representing various Protestant denominations held at Adrian, Michigan, where on 1 October 1835 a resolution was passed declaring war an unmitigated evil and urging that Christians "decline military service on conscientious grounds."

[50] See his letter, dated 23 Jan. 1845, in Coues's "Peace Album." See also Curti, *American Peace Crusade*, p. 45.

prominent Massachusetts politician. He had been introduced by a friend to Ladd's *Calumet* shortly after it started publication, and he became a subscriber to the paper. Reading its articles, he soon became convinced that war was not only the greatest calamity that could befall man but, as he wrote later, "that it was under all circumstances, and in every degree and form sinful." Total abstinence from war and preparation for war was a Christian's duty, as much as total abstinence from intoxicating liquor. He brought the question up at a meeting of the Massachusetts Peace Society, which he had recently joined, seeking to persuade its members to come out "openly and boldly" against all war and to abandon the temporizing policy which, he believed, would get it nowhere. He was not successful, of course; despite the rising strength of radical peace views in the constituent societies of the movement and the growing impatience of some of the more active elements in it, the rank and file were as yet unready to follow so far.

Equally interesting is the story of the conversion to pacifism of the young Unitarian minister, the Rev. Andrew P. Peabody (1811-1893), later to become a professor of theology at Harvard.[51] It was not until 1834, when he had to give a series of discourses on the Sermon on the Mount, that he came to think seriously about the relationship of Christianity and war. "I had taken for granted," he writes, "the current opinions of the Church and the world in general, supposing the Quakers to be labouring under a hallucination of mind as to those matters." When he came to prepare his sermon and read through the relevant chapters of scripture, he was surprised to find his old views on the legitimacy of wars of defense giving way to a conviction of the indefensibility of war in general. He astonished his congregation the following Sunday when he preached to this effect; at that date, he records, he found only two male members of his parish who expressed agreement with his sentiments. "I at that time supposed myself to stand entirely alone. I knew of no Christian, out of the sect of Quakers, who maintained the views, at which I had arrived, though I convinced myself that primitive Christian antiquity was on my side." However, he soon afterward became a member of the American Peace Society, another recruit to the band of those who were striving to bring the Society openly to the higher ground of opposition to all wars.

It was Grimké who had given them courage and confidence. This high-minded Southern lawyer, for all the overblown and artificial rhetoric of his style, had spoken to the condition of many earnest enthusi-

[51] See his letter, dated 28 Oct. 1845, in Coues's "Peace Album."

asts for peace up and down New England. He had shocked and shaken some of the more conservative members of the peace movement, as well as the outside public, who saw in his doctrines a threat to the security and stability of the state. The limits of pacifism had become a live issue, a subject of animated discussion, in peace circles —as was shown, above all, in the large amount of space now being devoted to it in the columns of the *Calumet*. It was more than eighteen months, however, before an effective counter-blast to Grimké appeared in the form of an article entitled "Defensive War Vindicated" by the redoubtable Dr. William Allen (1784-1868), president of Bowdoin College and a vice-president of the American Peace Society. It was published in the *Calumet* at the beginning of 1834.[52]

Allen prefaced what he had to say by stating that he regretted that the question of defensive wars had been raised within the Society at all. Since it was being discussed, however, he said he wanted to set forth the Christian case for the rightness of such wars. This case he based mainly on the comparison of defensive war with the enforcement of justice. Killing in such conflicts was equivalent, not to murder, but to the execution of a murderer after due process of law. He was not convinced, either, by Clarkson's evidence for the pacifist stand of the early church. And anyhow, he asked, what would Grimké, learned as he was in the law, actually do if he were the chief magistrate of a city attacked by pirates? "What is there in Christianity to discountenance such a defensive war, any more than there is to prohibit the killing of a mad bull or a hungry wolf?"

Allen's article was a serious challenge to the pacifists, not only because of the cogency of many of its arguments but, equally, because of the authority its author enjoyed as a leading educationalist and one of the foremost figures in the peace movement. The first to rush into the breach was Ladd himself.[53] "It is the most forcible defence of the right of defensive war I have ever seen," he readily admitted. "In short, it reasons in the same manner as I myself reasoned, though much more forcibly, for many years after I was an advocate for peace." Explaining that his present comments would be brief, a stopgap only until Grimké had had time to compose a considered reply, Ladd stated his objection, in the first place, to Allen's comparison between international war as it had existed hitherto and the judicial process. A closer parallel, in Ladd's opinion, would have been with the medieval institution of trial by combat or with the custom of dueling. If a congress of nations and an international court of justice administering an inter-

[52] *Calumet*, I, no. 17 (Jan.-Feb. 1834), 324-32.
[53] *Ibid.*, I, no. 18, 553-56.

national code of law were established, then, he said, he would be prepared to concede some validity in Allen's reasoning here. "The argument will have some force to prove the necessity of physical power to carry into effect the sentiments of the court"—if, however, as was indeed most likely, the nations had not by that time outgrown the need for using physical force. Secondly, Ladd accused Allen of ignoring the injunctions of the New Testament which, if followed, seemed to him clearly to debar Christians from ever resorting to war. "The great error [in Allen's presentation] is, putting the doctrine of expediency in place of the precepts of the gospel." Abandoning the higher ground of scripture for the quagmire of expediency, the doctor made far too much play of the argument from supposition. "If such and such happened, what would . . . ?" seemed to Ladd of only secondary importance beside the gospel imperative.

In the following issue,[54] Allen reiterated his belief that the early church had not, in fact, been pacifist. And Ladd retorted with the comment that the attitude of the Christians of those times, especially in view of the uncertain nature of the evidence, should not, indeed, be made the touchstone of conduct for contemporary Christians, who were as able as the early fathers themselves to reach their own conclusions—a line of reasoning that could, of course, be turned as much against pacifist writers as against their opponents.

The *Calumet*'s editor, however, was still merely marking time while he waited for the busy Grimké to complete his authoritative reply to Dr. Allen's onslaught. It was never to be finished, for in October 1834 Grimké died suddenly and unexpectedly in the course of a lecture tour in the West. His death at the comparatively early age of 48 was a big loss for the pacifist cause and, indeed, for the whole reform movement. Still at the time of his death an owner of slaves, he was just beginning to give the whole question of slavery his serious consideration, and his reforming friends were almost certainly right in believing that, if he had lived, he would eventually have come around—as his two sisters, Sarah and Angelina, were soon to do—to the full abolitionist position.[55] In the nineteenth century, at any rate, absolute pacifism and slaveholding could surely not lie long together in a man so conscientious as Thomas Grimké.

Ladd was able to print some 25 pages of the manuscript which Grimké had left unfinished. They appeared in the *Calumet* in the first half of 1835,[56] reproduced at the latter's special request in his own re-

[54] *Ibid.*, II, no. 1 (May-June 1834), 12-23.
[55] See, e.g., May's letter cited above in Coues's "Peace Album."
[56] II, no. 5 (Jan.-Feb. 1835), 140-51; no. 6 (March-April 1835), 165-80.

formed system of spelling. Grimké is mainly concerned here with the relationship between civil government, the office of the magistrate which he recognized as one worthy of the Christian citizen, and the armed defense of the community against external attack. It was at this point that Allen had made his most pertinent sallies against the pacifists' position, and Grimké began by pointing out the opposing concepts the two men held of the functions of the magistrate. Allen took it almost for granted that the magistrate, the ruling authority, had a right to take life. Grimké was inexorably opposed even to capital punishment: "the *first* duty of the Magistrate is *the reformation of the offender.*" How would this be possible if the offender was to be punished by death? Certainly, St. Paul had said of the magistrate: "He beareth not the sword in vain" (Rom. 13:4); but this Grimké interpreted as a metaphor for the general right of government to punish citizens for breaking the law, and not as a sanction for the infliction of the death penalty. In any case, he went on, a parallel could not fairly be drawn between the legitimate functions of civil government and the waging of even a defensive war, since no supranational community, no international code of law, was then in existence.

Finally, Grimké took up Allen's challenge to explain what course he would pursue if in the position of chief magistrate of a city attacked by pirates. If the people were unwilling to follow him, he said, he would resign. If they were ready to give him their confidence and support, on the other hand,

> I should make proclamation, that all the churches be opened, and that prayer be offered by the clergy, and all the pious, that God would be pleased to change the hearts of our invaders, and to manifest his power and mercy in our deliverance. That done, I should throw open the gate that fronted the enemy. Thence would I issue forth . . . with all the clergy, and a long line of Sunday School Teachers and Scholars, dressed in the white robes of peace, and chanting . . . the hymn of Christian faith and hope.

They would either die as Christian martyrs or, with God's grace, melt the hearts of the invaders. If they put up armed resistance, however, they might still have suffered defeat and all its horrors or, as victors, have conjured up a train of revenge and retaliation on the part of their enemies. For all its air of fantasy, Grimké's reply had made some telling points in refuting the analogy between international war and the police functions of national government.

This discussion of the limits of pacifism in the pages of the *Calumet* had not been confined to Grimké, Ladd, and Allen. Many readers joined in, and almost all supported the opposition to defensive wars. While still backing the Society's officially neutral stand, with freedom of discussion of the issue among its journal's readers, Ladd now felt "that articles in favour of war in any shape, should not" be "published, without . . . answer."[57] Most of the Society's leaders, he was able to claim, had taken "the high ground" of opposition to all forms of war as contrary to Christianity.[58] The majority of members, however, obviously less vocal than the energetic group of radical pacifists who were writing to the *Calumet* and making their influence felt in the counsels of the Society, still continued to cling to a belief in the legitimacy of war in certain circumstances.

In the mid-thirties the absolute pacifists had gained powerful allies in the persons of two prominent academic philosophers: Dr. Francis Wayland, D.D. (1796-1865), president of Brown University and a Baptist minister, and the young Bowdoin professor, Thomas C. Upham (1799-1872). Dr. Wayland's support, it is true, was somewhat hesitant, and he was never very closely associated with the work of the peace movement. He was, in fact, no more sound in his views (in the eyes of the strict reformers) on the question of capital punishment, for instance, which he regarded as appropriate for at least the crime of murder,[59] than he was on the issue of slavery when asked whether slaveholding was not incompatible with Christianity. Nevertheless, his explicit defense of nonresistance in the pages of his very popular textbook of moral philosophy, *The Elements of Moral Science*, first published in 1835 and repeatedly reprinted for many decades to come (though today it appears to us a turgid production), gave the doctrine respectability in circles where it would otherwise have been looked at askance and brought it to the attention of young men who might otherwise have passed it by.

The doctor deals with the problem of war and its relation to morals (Christian, of course) in half a dozen pages of his chapter on "Benevolence toward the Injurious."[60] Here Wayland posits a "law of benevolence" deriving from the precepts of the gospels, whereby not only individuals but nations, too, must return good for evil. "Hence it would seem," he goes on, "that all wars are contrary to the revealed will of God, and that the individual has no right to commit to society, nor society to commit to government, the power to declare

[57] *Calumet*, II, no. 6, 163.   [58] *Ibid.*, II, no. 5, 138.
[59] Francis Wayland, *The Elements of Moral Science*, 1835 edn., p. 440.
[60] *Ibid.*, 1835 edn., pp. 441-46. See also the introduction by Joseph L. Blau to the 1963 edn. of Wayland's tome, pp. xlviii-xlix, for the latter's views on war. Blau also reviews the previous editions published.

war." So much may be generally admitted. But how must a nation act until the day when all governments are ready to accept the benevolent principle? Answer: a Christian nation must not wait until all are agreed. Abandoning all weapons of defense, as well as of offense, and relying solely on "the justice of its own conduct, and the moral effect which such a course of conduct would produce upon the consciences of men," such a nation would most likely emerge unscathed from the aggressive designs of its neighbors. "There is not a nation in Europe that could be led on to war against a harmless, just, forgiving and defenceless people." "But suppose this method to fail. Why, then, let us suffer the injury. This is the preferable evil of the two. . . . I answer, suffer injury with forgiveness and love, looking up to God, who, in his holy habitation, is the Judge of the whole earth." He will not try us beyond our powers of endurance, because He could never demand of us the impossible. If we have to suffer aggression, it will come as a punishment and an object lesson for departing from "the law of benevolence," as a result of our nonloving actions in the past.[61] Such were the lessons which Wayland in his textbook placed before several generations of students of philosophy.

Thomas Upham was never the figure that Wayland was in the world of American learning. His textbook of pacifism, however, is of much greater importance in the history of the peace movement than the few pages which Wayland devoted to peace in his textbook of moral philosophy. Upham's *Manual of Peace*, which he published in 1836 (and which sold out in a few months), was a kind of encyclopedia of peace, a century before Aldous Huxley's attempt at something similar in the 1930's and on a much more ambitious scale. (It runs to more than 400 pages.) It is, in fact, one of the first attempts to give a full-scale exposition of pacifist ideology. In this aim it is not altogether successful, but it is as a pioneer work that it must be judged and its defects assessed. As Devere Allen aptly remarks of Upham: "He, too, was subject to the inadequate critical knowledge of his time, yet his vocabulary seems less

---

[61] In 1865 Wayland, then retired, published in Boston a "revised and improved edition" of his *Elements of Moral Science*. While still maintaining the duty of Christians, even in a collective capacity, to return good for evil and still condemning war as a method of settling disputes, the doctor made certain small but significant changes. The use of armed force, he now asserts, may be necessary against a nation which fails to respond to a policy of benevolence and enters on a course of aggression. "Force must be repelled by force, just as far as it is necessary to resist their evil design" (p. 394). Thereafter, with the defeat of the aggressor, love and friendship should again prevail toward the former enemy. For an account of Wayland's fervent, though reluctant, support of the Northern cause in the Civil War, see Francis Wayland and H. L. Wayland, *A Memoir of Francis Wayland*, vol. II, chap. XI. His antislavery feelings had increased during the antebellum years.

colored with theological phantasms than that of some pacifists who were contemporaneous."[62]

Upham conducts his argument on two planes. On the lower one, he confines himself to an indictment of the institution of international war, familiar to us from the writings of Worcester and the orthodox peace men, depicting its wastefulness, futility, and moral evil. To the general case against war he devotes his first seven chapters. In the last two parts of the book, a little over a third of the whole, he returns to this theme and suggests ways of mitigating the horrors of war, if it should unfortunately break out, and of eventually eliminating it altogether from the intercourse of nations. The reforms he proposes in international law in regard to the right of blockade, the confiscation of enemy and neutral property on the high seas and the like, and the establishment of a congress of nations as the nucleus of a world organization are not put forward as alternatives to "the doctrine of nonresistance," which he regards as the core of the peace idea but rather as necessary concessions to the fact that, as he has to admit, the overwhelming majority of even the civilized peoples of the world are as yet far from accepting this doctrine. International law will disallow war altogether only when mankind is further advanced on the road to peace.[63]

In the central portions of his *Manual*, therefore, he concerns himself with the relationship between Christianity and war on both the national and the personal levels. Here he occupies the higher ground. Here "the doctrine is, that human life, both in its individual and corporate state, as one and as many, is INVIOLABLE; that it cannot be taken away for any purpose whatever, except by explicit divine permission; and that war, in every shape and for every purpose, is *wrong*, absolutely *wrong*, wholly *wrong*." Any position which stops short of this will be ineffective in ultimately removing the curse of war from mankind. "The principles of the gospels [to the discussion of which he devotes a couple of chapters] are binding upon men in their social capacity."

Where Upham grapples with the problems connected with the practical application of noninjurious force, we see clearly the influence of Dymond and especially of Grimké. Missionaries, unarmed travelers, Quakers and other peace sectaries, even Switzerland and San Marino, are cited as examples of successful nonviolence, nonviolence in practice. He is careful to explain that the nonviolent method does not threaten "the existence of civil government" and "the exercise of its authority to control and to punish" within the limits of the inviola-

[62] *The Fight for Peace*, p. 381. [63] Upham, *Manual of Peace*, p. 267.

bility of human life. "There are some extreme cases, (very few indeed, but still some *extreme* cases,) where resistance and the use of force, so far as is necessary to disarm and confine the assailant, are justifiable and a duty." He recommends, in addition, what he calls "the practice of Non-Intercourse," in effect, a cross between boycott and economic sanctions, as a nonviolent method for enforcing treaties, trade agreements, repayment of debts, and even on the level of personal relations (rather on the model of the Mennonite "avoidance").[64]

What, the professor asks, can we do for peace now? At this stage of the peace movement's evolution, his suggestions are of considerable interest. Let us set up peace societies, he proposes, in each of the Protesttant denominations on the basis of complete pacifism, of a renunciation, that is, of all defensive as well as offensive wars. Members would pledge themselves (in the manner of the teetotal pledge, says Upham) not to participate either by personal service[65] or in any other manner in a military organization. The problem of paying a sum of money in lieu of service—which, as we have seen, was the traditional solution used by many state legislatures to relieve the conscience of the occasional objectors to the militia, the "Pacific Exempts," as Upham calls them— was a complicated one. Should such fines be paid? "Certainly not," replies Upham, "if the fines, as is generally the case, are exacted and are applied for military purposes." But should the authorities in granting exemption "at the same time impose on the Pacific Exempts, in consideration of their exemption, a tax, which should be expended on roads, schools, the poor, civil officers, hospitals and the like, it might be a question, whether it would not be a duty to pay it." This must be something for each to decide for himself according to conscience.

[64] *Ibid.*, pp. 80, 81, 96-125, 146-60, 211, 217.
[65] Upham recommends the refusal by pacifist ministers of chaplaincies in any of the armed services, since the office only helps to give the cloak of religion to an essentially antichristian activity. Cf. Allen, *The Fight for Peace*, p. 19, who quotes from a letter of the Rev. Stephen Thurston (of Maine) published in the *Christian Mirror* (19 March 1835), explaining why he would not accept the offer of a chaplaincy for the local militia. "If it is right for me to act as chaplain to the militia at home," Thurston wrote, "it would be right for me to join the army in that capacity in time of war. . . . If I were to join the army in this capacity, I should be expected to impart, on all suitable occasions, moral and religious instructions to the soldiers. Suppose that on the eve of some important battle, I should preach from the well-known words of our Saviour, 'Put up thy sword in its place; for all they that take the sword shall perish by the sword'; or the words 'Love your enemies'; . . . should I be considered as acting the part of a good chaplain? Would it be a suitable preparation for a work of slaughter upon which they were soon to enter? But would not such preaching be in perfect accordance with my duty as a minister of the gospel of peace? And is it not evident that my duty as chaplain to an army would be quite inconsistent with my duty as a minister of Christ?"

He himself was inclined to favor payment. "It would probably tend to satisfy public feeling, and to hush complaints; it would be an evidence of our sincerity; and would discourage those, (for undoubtedly some such would be found), who might for the sake of saving their time and money, hypocritically pretend conscientious scruples in regard to war." But, torn between the fear of strengthening the military spirit and a desire to fulfill so far as was consistent with conscience the duties of a loyal citizen, he still retained doubts about the rightness and feasibility of payment.

> If by paying any tax whatever, on the principle of commutation, (that is to say, on the principle of *purchasing* an exemption from military duty,) we find that we are promoting, even in the least degree, the cause of war, we cannot rightfully do it. And if we are forced to pay such a tax, then there is a violation of religious right. Going on Gospel principles, no military service is to be performed; no military fine is to be paid; nor is there to be a payment of any commutation tax, imposed for exemption from military services, so long as such payment is in any degree subservient to the purposes of war.

Talk of conscientious objection and nonresistance, Upham fully realized, might frighten the majority of people away. A peace movement grounded on such principles would long remain small. But it must persist in them, since they alone accorded with the precepts of Christianity.[66]

Upham contributed nothing original to the theology of Christian pacifism. He was content to repeat, and elaborate, the thoughts of his predecessors. He wrote within the rigid framework of the fundamentalist, literalist viewpoint. The historical approach to Biblical studies was alien to his outlook. His work is important, however, for the systematic way in which he presents, from the complete pacifist position, many of the ideas which had been the stock in trade of peace advocates for at least two decades. It represents, too, a significant landmark in the history of the peace movement in the case it presents for a transformation of the movement from one uniting all varieties of peace sympathizers to one based on a pledge of personal war resistance and active conscientious objection. Upham, like Ladd and even Grimké,[67] was es-

---

[66] Upham, *Manual of Peace*, pp. 167-69.

[67] In the interesting notes he appended to his edition of Jonathan Dymond's *Inquiry into the Accordance of War with the Principles of Christianity* (published posthumously in 1834 just after his death), Grimké stressed (pp. 158-61) that in his view condemnation of all war did not undermine and was not in any way opposed to civil government—except insofar as government might involve the

sentially a moderate; he had little liking for the anarchistic hostility to the state that was shortly to make such headway in the movement's ranks. Like the Quakers, he found a place for the use of some degree of coercive force by government, if not for the sword of the magistrate; like them, he, too, did not deny the usefulness, so long as world opinion had not opened to the truth of the Christian law of love, of wider schemes of international order from which armed force would not be entirely excluded. But—and this was important—he had broken with the practice of the peace societies hitherto by advocating a new (and, some might think, a narrower) basis for their activities. As we shall see, the idea was welcomed enthusiastically by some peace workers, especially among the younger men and women; for other, and many of them older, heads however, it remained unacceptable. The seeds of schism latent in the movement from the beginning had now ripened.

We shall now see how, with little groups based on the absolutist position (and undoubtedly influenced in part by Upham's work) coming into existence in different parts of the country, the more radical ideas were fermenting among the rank and file of the peace movement. Not surprisingly, Upham's own Brunswick, Maine, produced two societies which took up this position, one in the town and the other among the students at Bowdoin College. The student pacifists, having adopted "the most thorough principles," reported that they were "resolved to carry out their principles, in their intercourse with their fellow-men, so far as to decline all military service, or the payment of military fines." The resolution, of course, rejoiced the heart of their philosophy professor. "When *young men* of character and station," he wrote, "occupying places of influence in the community, and enjoying the confidence and respect of the Christian public, come boldly forward to advance and maintain, in the face of contumely and reproach, the grand principle of *total abstinence from all war*," then surely the success of their cause must be approaching.[68]

Down in Boston we meet with similar developments. After heated debate lasting three evenings, the newly established Boston Free Church Peace Society had included in its constitution an article asserting its opposition to "all wars, both offensive and defensive, and all preparations for war," as "sinful and inconsistent with the spirit and

---

taking of human life. The Christian pacifists, he asserted, must always be ready to obey the decrees of the government, except where the act—whether military service or the payment of war taxes or the undertaking of work connected with war—went against conscience.

[68] Rufus P. Stebbins, *Address on the Subject of Peace*, p. 32.

precepts of the gospel." Members expressed, too, their determination to fight the inculcation of "a military spirit and education" among the youth of the city. "It will be noticed," wrote a commentator on the Society's constitution, "that it is one step in advance of any movement which has yet been made. All *preparations* for war are subject to the pledge; consequently no member can do military duty." After the adoption of this constitution, "a committee of three was appointed to draft and circulate a petition to the legislature, praying to be exempted from military duty, as such duty is inconsistent with a Christian profession."[69]

In February 1835 another Boston peace society had been formed—the Bowdoin Street Young Men's Peace Society—and a ladies' branch had been added in March. The young Boston pacifists were perhaps more plebeian than the Bowdoin College boys, but the roster of members included such future stalwarts of American pacifism as the well-connected Amasa Walker, who was elected chairman, Charles K. Whipple, William S. Heywood, Isaac Knapp the publisher, and that stormy petrel of the movement, the Rev. Henry C. Wright. All these young men will figure in our story shortly. The Society was affiliated to the American Peace Society, and it seems to have been in the forefront of the struggle to get the parent organization to come out squarely against all war. To give its first anniversary address, the Bowdoin Street Society had invited the Rev. Rufus P. Stebbins (1810-1885) from the Harvard Divinity School, and he had proceeded to deliver a frontal attack on the concept of defensive wars. "Go to the head of an army," he told the young men, "and read to them Christ's sermon on the mount.... Our religion forbids fighting."

The Bowdoin Street group proposed, among other activities, to distribute peace tracts among the pupils of Boston's 62 Sunday schools as soon as suitable literature was available.[70] We do not know if this plan

[69] *Ibid.*, p. 31.
[70] *Ibid.*, pp. 14, 15, 25, 27, 28, 30. Information concerning these peace societies is taken from the appendices to Stebbins's *Address on the Subject of Peace*. On 4 July 1838 we find Stebbins delivering, on this anniversary of independence, another strongly antimilitarist *Address*, this time before the peace society at Amherst College, of which he was an alumnus. "To prevent war," he told the college boys, "be unprepared for it; so when the passions are up they will have time to subside, ere we can act" (p. 8). In the course of his talk he gave support to Upham's proposals for "non-intercourse" with any country refusing to abide by the decisions of an international tribunal. A little earlier Stebbins had written of himself that he had come to his new parish at Leominster (Mass.) "all ablaze," to use his own words, "with enthusiasm, flaming with zeal to correct all evils and perfect all good in a day ... restless, dissatisfied, aggressive, belligerent" (quoted in *Dictionary of American Biography*, XVII [ed. Dumas Malone], N.Y., 1935, 550, 551).

was actually carried out. But the group did publish in pamphlet form a couple of years later a fascinating little dialogue between two brothers; in it the older, William, instructs young Frank in "the Principles of Peace." The work had originally appeared anonymously in a juvenile paper, *Youth's Cabinet* and it was now reprinted with supplementary material. The avowed object of the pamphlet was said to be to help mothers to train their offspring to follow the ways of peace. Even the best behaved children, states the author, may show bad temper and bellicosity at times (though it is perhaps hard to believe this could ever have been the case with the pious, sanctimonious William, who appears to us a terrible prig). Therefore, by means of the dialogue between the two boys and for the edification of parents as well as children, the writer outlines the nonresistant doctrine: the law of love and its scriptural foundation, the need to practice nonretaliation in respect to injury done us, and the consequent renunciation of all recourse to violence and war or preparation for it.

This long-forgotten pamphlet is seemingly the first attempt at peace education of youth in a consciously pacifist spirit. As propaganda, it is really not particularly good, with its stilted and didactic style. But it deserves some attention as a pioneer work in a field where in our century there were to be many successors. Let us concentrate on its treatment of two topics of special interest to our theme: the problem of law enforcement, of civil government, and the problem of conscientious objection.

As the law now stands, William explains to Frank, a magistrate, at least in his official capacity, cannot act in a spirit of Christian love and forgiveness. Justice demands the imposition of harsh penalties, including death itself for some crimes. A Christian should, therefore, refuse to accept office until the penal system is changed—and this it can be, William goes on, in a country like theirs if enough people desire it. We must do all in our power to persuade public opinion and the legislature to bring into effect much needed reforms in the laws. "How would you have them changed?" asks Frank. William replies: "I would have them always designed and suited to promote the interest, reformation, and permanent welfare of the criminal; and if an offender cannot be seized and punished without violating this principle, I think it is better that he should escape for the time." Next, Frank asks his brother what should be the attitude, in case of an armed invasion of his country, of a Christian pacifist magistrate (who, presumably, before accepting office had first satisfied himself that he would not have to act against his conscience in the exercise of his authority). William's answer follows closely, indeed is obviously copied from, Grimké's reply to Dr. Allen in their recent controversy. "We are never released from the obligation to obey God's rules. We have no more right to render evil for evil to an army than to individuals," William says in summing up his standpoint here.[71] But obviously government, some measure of restraint and degree of force, is not incompatible with the profession of Christian pacifism.

A little further on, we find William explaining to Frank that training to fight is as wrong, as unchristian, as the act of fighting itself. Their discussion of this topic is worth quoting in full:

Frank ... But I thought they could compel you to train, whether you wanted to or not.

William That would be a difficult matter. How would they go to work to compel me to buy a gun and cartridge box tomorrow morning, and to go to the common, instead of going to my store as usual?

F. I thought they could prosecute you if you did not go.

W. Very well. Then according to your own account, I can choose which I please, either to train or to be prosecuted. I prefer the latter.

F. But they will put you in prison.

W. Very well. Still I have the choice of training or going to prison, just which I like best. This is not compulsion; and I had much rather go to prison than train.

F. Oh, William! Go to prison?

W. Certainly, Frank. And I hope *you* would go to prison, if necessary, rather than deliberately do something you knew to be wrong. I see you are shocked at the idea of a prison, because you think that none but bad men are put there. But men have sometimes been sent to prison for being good, and when that is the case, it is no shame, but rather an honor.

F. But do men ever go to prison rather than train?

W. Yes. A friend of mine was put in Leverett Street jail last year for that very reason. I went to see him there two or three times. He was confined in the prison about a week.

F. Was he not very dull and miserable?

W. On the contrary, he was remarkably cheerful. He carried his books and papers there, and occupied himself pleasantly in reading and writing. And above all, he carried with him a good conscience, which can make even a jail pleasant.

F. But is everybody put in jail that refuses to train?

[71] *Dialogue between Frank and William*, pp. 36-38.

W. No. Many people escape by paying a fine.
F. Why then should you not pay the fine?
W. I do not think it would be right. These fines are paid to the companies, and go to support the military system. I must not escape doing a wicked thing by paying other people to do it for me.

Here Frank inquires if it is not true that Quakers are granted exemption from militia duties. Yes, William replies, and goes on to explain that they had won this right only after having long and patiently borne persecution on account of their refusal to fight.

F. But if you have the same scruples, why should not you be excused too?
W. There is no good reason why I and all who think thus should not have the same exemption.[72]

Finally, we may mention the peace group formed in the summer of 1836 by some of the students at the Oneida Institute in upstate New York. They too, like the student pacifists at Bowdoin College, adopted Upham's idea of a peace pledge, a pledge to renounce war and military service in any form, including the hiring of substitutes or the payment of fines in lieu of service. "We cannot," they state, "in these days of violence, keep silence on this great question without incurring the guilt of shedding the blood of men." A novel feature of the Oneida group's constitution was the article it contained allowing for the expulsion, on a two-thirds vote, of any member who continued to violate its provisions after visitation and kindly admonishment to repent.[73]

The groups we have been discussing were small and ephemeral. The mainstream of pacifist effort still ran within the confines of the American Peace Society, and here radical ideas were gaining increasing support among the more active members. Ladd in his "Farewell" as editor of the *Calumet* had declared: "I am myself opposed to all war in every form, as utterly inconsistent with the spirit of the Gospel."[74] Despite his continued desire to accommodate all shades of peace opinion under the Society's umbrella, he looked with a sympathetic eye on the aspirations of the young enthusiasts—some would call them firebrands—who were beginning to speak out in favor of getting the Society

---

[72] *Ibid.*, pp. 41-43.
[73] William Lloyd Garrison, Scrap-book, B.P.L., *4261.64, p. 1, cutting from the *Friend of Man*.
[74] *Advocate of Peace*, II, no. 6 (March-April 1835), 163. See also *The Duty of Women to Promote the Cause of Peace* (1836), pp. 8-11.

to take a more unequivocal stand against all varieties of war and violence.

There was, for instance, young Henry Clarke Wright (1797-1870), a Congregational minister (about whom more will be said in the next chapter). In 1836 he was employed by the Society as one of its agents. An early convert to absolute pacifism, he had been agitating within the Society for several years now for its adoption as the Society's platform. Intensely idealistic and religious, Wright found it impossible to compromise on any issue; a certain rigidity in his character also made it difficult for him to understand sympathetically the motives of those unable to "go the second mile." He has been called a "persistent trouble-maker," "a conceited, mischief-making incompetent."[75] Disliked intensely by his political adversaries, he was, nevertheless, always highly respected by a small circle of admirers. He soon came to feel that the doctrine of complete nonresistance and "no-government" was the only consistent position for a practising Christian. "I made up my mind when I embraced the peace principle some years ago," he wrote in 1836, "that in this cause I might be called to lay down my life; and in endeavoring to gain converts to this cause, I have uniformly impressed on men the necessity of making up their minds to die, unresisting and unprotected, except by the arm of that God who is almighty to save."[76] It was to the American Peace Society's shilly-shallying on the question of defensive war that he, along with a number of others, as we have seen, attributed the slow progress the movement had been making up to that time.

Ladd certainly followed Wright a good part of the way and was probably to some extent influenced toward radicalism by his young colleague, but he drew back at the thought of the eventual alienation of conservative opinion within the ranks of the movement, which might result from too startling a change in the Society's platform. "I am myself what they would call an ultra," he admitted to Wright in a letter of 20 September 1836. "The members of our Executive Committee are very moderate peace men and are very much afraid of ultraism."[77] He warned Wright against the probable consequences of being too outspoken in this question in another letter written about this time. In it Ladd told his younger colleague: "You should preach against war generally and not . . . specify *defensive* war unless you are asked—but let your arguments go against all war offensive and defensive

[75] Barnes, *The Antislavery Impulse*, p. 252.
[76] Scrap-books of Henry C. Wright, I, 2-4, 9, quoting from the *New England Spectator* (1836).
[77] Galpin, *Pioneering for Peace*, p. 109.

without specifying either." And he warned Wright not "to mix up with your public exercises the subject of capital punishment. . . . If you are asked your own private opinion give it, but do not implicate the American Peace Society as though they commissioned you to preach against capital punishment or any other punishment." And he added that he much doubted "the *expediency* of declaring it to be a sin against God for a man or nation to defend itself as the case may be, when attacked. This is your opinion and mine also but neither of us adopted it at once and the world is not prepared for such a leap."[78]

Ladd had, indeed, been alarmed by reports of Wright's activities during the summer months of 1836, when the indefatigable agent had traveled nearly 2,000 miles through the northern parts of New York state and in New England lecturing on peace and preaching non-resistant doctrines to all and sundry, to adult and child, indeed, to all who would listen. "I have much discussion on the subject of peace," Wright wrote in September, "in the stage, in the cars, in the boats, in the house, by the way-side, and in hotels."[79] Included in his itinerary, for instance, was a visit to the Springfield arsenal, where he addressed the munition workers on peace and the duties of Christian nonresistance, telling them "that they ought to engrave on every lock, barrel, and bayonet of every musket, 'love your enemies,' 'overcome evil with good,' 'thou shalt not kill.'" They listened to him attentively and courteously, he reported.[80] Elsewhere, however, he met with a less friendly reception. In one church where he was preaching, two members of the congregation, a general and an elder, walked out angrily.[81] The usual reaction seems to have been puzzlement rather than anger; the chief objection urged against his views was that they were not applicable in the world as it then existed. But the danger was obvious that the Society might be credited with the extreme opinions of its agent.

"Notwithstanding this difference of views," wrote Ladd at this time in reference to the divergence that had arisen in the Society between the protagonists of defensive war and the absolute pacifists of the Wright variety, "the friends of peace move harmoniously along together."[82] Nevertheless, that some change in its platform was called for, if the Society was not to lose the support of the radical wing, and that a more outspoken condemnation of war in general was necessary before new life could be pumped into the already somewhat mori-

---

[78] *Ibid.*, pp. 107, 108.   [79] Scrap-books, I, 62ff.
[80] *Ibid.*, I, 61, quoting from the *New England Spectator* (July 1836).
[81] Curti, *American Peace Crusade*, p. 74.
[82] Ladd, "History of Peace Societies," in *Scientific Tracts for the Diffusion of Useful Knowledge*, p. 190.

bund organization was readily admitted by many members, even though they looked at Wright's activities with some misgivings and were not very sympathetic to his suggestions that the peace society should be transformed into a nonresistant association. At the Society's annual meeting of 1836 a committee (with Ladd as one of its members) had been set up to revise the constitution. After weighing the pros and cons, this committee—undoubtedly under the guidance of Ladd, who felt strongly that the time had come for some fairly drastic step if the Society was not to decline in influence and numbers[83]—had concluded not only that sentiment within the Society, at least among the leadership and active workers, favored a total condemnation of international war in all its forms, but that this position was in fact the truly scriptural one. At the next annual meeting, therefore, it recommended that changes be made in the Society's constitution to this effect.

As Ladd wrote around this time:

> It ought not . . . to be suppressed, that most of the leaders in the peace cause are in favour of total abstinence [i.e., from war]; and that almost all of those who have looked into the subject by the light of the gospel, have been brought, often reluctantly and to their own surprise, to adopt the total abstinence principle as the only safe one for a Christian. Let any one who has any doubts on this subject take the gospel, and study it prayerfully and diligently in reference to peace and war, and let him improve what light he has by *acting* in the cause of Peace, and he will have more light, and will find that his dreaded difficulties were but bugbears, and that it is safest to follow the precepts of Christ, wherever they may lead us.[84]

Taken by surprise perhaps, the members present showed no opposition to the committee's proposals, which were accepted unanimously.[85] Article II of the newly adopted constitution now read as follows: "This society, being founded on the principle that all war is contrary to the spirit of the gospel, shall have for its object to illustrate the inconsistency of war with Christianity, to show its baleful influence on all the great interests of mankind, and to devise means for insuring universal and permanent peace." Article III, however, went on to add: "Persons of every denomination, desirous of promoting peace on earth, and good-will towards men, may become members of this society."[86] Thus, although the Society had now taken its stand publicly against de-

---

[83] Hemmenway, *The Apostle of Peace*, p. 63.
[84] Ladd, *Obstacles and Objections*, p. 4.
[85] *Advocate of Peace*, I, no. 3 (Dec. 1837), 120.
[86] *Ibid.*, I, no. 1 (June 1837), 30.

fensive wars as well as against wars of aggression, although it had denied the possibility from the Christian point of view of such a thing as a just war, the nonpacifists were still welcome to join its ranks. In fact, almost all those nonpacifists holding office within the Society continued on in their positions.

In its first issue the Society's new periodical, the *Advocate of Peace*, hastened to explain that *plus se change, plus c'est la même chose*. "This step is less a change than a distinct avowal of sentiments long cherished. The society has never taken any ground at variance with this position; it has merely left the point for its members to settle, each for himself in the light of revelation; while the tone of its appeals, the drift of its measures, and the deep-seated convictions of its leading friends, have always been against every species of war as repugnant to the Sermon on the Mount." Those members who now accepted the full pacifist position had "been brought upon this high ground, not by the ultraism of the age, nor yet by the impulses of a blind or visionary enthusiasm, but by a calm, prayerful examination of the gospel."[87]

As later issues reiterated,[88] all who strove for universal and permanent peace—as in the London Peace Society, which had taken the "high-ground" as its official position from the outset—would continue to be welcome within the Society's ranks, whatever their views on such subjects as defensive wars, capital punishment, the proper limits of the use of force in government, or the inviolability of human life. The change had become necessary it was explained, owing to the idea becoming current outside the Society that it positively approved of defensive wars. This state of affairs, in turn, had begun to alarm the absolute pacifists, those, in fact, who were most active in the promotion of the Society's activities, and voices had more and more been raised in favor of having the Society take a clear stand against war in all its forms. "The demand appeared so reasonable, that the revised constitution gave such a pledge, by recognizing for its basis the contrariety of *all* war to the *spirit* of the gospel." This statement was not intended as a test of membership, as an instrument by which to measure the purity of the principles of its followers. "We merely give it as a guarantee, that our influence as a society shall never go to countenance *any* form of war. Our *general* course is still the same." There must still be unity between the two wings of the movement united together under the Society's banner. No good would come, either, from denouncing the absolute pacifists as "ultraists" or abusing those who clung to the need for some measure of defense as "time-servers."

[87] *Ibid.*, p. 8.
[88] See, e.g., *ibid.*, vol. I, no. 3 (Dec. 1837).

One man, at least, remained unconvinced by such arguments. In August 1837, soon after the changes had been introduced, Dr. Allen, president of that center of radical student pacifism, Bowdoin College, a vice-president of the American Peace Society, and Grimké's doughty opponent in the recent controversy, wrote Ladd an angry letter of resignation.[89] "I am not," he wrote, "a believer in the Quaker principle of the criminality of defensive war. I ought not, therefore, to lend even the poor support of my name to a principle which I think not founded upon the gospel, not true, and blasting to the prospects of usefulness of a society . . . which I hoped would tend to correct the public opinion concerning war." With its present constitution, he continued, the American Peace Society set itself in effect, if not in intent, against all civil government. This stance would prevent it from spreading further among sound Christian ministers and laymen, its best source of support, and would damage its reputation with the public at large.

Ladd replied mildly in his usual conciliatory style, at the same time not concealing where his own sympathies lay.[90] "A peace society," he told Allen, "which should allow its members to fight when they thought it necessary . . . would have no more effect in banishing war from the world, than a temperance society which should allow its members to drink rum when they thought it necessary, would have in banishing intemperance." While answering Allen's arguments point by point, he was, however, ready to concede that the pacifist position had its problems, too. "In the transition state of society from war to peace, there are difficulties to be encountered similar to temperance." But, in any event, there was no need at all, in Ladd's view, for Allen to have resigned because the leaders of the Society had declared themselves in favor of total abstinence from war. Diversities of opinion would still be tolerated within its ranks, and there was more than enough work for persons of varying peace views to do in helping to bring about a warless world.

Although Dr. Allen had withdrawn altogether, it is clear that most of the nonpacifists in the Society had not followed his lead. At the annual meeting of 1838, held as usual in Boston in May, an attempt was made to water down the declaration against all war taken in the previous year. Its leader was the Rev. George C. Beckwith, a Congregational minister whom Ladd himself had selected to take over his own duties as secretary of the Society and to edit the *Advocate of Peace*. In fact, Beckwith, who was to play a very important role in the Society

[89] *Ibid.*, I, no. 3 (Dec. 1837), 111-19.   [90] *Ibid.*, pp. 119-25.

for several decades to come, far outdid Ladd in his conservatism and caution and in his anxiety to appease the moderate elements within the movement. He now came forward with a resolution to amend the wording of Article II of the new constitution to read as follows: "The object of this society shall be to illustrate the inconsistency of war with Christianity, to show its baneful influence on all the great interests of man and to devise means for insuring universal and permanent peace." Thus, by omitting the offensive clause—"all war is contrary to the spirit of the gospel"—the sting would be removed from the article and the Society would return to its position prior to the revisions of 1837. A majority, however, rejected the motion; even Beckwith's mentor, Ladd, voted against it, and it was finally agreed to leave the existing constitution as it was. But, not unnaturally, the radicals were disturbed at the rapid resurgence of conservatism within the Society, and, after the annual meeting had adjourned, a further and informal meeting of members was held on the following day. At this time, a motion proposed by Henry C. Wright was carried, calling for a peace convention later in the year to thresh out some of the pressing problems which were besetting the peace movement. Attendance was not to be confined to members of the American Peace Society: all interested in peace might come. An arrangements committee was also appointed. But, since both Ladd and Beckwith refused to serve on it—ostensibly, on the grounds that the Society should not be connected officially with such a convention, more likely in reality out of well-grounded fears that such an assembly would be far to the left of the existing Society leadership—members of this committee were chosen entirely from the radical camp.[91]

A new crisis was now approaching. Hitherto, moderates and radicals had been kept in uneasy partnership within the framework of the American Peace Society. Credit for this achievement was largely due to William Ladd, who had succeeded in maintaining the respect and allegiance of the moderates even after declaring himself in favor of radical pacifism. The constitution as reframed in 1837 made concessions to both camps, but it did not succeed in satisfying either the left or the right wing. The more extreme among the radicals were the least contented, and their discontent was fanned by intellectual influences and by personalities standing apart from, and even outside, the organized movement, who wished to broaden the range of discussion from its center hitherto in the problem of war between nations so as to embrace also the whole issue of the use of force in the do-

[91] Galpin, *Pioneering for Peace*, pp. 109-13, 121-23; Curti, *American Peace Crusade*, pp. 75-79; Allen, *The Fight for Peace*, pp. 383, 384.

mestic arena by either government or individual citizen. Nonresistance and "no-government" were now being propounded as the slogans of a radical peace movement, in place of the narrower (and less inflammatory) principle of the incompatibility of international war with Christianity. This new battle of the peace men would lead shortly to a split in the movement; then some of the more fervent among the radical pacifists would break with the old Society and create their own organization, the New England Non-Resistance Society.

Chapter 3

The Genesis of the Garrisonian Formula: No-Government and Nonresistance

The first generation of American peace men, the absolute pacifists as much as the relativists, were on the whole a socially respectable group of people. This did not mean that they did not come in for their fair share of abuse, that they were not accused of subversion and of lack of patriotism and did not have to suffer a certain amount of inconvenience on this account. But they were, as we have seen, almost to a man solid citizens, upholders of the existing political and social order, protagonists of civil government insofar as it did not infringe upon the rights of private conscience. They did not deny a rightful place in God's order to the magistrate. In the tradition of Quaker pacifism, law and order, with perhaps some degree of coercive force, were not deemed irreconcilable with the Christian law of love. This opinion was held equally as much by those who called themselves nonresistants as by their moderate and conservative brethren who balked at the implications of full pacifism. The prosperous, well-to-do middle-class from which the peace movement drew the overwhelming majority of its members gave it also its most prominent absolutists: Ladd the wealthy farmer, Grimké the successful lawyer, Blanchard the substantial merchant, Amasa Walker the banker, Upham the college professor, the sprinkling of worthy Quakers (too few, it is true, to reflect much credit on the foremost peace church in the land), and the numerous clergymen drawn from all denominations, from Episcopalians to Unitarians. However, none of these men, for all their renunciation of defensive wars and the use of armed force in the protection of person and property, ever went so far as to contest the necessity of government or the moral rightness of political action, when directed toward desirable ends and if carried on by proper means.

Perhaps old David Dodge (still active in New York but no longer in the forefront of the peace movement) had come nearest, with his refusal to vote in elections, to doubting the compatibility of a belief in nonresistance with collaboration in even the beneficial aspects of government as then constituted. It is true, however, that this problem of government had been at the back of all these men's minds as they wrestled with the implications of their peace beliefs. (They were, for instance, opposed almost to a man to the state's imposition of the death penalty for the most serious crimes.) And even if they had not already been aware of the problem themselves, their opponents, like President Allen of Bowdoin, hastened to bring it to their attention. Briefly stated, the problem amounted to this: could a man who had renounced the use of armed force in international affairs and in his own personal relations approve or, indeed, voluntarily collaborate in any way with the machinery of state, so long as this was connected with violence and the military? And, conversely, could national governments ever be so ordered as to dispense with the use of armed force; were not, perhaps, Christian pacifism and Christian government mutually contradictory concepts? There is no doubt that the answer that they were, that no true Christian might participate in the work of the state, had been the traditional attitude of members of the pacifist sects before the Quakers made their attempt to reconcile pacifism and the political order, and that it had remained the belief of those of the sects' descendants who still clung to their forefathers' pacifist faith. Therefore, "no-government," to use the phrase current at this time, was not something new in the history of pacifism. What was novel was the effort now to extend the doctrine outside the narrow limits of the more conservative peace sects, the attempt to spread it among the clergy and laity of the Christian church at large.

By 1838 these ideas were acting as a ferment within the American Peace Society. We can see their effect, for instance, in the case of the famous essayist and poet, Ralph Waldo Emerson, who, though never intimately associated with any peace group or committed unreservedly to either moderate pacifism or radical nonresistance, was yet strongly attracted to pacifist and nonresistant ideas during the thirties and forties. For the transcendentalist, love was the cement that would bind all human souls in a oneness of spirit. On 3 October 1831 the young Unitarian minister (as he then was) had entered in his journal:

> I wish the Christian principle, the *ultra* principle of nonresistance and returning good for ill might be tried fairly. William Penn made one trial. The world was not ripe and yet it did well. An angel stands a poor chance among wild beasts; a better chance among men; but among angels best of all. And so I admit of this system that it is like the Free Trade, fit for one nation only on condition that all adopt it. Still a man may try it in his own person and even his sufferings by reason of it shall be its triumphs. . . . Love is the adamantean shield that makes blows ridiculous . . . it is said that it strips the good man bare and leaves him to the whip and license of fools and pirates and butchers. But I suppose the exaltation of the general mind by

the influence of the principle will be a counteraction of the increased license. Not any influence acts upon the highest man but a proportion of the same gets down to the lowest man.[1]

In 1838 we find Emerson lecturing on the topic of "War," the last in a series of addresses sponsored by the American Peace Society.[2] As before and later in his life, he did not deny that warlike instincts were deeply embedded in man and that war's heroic qualities had value at a certain level in mankind's development. It was, however, "a juvenile and temporary state," which the human race must outgrow. He spoke appreciatively, though not without some ambiguity, of those who advocated both the repudiation of war, even of a defensive kind, and personal nonresistance. Should one be ready, then, to stand by and see his family slaughtered by thugs? To such inquiries Emerson, who avoided recourse to specifically Christian arguments, gave a twofold answer. In the first place, such a formulation of the question tended to ignore the positive aspect of absolute pacifism while concentrating on "the passive side of the friend of peace." "If you have a nation of men who have risen to that height of moral cultivation that they will not declare war or carry arms, for they have not so much madness left in their brains, you have a nation of lovers, of benefactors, of true, great and able men." Such men would generate an all-conquering moral force. Secondly, in regard to individual nonresistance, "the good and just man" who adopted this position would, Emerson thought, only very rarely be subject to attack. However, such a man, if he was also wise, would not "decide beforehand what he shall do in a given extreme event. Nature and God will instruct him in that hour." Finally, Emerson declared in his address his disbelief that universal peace would come merely through organizing societies, for, if in the meantime war should break out, most members would be swept up in the martial enthusiasm of the conflict—a prophetic vision of what did, indeed, take place in the case of the peace society he was then addressing. Instead, what was needed, in his view, was individual conversion to the concept of peace: "private, dear and earnest love."

Among those who were most impressed by Emerson's stand was Garrison himself, who was soon to become the chief apostle of radical nonresistance. To friends Garrison "expressed . . . his hopes in

---

[1] *The Journals and Miscellaneous Notebooks of Ralph Waldo Emerson*, III (1963), 295, 296.

[2] The address on "War" is printed in XI (*Miscellanies*) of Emerson's *Complete Works*, 1904 edn., 149-76.

[Emerson] as a man of the new age."[3] True, Emerson had dealt only with the question of war and personal self-defense, and not with the problem of organized government: he had said kind things about the Quakerlike brand of pacifism while refraining from discussion of its relation to the institution of the state. Yet, by implication, at least, Emerson had appeared to commend the "no-government" perfectionism that was being broached now by Garrison and his friends.[4]

These ideas had indeed begun to attract many of the most vigorous and capable of the younger peace men, who had come more and more to feel that the middle-of-the-road policy represented by Ladd and his associates was, despite the more radical constitution adopted by the American Peace Society in 1837, in general stultifying to the Society's growth and that the attempt to conciliate the nonpacifists would lead to its speedy decay. These dissenters within the peace ranks were not all of one mind on the limits and obligations of radical pacifism. Some were well advanced along the road to thoroughgoing nonresistance and the renunciation of all association with the state; others went little beyond Ladd himself in their position on the duties of absolute pacifism. That their strivings and searchings crystallized to form an independent peace society dedicated to the twin principles of no-government and nonresistance, and divided from the older Society by its attitude toward the state, was attributable in particular to the efforts

---

[3] *Ibid.*, XI, 578 (quoted from A. Bronson Alcott's diary).

[4] Emerson's conversation with Carlyle and some English acquaintances in 1847 on the subject of nonresistance was recorded in his essay "Stonehenge" (in V [*English Traits*] of the *Complete Works*, 1903 edn., 286, 287). Upon the Englishmen's inquiring if he knew of any Americans "with an American idea—any theory of the right future of that country," Emerson thought at once of his friends in the New England Non-Resistance Society: "the simplest and purest minds," he called them. Many might think them fanatics, regard their theories as visionary or ridiculous. Nevertheless, he goes on, "I opened the dogma of no-government and nonresistance, and anticipated the objections and the fun, and procured a kind of hearing for it. I said, it is true that I have never seen in any country a man of sufficient valor to stand for the truth, and yet it is plain to me that no less valor than this can command my respect. I can easily see the bankruptcy of the vulgar musket-worship,—though great men be musket-worshippers;—and 't is certain as God liveth, the gun that does not need another gun, the law of love and justice alone, can effect a clean revolution." By the 1850's, however, Emerson's sympathies with nonresistance had almost ebbed away. We find him supporting the purchase of "Sharp's rifles" for Kansas; in the Civil War he was enthusiastically and unqualifiedly in favor of the Unionist cause. "The brute noise of cannon," he told the students at Tufts College in July 1861 in words that might, indeed, have been spoken by Carlyle himself, "has a most poetic echo in these days, as instrument of the primal sentiments of humanity" (*Complete Works*, XI, 579). For Emerson's attitude toward the Civil War, see William Allen Huggard, *Emerson and the Problem of War and Peace*, chap. IV; Merle E. Curti, "Poets of Peace and the Civil War," *World Unity*, X, no. 3 (June 1932), 154, 155.

of a handful of men led by that stormy petrel of mid-century reform, William Lloyd Garrison (1805-1879). It is to their story that we must now turn.

Garrison's role was central in the history of New England nonresistance. He dominated it by his moral conviction as well as by the strength of his personality, his gift for leadership, and his ability to inspire unswerving confidence in his disciples. Garrison, it has been aptly remarked, was essentially "a man of action, . . . a man to whom ideas were revealed in relation to passing events, and who saw in ideas the levers and weapons with which he might act upon the world."[5] He contributed little to the formulation of the ideology of nonresistance; yet he gave it its shape and its drive, and his energy made of it for a brief while a force that attracted many of the best minds and finest spirits in the New England of that day. Although we cannot at all ignore the other figures in its history, we would not be wrong in calling this radical peace movement "Garrisonian" pacifism, just as the same epithet is applied to one branch of the radical abolitionism of the period.

In his very background and early upbringing we find a striking difference between Garrison and the peace leaders we have been studying until now. The grinding poverty of his home, the small boy's weary hours first as a cobbler's and then as a cabinetmaker's apprentice, and later the possibility for self-education and self-improvement that employment in the printing trade afforded him contrast sharply with the middle-class affluence and the educational opportunities of the older generation of peace leaders. Even when in his early twenties Garrison was able to exchange the printer's shop for the editor's office, he still remained desperately poor, a struggling young journalist without money or social connections or educational qualifications. Much of the later Garrison, of Garrison the pacifist as much as of Garrison the abolitionist (for it is, of course, in the history of the antislavery movement that his major claim to fame lies), can be traced back to these early years. His mother, who brought him up by herself, was a Baptist, and his early church ties were with the Baptists; from the religious upbringing in his home derive that rigidity and inflexibility, that uncompromising mark, that rests on his whole character and on all his manifold activities. Next, let us note his intense Biblicism, the profound knowledge of the scriptures that he constantly drew upon —and with such effect—in his speeches and writings, continuing to do so, indeed, long after he had abandoned his early fundamentalist views

---

[5] John Jay Chapman, *William Lloyd Garrison*, 2nd edn., p. 162.

and had broken finally with organized Christianity. "The source of Garrison's power," to quote John Jay Chapman again, "was the Bible. ... From his boyhood upward Garrison's mind was soaked in the Bible and in no other book."[6] It was his reading of the New Testament, and perhaps some contact with Quakers in his neighborhood, that brought Garrison as a very young man, even before he left his native Newburyport for good at the beginning of 1827, to the conviction that all connection with war was a sin, as sinful, indeed, as indulgence in alcohol. His pacifist convictions, therefore, predate his allegiance to the abolitionist cause.[7]

When, at the age of 23, he was appointed editor of a small and vegetating temperance sheet in Boston, the *National Philanthropist*, its publisher generously permitted him, in addition to pushing his main theme of the evils of strong drink, to use its columns as a platform from which to launch vigorous attacks on war as well as on a multitude of other iniquities: smoking, Sunday postal deliveries, and immorality in general. It was in 1828, while he was engaged in editing the *National Philanthropist*, that Garrison first met the gentle Quaker, Benjamin Lundy (1787-1839), who roomed for a short while in the same house as Garrison. Contact with Lundy led to a radical change in the young man's views on the slavery question. Soon he had developed from an advocate of colonization to become the fiery apostle of immediate emancipation. Probably, too, conversations with Lundy led to a strengthening of Garrison's burgeoning pacifist convictions. Both his abolitionism and his pacifism, in fact, flowed from the same source: his belief in the freedom and dignity of man, all men, as the necessary outcome of his religious faith.

During the winter months of 1828-1829, Garrison spent a six months' period as editor of a short-lived paper, the *Journal of the Times*, which had been started up in Bennington (Vt.) to support the candidacy of John Quincy Adams, who was then running for the presidency against Andrew Jackson. Garrison, whose journalistic talents were beginning to attract notice—and whose political sentiments were then Federalist—accepted the invitation to Bennington on condition that he could continue as before his advocacy of his favorite reform causes. His object as editor, he wrote in the first number, would be to promote "the suppression of intemperance and its associate vices,

---

[6] *Ibid.*, pp. 164, 165.

[7] Garrison's first known contact with the peace movement was in the summer of 1826, when William Ladd visited Newburyport and the young journalist wrote approvingly of Ladd's views on war in the local *Free Press* he was then editing. See John L. Thomas, *The Liberator*, pp. 49-51.

the gradual emancipation of every slave in the Republic, and the perpetuity of national peace"—in addition, of course, to the support of Adams' candidacy.[8] Antislavery and peace had already become the dominant themes in Garrison's life.

Since his first arrival at Boston, the young man had been receiving repeated summonses to serve in the state militia. These he had always refused, but until the summer of 1829 (a witness, indeed, to the laxity with which militia regulations were then enforced) he had not been called upon either to pay the customary fine which exempted from actual service or to provide any explanation of his nonattendance at drill. In 1829, however, the authorities caught up with him, and he received a visit from the clerk of his militia company back home, who was the local blacksmith ("a saucy, smutty faced son of Vulcan, as well as an ambitious follower of Mars" and "a poor, worthless scamp" are Garrison's descriptions of him). After pleading both nonresidence and his nearsightedness to no effect, Garrison submitted to the payment of the small fine. As he wrote of himself shortly afterward:

> I am not professedly a Quaker; but I heartily, entirely and practically embrace the doctrine of non-resistance, and am conscientiously opposed to all military exhibitions. I now solemnly declare that I will never obey any order to bear arms, but rather cheerfully suffer imprisonment and persecution. What is the design of militia musters? *To make men skilful murderers.* I cannot consent to become a pupil in this sanguinary school.[9]

Six months after penning these words, Garrison was, indeed, to find himself in a prison cell—not, however, as a result of his conscientious objection to military service, but on account of the fiery campaign he had commenced for the immediate abolition of Negro slavery. The story of his prosecution in the spring of 1830 by a Massachusetts slave-trader for alleged calumniation of character in the columns of the *Genius of Universal Emancipation,* the antislavery paper which Lundy had invited Garrison to help him edit in Baltimore, and of his conviction and subsequent imprisonment in the Baltimore city jail is well known, and it need not be retold here. In prison he penciled on his cell walls a sonnet entitled "The Guiltless Prisoner," not very good poetry perhaps, but often quoted in later years:

[8] Russel B. Nye, *William Lloyd Garrison and the Humanitarian Reformers,* pp. 13, 21, 22.
[9] *Genius of Universal Emancipation,* N.S., IV, no. 2 (16 Sept. 1829), 14, quoted in part in *W.L.G.: Story of His Life told by his Children,* I, 124, 125.

Perchance thy fault was love to all mankind;
Thou didst oppose some vile, oppressive law;
Or strive all human fetters to unbind;
Or wouldst not bear the implements of war. . . .

Soon after his release, Garrison parted company amicably with Lundy, whose Quaker mildness made it hard for him to stomach the violent tone that Garrison was giving to his attacks on slavery and the slaveholders. Now Garrison began on the great venture of his life. Returning to Boston, he started up, with scarcely any funds but with unbounded faith in his cause and confidence in himself, a paper devoted primarily to the policy of immediate emancipation. The first issue of the *Liberator* appeared on 1 January 1831; in the following year an obscure group of enthusiasts inspired by Garrison formed an antislavery society in New England to support the work of the *Liberator*, and the end of 1833 saw the foundation at a conference in Philadelphia of a national organization dedicated to the policy of immediate abolition. The abolitionists, though still a handful, were slowly beginning to make their influence felt, and Garrison's name, especially after the slave revolt led by Nat Turner in Virginia in 1831 (with which, of course, the pacifist Garrison had not had the slightest connection) had alarmed the South into creating a bogey out of the *Liberator's* editor, soon became known up and down the country.[10] For most, he was just a professional troublemaker, the epitome of reckless extremism, if not of downright incendiarism; for a few, he became the acknowledged leader of reform. These Garrisonian abolitionists were to form the nucleus of the New England nonresistance movement.[11]

The delegates assembled at the Philadelphia conference of December 1833 adopted for the newly founded American Anti-Slavery Society a "Declaration of Sentiments." Although the initiative for the conference had come more from the abolitionist group centered in New York led by the Tappan brothers than from the New England (later Massachusetts) Anti-Slavery Society that Garrison had founded

---

[10] It is true, however, that now, as later, Garrison the nonresistant asserted that, *if* "white men" were justified in revolting against oppression, black men were equally entitled morally to rise in arms against those who held them in slavery. See Thomas, *The Liberator*, p. 136; Walter M. Merrill, *Against Wind and Tide*, pp. 50-52.

[11] "It was by no means a mere coincidence," writes John R. Bodo, "that the leadership of the abolitionist societies and of the peace societies overlapped to a considerable extent: the fiercest abolitionists . . . were also the champions of the most uncompromising antiwar platform" (*The Protestant Clergy and Public Issues*, p. 229).

at the beginning of the previous year, the Declaration itself emanated almost entirely from Garrison's pen. It has quite a lot to say that bears on the use of nonviolent methods in combating evil, passages that were later to be the subject of controversy within abolitionist ranks. Stressing the efficacy of propaganda by the written and spoken word for promoting the cause, the Declaration compares the methods of the patriots of the American Revolution with their own today as they struggled against the infinitely greater evils of the slave power. Referring to the men of the Revolution, it declared:

> Their principles led them to wage war against their oppressors, and to spill human blood like water, in order to be free. Ours forbid the doing of evil that good may come, and lead us to reject, and to entreat the oppressed to reject, the use of all carnal weapons for deliverance from bondage; relying solely upon those which are spiritual, and mighty through God to the pulling down of strongholds. Their measures were physical resistance—the marshalling in arms—the hostile army—the mortal encounter. Ours shall be such only as the opposition of moral purity to moral corruption—the destruction of error by the potency of truth—the overthrow of prejudice by the power of love—and the abolition of slavery by the spirit of repentance.[12]

Was this disavowal of the use of force in fact a declaration in favor of nonresistance? Though admittedly it says nothing either of international war or of civil government (both these subjects were, indeed, only indirectly related to the matter at hand), the implication seems to be against the use of force for even righteous ends. Most of the Garrisonians, Samuel J. May and David Lee Child, for instance, understood it thus. The numerous Quaker delegates, who made up a considerable proportion of the conference's membership, must have interpreted it thus, too. However, Garrison himself, the virtual author of the Declaration, while conceding that the doctrine of nonresistance might not unfairly be read into it, admitted at the same time that it would not be correct to consider it as a purely pacifist document.[13] And it is fairly certain that it was not understood in this way by some influential members of the new Society, those in particular, like the wealthy Tappan brothers, who were to be most active in the Society's New York headquarters and were always to remain critical of Garrison's policies and his Bostonian group.

The issue of nonresistance, however, was not to stir the abolitionist

---
[12] Garrisons, *W.L.G.*, I, 409, 412.
[13] *Ibid.*, II, 303, 304. See also *Liberator*, 5 Jan. 1838.

movement for several years after the founding of the American Anti-Slavery Society. Before discussing the Lovejoy case of 1837, which brought out into the open the deep differences of opinion that divided the movement on this subject, let us turn our attention to the small band of men and women gathered around Garrison and the Boston *Liberator*.

Nearest to Garrison himself in spirit, in the intensity of his hatred for both war and slavery, was the Rev. Henry Clarke Wright.[14] Originally a hatmaker from Connecticut, Wright, after being ordained a Congregationalist minister, had worked for the American Sunday School Union and, as we have seen, for the American Peace Society. His pacifism stemmed directly from his sternly Puritan and Bible-centered religion, from his study of—and reflections on—the books of the New Testament. He had been greatly impressed, too, by the arguments put forward by Grimké in his 1832 *Address* in favor of thoroughgoing nonresistance. We have already watched Wright causing alarm and embarrassment in the summer of 1836 to the officers of the American Peace Society by the vehemence with which he propounded radical nonresistant views while acting as the Society's traveling agent. In debate with moderate peace men like Wayland and Beckwith (the Society's secretary since 1837), he ridiculed the idea of opposing all forms of international war while maintaining the validity in the last resort of the magistrate's use of the sword in domestic relations. "A glaring absurdity" he called such views. Wright early became associated with Garrison in his campaign for immediate abolition. For him, as for Garrison, antislavery and pacifism were but facets of the same underlying principle: "How can anyone," he wrote in April 1837 in an article in *Zion's Watchman*, "plead the cause of the slave, on *Christian* principles, and not oppose the law of violence, the basis of all war? And, what is slavery but the carrying out of the war principle and spirit to the end."[15] Thus, in the second half of the thirties, Wright took his place alongside Garrison in combining militant abolitionism with extreme nonresistant views and in giving direction and meaning to the efforts of those within the orthodox peace movement who had become discontented, even after the changes in 1837, with the conservative inclinations of the American Peace Society's leadership.

A very different character from the belligerent Wright, but also one of the shaping influences on New England nonresistance, was the saint-

[14] See M. E. Curti, "Non-Resistance in New England," *NEQ*, II, no. 1 (Jan. 1929), esp. 35-39, for Wright's early pacifism.
[15] Scrap-books of Henry C. Wright, I, 9, 54.

ly Unitarian minister, the Rev. Samuel J. May.[16] "One of heaven's own," the Quaker Lucretia Mott called him;[17] he was more successful in embodying nonviolence in the practice of everyday life than some of the other, and more militant, contemporary nonresistants.[18] Unlike Wright—or, for that matter, Garrison—May came from a distinguished Massachusetts family related to many of the other clans of the social elite, and he moved with ease in society circles, even while prepared to make himself unpopular by his advocacy of radical views. Already an absolute pacifist by the late 1820's, May had been converted by Garrison to abolition early in the next decade. May, writes Chapman, "had not Garrison's strategic understanding of the fight, nor Garrison's gift of becoming the central whirlpool of idea and persecution. But he was the diviner spirit of the two."[19] With the ardent espousal of peace and antislavery May united the advocacy of temperance, penal reform, and women's rights, and, in fact, the cause of all the oppressed, from native Indians to immigrant Irish. In the 1830's, under the influence of Garrison and Wright, though without following them all the way in their arguments concerning "no-government," he more and more became the spokesman within the American Peace Society of those elements who believed the Society should come out unequivocally on a fully pacifist platform.

All these men, then—Wright and May and a number of lesser figures, mostly from within the Massachusetts Anti-Slavery Society, always the most important stronghold of Garrisonism, or in the ranks of the American Peace Society—had begun to look more deeply into the bases of pacifism and to see to what conclusions peace principles might lead. From Garrison they drew much of their inspiration, and along with him they eventually came to accept, to a greater or lesser degree, an extension of nonresistance to include the renunciation of civil government altogether. Political anarchism, in other words, was to appear to most of them the only logical outcome of Christian pacifism.

Many writers have emphasized the influence on Garrison's thinking from around 1836 of John Humphrey Noyes, Christian perfectionist, Utopian socialist, and founder of the famous Oneida Community,[20]

[16] See W. Freeman Galpin's MS life of May: "God's Chore Boy"; Joseph May, *Samuel Joseph May: A Memorial Study.*
[17] Otelia Cromwell, *Lucretia Mott,* p. 101.
[18] See *Memoir of Samuel Joseph May,* pp. 254-56, for the story of how May courageously consented to sleep beside a lunatic with homicidal tendencies in order to calm him.
[19] Chapman, *Garrison,* p. 81.
[20] See Nye, *William Lloyd Garrison,* p. 105; Galpin, *Pioneering for Peace,* pp. 114-16; Thomas, *The Liberator,* pp. 227-35.

whose views on war are considered in my *Pacifism in the U.S.* Though unwilling to accept Noyes's later communitarian views (or his ideas on sex), Garrison did at this time imbibe much of his thinking on the problem of government. In particular, Noyes's rejection of all man-made laws and civil government as superfluous, as a hindrance for all who strove perfectly to follow the law of God as set forth in the Bible, appealed to Garrison. Let man only be guided by the voice of God within him and all the paraphernalia of church and state would be revealed as an encumbrance, which must be thrown aside as soon as possible. For Garrison now, the position he had already reached concerning the validity of Christian nonresistance seemed to lead logically to the fuller perfectionism of the "no-government" doctrine. Christians, he wrote to Henry Wright early in 1837, "are not authorized to combine together in order to lacerate, sue, imprison, or hang their enemies, nor even as individuals to resort to physical force to break down the heart of an adversary. And, surely, if they cannot do these things as a body, or in their private capacity, they have no right to join with the ungodly in doing them." They must peacefully await the inauguration of "the Kingdom of God's dear Son." "It has no swords, for they are beaten into ploughshares—no spears, for they are changed into pruning-hooks—no military academy, for the saints cannot learn war any more—no gibbet, for life is regarded as inviolate—no chains, for all are free. And that kingdom," Garrison concludes, "is to be established upon the earth—for the time is predicted when the kingdoms of this world will have become the kingdoms of our Lord and of his Christ."[21] It was several years, however, before Garrison and his friends sought to create an institutional framework for propagating their ideas.

Among the most enthusiastic converts to Garrisonian views were the two Grimké sisters, Sarah (1792-1873) and Angelina (1805-1879). No doubt, before his premature death, their brother Thomas had been influential in their spiritual quest, which took them from the family plantation in South Carolina into the ranks of Philadelphia Quakerism and the abolitionist movement. Their appearance on antislavery platforms did indeed cause a sensation at a time when such conduct was considered unbecoming in a member of the weaker sex. Soon the two sisters had been won over by Henry Wright to the full nonresistant gospel as well.[22] And we see them in their voluminous correspondence seeking, with all the zeal of the newly converted, to bring over other abolitionist leaders to nonresistance and "no-government."

Their letters are revealing of the crusading spirit which made a

[21] Garrisons, *W.L.G.*, II, 148, 149.
[22] Benjamin P. Thomas, *Theodore Weld: Crusader for Freedom*, pp. 142-46.

vital force of Garrison and his circle during this period. To Gerrit Smith (1797-1874), a wealthy and influential abolitionist and reformer of New York state, Sarah writes in April 1837 deploring the lack of trust in God among abolitionists "on the great subject of self-defense." For her, to yield to the desire to resist by physical force is similar to the impulse to drink with the drunkard. "This doctrine of non-resistance is the greatest test of our faith." In a further epistle she describes to Gerrit Smith the liberating effect which "the sublime doctrine of acknowledging no government but God's" has had upon her. It has made her feel free with Christ. "I cannot describe to thee the blessed influence which my ultra Peace Principles have had upon my mind." Slavery is the outcome of war, the war spirit lodged within the domestic life of the nation. "It does appear to me," she writes in a letter to Henry Wright, "that if the simple precept 'resist not evil' were once entrenched in the hearts and consciences of men, slavery and war and oppression and domestic tyranny and the usurping of authority over one another must wholly cease."[23]

For the Grimké sisters, then, as for men like Garrison and Wright and many of their friends, the fight against oppression was one. A person could not oppose war, or renounce violence for himself and urge its rejection by his community, without opposing slavery and working actively for its abolition. That was common ground with the older generation of pacifists. Now, the state, the instrument and incarnation of violence, must go, too; it had failed to pass the test when the principles of the gospels were rigorously applied to its actions.

The Grimké sisters seem to have received a sympathetic hearing from Gerrit Smith—though ultimately, as we shall see, he was not won over to nonresistance. With another leading figure among the abolitionists they had to acknowledge defeat. While stating his belief in returning good for evil on the personal level, Theodore Weld (1803-1895) told them bluntly his opinion of the "no-government" idea as thoroughly unsound from a Christian point of view. "*That* doctrine fills me with shuddering and I pray for you and all who are bewildered in its mazes and stumbling on its dark mountains."[24] Moreover, Weld finally succeeded in winning the younger Grimké sister, Angelina, for his wife, a marriage that led to the disownment of both sisters from the Society of Friends—Angelina for "marrying out" and Sarah for attending the wedding—and to their eventual withdrawal from active interest in the peace movement.

[23] *Letters of Theodore Dwight Weld, Angelina Grimké Weld and Sarah Grimké*, I, 377, 407-9; II, 614.
[24] *Ibid.*, II, 513, 706, 707, 856.

Meanwhile, however, late in 1837 the question of the relationship between abolitionism and nonresistance, and of the validity of the latter for the Christian citizen, was brought to the forefront by events cut in frontier Illinois. The murder of the Rev. Elijah P. Lovejoy (1802-1837) at Alton in November 1837 constitutes a landmark in the history of the freedom of the press, as well as in the history of abolitionism. It also led to repercussions in the development of the pacifist movement in America. His death marked a climax in the long series of violent acts directed against the protagonists of abolition by mobs and individual supporters of slavery, who felt increasingly menaced by the rise in antislavery feeling. In October 1835 Garrison himself had barely escaped death at the hands of an enraged crowd in the city of Boston. He had refused to defend himself by arms, though urged to do so. "I will perish sooner than raise my hand against any man, even in self-defence," he had said, "and let none of my friends resort to violence for my protection."[25] He was finally rescued by the somewhat dilatory police force headed by the mayor. Henry C. Wright, on another occasion, had refused to strike back when attacked in a Philadelphia hotel, telling his assailant: "I feel no unkindness toward you, and hope to see you at my house," whereby he succeeded in winning the man over.[26] In many parts of the country nameless abolitionist speakers had acted in the same way. But none had been tested to the same degree as Lovejoy, whose attempts to publish an abolitionist paper, first at St. Louis (Mo.) and then across the state border at Alton (Ill.), were frustrated by repeated mob attacks on his press and even on the persons of himself and his family.

In Lovejoy's case two new factors were present: the absence in the area of an effective police force along with the connivance of the authorities and most of the community at mob violence and, secondly, the effect of the continuous threats on Lovejoy's own family, especially on the health and even sanity of his ailing wife. Lovejoy had started out as a convinced Garrisonian nonresistant but had finally abandoned his pacifism and, with the sanction of the mayor of the town, had armed himself and his family and friends. It was in repelling an attack by the mob on his printing press that Lovejoy met his death.[27] Not long before the end, Lovejoy wrote to a friend:

It is now Tuesday night. I am writing by the bedside of Mrs. L., whose excitement and fears have measurably returned with the dark-

[25] Fanny Garrison Villard, *William Lloyd Garrison on Non-Resistance*, p. x.
[26] Curti, "Non-Resistance in New England," p. 37.
[27] John Gill, *Tide Without Turning*, pp. 108, 137, 142, 143, 167; Merton L. Dillon, *Elijah P. Lovejoy, Abolitionist Editor*, pp. 114, 115, 123, 124, 153.

ness. She is constantly starting at every sound, while her mind is full of the horrible scenes through which she has so lately passed. . . . A loaded musket is standing at my bedside, while my two brothers, in an adjoining room, have three others, together with pistols, cartridges, etc. And this is the way we live in the city of Alton! I have had inexpressible reluctance to resort to this method of defence. But dear-bought experience has taught me that there is at present no safety for me, and no defence in this place, either in the law or the protecting aegis of public sentiment. I feel that I do not walk the streets in safety, and every night when I lie down, it is with the deep settled conviction, that there are those near me and around me, who seek my life. I have resisted this conviction as long as I could but it has been forced upon me. Even were I safe from my enemies in Alton, my proximity to Missouri, exposes me to attack from that state. And now that it is known that I am to receive no protection here, the way is open for them to do with me what they please.[28]

Thus Lovejoy stated the agonizing dilemma in which he had been placed as a result of his stubborn refusal to retreat before mob rule.

The reaction of the antislavery movement (and of many other fair-minded men outside its ranks) was unanimous on one point: that Lovejoy had died a martyr to the cause of liberty and of the freedom of the press. They united in their abhorrence of the murderers and in their admiration for Lovejoy's courage. But was he justified as an abolitionist in abandoning the weapon of moral suasion for armed defense of the cause? And, moreover, how should a professed nonresistant react to this abandonment of nonviolence?

The executive committee of the American Anti-Slavery Society, representing the New York group in particular, took the view that abolitionists in general were not pledged to the nonresistant way. For once, Garrison himself went a long way in agreement with them. Abolitionists—unless they happened also to be "no-government" men like himself—had not, in his view, renounced the use of force in support of the law. "I wish it were otherwise," he wrote; "I wish all in our ranks could be led to see, that civil government—a government upheld by military power—is not justified *among Christians*."[29] But his followers continued to press the point—though with some hesitation, for fear that any criticism of Lovejoy's conduct might be construed as justi-

---

[28] Joseph C. and Owen Lovejoy, *Memoir of the Rev. Elijah P. Lovejoy*, pp. 257, 258.
[29] W. L. Garrison to S. J. May, 30 Dec. 1837, Garrison Papers, B.P.L., MS A.1.1., vol. 2, no. 74. See also the *Liberator*, 5 Jan. 1838.

fying his enemies—that Lovejoy, though a martyr, had not died "a *Christian* martyr." The board of managers of the Massachusetts Anti-Slavery Society (followed a little later by the Rhode Island abolitionists) declared:

> That while it is not the province of their Board to determine for the friends of universal emancipation, how far and under what circumstances it is right to use arms in self-defence; ... yet, as abolitionists, we are constrained to believe, that if the doctrine of non-resistance had been practically carried out by our brethren in Alton ... victory would, in the providence of God, have been the result; or, if not, that the spilling of the blood of defenceless men would have produced a more thrilling and abiding effect.[30]

Even Dr. Channing, who was far from being an absolute pacifist, took much the same view, and so did William Ladd of the American Peace Society.[31] The *Liberator*, whose columns Garrison opened to discussion of the issue,[32] showed the distress and pain which Lovejoy's defection had caused his fellow nonresistants, torn between admiration for his bravery in the face of overwhelming opposition and regret that he had not been willing to crown it with a nonresisting martyr's death. "I think I never received so great a shock to my feelings as in the intelligence of the death of Elijah P. Lovejoy," wrote Angelina Grimké. "It was not because an abolitionist had fallen.... Oh no! ... it was because he did not fall the unresisting victim of that fury." Her sister, Sarah, in a private letter of lamentation to a friend, wrote: "How appalling the spectacle! a minister of Jesus Christ engaging in the work of killing his brother man, of sending to the bar of judgment beings who were mad with fury."[33] Even the mild Samuel J. May expressed his regret at "the unchristian spirit which he [Lovejoy] manifested."

Although the lines of demarcation were by no means clear-cut, the

---

[30] *Liberator*, 24 Nov. 1837.

[31] *Ibid.*, 22 Dec. 1837; John Hemmenway, *The Apostle of Peace*, pp. 66-69. The Rev. Leonard Worcester, brother of the late Noah Worcester and himself a near pacifist, who roundly condemned Lovejoy's assailants as well as the whole institution of slavery, considered that "it was no ... sudden and unavoidable peril in which the victim of the Alton mob was placed. The evil which he resisted had long been threatened and foreseen." His death was, therefore, avoidable. Lovejoy, in his view, had died, not in strict self-defense, which was permissible even in a follower of Christ, but "in defence of his rights, and of his property." This action, although legally justifiable, was contrary to Christ's precepts, which urged nonresistance in such circumstances. See L. Worcester's *A Discourse on the Alton Outrage*, pp. 6-9.

[32] *Liberator*, esp. 1 Dec. 1837; 8 Dec. 1837; 22 Dec. 1837; 5 Jan. 1838; 16 Feb. 1838.

[33] *Weld-Grimké Letters*, I, 481.

discussion on Lovejoy's death which ensued made it plain that large sections of the abolitionist movement rejected nonviolence, not merely as a principle but also as a practical tactic. Nor were all of Garrison's followers, for that matter, supporters of no-government and nonresistants in the strict meaning of the word, although all eventually came to reject political means for bringing about abolition. Henceforth these doctrines were more or less confined to the Garrisonian division of the movement.

Protagonists of nonresistance and no-government had so far not formed an organization of their own. Belief in the inviolability of human life and the unchristian nature of all human government had begun to make headway among reforming circles in New England, even outside Garrison's group of personal followers. We have noted in the previous chapter the restlessness among the more radical members of the American Peace Society at what they considered the unduly circumspect policy of Ladd and the leadership. It was this feeling that gave the impulse to prepare a grand peace convention in the autumn of 1838 to thresh out a new and, it was hoped, nonresistant policy for the peace movement. We have mentioned that the committee in charge of preparations was manned by nonresistants and their sympathizers, Henry C. Wright and Samuel J. May among them. "A number of deeply interesting radical questions will be presented for debate," stated the committee in outlining the forthcoming convention's program. Its main task was to be a searching examination into the question whether, according to the Christian gospel, defensive war—or even war for some holy cause—was not totally excluded and nonresistance commanded in its place. "We propose," they concluded, "not to evade any question that may be found incidental to the decision of this one, namely; how is the evil that is in the world to be overcome? By violence, or sacrifice?"[34] Wright, in particular, was busy all the summer in organizing meetings in Boston and the surrounding country at which the radical case was presented and fresh converts made to the cause.[35]

Garrison, meanwhile, was backing Wright's efforts in the field by devoting a considerable amount of space in his *Liberator* to nonresistance and no-government, alongside news of the abolition movement, which had been the main concern of the paper hitherto. He had by now become as stern a critic of the conservative elements which still continued to dominate policy in the American Peace Society as the ebullient Wright. Despite mutual respect for each other, which they succeeded in maintaining to the end, Garrison and Ladd were poles apart in

[34] *Ibid.*, II, 685-88.
[35] Curti, "Non-Resistance in New England," pp. 42, 43.

temperament. For Garrison (and even more so for Wright, of course) moderate reform was a contradiction in terms. It was almost worse than useless to write absolute pacifism into a peace society's platform if one still admitted nonpacifists into the membership, for the effect was to water down the testimony for truth. "Be assured," he once told Ladd, "that until . . . your cause is honored with lynch law, a coat of tar and feathers, brickbats and rotten eggs—no radical *reform* can take place." This was as true for the peace cause as it was for antislavery. In the *Liberator*, early in September 1837, Garrison drew a comparison between the American Peace Society and the American Colonization Society, which he had done so much to discredit in the eyes of antislavery opinion both in America and back in Britain. Such bodies, he said bluntly, "are mischievous, instead of being beneficial, because they occupy the ground without being able to effect the object. What a farce it is to see a Peace Society enrolling upon its list of members, not converted, but belligerent commanders-in-chief, generals, colonels, majors, corporals, and all! What a wonderful reform may be expected where there are none to be reformed!" He concluded his attack with the following threat: "I hope to be more deeply engaged in the cause of Peace by and by, than I can at present; and unless they alter their present course, the first thing I shall do will be to serve our Peace Societies, as I have done the Colonization Societies."[36] No wonder then that, within a few months, the hapless Beckwith was complaining publicly of Garrison's and Wright's pugnacity as a serious obstacle to the success of the peace cause![37]

And so, as September approached, the radicals went ahead with high hopes of winning over to their platform the most active sections of the peace movement, the only ones that really mattered in their view. Opinion was not unanimous, however, even among the members of the preparative committee. We find Samuel J. May, for instance, writing to Garrison in July: "You and brother Wright have startled me, but I am determined to follow wherever *truth* may guide. I look forward to the Convention with high expectation. If we do not drive off the timid ones by broaching our ultra doctrines in the beginning, but lead them along through the preliminaries,—getting them to concede certain fundamental truths,—we may at last surprise many into the acknowledgment of a faith from which at first they would revolt." May him-

---

[36] *Liberator*, 8 Sept. 1837. Cf. *Advocate of Peace*, I, no. 4 (March 1838), 189, where Garrison is described charitably as "a devoted friend of peace," although it is pointed out that nonresistance and no-government are "political reforms," with which matters the A.P.S. has no concern officially.

[37] Scrap-books of H. C. Wright, vol. I, quoting from the *Morning Star* (Feb. 1838).

self seems to have been hesitant about whether Garrison and Wright were in fact correct in their belief that the infliction of imprisonment on the criminal was not consistent with the Christian gospel of love.[38] And even Garrison agreed that, while many who came to the convention might be prepared to accept the validity of nonresistance (especially since, as one of his colleagues reported, they might expect "the attendance of only pretty thorough men"),[39] it might be harder to get them to oppose the whole institution of civil government. As he confided to May: "We shall probably find no difficulty in bringing a large majority of the Convention to set their seal of condemnation upon the present militia system, and its ridiculous and pernicious accompaniments. They will also, I presume, reprobate all wars, defensive as well as offensive. . . . But few, I think, will be ready to concede, that Christianity forbids the use of physical force in the punishment of evildoers; yet nothing is plainer to my understanding, or more congenial to the feelings of my heart."[40]

The peace convention opened on 18 September in Marlboro Chapel in Boston.[41] Between 150 and 200 persons attended, almost all New Englanders, and of these the greater number were from Massachusetts. The delegates included a contingent of moderates from the American Peace Society led by Beckwith, who had met the previous day in conclave to decide on the tactics to be pursued at the convention. It seems that they had some hopes, despite the radical initiative, of being able to secure a majority for their point of view and thus protect "the cause . . . from the extravagance of the ultra men."[42] However, their hopes were disappointed, and they withdrew after a few hours, using as a pretext (though they were undoubtedly also genuinely shocked by) the admission of women to full membership in the convention and its committees.

The "women's rights" question, indeed, was already beginning to split the abolitionist movement, though the final schism was not to come until 1840. Garrisonian nonresistance had won the enthusiastic support of a number of capable and energetic women who did much to further its spread. We have already mentioned the Grimké sisters (who were unable to be at the convention). The well-known novelist,

---

[38] Garrisons, W.L.G., II, 223.   [39] *Ibid.*, II, 223, 224.
[40] *Ibid.*, II, 225.
[41] See *Proceedings of the Peace Convention* and the *Liberator*, 26 Sept. 1838, for the official account. See also Garrisons, W.L.G., II, 222-42; Curti, *American Peace Crusade*, pp. 81, 82; "Non-Resistance in New England," pp. 43-50; Galpin, *Pioneering for Peace*, pp. 124-131.
[42] Garrisons, W.L.G., II, 226.

Lydia Maria Child (1802-1880), one of the most popular writers of her day, the stalwart abolitionist Mrs. Maria Chapman (née Weston; 1806-1885), the two unmarried Weston sisters, scions of patrician Boston, and the fiery Quakeress and advocate of women's rights, Abby Kelley (1810-1887), were all to do the new movement yeoman service over the next few years. New England nonresistance owed much to its women devotees.

The convention lasted three full days, and, even after the withdrawal of Beckwith and his associates (mostly clerics), there was no lack of animated and sometimes heated discussion. Aside from the presence of a few nonpacifists, like Wendell Phillips (1811-1884), attracted to the meetings through their association with Garrison in one or another of his other causes, and in spite of the predominance of Garrisonian abolitionists among the delegates, there was still much diversity of opinion in the ranks of the pacifists present. The main debate was over the resolution introduced by the banker Amasa Walker, who was later prominent in Massachusetts politics. It ran as follows: "Resolved that human life is inviolable, and can never be taken by individuals or nations without committing sin against God."[43] Eventually the motion was carried, and the convention passed on next to set up a society based on the principles of nonresistance. A committee of nine headed by Garrison was chosen to draft a Constitution and a Declaration of Sentiments for the new organization, which was given the name of the New England Non-Resistance Society. Before concluding its business, the convention accepted the reports of the committees appointed to examine, among other matters, the rights of conscience in relation to the existing militia laws in Massachusetts and to inquire into the practical results of the adoption of a nonviolent policy. Orders were given for the Declaration of Sentiments to be "engrossed upon parchment" —those in sympathy with its aims were to append their signatures—and for the proceedings of the convention to be published. Thereupon the delegates dispersed to spread the good word throughout the limits of New England and beyond.

The key document produced at the convention was undoubtedly the Declaration of Sentiments. There is some evidence that the Declaration, and the Constitution as well, had been prepared in outline by Garrison and his friends before the convention opened.[44] It certainly

---

[43] *Proceedings*, pp. 4, 5.
[44] On 10 August 1838 Edmund Quincy wrote to Garrison (Garrisons, *W.L.G.*, II, 223, 224) as follows: "Brother Wright was in town yesterday, and we talked over together the approaching Peace Convention and its probable results. . . . The result of the Convention will probably be a new organization on the principle of

goes a good way beyond the mere faith in the inviolability of human life, for it takes up a negative position toward the whole apparatus of government along with the armed forces and police. Garrison, who was most responsible for its style and contents, wrote proudly to his wife at the conclusion of the convention:

> Never was a more "fanatical" or "disorganizing" instrument penned by man. It swept the whole surface of society, and upturned almost every existing institution on earth. Of course it produced a deep and lively sensation, and a very long and critical debate; and, to my astonishment was adopted by a vote of more than five to one.[45] ... It will make a tremendous stir, not only in this country, but, in time, throughout the world. All who voted for it were abolitionists.

The tempo of persecution, he added in a letter to his sister-in-law, was likely to increase when its message became known, and they would have to face afresh the fury of the mob. "But my soul is in perfect peace, for my trust is in the living God."[46]

"We cannot acknowledge allegiance to any human government," states the Declaration at the outset.[47] Christ is our only ruler and lawgiver, and we must obey him and his laws rather than any earthly king or government. We can make no distinction among ourselves according to rank or sex or national origin. "Our country is the world, our countrymen are all mankind" (the now familiar words that Garrison had adapted from Tom Paine to use in black-letter type as the masthead in his *Liberator* were repeated here). Nonresistants do indeed love their native land, but neither more nor less than the other coun-

---

the Inviolability of Human Life. Now, as it will be well to be prepared for such a result, I write you, at his request, to ask you and your brother [-in-law], G. W. Benson, to lay your heads together and concoct a Declaration of Sentiments and Constitution, or a Constitution, including the emphatic annunciation of this great principle. Especially try to fix upon a *name* for the association—something that shall convey the idea of the principle of the movement: the anti-man-killing principle. This last has puzzled us a good deal. Brother Wright is going to Scituate to spend a week with Bro. May, with whom he is to attempt what we ask of you. I shall apply to Amasa Walker here to assist me in concocting something of the kind; so that when we come together at the time of the Convention, we shall be tolerably well prepared for the emergency. Please do not neglect this."

[45] The Declaration was carried toward the end of the third day by a vote of 27 to 5, while the Constitution had been passed on the second day 28 to 5. Though voting for the former took place fairly late in the proceedings, the small numbers of those who took part is still surprising.

[46] Garrisons, *W.L.G.*, II, 228, 229; W. L. Garrison to Mary Benson, 22 Sept. 1838, Garrison Papers, B.P.L., MS A.1.1., vol. 3, no. 19.

[47] Printed in *Principles of the Non-Resistance Society*, pp. 3-9. The Declaration has been reprinted in full by Devere Allen, *The Fight for Peace*, pp. 694-97.

tries of the world and their inhabitants, who are all God's children. For that reason,

> We register our testimony, not only against all war, whether offensive or defensive, but all preparations for war; against every naval ship, every arsenal, every fortification; against the militia system and a standing army; against all military chieftains and soldiers; against all monuments commemorative of victory over a foreign foe, all trophies won in battle, all celebrations in honor of military or naval exploits; against all appropriations for the defence of a nation by force and arms, on the part of any legislative body; against every edict of government requiring of its subjects military service. Hence, we deem it unlawful to bear arms, or to hold a military office.

But this protest alone was not sufficient. To deny the use of physical force by national states to ward off attack by external enemies while retaining its use within the country to deal with domestic evildoers was a contradiction that must not be allowed. "The unit cannot be of greater importance than the aggregate." No domestic government was to be found at present ready to renounce its trust in armed might to enforce the law. It was therefore incumbent upon nonresistants to voluntarily dissociate themselves from government so far as possible. Refuse all public offices, the Declaration goes on, and refrain from voting or sitting in any legislative body or acting in any judicial capacity. Eschew politics altogether. Otherwise, the guilt of blood shed will be upon you, too. "It follows, that we cannot sue any man at law to compel him by force to restore anything which he may have wrongfully taken from us or others; but, if he had seized our coat, we shall surrender up our cloak rather than subject him to punishment." Prisons and punishments could form no part of Christ's order; this was not the way to the moral regeneration of mankind. By meekness and love and long suffering alone would evil be overcome in the end. "We advocate no jacobinical doctrine. The spirit of jacobinism is the spirit of retaliation, violence and murder." They were ready to suffer for their opinions, while fearlessly putting their ideas before their fellowmen. The Declaration ended on a note of confidence, with the belief that time and God were on their side. "Having withdrawn from human protection, what can sustain us but that faith which overcomes the world?"

The document has vigor and considerable rhetorical force; it is not mere verbiage covering empty sentiments but has an authentic ring about it. It does not so much argue as state what it believes to be moral truth. It has its fair share of the sententiousness current at the time, its tone is too often priggish and moralistic, and it has little or nothing to say about the relationship of nonresistance and no-government to the social order. Its Christian anarchism is of the individualist variety. In relation to the state the Declaration takes an extremist view that has not usually been shared by the modern pacifist movement. But here, indeed, there is some ambiguity as to its exact position. Was the state as such condemned root and branch? Or was it to be regarded as unchristian only so long as it was tied up with the instruments of oppression and war and punishment? If—to paraphrase its wording —the state ceased to be upheld by physical strength, or its laws enforced by the bayonet, would the way then be open for the genuine nonresistant to participate in the work of human government?

In fact, while stating the obligation incumbent upon its members to refrain from violence and from all attempts to punish the wrongdoer, a matter to be left to God's judgment, the synopsis of the new Society's principles goes on to say: "All human governments *at present existing* are based on the principles of violence and retaliation. Therefore I cannot approve or maintain any of them."[48] Was a constitution, an administration, a legislature and judiciary that would in the future have shed the trappings of military might and coercive power and have thereby become acceptable to a simon-pure nonresistant really conceivable? Perhaps, as for the earlier peace sects, such questions were not quite relevant since, in the eyes of men like Garrison, such a state of affairs was not likely to come to pass until "the kingdoms of this world will have become the kingdoms of our LORD and of his CHRIST, and he shall reign forever."[49] Without reference to the perfectionist and millenarian ferment of that time, in which Garrison and his friends fully participated, a proper understanding of the document is impossible. For all its exaggeration, it has remained a landmark in the evolution of pacifist thought. Tolstoy was greatly influenced by it (and so, through him, was Gandhi, too); Tolstoy reprints lengthy extracts from it in his famous treatise *The Kingdom of God is within you* (1893).[50] "On the face of it erratic, contradictory, ill-considered," writes Devere Allen of the Declaration, "yet a study of it will induce only respect,

[48] *Proceedings*, p. 29. My italics.   [49] *Principles*, p. 7.
[50] See Leo Tolstoy, *The Kingdom of God and Peace Essays*, pp. 5-11, 22, 575-82, for details concerning Garrison's impact on Tolstoy. The Russian learned of the writings and activities of Garrison and other American nonresistants only after the publication in 1884 of his *What I Believe*, the first public statement of his own nonresistant faith. In the introduction he wrote in 1904 to the condensation of the four-volume life of Garrison by his sons, which was undertaken by Vladimir Chertkov and Florence Holah, Tolstoy (*The Kingdom of God*, p. 575) speaks of "the spiritual joy" he experienced at his first encounter with the New England nonresistants.

if not agreement.... It is a great historic paper."[51] It is important rather for the striking challenge to accepted ideas on war and society that it threw into the arena than for logical thought or original argument.

Let us now turn for a moment to a second document emanating from the convention, which is of considerable interest to our study. In July, Samuel May had written to Garrison that Edmund Quincy (1808-1877), a young Boston patrician and a recent convert to abolition and nonresistance, would prepare a report for presentation at the forthcoming convention "on the right of others, as well as members of the Society of Friends to have their conscientious scruples respecting military training, etc., duly regarded."[52] On the second day of the convention Quincy was elected to lead a committee to consider this subject, and the committee's report, or rather Quincy's, was accepted by the convention.

The payment of a small monetary fine in lieu of militia service, which was then the penalty for nonattendance at musters, was not a trifling question, Quincy stated in his report.[53] It was one that raised important matters of principle. What purpose did the proclamation of religious liberty serve if a man were not free to put his religious beliefs into practice in a matter like military service? He recommended that the various state legislatures be petitioned on behalf of liberty of conscience; a number of nonpacifists, he thought, would probably be glad to sign, since the matter concerned the principle of religious freedom as fully as it did the narrower one of nonresistance. Four additional considerations, he said, should be urged on the state lawmakers in support of the petitions. In the first place, the existing law penalized the genuine conscientious objector who was unwilling to submit to a fine, while the shirker got off with paying a few dollars. Secondly, it was unlikely that an exemption clause would be abused by the unconscientious, for (and here we meet again the same argument used by Thomas Grimké in his unsuccessful petition to the South Carolina legislature, discussed earlier) "it is not probable that the profession of peace principles will be for some time to come so popular, that many worldly-minded persons will be willing to incur, the odium of being of that sect everywhere spoken against, for the sake of saving a few dollars." Next, Quincy pleaded the exemption already granted Quakers in Massachusetts and several other states.

[51] *The Fight for Peace*, p. 395.
[52] Garrisons, *W.L.G.*, II, 223. In his diary Quincy wrote enthusiastically of the acceptance of "that immortal instrument," the nonresistants' Declaration of Sentiments (Merrill, *Against Wind and Tide*, p. 146).
[53] *Report on the Injustice and Inequality of the Militia Law* . . . , esp. pp. 6-11.

Were not the grounds of objection and the right to consideration of their conscientious scruples the same in the case of those Christians in other churches who rejected war? Lastly, he pointed out that exemption on conscientious grounds from the taking of oaths had been extended, at least in Massachusetts, to non-Quakers.

Quincy and his colleagues thought that petitions of this kind, if properly organized, would in the end bring the desired exemption. But what should objectors do before this is achieved? They must "firmly, though meekly . . . refuse to comply with the requisitions of the military laws." Some in the movement would consider that it was enough to make their protest by refusing to drill and would then voluntarily pay the fine laid down by law. Others—and among them "some of the most consistent and honored of the friends of peace"—would feel bound to go further and would, as part of their peace witness, refuse to pay the fine and either have their property distrained by law or go to prison for a time. Quincy and his committee, while feeling that at present the payment of the fine could not be regarded as a compromise of principles, stated their belief that the more radical witness would become, as time passed, increasingly effective as a protest against war.

Another report which the convention approved was one on "the tendency and effects of the pacific principle." It was prepared and presented by a committee of three otherwise obscure members of the convention.[54] It is interesting as an attempt to investigate the practical effects of the adoption of a nonresistant policy. The convention had already passed a resolution that "to doubt its safety and expediency is to deny the wisdom and goodness of Jehovah."[55] But it was evidently felt that more tangible proofs of the efficacy of nonresistance would be helpful. "Has this principle," the authors of the report inquire, "when carried out agreeably to the precepts and example of Christ, a natural tendency to secure, and would it result in the general safety and happiness of mankind?" That is, was nonresistance expedient as well as moral? On the positive side, the report pointed to instances, most of them extracted from Biblical history, where love, kindness, and forbearance toward evilly inclined persons had finally succeeded in winning them from their course. "These examples on divine record, being the natural and legitimate effect of the pacific and kind course, afford a strong and conclusive argument in favor of the utility and expediency of perfectly following the precepts and example of Christ in respect to non-resistance, and overcoming evil with good." It was

[54] *Report on the Tendency and Effects of the Pacific Principle* . . . , pp. 3-20.
[55] *Proceedings*, p. 9.

argued, too, that the "pacific principle" was capable of evoking feelings of shame on the part of an aggressor and leading him to make amends for wrong done. Or, again, when followed fearlessly, nonviolence had been known to win the respect and love of savages: this was shown in the relations of Penn and the Quakers with the American Indians, who, on the other hand, reacted with hatred and deadly enmity to attempts to molest them. On the negative side, it was urged that the risks of living according to this pacific principle were far less than those incurred by following the way of self-defense in violence and war. There would be martyrs for peace: indeed, defense by means of arms did not always succeed—as the case of Lovejoy clearly showed. "Almost all the wars which have . . . desolated the earth, have owed their existence to some kind of bloody self-defence, in returning evil for evil, and would have been avoided in returning good for evil." Let a beginning be made somewhere, the report concluded: violence and wars will only cease if men refrain from sanctioning them.

Like every self-respecting society of that day, the New England Non-Resistance Society was furnished not only with a Declaration of Sentiments, embodying the leading principles which were to guide its action, but also with a Constitution, which concerned itself mainly with organization. The author of this document was once again Garrison himself. "I first wrote the Constitution, radical in all things, and presented it without delay," he reported to his wife at the convention's conclusion.[56] According to its provisions, a majority of the executive committee was, for practical reasons, to be drawn from the Boston area. But membership and full voting rights in the Society were to be open to all, irrespective of color or sex or creed, who were prepared to assent to Article II of the Constitution, which ran as follows:

> The members of this society agree in opinion, that no man, or body of men, however constituted, or by whatever name called, have the right to take the life of man as a penalty for transgression; that no one, who professes to have the spirit of Christ, can consistently sue a man at law for redress of injuries, or thrust any evil-doer into prison, or fill any office in which he would come under obligation to execute penal enactments—or take any part in the military service— or acknowledge allegiance to any human government—or justify any man in fighting in defence of property, liberty, life or religion; that he cannot engage in or countenance any plot or effort to revolutionize, or change, by physical violence, any government, however corrupt or oppressive; that he will obey "the powers that be,"

[56] Garrisons, W.L.G., II, 228.

except in those cases in which they violate his conscience—and then, rather than to resist, he will meekly submit to the penalty of disobedience; and that, while he will cheerfully endure all things for Christ's sake, without cherishing even the desire to inflict injury upon his persecutors, yet he will be bold and uncompromising for God, in bearing his testimony against sin, in high places and in low places...."[57]

For the honorary position of president of their Society, the nonresistants chose Effingham L. Capron, "a Friend," it was said, "of the straitest kind,"[58] who had been converted early in the decade to abolitionism by reading the *Liberator*. Several other Quakers served as officers, including Garrison's brother-in-law, George W. Benson of Brooklyn (Conn.), though—as we know—official Quakerism was extremely cool, in some cases downright hostile, to the Non-Resistance Society. Garrison and Henry C. Wright, the most energetic and dynamic of the Society's leaders, were chosen as corresponding secretary and vice-president, respectively. Among its other officers, the names of Mrs. Maria Chapman (who acted as recording secretary), Charles K. Whipple (the treasurer), Oliver Johnson (who eventually became Garrison's biographer), Edmund Quincy, and Miss Anne W. Weston are worth recording for the part they played in the Society's counsels in its early days.

Garrison, at least, had felt very satisfied with the outcome of the convention. The immediate preparations for it he had left mainly to Henry C. Wright and others, owing in part to his continuing preoccupation with the antislavery question and, also, to illness in his own family, which had taken up much of his time. However, as it turned out, he writes, "I took a much more active part [in the sessions of the convention] than I thought of doing."[59] "The three days of the past week in Boston," he prophesied after its conclusion, "are destined to become more memorable in history, than the famous 'three days in Paris.' They will constitute an important chapter in the annals of Christianity. Mankind shall hail the TWENTIETH OF SEPTEMBER with more exaltation and gratitude, than Americans now do the FOURTH OF JULY."[60] He had good reason to be pleased with what had been achieved. From the strange assortment of saints and fanatics, selfless reformers and professional agitators, who had made up the convention's membership, a majority had been found to vote into existence an organization dedicated to Garrison's program and based on the sentiments and constitu-

[57] *Principles*, pp. 11, 12.
[58] Garrisons, *W.L.G.*, I, 398.
[59] Garrison Papers, B.P.L., MS A.1.1., vol. 3, nos. 17 and 19.
[60] *Liberator*, 26 Sept. 1838.

tion which he had himself drawn up for it. His disciples had shown themselves ready to follow him, and not only in his crusade to emancipate the slave; they were willing, moreover, to outdistance the ordinary run of Christian nonresistants and challenge the right of the mighty state power itself to exercise coercive authority over men.

It was hardly surprising, then—even though a few voices of sympathy were heard[61]— that almost the whole press of New England and beyond, especially the church journals, raised a hue and cry against Garrison and his Society. "The most fanatical ultraist in New England," "ultra beyond ultra," "truly, Jack Cade is come again"[62] were typical of the reactions among the educated classes at large.

There was considerable hesitation, even in the ranks of the radical pacifists, at accepting the full nonresistant creed as presented, in particular, in the Declaration of Sentiments. It was certainly too strong a medicine for some to swallow at a gulp; others came to accept it only after lengthy consideration and much soul-searching. It is interesting to note, for instance, that the Hon. Sidney Willard (1780-1856), a prominent Harvard scholar and provincial politician who had been elected to act as president of the convention, took no further part in the movement. We know quite a lot, from their correspondence and other writings, of the tussle that was going on in the minds of several leading pacifists, who had hesitated to sign the Declaration when the invitation came at the conclusion of the proceedings. This inner debate is extremely revealing of some of the problems which faced the radical section of the pacifist movement at this time.[63]

Let us take first the case of the Rev. Samuel J. May.[64] We have already seen him actively participating in the preparations for the convention and in its sessions. He had long been a nonresistant. But the relation between pacifism and politics did not present itself to him in the simple, black-and-white terms in which men like Garrison or Wright viewed it. May, as contemporaries witnessed, was more than half a

[61] Orestes Brownson's *Boston Quarterly Review*, for instance, in its March 1839 issue (quoted in *Principles*, p. 14), considered that the nonresistants were quite correct in regarding no-government as the logical outcome of Quaker pacifism. Garrison, it is interesting to note, had disciples in the editors of the *Vermont Telegraph* (the Rev. Orson S. Murray) and the *Herald of Freedom* (Nathaniel P. Rogers). For the nonresistant movement in Vermont from 1837 into the early forties, see David M. Ludlum, *Social Ferment in Vermont 1791-1850*, pp. 169-75. Murray was eventually disfellowshipped by the Baptists in 1841 for his unorthodox utterances.

[62] *Greenfield Gazette*, *Concord Baptist Register*, and *Christian Statesman*, respectively, as quoted in the *Liberator*, 18 Oct. 1838; 16 Nov. 1838. See also Galpin, *Pioneering for Peace*, pp. 131, 132.

[63] See Galpin, *Pioneering for Peace*, pp. 129, 130.

[64] See Galpin, "God's Chore Boy," chap. V.

saint, a man overflowing with charity toward his fellow creatures, who was often irked—despite his genuine admiration for the man—by Garrison's bitter personal attacks on those he believed to be in the wrong. Now, toward the end of the convention, May came forward with a resolution, as circumlocutory in diction as it was tolerant in spirit, which was adopted by the delegates: "That, while our perceptions of the truth as it is in Jesus impel us to announce other principles and pursue other measures than those pursued by other friends of peace, we feel no hostility to them, but cordially wish them success in all their endeavors to promote the cause of our Lord and Savior Jesus Christ."[65] Shortly afterward, when a vote was taken on the Declaration of Sentiments, May abstained along with a few others. "Though almost ready to swallow it entire . . . Bro. May acted very inconsistently, got frightened, confused and did some harm." Thus writes Garrison.[66] But this judgment fails to appreciate May's dilemma. May felt profoundly at one with the thoroughgoing rejection of violence, which was at the basis of the principles enunciated in the Declaration. But that this rejection necessarily entailed for the nonresistant a withdrawal from the whole political order, and not merely from those sectors of it clearly connected with violence, was not so obvious to May. Nor did he feel satisfied that the apparatus of justice was inevitably only a synonym for oppression and coercion. He was, indeed, apprehensive of the farfetched conclusions that might be derived by some from such premises. And lastly, he may have drawn back, sensitive and modest as he always was, from a sense of personal inadequacy. He was to write a few years later: "Non-Resistance is the gospel of the Cross. . . . I do not therefore presume to call myself a non-resistant. I am sure Jesus was one. I acknowledge that I ought to be one; and pray for faith and love and courage enough to make me one."[67]

Garrison was most anxious to gain May's adherence, and perhaps this explains the note of irritation Garrison displayed at May's behavior at the convention. Let him only give his agreement, Garrison pleaded a short time later, to the general principle of nonviolence that is the kernel of the Declaration of Sentiments—and, assuredly, he assented to this—and that would be enough in all conscience to justify his adding his signature to the document. "This instrument contemplates nothing, repudiates nothing, but the spirit of violence in thought, word and deed. Whatever, therefore, may be done without

[65] *Proceedings*, p. 12. [66] Garrisons, W.L.G., II, 229.
[67] Letter from May, 4 Jan. 1845, in S. E. Coues's "Peace Album," Harvard University Library, MS Am. 635*.

provoking that spirit, and in accordance with the spirit of disinterested benevolence, is not touched or alluded to in the instrument." The argument is a little disingenuous, and Garrison himself seems skeptical about the effect it would have on Brother May.[68] Finally, however, while not wholly abandoning his belief in the legitimacy of political action (as will be seen later in this story), and while also remaining unwilling to sever his connections completely with the American Peace Society May by the summer of 1839 had yielded to Garrison's entreaties and over the next few years was to give lavishly of his time and energy to the work of the Non-Resistance Society.

Instrumental, along with Garrison, in bringing May into the fold was his friend, Edmund Quincy,[69] who, like May, had himself had serious reservations about some of the sentiments in the Declaration, despite his active part in planning and carrying through the convention. Quincy is an interesting figure, typical perhaps of the aristocrat in reform. Born in 1808, the second son of President Josiah Quincy of Harvard, and related to most of the "best" families in Boston, Quincy had studied law, though he was never to practice it, and then had entered for a time on the life of a young man about town. The murder of Lovejoy had led to his conversion to abolition, and association with the Garrisonians soon brought his enlistment in a number of other humanitarian causes: women's suffrage, temperance and, by no means least, nonresistance. A wit, a man of elegant and cultivated taste who showed distinct talent as a writer, he now threw himself without reserve into the public arena alongside Garrison and Wendell Phillips and the others of their circle. "Every letter of his in the Garrison life," writes John Jay Chapman, "casts as much light as a bush-burner on the queer crowd of enthusiasts he spent his life with." With an ample private fortune he remained throughout his life to some extent a dilettante, one who devoted himself, in the words of the poet James Russell Lowell, "deliberately to the somewhat arduous profession of gentleman." But this profession he interpreted as demanding service and sacrifice for the welfare of the oppressed and in support of unpopular reforms. A Boston Brahmin by birth, he was, like Phillips, not afraid to risk the abuse and obloquy of his caste.

At the convention Quincy's legal training had been useful in drawing up the recommendations for amending the militia law in favor of conscientious objectors who did not belong to any of the peace

---

[68] Garrisons, W.L.G., II, 237.
[69] See J. P. Quincy, "Memoir of Edmund Quincy," *Proceedings of the Massachusetts Historical Society*, 2nd ser., XVIII (1905), 401-16; M. A. DeWolfe Howe, "Biographer's Bait: A Reminder of Edmund Quincy," *ibid.*, LXVIII (1952), esp. 377, 378.

churches. But for a lawyer, even if he did not have a legal mind, parts of the Declaration of Sentiments were indeed difficult to accept as they stood. Therefore, Quincy, like May, had not signed. He repudiated utterly all powers of government based on bloodshed and force, he explained to Garrison in a letter of 21 September; he trusted in the power of nonresistance. However, he went on, "there are certain things originating in Government, and sanctioned by it, which I think are innocent, and may be innocently used": the use of banknotes and coinage, for instance, and of legal contracts—life could not be carried on in a state of civilization without them. Garrison was apparently willing to meet some of Quincy's objections by making slight alterations in the text of the Declaration as it appeared in the *Liberator*.[70] It was not very long before Quincy, putting aside his reservations, took the decision to join the Society, and by the spring of 1839 he felt able to inform May: "I have been much happier since I have attained to the high and sound ground of Non-Resistance."[71]

In the following September, Quincy consummated his attachment to nonresistance by resigning his commission as a justice of the peace. In his letter to Governor Everett he wrote of his conviction of the incompatibility of officeholding with belief in the inviolability of human life. "I do, therefore," he stated, "in the presence of Almighty God, and before you, as Chief Magistrate of this Commonwealth, hereby abjure and renounce all allegiance which I may at any time have acknowledged myself to owe to any government of man's institution. And I call upon Him and you to witness that I have put away from myself this iniquity forever!"[72]

Quincy was to be extremely active in the work of the Non-Resistance Society and to do it yeoman service through his editorship of its paper, the *Non-Resistant*. Surprisingly enough, the two Grimké sisters, whose ardent advocacy of the nonresistant cause we have discussed a few pages back, were to take little part in the movement from now on. Perhaps the influence of Angelina's husband, Theodore Weld was partly responsible. Wrote Abby Kelley: "As for Theodore he is unsparingly severe upon us. Says all that Garrison, [Lucretia] Mott, Chapman and all others who have adopted the will o'wisp delusions of non-resistance, can do for the emancipation of the slave will be undermined and counteracted by these idle notions on this subject. He thinks however that there is to be no permanent harm apprehended, as they have been caught up by us without thought—and that we shall

---

[70] Garrisons, W.L.G., II, 234-37.
[71] Quoted in Galpin, *Pioneering for Peace*, p. 129.
[72] *The Non-Resistant*, 7 Dec. 1839.

soon abandon them—fact of our having embraced them is full evidence that we have not considered them with any *depth* of thought." However, he respected their sincerity, telling them, Abby reports, that "we should be untrue to our own souls did we not proceed in their dissemination. Indeed it seems to me that he looks upon the whole matter with deep contempt mingled with pity."[73]

In any case, we find Sarah Grimké in the middle of October informing her tutor in nonresistance, Henry C. Wright, that she did not believe that she would have felt herself able to sign either the Declaration of Sentiments or the Constitution had she been present at the convention in September. "Perhaps thou mayest be surprised at this, and query what change has taken place in my views." She was not herself conscious of any alteration, she goes on—unless it be a realization that the matter demanded "*deep searching of my own heart* and a fuller insight into the mysteries of God's kingdom, than I have yet attained." In particular, she was troubled—and what she writes here is interesting in view of similar difficulties experienced by the whole evangelical generation of pacifists—by the seeming discrepancy between the God of love as revealed in the New Testament and the God of battles as portrayed in the pages of the Old. "I have labored in vain hitherto to reconcile the Mosaic and Christian dispensations, yet I am persuaded they must be *reconcilable* in principle, however various in practice." And so, "until this stumbling block is removed out of my way," however much her private sentiments might draw her toward absolute nonresistance, she felt unwilling to commit herself by endorsing these documents "to the principle that one of Jehovah's dispensations is contrary to the other in those principles of fundamental morality on which they are based." She wished Godspeed to those who had fully accepted the nonresistant covenant. And with womanly commonsense and some experience, perhaps, of the belligerence sometimes shown by pacifists in their private lives, she adds: "May they remember that home is the first place to exhibit the meekness and lowliness of Him whom they have called master."[74] Already, if but faintly, we can read in this letter from Sarah Grimké the dilemma that was increasingly to face the nonresistant abolitionists over the next two decades and right up to the outbreak of the Civil War. Were they to be the followers of the Lord God of Hosts ready to do battle with the unrighteous on behalf of the oppressed, or were they to be the long-

[73] Abby Kelley to A. W. Weston, 29 May 1839, Weston Papers, B.P.L., MS A.9.2, vol. 11, no. 112.
[74] *Weld-Grimké Letters*, II, 705-7.

suffering disciples of the meek and humble Jesus willing to wait for the righting of injustice until God's good time?

But this conflict of conscience lay in the future. The main focus of contention now centered in the belief of those, like Garrison and Wright, that nonresistant pacifism, if it was to be consistent with itself, necessarily involved a form of spiritual anarchism, a belief that proved unacceptable to many who shared these men's rejection of force in international and political life. As we have just seen, some who dissented were sooner or later led to throw in their lot with the Non-Resistance Society, considering that agreement on essentials was more important than their private reservations concerning the full implications of the "no-government" idea. Still others, on the other hand—among them some of the most dedicated of the absolute pacifists—saw in this idea an insuperable object to their collaborating with the new Society. As Ladd remarked: "There is such a thing as going beyond the Millennium."[75]

Take Amasa Walker, for instance, a sensible, practical man certainly, but one sensitive to the humanitarian call on conscience, who had at the September convention proposed the resolution in favor of the inviolability of human life. "For myself," he wrote to Garrison at the end of the year in a letter which the latter described as "catholic and gentlemanly in its spirit—just what we should expect from its author," "for myself I regard your Society with entire good will." But, he added, "I could not subscribe to the doctrines of the Non-Resistance Society, because I would not see my way clear to do so; I could not see that they were sound and correct." Was it reasonable on their part, as citizens of the state, to refuse to exercise their privilege of voting or to stand aside from all responsibility for the administration of the country even where coercive methods were not being used?[76]

It was, of course, William Ladd who, more than any other man then living, represented the peace cause in the public mind. We have watched the evolution of his views on the peace question from a qualified acceptance of defensive wars to the open avowal of absolute pacifism. Even Garrison, despite impatience at what he considered his appeasement of the nonpacifist element in the American Peace Society, treated Ladd with respect and tolerant affection. His role at the peace convention Garrison described amusingly in the following words: "The deep solemnity of the occasion was somewhat disturbed by the broad and irresistible humor of William Ladd. He is a

[75] Quoted in Hemmenway, *The Apostle of Peace*, p. 77.
[76] *Liberator*, 11 Jan. 1839; letter from Amasa Walker, 23 Jan. 1845, in Coues's "Peace Album."

huge and strange compound of fat, good nature, and benevolence. He went with us nineteen-twentieths of the way, and said he expected to 'go the whole' next year!"[77] In fact, however, Ladd was never to tread the remainder of the road, and the real extent of his difference with the Garrisonians was greater than perhaps either side realized at the outset.

Although Ladd had voted against the Constitution and had refrained from signing the Declaration of Sentiments and had, moreover, been somewhat shocked by the participation of women in the debate at a mixed gathering,[78] he wrote to a friend, not unenthusiastically, about the sessions of the convention, which had just ended the day before:

> If the American Peace Society are called ultra for adopting the principle that *all* war is contrary to the gospel, the new society must be called ultra beyond ultra. . . . I fully agree with many of their sentiments, and I bid them Godspeed so far as they follow Christ. . . . I consider the new society as ultra high; but almost the whole world are ultra low on this subject, and, if I must choose between the two ultras, give me the ultra high one; for I have always found it more easy to come down to the truth, than to come up to it.[79]

He spoke appreciatively of the ability and energy the nonresistants had shown, and he surmised that soon their Society would in all likelihood eclipse the American Peace Society as the mainspring of the peace movement. "I have no doubt that they mean well, and perhaps have more light on the subject than I have. I dare not say positively that they are wrong." His failure to accept their position wholeheartedly, he went on, was possibly due to an old man's caution, his failure to perceive a new truth. "If they are of God, they will prevail, if not they will come to naught. If the new society do [sic] anything, they will turn the world upside down! but the world has been wrong side up these six thousand years."[80]

After a few weeks, however, Ladd was to give a more detailed exposé of the serious misgivings that some of the "no-government" ideas had aroused in him. In a letter to the *Liberator* early in November, he expressed his disappointment at the withdrawal of his colleague Beckwith's contingent from the convention. If they had stood their ground, they would very likely have succeeded in giving a more moderate tone

---

[77] Garrison to Sarah Benson, 24 Sept. 1838 in *W.L.G.*, II, 229.
[78] Cf. Sarah Grimké's comment to Henry C. Wright: "I rejoice that you organized the Convention on the basis of humanity; it is one step, a great step towards the redemption of woman" (*Weld-Grimké Letters*, II, 707).
[79] Quoted in Hemmenway, *The Apostle of Peace*, pp. 73, 74.
[80] *Christian Mirror*, 22 Sept. 1838, quoted in the *Liberator*, 18 Oct. 1838.

to the declarations which were issued in the convention's name. (It seems probable that Ladd himself would have welcomed the coming into being, alongside his own somewhat unadventurous American Peace Society, of a spirited group embodying the radical pacifist idea, but without the admixture of antigovernment notions which Garrison and Wright had grafted on to it.) Turning now to the points at issue between himself and the Non-Resistance Society, Ladd declared his disapproval of capital punishment along with war, yet the question of its abolition, he felt, should not be attached to the peace question any more than abolitionism or the temperance cause, both of which he also supported, should. Again, the nonresistants were right in believing that lawsuits were symptoms of evil. They must be avoided by Christian people wherever possible. But Ladd did not believe that appeal to the law was forbidden in every instance; he could not feel that in all cases there was a contravention of gospel love. And as for the imprisonment of offenders, here again he had to register his dissent from the Garrisonian view. "I believe that . . . culprits may be seized and condemned without a necessary violation of that principle of love; consequently, that civil and criminal jurisprudence ought to be supported by Christians, to a certain extent. . . . I also believe that physical force may sometimes be used in the spirit of love, as in family government, and restraint of drunkards, lunatics, and criminals." Lastly, Ladd, even more forthrightly than May, took issue with the Society on the question of the franchise. To vote for the best man in an election, he felt, even where the choice lay between candidates not connected in any way with the peace movement, was not a surrender to war and militarism.[81] In other words, active citizenship and Christian pacifism were not mutually exclusive in his view.

The founders of the New England Non-Resistance Society, therefore, had failed to bring into existence an organization which would unite under its umbrella all absolute pacifists. The American Peace Society still retained the loyalty of a number of its more radical members. The new body was predominantly, as its name indicated, a New England group. In reality, at the outset at any rate, membership was confined mainly to the eastern districts of Massachusetts. In respect to both the leaders and the rank and file, it was essentially an organ of the Garrisonian abolitionists; the life and vigor of the new group came from the members of the Massachusetts Anti-Slavery Society. As we shall see, this was in some ways to have an unfortunate influence on the Non-Resistance Society's development.

[81] Letter of 7 Nov. 1838, reprinted in Hemmenway, *The Apostle of Peace*, pp. 75, 76.

Even more fatal in the long run to its chances of expansion than the narrow geographical base from which the Society operated at first was what we may call the anarchist slant given to the traditional non-resistant view by Garrison and his colleagues. Their idea had boldness, and it excited and attracted reformers of the time, including some of the best intellects of New England, by the moral force and the thoroughness of its attack on power, "THE POWERS THAT BE," the state power that sanctioned slavery and war and domestic coercion. Nearly fourteen years before Garrison's celebrated act, on the Fourth of July 1854, of burning a copy of the United States Constitution, he had in penning the Declaration of Sentiments of the New England Non-Resistance Society virtually renounced allegiance to that "covenant with death . . . and agreement with hell." Yet the Declaration was mainly a negative document. It remained to be seen whether the New England nonresistants could supplement it with a positive program of action such as the older generation of peace workers had endeavored to forge for the American Peace Society, whether they could develop a cohesive body of doctrine, which would offset to some degree the sectarian narrowness of the "no-government" view.

Chapter 4

The New England Non-Resistance Society

The founding of the New England Non-Resistance Society in September 1838 marked a dividing line in the history of the American peace movement. The radicals now had their own organization and the possibility of developing their ideas free from interference from the more conservative sections of the movement. The Society flourished for several years, attracting the allegiance of some of the most talented intellects of New England and a number of the most devoted spirits in its reform circles. Soon, however, the movement began to lose momentum, and by mid-century the Society had ceased to function altogether. Yet, during the brief years of its existence, it had showed considerable creativity and at first, at any rate, a many-sided activity.

Among the most immediate tasks facing the new Society was to define its relationship to the organizations with whose work its founders were most closely associated. With the American Peace Society, in which hitherto pacifists had worked with greater or less harmony alongside nonpacifists, as we have seen, relations were bad from the beginning, despite Ladd's attempts to bridge the gap. Ladd sincerely desired to reach a modus vivendi with the new Society. Both shared the same enthusiasm for the work of peace, and Ladd, though not quite a nonresistant, considered himself as much an absolute pacifist as the radicals. His attendance and conduct at the foundation convention and at subsequent annual meetings of the new Society testify to his genuine desire for good relations; at the same time, he did not ignore differences in outlook or conceal his own feeling that the nonresistants, though sincere, were carrying their principles to unwarranted extremes. Nevertheless, some members of the American Peace Society soon began to express doubts whether Ladd had not gone too far in trying to understand the nonresistant point of view.[1] And from the other side, too, it was not long before strong criticism of the American Peace Society was being voiced by the new Society's leaders.

Late in the summer of 1839 an editorial in the recently established *Non-Resistant* stated: "As to the services of the American Peace Society in the cause of Peace, we are not disposed to undervalue them. It has done much in the preparation of materials for a more scorching

---

[1] *Advocate of Peace*, III, no. 10 (Dec. 1840), 232-35.

reform. We cannot perceive, however, that it has made much impression on the martial spirit of the nation. We believe that it has accomplished its mission, and will ere long be no more."[2] In particular, the American Peace Society's panacea for universal peace, the establishment of a congress of nations to arbitrate international peace, in which Ladd was, as we have seen, particularly interested, met with no support from the nonresistants. "Impracticable" their organ called it. The editorial doubted whether the world's governments would be ready to honestly adopt the scheme and make it work: in any case, it would need military sanctions and not merely the backing of public opinion, if its decisions were not to be "but so much empty breath." Peace workers, the article concluded, must begin by working a revolution in the human conscience; to commence at the top with governments was to start at the wrong end.[3] The debate brings to mind the controversy on the question of sanctions inside the peace movement in our own day. A curious similarity, too, may be detected between the arguments used by the nonresistants and those of the American Peace Society's military-minded critics, who likewise maintained that the world was not yet ripe for such a scheme and that, anyhow, it would fail unless backed by armed force.

By the 1840's relations between the two peace bodies had deteriorated to the point where there was little, if any, contact between them—except for an occasional outburst of polemics. Personal friendships between many of the pacifists in each camp, of course, continued, and they worked together harmoniously on other reform platforms. Beckwith, however, correctly summed up the situation (from the American Peace Society's point of view) when he wrote toward the end of the decade: "There is a class of radical men whom we have never reached as a body; men who would never work harmoniously with our sort of peace men, even tho' we agreed with them in sentiment; a class of men who have seldom come near us, and when they did, were always sure to embroil us in difficulty."[4]

A second problem facing the nonresistants at the outset of their Society's existence was to sort out its relationship with the various other reform movements, besides the peace movement, in which both leaders and rank and file were actively involved. Most important of these, of course, was abolitionism. In the minds of most nonresistants, the two causes were expressions of a single principle: the brotherhood of man. As the novelist Mrs. Lydia M. Child wrote: "Abolition principles and nonresistance seem to me identical; . . . the former is a

[2] *Non-Resistant*, 7 Sept. 1839.   [3] *Ibid.*, 12 Feb. 1840.
[4] *Advocate of Peace*, VII, no. 2 (Feb.-March 1847), 34.

mere unit of the latter. I never saw any truth more clearly, insomuch that it seems strange to me that any comprehensive mind can embrace one and not the other."[5] Garrison, who shared this belief, was yet at the same time always careful to point out that the activities of the nonresistants in no way committed the abolitionist movement. It was, however, not so easy for him in practice to keep his two concerns separate. As editor of the *Liberator*, he had given over a considerable amount of space to discussion of nonresistance after his conversion to the radical position and, especially, after the founding of the Non-Resistance Society. His statement that the peace question was "merely incidental"[6] in the paper's policy began to look a little disingenuous. Some of his antislavery followers, even among those who were also convinced nonresistants, began to fear that the abolition cause would suffer from too close an identification with the still more unpopular nonresistance; for many others, Garrison's "non-combatism and his perfectionism" were "downright fanaticism." For them—to use the words of the abolitionist Elizur Wright—"the wind of perfectionism" had "blown off the roof of his judgment."[7] Indeed, the "no-government" views of Garrison and his associates became one of the factors, along with their advocacy of woman's rights and other reform causes, contributing to the split in the abolitionist movement finally consummated in 1840, which left it divided between the Garrisonian apolitical wing centered in Boston and the supporters of political action with headquarters in New York.

Discontent at the prominent place given to nonresistance in the columns of the *Liberator* was felt, as we have said, not merely among Garrison's opponents among the reformers but inside his own circle, too. Part of the trouble lay in the fact that in the early months of its existence the Non-Resistance Society as yet lacked a journal of its own. It was natural, therefore, for Garrison not only to include in the *Liberator* his own pleas on behalf of the new faith but to open the

[5] *Letters of Lydia Maria Child*, p. 44. Letter written on 27 May 1841.
[6] *Liberator*, 26 Sept. 1838.
[7] W. Freeman Galpin, *Pioneering for Peace*, p. 116. See John Demos, "The Antislavery Movement and the Problem of Violent 'Means,'" *NEQ*, XXXVII, no. 4 (Dec. 1964), 502, 515-19, and John L. Thomas, *The Liberator*, pp. 266-71, for the nonresistant issue in the relations between the two wings that eventually emerged within the abolitionist movement. Among those who became Garrison's opponents there were antislavery men like the Rev. William Goodell (1792-1878), editor of the abolitionist *Friend of Man* published at Utica (N.Y.), and the Quaker poet, John Greenleaf Whittier (1807-1892), who held pacifist—though not, of course, thoroughgoing nonresistant—views, just as there were a number of fervent Garrisonians who, like Wendell Phillips, were never pacifists. For Goodell's belief in "the peace principle as generally held by the Society of Friends," see the *Liberator*, 14 Aug. 1840; *Non-Resistant*, 22 July 1840; 12 Aug. 1840.

columns of the paper to other devotees of "the non-enforcing principle," like the prolific Henry C. Wright, and to publish news there of the Non-Resistance Society's activities.

The position was obviously unsatisfactory. We find dissatisfaction expressed, for instance, in a letter written to Garrison by one of the Weston sisters, who were all enthusiasts for both nonresistance and antislavery. Mixing the two causes in the *Liberator*, Anne Weston now told Garrison, was fair neither to the abolitionists who were not nonresistants nor to the nonresistants who felt that, nevertheless, their cause was not being given the attention it deserved. Both were discontented. She went on to suggest that henceforth the *Liberator* be devoted solely to antislavery matters and that at the same time steps be taken to start a new paper devoted exclusively to promoting nonresistance—with Garrison as editor, if he still felt able to combine this task with running the *Liberator*. "The idea has originated wholly with myself," Miss Weston concluded.[8]

Probably others, too, had been thinking along the same lines, for in January 1839 the first number of the *Non-Resistant* appeared.[9] It was published as the official organ of the Society: the words "Resist not Evil—Jesus Christ" stood underneath the title in each issue. Evidently, Garrison felt that the work of running two papers would exceed even his capacities, for Edmund Quincy was chosen as editor instead. The paper was to appear twice monthly from January 1839 until June 1842, with each issue consisting of four pages. It was printed for convenience' sake from the same type that was used for the *Liberator*. Unlike Garrison's paper, which long remained a byword for antislavery radicalism, the *Non-Resistant* was soon forgotten after being either ignored by contemporaries or subjected to ill-informed abuse and ridicule. Yet it was in many ways a lively little paper, and in its columns were aired many of the problems which have occupied the peace movement since that time. It was not until after the outbreak of the First World War that we find another American paper carried on in the spirit of absolute pacifism. The relationship of pacifism to government, penal reform, and capital punishment were discussed, along with articles on the more familiar themes in the arsenal of the antiwar movement. Most of the prominent nonresistants contributed to its pages, including Garrison himself and the indefatigable Henry C. Wright, who sent in periodic and detailed reports of his journeys up and down New England and beyond as the Society's general agent. It also print-

[8] Garrisons, *W.L.G.*, II, 240-42 (letter dated 11 Nov. 1838).
[9] See Fanny Garrison Villard, *William Lloyd Garrison on Non-Resistance*, pp. 42-45.

ed countless letters and a good number of articles from ordinary members and sympathizers—quite a few of whom, it would appear, had reached the nonresistant stand independently many years before coming into contact with the peace movement—and it served to keep them in touch with the activities of the Society and the thinking that was going on in its ranks. The editor did not hesitate to print hostile comment at length (though from the nature of most of these attacks it would seem that printing them may well have served rather to discredit the critics than to injure the Society).

"The warrior, as well as the man of peace, shall be entitled to a respectful hearing," Quincy wrote in the first number. Earlier in the same editorial he had defined the object of the new paper in the following words: "Such a periodical, in this seditious, warring, anarchical age, is greatly needed; . . . it cannot fail to exert a most salutary influence upon individuals, communities, governments, restraining what it may not wholly reform, and making that which is rigorous or despotic in power lenient and tolerable."[10] Even such a modest, almost reformist aim was not in fact to be realized. For the failure of the *Non-Resistant* to weather more than a brief three and a half years, both personal and financial factors were responsible. Although in the very early days the paper almost seemed to prosper, with the rabid attacks and ridicule meted out to it by opponents proving less effectual than had been feared, it soon ran into financial difficulties. The nonresistants certainly made up in enthusiasm (some would say fanaticism) what they lacked in numerical strength. But in 1840 the paper had only about 1,000 subscribers.[11] Since the nonresistants were not a wealthy group and since the paper failed to attract a large number of subscribers, it had to rely more and more on its few well-to-do backers. Ultimately, the breaking point was reached. But there was a second factor which contributed as much, if not more, to the eventual closing of the paper: the increasing absorption of its chief sponsors and of many rank-and-file members, from the beginning of the forties on, in the antislavery struggle, a shifting of emphasis that was particularly true of Garrison. We find him telling his friend H. C. Wright: "Our time, our means, our labors are so absorbed in seeking the emancipation of our enslaved countrymen, that we cannot do as much specifically and directly for non-resistance as it would otherwise be in our power to perform."[12] This was written late in the winter of 1843, but already, several years earlier, Garrison's main interests had again begun to center in his antislavery crusade.

[10] *Non-Resistant*, 1 Jan. 1839.   [11] *Ibid.*, 14 Oct. 1840.
[12] Garrisons, *W.L.G.*, III, 80.

Wright himself continued to put the energies of several men into his work for the Non-Resistance Society, and, as we shall see, it was partly due to him that its life was protracted until the end of the decade. The efforts of one man, however, were insufficient to keep the paper solvent; Quincy was finding it an increasingly trying task to battle with financial deficits and the reluctance of his most prominent supporters to take time off from their other reform interests to help the paper. In August 1841 we find him writing to Mrs. Maria W. Chapman to ask her to supply an editorial later that month, as well as further contributions at a subsequent date: "The truth is," he confided, "the N.R. is getting [to be] a dead loss to me, and sometimes I am almost disposed wickedly to wish that it might fall through. But with an occasional article from you and the other friends, I will try to keep it along for the present." When no article was forthcoming, he wrote in a tone of reproachful banter to Mrs. Chapman at the beginning of the next month: "It was indeed enough to make a perfectionist swear after he had attained a sinless state."[13] Though both the editor and the editorial board served without pay, the paper was running with a steady deficit, which was made up by voluntary contributions from members. Appeals for help were published in each number, and for a time financial disaster was staved off by this means. Since the editorial board's policy was rather to close the paper than to carry on at the price of running into debt, its position was indeed precarious. At last, a notice appeared in the number of 29 June 1842: "The treasury of the Society is entirely empty. No other paper can be issued until the means are supplied by the friends of the cause." Thus expired the first, and for many decades the only, pacifist journal in America.

Once again, the New England nonresistants were without a press organ of their own. The *Liberator* had still continued to give prominence to the subject of nonresistance for a year or two after the appearance of the *Non-Resistant*. But at the time the latter ceased publication, articles on pacifism had become rare in Garrison's journal, and he did not choose to reverse this trend. Although meetings of the Non-Resistance Society were still reported fully and regularly and its editor remained an ardent nonresistant, the *Liberator* had returned to being primarily an antislavery organ. Adin Ballou twice attempted to revive the *Non-Resistant*, carrying on the editorial work from his Hopedale community, but without success. By this time enthusiasm had ebbed, the number of active sympathizers had dwindled, and the nonresistant movement was on the decline.

Even at the outset the Society had had to rely rather on the high

[13] Weston Papers, B.P.L., MS A.9.2, vol. 15, nos. 54 and 59.

intellectual quality of its leadership and the fiery enthusiasm of many rank-and-file members than on numerical strength, which was clearly lacking. On 29 September 1838, Garrison wrote to his brother-in-law, George W. Benson, the Quaker nonresistant: "We shall not have a *great* and *sudden* rush into our ranks! There are very few in this land, in this world, who will be able to abide by the principles we have enunciated; though there may be many whose consciences must assent to their correctness."[14] Indeed, even a conscientious Quaker sympathizer like Elizabeth Buffum Chace (1806-1899) hesitated to accept all the conclusions to which the nonresistants pushed their doctrine. "I am ready to join the Non-Resistance Society as far as entire belief in the doctrines goes," she wrote to Mrs. Chapman on 26 October 1839, "but I feel that I am not ready to promise to obey them always in spirit as well as in letter." Though she finally joined the Society, the decision came only after many months of hesitation stemming, as she expressed it, from "a solemn sense of the responsibility" such a step entailed.[15]

[14] Garrisons, *W.L.G.*, II, 237. For the conversion to full "no-government" nonresistance of one who had taken the C.O. stand as early as the War of 1812, see Thomas Haskell's account in the *Voice of Peace*, 1st ser., vol. II, no. 8 (Aug. 1873), printed on the unpaginated inside end cover. Haskell was a Massachusetts man from West Gloucester and a farmer by calling. During the war he had been introduced to pacifism by his brother. After two years of thought and study of the New Testament, he felt compelled to refuse both militia service and the fine. "I practiced giving to the different commanding officers my reasons for not training. They said the laws must be obeyed, but after a number of years they became ashamed and left off warning me, thus I was delivered of this burden." However, it was only with the advent of the Non-Resistance Society that he became convinced that pacifism entailed rigorous nonparticipation in government. Within a year we find him refusing to serve as a juror. "I then saw," he goes on, "that I could not apply to government for protection, nor voluntarily give it any support. Thus I have lived an outlaw for thirty five years, and am now fully convinced that moral power is the only sure protection." Haskell also became (like Garrison) a spiritualist and a worker in a multitude of reform causes. In his old age he was elected a vice-president of Alfred H. Love's postbellum Universal Peace Union. See the *Voice of Peace*, 1st ser., II, nos. 11-12 (Nov.-Dec. 1873), 12. It is also interesting to note the accession to the nonresistance movement of several army veterans, who had earlier renounced the sword for the ploughshare. This, indeed, was almost literally the case with Samuel Ledyard of Pultneyville (N.Y.), son of a Revolutionary War hero and, as a young man, himself a keen militarist. On conversion to pacifism in the early 1820's, he had taken the sword to the local blacksmith and himself converted the weapon into a pruning hook. "His minister and his family called him crazy." See the *Non-Resistant*, 28 Oct. 1840. A parallel case is that of the two brothers, Elisha and Joseph Bradley of Williston (Vt.), both Revolutionary War veterans, who since about 1808—to quote the *Practical Christian* (20 Jan. 1849)—"were so conscientious in their peace doctrines that they strenuously opposed all attempts to gain for them their pensions," maintaining that for them to accept would be tantamount to receiving "the price of blood."

[15] Weston Papers, B.P.L., MS A.9.2, vol. 12, no. 63; vol. 13, no. 32.

Another earnest Christian who, though of a very different temperament from Mrs. Chace, long toyed with the idea of linking up with the nonresistants but finally decided against doing so was the New York landowner and philanthropist, Gerrit Smith, whose interest in the peace movement dated back several years. His influence and affluence would have made his adherence to their Society an important asset to the nonresistants. Garrison, Wright, and Quincy did all they could to attract him into their orbit.[16] In March 1839, Smith sent $100 for their paper, the *Non-Resistant*—the largest donation ever received by the Society[17]—expressing at the same time his keen interest in its work. A couple of months later he wrote to Wright of "the unsettled state of my peace views." "I was not alarmed at the organization of the New England Non-Resistance Society," he went on. "I had a strong impression at the time, that its principles were right. The impression has become stronger." Yet at the end of the letter we still find him hesitating to embrace the full doctrine.

Not long afterward, Wright during one of his propaganda tours as the Society's agent visited the Smiths at their home at Peterboro in upstate New York. He found Smith's wife Nancy already a convinced nonresistant, and he had lengthy discussions with them on the subject during his stay. "We took up the Constitution [of the Non-Resistance Society], paragraph by paragraph, and compared it with the Divine Will" as shown in the Bible, which lay open before them the whole time. Agreement seemed to have been reached; Smith soon afterward even went so far as to display the nonresistants' "Declaration of Sentiments" prominently in one of his rooms. "Brother Smith says," Wright reported, "no man can become in heart and life a non-resistant, till the lust of *dominion over man is eradicated*." Realizing the close connection between the abolition of slavery and the abolition of war, Smith, it appeared to Wright, had come to accept the nonresistant arguments with his heart and not merely with his head.[18]

But Smith's doubts seem to have increased rather than diminished over the ensuing months, and by September 1839 he felt unwilling to attend the Society's first annual meeting. His state of mind at that

[16] On 25 February 1839, Anne W. Weston wrote to her sister, Deborah, that she had learned confidentially "that G. Smith is very friendly to non-resistance. We really feel alarmed lest there should not a single fighting man be left to us, for Collins is a non-resistant" (*ibid.*, MS A.9.2., vol. 11, no. 46). John A. Collins (ca. 1810-1879), a man of a militant temperament, was one of the few agnostics who attached themselves to the Non-Resistant Society. He later became a communitarian.

[17] Galpin, *Pioneering for Peace*, pp. 137-39.

[18] *Non-Resistant*, 6 April; 4 May; 18 May 1839; *Practical Christian*, vol. V, no. 9, 14 Sept. 1844.

time distressed Edmund Quincy, who wrote him: "I regard the position in which you stand, . . . as one of imminent moral peril. I tremble for your soul. . . . May God give you the victory, the greatest of victories, the victory over yourself."[19] Smith in the end did not throw in his lot with the nonresistants. Instead, in the very next year he accepted, somewhat reluctantly it is true, nomination for the governorship of New York on the new Liberty Party ticket. Wright made one last effort to prevent Lucifer's fall, begging him to issue a categorical statement that, if elected, he would refuse to act in the capacity of commander-in-chief of the state militia. Smith parried by replying that, as he had in fact no chance of election, the gesture would be pointless.[20]

Despite Smith's renunciation of nonresistance in his actions, his unwillingness to abdicate from the political road to moral reform, and his inability to quell his doubts about the efficacy of nonviolent means for overcoming internal disorder or foreign aggression, his heart continued to hanker after the certainties of radical nonresistance. "If my mind should supply me with any arguments, my heart would be too much on your side to let me utter them," he wrote.[21] Smith continued to support the activities of the peace movement and to respect the radical nonresistants as persons, but his flirtation with their ideas was only a short interlude in a career which finally led him to back unequivocally the militancy of the free-soil guerrillas in Kansas and of John Brown at Harpers Ferry.

Gerrit Smith may be taken as typical of the reforming intellectual, who supported the nonresistant impulse with his heart but drew back because his head refused to give its allegiance. Smith had also been attracted to the Non-Resistant Society by his strong evangelical faith; indeed, for all the opposition of the churches and their cry of "infidelity," the Society drew some of its staunchest members from the theologically orthodox. On the other hand, paradoxically, it also attracted some of the most vocal religious rebels of that religiously ebullient generation. Edmund Quincy summed up the kaleidoscope of religious belief that went to make up the Society well when he wrote: "The number of professing non-resistants is not large—but is large enough to embrace almost every shade of belief from the highest Calvinism to the simplest rationalism. The great majority, however, hold the sentiments of the stricter 'evangelical' denominations."[22] Although

---

[19] Quoted in Galpin, *Pioneering*, p. 142.
[20] Ralph Volney Harlow, *Gerrit Smith*, p. 150. See also pp. 108, 109.
[21] Quoted in Galpin, *Pioneering*, pp. 142, 143.
[22] *Non-Resistant*, 28 April 1841. As is shown in my *Pacifism in the U.S.*, the nonresistant cause even found supporters among the millennial second Adventists, who

some of these evangelical nonresistants remained lifelong members of their churches, coldness and sometimes downright hostility drove others, like Garrison himself, to leave. Even the Society of Friends, as we have seen, remained at best extremely cool toward what they considered the extremism of the New England nonresistants. Several stalwarts of the nonresistant cause of the caliber of Samuel J. May came from the Unitarian fold, which had contributed many prominent workers, beginning with Noah Worcester, to the more conservative wing of the peace movement. But the liberal religious groups, Unitarians and Universalists, whose stronghold was in New England, remained on the whole indifferent to the persuasions of the nonresistants. The Universalists in particular, despite their broad humanitarian faith and opposition to capital punishment, were tardy in taking up a radical stand against war. One of the very few Universalist nonresistants expressed his surprise at the attitude of his church. The doctrine of nonresistance, he told the Vermont Universalist convention in 1846, "lies at the foundation of practical Universalism, ... no man can be a true genuine Universalist, who is not a non-resistant in theory and practice. Why should it be deemed any more out of order for a Quaker to fight than for a Universalist? Judge ye."[23] But his plea seems to have evoked no response.[24]

Most typical of the nonresistants in the public mind were the radical "come-outers," those militants who had withdrawn from one or another of the churches in symbolic protest against their failure to condemn the institutions of slavery or war as sins against God and who spent much of their time subsequently in denouncing what they regarded as the treason of the clerics. Not all the "come-outers" were pacifists, and many who were abandoned their belief in nonviolence in

---

had succeeded in weathering the debacle of 1844 when Christ's second coming, foretold by their leader, William Miller, had failed to come about.

[23] John Gregory, *Anti-War*, pp. 8, 69, 94-96, 98. Gregory might have found support for his assumptions in an unexpected quarter. A decade earlier Dr. Samuel Hanson Cox, a former Quaker turned Presbyterian minister, had written in his book *Quakerism not Christianity* (p. 240): "It comes to pass observably that many opposers of the plainly revealed doctrine of eternal punishment (as universalists, unitarians, infidels, pseudo-philanthropists of every description) grow very specially tender in their clemency on the topics of capital punishment, war, ... and the superlative excellence of the ethics or creed of passive endurance!"

[24] Gregory also made the interesting suggestion (*Anti-War*, p. 49) that pacifists should adopt the "white feather" as a badge, "showing to the world that we cannot and will not war against any portion of our fellow men—that we cannot be induced by any consideration to take up arms against our brother man." The adoption of a distinctive emblem is common to most twentieth-century pacifist organizations; this appears to be the first time such a proposal was put forward.

the stormy fifties. But in the previous decade we find them prominent among the Garrisonian nonresistants: men like farm-bred Parker Pillsbury (1809-1898), who was (in Emerson's words) "a tough oak stick of a man not to be silenced or intimidated by a mob, because he is more mob than they; he mobs the mob";[25] or Stephen S. Foster (1809-1881), "the modern 'steeple-house' troubler," as a contemporary aptly dubbed him,[26] who had been put in prison as a conscientious objector against militia service while a student at Dartmouth College and in jail both had won the confidence of the debtors, thieves, and other felons sharing his incarceration and had succeeded in exposing the bad conditions to which they were subjected while serving their sentences;[27] or Nathaniel P. Rogers (1794-1846), who made his Concord (N.H.) paper, the *Herald of Freedom*, a bastion of abolitionism and nonresistance—and, indeed, of a multitude of other reforms—until his premature death in 1846;[28] or—to mention yet another—the redoubtable Austin Bearse, New England sea captain and owner of the *Moby Dick* which carried out a number of armed rescues of fugitive slaves during the fifties, who had acted as one of the *Non-Resistant*'s agents in the previous decade. These were fighting men even when they were preaching nonresistance, men who did not hesitate to disturb church services, including Quaker meetings, in an attempt to show up what they believed was the church's apostasy. And in due course they were forcibly ejected from these churches by infuriated parishioners (and even, on occasion, by angry Quakers).[29] At the same time, they

[25] From Emerson's *Journal* for 1846, quoted in Louis Filler, "Parker Pillsbury," *NEQ*, XIX, no. 3 (Sept. 1946), 315.
[26] *Practical Christian*, 29 Oct. 1842, p. 47.
[27] Parker Pillsbury, "Stephen Symonds Foster," *The Granite Monthly*, Aug. 1882, p. 370.
[28] Pillsbury, *Acts of the Anti-Slavery Apostles*, pp. 33, 43, 44. Rogers helped to found the New Hampshire Non-Resistance Society in 1841. See Robert Adams, "Nathaniel Peabody Rogers," *NEQ*, XX, no. 3 (Sept. 1947), 365-76. "I would quit the ballot box, as I would the militia," Rogers wrote (p. 374). "It is as immoral to vote or be voted for, for political office, as to train or enlist in the army. . . . The spirit of them is the same. . . . The weapons of both are violence, and the instrumentalities of both, bloodshed and murder." Rogers eventually split with Garrison on account of his own extreme aversion to all kinds of organizational activity, even in the cause of nonresistance or antislavery.
[29] Instances of this are given by Pillsbury in his *Acts*, pp. 303, 305, 312-15. One of those who ended with three months in jail for disturbing the Quaker meeting at Lynn (Mass.) was the Garrisonian nonresistant and former Congregational minister, Thomas P. Beach. For such men as this, the Society of Friends was indeed a "wicked body" in its failure to support the abolitionist movement. And Beach himself wrote as follows of the Lynn Friends (quoted in *Acts*, p. 318): "Those quiet, meek, peaceable, persecuting followers of Jesus have marched up and bowed their joints at the door of the court house and begged the state to stretch out the bayonets, load up the big guns and rifles, and drive this blood-

were men of courage, who put nonviolent resistance into practice when they faced angry mobs alone and without arms (despite Lovejoy's example a few years back) and who took a beating and countless manhandlings without attempting to retaliate. "We never doubted that our non-resistance principles saved our lives in many a desperate encounter," wrote Parker Pillsbury.[30] For their abolitionist militancy, too, they were assaulted by irate mobs and jailed by the authorities. Their reply was to practice the techniques of Gandhian *satyagraha*. Of Stephen S. Foster, for instance, it was said that, when physical force was being used against him, he always put himself "into a perfectly passive state,"[31] a state, that is, of complete physical passivity such as we find being used in the contemporary practice of direct nonviolent action.

These advocates of direct action, however much they may have figured in the public mind as typical of the Garrisonian radical nonresistant, were not, in fact, representative of the Society's membership. Rather was it the grave, respectable churchman, conventional in behavior if not in outlook, a man like the Unitarian minister, Samuel J. May, who gave the tone to the Non-Resistance Society. It was the direct actionists, however, who brought the Society publicity and tended to form in the public mind, and among many conservative peace workers, too, an image of the nonresistant as a wild fanatic intent on disrupting society.[32]

---

thirsty Beach to prison *sine die*, or till he pays a fine of a hundred dollars, which he has no means of paying, and could not pay conscientiously if he had. . . . I am not astonished that . . . Baptist majors and captains should fly to the courts and the forts, but that meek, loving, forgiving Quakers, who cannot *bear arms*, which are the only possible support of human governments, can step forward and say to the state, 'Please imprison Thomas Beach. . . .' Spirits of George Fox and Edward Burroughs, awake! awake!" The situation was, of course, more complicated than Beach could perceive. See Appendix for a discussion of the differences between Quakers and the New England nonresistants.

[30] *Acts*, p. 194.   [31] *Acts*, pp. 310, 311.

[32] That the Society's leaders cannot be acquitted altogether of overindulgence of the less balanced section of the movement is clear, for instance, from a letter Edmund Quincy wrote Anne Weston in 1839, supporting the candidacy of one James Boyle, ex-clergyman, faith healer, and general eccentric, for the post of agent for the Society. Boyle might not be quite the man they were looking for, Quincy admitted, but "we cannot afford to be too particular as to the entire eligibility of our agents," provided they show evidence of a nonresistant spirit in their thought and conduct. "What we want," Quincy went on, "is a man or men who will startle the community, now dead in trespasses and sins, from their living death. . . . And I am mistaken in the man if James Boyle will not sound a blast that will break the fat slumbers of the church and the iron sleep of the world . . . be assured, my dear sister, that the most hateful and odious man, hated and feared for his fearless denunciation of sin and exposure of iniquity, is the very man to give an impulse to our holy enterprise. He will doubtless bring down upon us all

How far this attitude was mistaken when applied to nonresistants without distinction comes out clearly in the case of that cultured and refined Boston gentleman, Edmund Quincy, whom we have already met as the editor of the *Non-Resistant*. At the end of February 1839 we find Miss Anne W. Weston writing to her Aunt Mary: "Edmund Quincy took tea here and we had much interesting conversation. Edmund has written a letter, begging for money for the N.R. Society. It is a beautiful letter, as I think you will say when you see it. I think very highly of Edmund as a good man."[33]

The letter referred to here came out in lithographed form on 1 March;[34] in addition to the appeal for funds ("our efforts, hitherto, have been cramped by the narrowness of our resources"), it exhorted the followers of nonviolence to stand firm against the unfair and often untrammelled criticism that had been unleashed against the Society. Lack of money to carry out necessary tasks ("we have materials for a mighty array of tracts," the letter stated), recognition that they formed a tiny band pitted against a hostile world, and consciousness at the same time of being crusaders called to fight a "holy warfare," all emphasized in this early address, continued to be characteristic of the Society throughout its existence.[35]

At the end of September 1839 the Society held its first annual convention under the chairmanship of its president, the Quaker Effingham L. Capron, and with the charming Mrs. Maria W. Chapman as its recording secretary. Almost all those attending came from Massachusetts; but Lucretia Mott was there from Philadelphia, risking the displeasure of her conservative Hicksite brethren, and the Midwest was represented in the person of the Rev. Amos Dresser, whose ill-treatment in the South four years earlier had made him something of a public figure outside antislavery circles.[36] Naturally, the interminably

---

manner of calumnies and slanderous misrepresentations, perhaps persecution, and make us more and more hateful for a season to the world; but is not this the baptism with which our Lord was baptized, and which He ordained for the proof of his disciples in all ages?" Quoted in J. P. Quincy, "Memoir of Edmund Quincy," *Proceedings of the Massachusetts Historical Society*, 2nd ser., XVIII, 405. For Boyle's "ultraism," see Whitney R. Cross, *The Burned-over District*, 1965 edn., pp. 189, 190. On p. 236, Cross draws attention to the influence of religious "ultraism" in the "Burned-over District" of upper New York state in producing pacifists and nonresistants, although its Biblicism might also have had an opposite effect.

[33] Letter of 27 Feb. 1839, Weston Papers, B.P.L., MS A.9.2, vol. 11, no. 48. See also A. W. to D. Weston, 25 Feb. 1839, *ibid.*, no. 46.
[34] Garrison Papers, B.P.L., MS A.1.2, vol. 8, nos. 12, 13.
[35] These features are evident in almost every number of the *Non-Resistant*.
[36] For Dresser's pacifism, see below, chap. 6. In a letter published in the *Non-Resistant*, 16 March 1839, Dresser declared his support for the aims of the Society,

loquacious Abigail Folsom, the bane of every reform meeting in Boston (until, finally, one day patience was lost and she was carried bodily out of the hall by two stout nonresistants), was in attendance; among a number of well-known figures in Boston reform circles present we may mention the name of Amos Bronson Alcott (1799-1888) of "Fruitlands" fame, who took an active part in the debates at this and subsequent annual meetings. The main resolution—"that human life is inviolable; and that no man can rightfully take, threaten, or endanger life"—was moved by Henry C. Wright, who in addition debated the subject of nonresistance in open session on two successive evenings with the Rev. Nathaniel Colver, a Baptist minister well known as an abolitionist and reformer. Although the meeting showed little evidence of any considerable increase in the strength of the nonresistant cause, Garrison at any rate felt able to pronounce it a success. "Our Non-Resistance Convention is over," he wrote to his brother-in-law, George W. Benson, "and the peace and blessing of heaven have attended our deliberations. Such a mass of free mind [sic] as was brought together I have never seen before in any one assembly ... there was much talent, and a great deal of *soul*. Not a single *set* speech was made by any one, but every one spoke in a familiar manner, just as though we constituted but a mere social party." "The resolutions that were adopted," he added, "were of the most radical and 'ultra' stamp, and will create, I think, no little agitation in [the] community."[37]

The winter of 1839-1840 marks perhaps the peak of Garrison's enthusiasm for the cause of nonresistance. In June 1840, on the high seas en route for England to attend the international antislavery convention in London, we find him writing to Edmund Quincy on the subject in exalted tones:

> My mind has been greatly exercised on the subject of non-resistance since I left New York. It magnifies itself wonderfully as I reflect upon it. It is full of grandeur, sublimity, glory. It is a mine, the riches of which are inexhaustible, an ocean of disinterested benevolence, at once shoreless and fathomless. Aside from it there is no such thing as our being "crucified unto the world, and the world unto us." It is the consummation of the gospel of peace, for it is that perfect reconciliation which the Messiah died to make between God and

---

describing, too, his efforts to spread nonresistant ideas in his part of the world. "There is another little church," he wrote, "with whom I have labored some the winter past, most of whom come fully into the peace principles of the *ultra stamp*."

[37] Letter dated 30 Sept. 1839 in W.L.G., II, 328. The convention was reported in the *Non-Resistant*, vol. I, nos. 19-23.

man, and among the whole human race. It makes babes and fools more sagacious and intelligent than the wisest statesmen, the deepest philosophers, and the most acute political economists. Its principles and doctrines receive the cordial detestation of all that is selfish, ambitious, violent and lustful on earth.[38]

Contacts with sympathizers like Dresser in the Midwest (noted above) were bearing fruit around this time in the establishment in these still pioneer areas of a small number of local groups. On 18 June 1840, for instance, we find a nonresistance society being formed at Oberlin, which became quite a center of nonresistant sentiment. Its constitution was based on that of the parent Society, and it accepted, too, the latter's Declaration of Sentiments. Its members, about thirty in all, were mostly students from the college with a sprinkling of faculty; a few local clergy and church people, some of whom, we learn, had held pacifist sentiments for several decades without being in any sort of contact with those of like views, also supported the work. According to the secretary, the overwhelming majority of students and faculty, however, were either indifferent or actually hostile to the idea of nonresistance, and, evidently, some heated arguments took place on the subject both on the campus and at meetings in the town. The group felt obliged to disclaim the "unchristian spirit manifested by some who sustain our views in part," protesting that its members were not "anarchists" or "disorganizers" as their opponents were trying to prove. Perhaps because of their isolation (or was it a means of quenching the excessive fervency of some of their young recruits?), the Oberlin nonresistants took a milder stand than many of their New England brethren who, like Garrison himself at times, gloried in the task of —nonviolently—"disorganizing" a corrupt society.[39]

We hear, too, of other small groups being formed in Ohio as well as in Michigan.[40] At Greenfield, in Lagrange County (Ind.), those who shared nonresistant views had banded together to form a pacifist church, accepting the nonresistant Declaration of Sentiments as their covenant. Their leader was one Samuel Bradford, according to Garrison "a self taught, uneducated man," who had, however, "an excellent simplicity of character, and a naturally rigorous and philosophical cast of mind." Although Garrison was unable to agree with what he con-

[38] Letter dated 13 June 1840 in the Garrison Collection, Sophia Smith Collection, Smith College, Northampton (Mass.).
[39] *Non-Resistant*, 9 Sept. 1840. The Oberlin society also reprinted its foundation documents as a separate pamphlet.
[40] See the *Non-Resistant*, 6 July 1839; 11 March 1840; 12 Aug. 1840; 27 April 1842.

sidered the sectarian spirit of the little group, its emphasis on outward observances such as baptism by immersion or breaking of bread each Sunday, he did admire their courageous stand for peace. "Though they reside in a frontier state, where they are continually exposed to outrage and danger, the Lord has protected them from all harm."[41]

These Midwestern nonresistants, small in numbers and scattered over a vast area, had to contend with spiritual isolation and the hostility or indifference of their environment to a larger degree than their brethren in New England.[42] We do not hear much, however, of their suffering disabilities on account of any refusal of service in the militia. Even in the East, cases of conscientious objection were seemingly rare among nonresistants. Certainly, the comparatively small size of the movement would preclude its producing as many conscientious objectors against militia service as the Quaker communities did. Some nonresistants undoubtedly were prepared to pay the commutation fine—as the young Garrison had been a decade earlier. Others must have been exempt on account of age or occupation (there were not a few clergymen, as we have seen, among the Society's supporters). Still others, known to have held peculiar views on the subject of war, may just have been left alone by sympathetic neighbors who understood to some extent the grounds of their objection, even though they did not share their views. Nevertheless, it is puzzling that—if we may judge by the columns of the movement's organ, the *Non-Resistant*, or of Garrison's *Liberator*—so few when called upon by the authorities for military service took the absolutist stand of preferring prison to all alternatives in the way of fines, etc. The Non-Resistance Society, indeed, left it up to the conscience of each of its members to determine how far he might rightly go along with the requirements of the state, while demanding, as we have seen, the same right to complete exemption for non-Quaker conscientious objectors as the commonwealth of Massachusetts had already granted to those of its citizens affiliated to the Quakers and Shakers.

Some absolutists were to be found among nonresistants of military age (most of the cases reported in the *Non-Resistant* or *Liberator* come from the late 1830's or early 1840's). To begin with, let us take the case of David Cambell, an ardent health reformer and publisher of

[41] Garrison to S. J. May, 22 June 1839, Garrison Papers, B.P.L., MS A.1.1., vol. 3, no. 35. Bradford was living in an area shortly to be settled by Amish and Mennonites, but they did not begin to move in until 1841.

[42] Some attempt seems to have been made during the forties to organize Midwestern nonresistants into a Western Peace Society. See *Non-Resistant and Practical Christian*, 9 Dec. 1848, where the former Lane seminarist Marius R. Robinson is mentioned as president.

the *Graham Journal of Health and Longevity*. Cambell first found himself behind the bars of the Leverett Street jail in Boston in the 1830's; in 1840 we still find him undergoing his annual term of six days in the city prison. In 1838 he had written to Garrison that he was not concerned about any hardship he might be suffering, "but I feel a solicitude for the young men who are just entering our ranks. To them the trial may be somewhat severe, not having been so thoroughly disciplined as those soldiers who enlisted [in] the service fifteen or twenty years ago"[43]—a reference to the thin trickle of men who had taken an absolutist stand in the past and been subjected to a mild form of "cat-and-mouse" treatment. The penalty was light; more difficult to face perhaps was the lack of understanding from associates and friends. Amos Wood, a Congregational deacon, for instance, was sent to the Hopkinton jail in Merrimack County (N.H.) by a justice who was a member of his own church.[44] Again, the situation was complicated, as we have seen, by the fact that exemption might be obtained by merely paying the fine laid down by law. In January 1840 we find young Charles Stearns, a clerk in the local Anti-Slavery Depository, writing to Garrison from the Hartford County jail (to which he had been committed for an undefined term, as was then possible under Connecticut state law) to ask his advice "not only for my own sake, but for that of others, who may be placed in the same circumstances." "Since I have been here," he explained, "some of my friends have tried to persuade me, that I am in the wrong concerning this matter; that by paying the fine, I do *not* countenance the military system, as I do it unwillingly; I as much countenanced it by coming to jail as by paying the fine." While admitting that it was "something of a gloomy prospect for a young man just commencing life, to think of spending it in prison," Stearns nevertheless disagreed with his friends' arguments. He felt strongly that some clear-cut witness for peace was needed in the circumstances. Those with no scruples concerning war could gain exemption by way of a fine, so that in reality no testimony was being borne to peace principles by paying it.[45] Although he stuck to his absolutist position, Stearns did not, however, have to spend the rest of his young adult life in jail, and we shall meet him again later in the fifties out in "bleeding Kansas," where he was to undergo a change of heart in respect to his pacifist views.

Although few had to witness to their faith by going to jail like Cambell or Stearns, the nonresistants were busy during these early years,

[43] *Liberator*, 27 April 1838; 14 Feb. 1840.
[44] *Non-Resistant*, 23 Dec. 1840.
[45] *Liberator*, 14 Feb. 1840; *Non-Resistant*, 12 Feb. 1840, 11 March 1840.

when enthusiasm was still high and the effects of a dwindling treasury not yet fully apparent, in putting their case over to the public as best they could by means of public meetings or the distribution of literature. Each year, at the end of September, they gathered for a few days in Boston for their annual convention, coming up for the occasion from the towns and villages of Massachusetts and some from further afield in New England. William Ladd has left us with an amusing description of the 1840 convention. In April, H. C. Wright had written in his journal: "William Ladd does not differ from me at all in principles,"[46] and Ladd, as we have seen, was indeed ready to pay tribute to the devotion of the Society's adherents and to their good intentions. But the waywardness, amounting sometimes to fanaticism, of some of the convention's participants aroused his wry sense of humor. On the debate on that perennial issue—the inviolability of human life—for instance, he had this to say: "The discussion took a wide range, . . . far from the resolution . . . Arminianism, Transcendentalism, and all kinds of radicalism were drawn into the debate." At another session he described how "one speaker denounced all governments, ministers, churches, Sabbaths and ordinances, and pretended to be as much inspired as any man ever was." Of a woman orator he wrote: "There was a breathless silence while she soared away into the regions of transcendentalism, far, far beyond my ken. She seemed to rejoice in the approaching abolition of all orders, days and ceremonies, and fully accorded with the brother who had preceded her, in his transcendental notions of pantheism." Ladd, in fact, had earlier shown his hesitations concerning the active participation of women in public assemblies; as full equality between the sexes was among the most cherished principles of the Society, he was not an entirely impartial witness here. However, on this occasion he noted that the ladies rarely spoke ("Miss Folsom twice, in all not exceeding five minutes"), "but employed themselves with knitting, sewing, embroidery, etc."[47]

[46] M. E. Curti, "Non-Resistance in New England," *NEQ*, II, no. 1 (Jan. 1929), 48.

[47] *Non-Resistant*, 28 Oct. 1840 (reprinted from the *Christian Mirror*). Cf. the somewhat similar tone of the report on the Society's annual meeting of 1842 in the *Practical Christian*, 29 Oct. 1842. Its author, a member of the Hopedale Community and therefore, like Ladd, an absolute pacifist, was disturbed by the extremism manifest during the sessions. The Society he dubbed "a mere agitation club." "It breathes out such a spirit of antagonism and defiance; it speaks a language of such burning damnation against all who in any way uphold the prevailing institutions of government and religion; it rides on such a whirlwind of disorganizing radicalisms, and puts on so forbidding an aspect to the great mass of gentle and tender minds, that the genuine non-resistance of Christ will in our opinion gain little more by its movements than the mere excitement of public attention to the general subject."

Next year the *Non-Resistant* reported the annual convention as being "on the whole a very well attended, well conducted, profitable meeting," the most successful of the three held thus far. Ballou, who wrote the report, expressed the hope that the Society would be able to maintain its specifically Christian character and not go over to "a deistical or pantheistical philosophy, however sublimated and refined."[48] Bronson Alcott, on the other hand, left the convention "with the conviction deepened that a few years will bring changes in the opinions and institutions of our time of which few now dream. All things are coming to judgment, and there is nothing deemed true and sacred now that shall pass this time unharmed. All things are doomed. . . . A band of valiant souls is gathering for conflict with the hosts of ancient and honorable errors and sins. . . . I would be of and with them in their work."[49] At any rate, for the time being the Non-Resistance Society could provide a meeting ground for Christian communalist and communalistic transcendentalist.

The presence of a "lunatic fringe" on the periphery of the Society, which was especially vocal on the occasion of public meetings and conventions, was perhaps inevitable. Almost all radical reform movements have suffered from this burden. As will be seen, the primary causes of the Society's decline lay elsewhere however. That its life was prolonged until the end of the decade was due largely to the efforts of two men: Henry C. Wright and Adin Ballou. Wright was indefatigable as the Society's traveling agent, facing hostile audiences and exhausting journeys in all types of weather, ready to engage all and sundry in conversation on the subject of peace and ready to take any platform at a moment's notice if it gave him the opportunity to plead the cause. His extremism offended many of his contemporaries,[50] and later writers are divided as to the value of his contribution to the reform movement. But there can be little doubt that his vigor injected new energy into the flagging Non-Resistance Society, to the extent that, when he departed for a prolonged visit to Europe in 1843, the Society began to show increasing signs of inertia. Garrison was in a good position to observe the situation. In December 1843 he confided

---

[48] *Practical Christian*, vol. II, no. 13, 30 Oct. 1841.

[49] Quoted in Odell Shepard, *Pedlar's Progress*, p. 279, where it is dated ca. Oct. 1839. Extracts from a different draft of this letter are given in F. B. Sanborn and William T. Harris, *A. Bronson Alcott*, I, 324, 325, with the date 28 Sept. 1841. This appears to be the correct one.

[50] In his *Autobiography* (p. 381) the moderate nonresistant Ballou gives the following verdict on Wright: "His zeal and activity were preeminent, his devotion to the cause unquestionable, his pen prolific, but his discrimination and soundness of exposition did not always command my admiration or satisfy my judgment."

in a letter to Wright, then on a speaking tour in Great Britain: "Little has been done, directly, to promote the heaven-born cause of non-resistance since you left. No agent has been found to take the field, and the Executive Committee of our little Non-Resistance Society are so occupied with their antislavery labors and responsibilities, that they have neither the time nor the means to put any efficient machinery into motion."[51] A year later he was writing in the same strain: "The Society, I regret to say, has had only a nominal existence during the past year —and, indeed, ever since your departure. It is without an organ, without funds, without publications."[52] Another year passed, and Garrison was still sounding the same note: no replacement for Wright in the field, most of the stalwarts like Abby Kelley, Stephen S. Foster, and Parker Pillsbury (and, of course, Garrison himself) almost completely absorbed in the work of abolitionism.[53]

In England, Wright had closest contacts with radical antimilitarists like John Scoble or antislavery men like George Thompson or the Quaker Joseph Sturge, who were also pacifists. Although his lecture tours on peace understandably did not do much to bridge the gap between the New England nonresistants and the somewhat conservative London Peace Society, which had taken the side of the American Peace Society in its dispute with the nonresistants, they do appear to have made a considerable impact on the burgeoning antimilitarist movement in Great Britain.[54] On the European continent, where the military spirit was everywhere in the ascendant and the peace societies, where they existed, did not renounce the possibility of defensive war, Wright's message was less effective. We do find him, however, arguing the nonresistant case assiduously with his fellow patients while spending six months in 1844 taking the water cure at Graeffenberg in Silesia.[55] "They were astonished to find," wrote Garrison, "that they could not excite in him any *American* feeling of exultation or exclusiveness; that he truly embraced all mankind as his countrymen."[56]

Wright was, indeed, almost indispensable to the Non-Resistance Society—at least in view of the absorption of its other capable leaders in antislavery activities. In part, however, his place was filled during

[51] Garrison to Wright, 16 Dec. 1843, Garrison Papers, B.P.L., MS A.1.1., vol. 3, no. 114.
[52] Garrison to Wright, 1 Oct. 1844, quoted in *W.L.G.*, III, 80.
[53] Garrison to Wright, 1 Nov. 1845, Garrison Papers, vol. 4, no. 17.
[54] See, e.g., the Manchester Peace Society's quarterly report to the London Peace Society for the spring of 1843 (B.P.L., MS G. 31.26.).
[55] See H. C. Wright, *Six Months at Graeffenberg*, for an account of his sojourn in Europe generally.
[56] *Practical Christian*, 7 Dec. 1844.

the years of his absence by Adin Ballou, who succeeded Quincy as the Society's president in the autumn of 1843 and was responsible for the two short-lived revivals of the *Non-Resistant* in 1845 and 1848. Yet, for all his greater intellectual depth, deeper spiritual resources, more stable temperament, and more balanced outlook, Ballou lacked the drive Wright had, which alone might have served to inject renewed energy into an already moribund organization. In addition, a considerable part of Ballou's attention had to be given to overseeing his Hopedale experiment. The communitarian leader was much less of an individualist, much less of an iconoclast, than either Wright or Garrison or many of their followers, even though his contribution to framing a coherent philosophy of nonresistance was unequalled (an aspect of his work that will be discussed in the next chapter). As chief organizer in the absence of Wright, Ballou was not, however, particularly effective.

"On your return," wrote Garrison to Wright toward the end of 1845, "we shall endeavor to give a new impulse to the cause of nonresistance. Its converts are steadily multiplying, and it has ceased to be assailed so wantonly and abusively as formerly."[57] That there was any increase in the number of adherents, however, was wishful thinking on Garrison's part, and the dying down of criticism and hostility was probably due more to lack of interest than to the growth of a greater understanding of nonresistance on the part of its opponents.[58]

Even the excitement of the Mexican War did little to reinvigorate the expiring Society. Garrison and his friends were, of course, among the most vehement opponents of the war and the administration's policy that had preceded it. Garrison himself, hoping for "success to the injured Mexicans and overwhelming defeat to the United States,"[59] for a moment almost appeared to grant, in the case of the former, that there could be a legitimate war of defense. And Thoreau (1817-1862) in 1845 had taken the step of offering passive resistance to the collection of taxes that might be used in the impending prosecution of what he regarded as an unjust war, "a peaceable revolution"[60] that landed

[57] Garrison to Wright, 1 Nov. 1845, Garrison Papers, vol. 4, no. 17.
[58] Cf., though, *Practical Christian*, 20 March 1847: "The cause [of nonresistance] is an unpopular and despised one, every where spoken against and treated with more or less contempt by the leaders of the people."
[59] Quoted in John L. Thomas, *The Liberator*, p. 343. See also Walter M. Merrill, *Against Wind and Tide*, pp. 209-11.
[60] "Civil Disobedience" in X (*Miscellanies*) of *The Writings of Henry David Thoreau*, 1893 edn., 150. This essay was first published in 1849. Thoreau's objection to the tax for which he was briefly jailed in 1845, on the eve of the war, however, stemmed more from his opposition to slavery than from his repugnance to war. We discover this, for instance, in a passage in *Walden* (1854) at the end

him for one night in the Concord jail. Thoreau, of course, was not a member of the Non-Resistance Society or of any other peace society, but the essayist's famous attempt to withdraw his collaboration from a warmaking, slaveowning state was certainly influenced to some extent by the example of the New England nonresistants.[61]

Wright, when at last he returned to the United States, was unable to turn the tide back in his capacity as "a voluntary, unhired lecturing agent of the Non-Resistance Society."[62] But he was able to achieve something, as we see from his account of his tour of Ohio in the late summer and early fall of 1848, in an area where, as he wrote in his journal, "war-making priests and churches have but little influence over the people."[63] Wright undoubtedly put new courage into the scattered handful of nonresistants in the state[64] and aroused considerable interest

---

of the chapter entitled "The Village," where he writes as follows of the motives of his refusal: "I did not pay a tax to, or recognize the authority of, the state which buys and sells men, women, and children, like cattle at the door of its senate-house." For the pacifist movement in this century, the essay on civil disobedience has served as a kind of brief manual of nonviolence. For Thoreau's impact on Gandhi and his philosophy and practice of *satyagraha*, see George Hendrick, "The Influence of Thoreau's 'Civil Disobedience' on Gandhi's *Satyagraha*," *NEQ*, XXIX, no. 4 (Dec. 1956), 462-71. Gandhi came upon the writings of Thoreau in the first decade of this century during his residence in South Africa.

[61] In 1843 Bronson Alcott, who was closely associated at this date with the Non-Resistance Society, had refused to pay his poll tax on grounds similar to Thoreau's. Another leading New England literary figure influenced by, though perhaps not entirely sharing the views of, the nonresistants was the poet James Russell Lowell (1819-1891), at that time a strong supporter of radical abolition. In his *Biglow Papers*, published in 1846, he makes Hosea Biglow say: "Ez fer war, I call it murder/ . . . I don't want to go no furder/ Than my testimony fer that." On 16 August 1845 we find Lowell writing Charles Sumner shortly after the latter had given his famous pro-peace Fourth of July oration (discussed in a subsequent chapter): "I only regret that you should have deemed it necessary to disavow any opposition to the use of force in supporting human governments. But I am willing to leave you entirely to the principle you yourself have advocated which will inevitably lead you to a different conclusion. *All* force is weak and barbarian, whether it sheds blood, or locks the doors of prisons and watch-houses" (Worthington Chauncey Ford [ed.], "Sumner's Oration on the 'True Grandeur of Nations,'" *Massachusetts Historical Society Proceedings*, L [1917], 266). Both Thoreau and Lowell, under the influence of their intense antislavery feelings, abandoned their pacifistic views in the next decade and in the Civil War became enthusiastic supporters of the Northern cause.

[62] *Non-Resistant and Practical Christian*, 22 Jan. 1848.

[63] *Ibid.*, 16 Sept. 1848.

[64] In his journal (reprinted *ibid.*, 16 Sept. 1848) Wright mentions meeting one such person, Valentine Nicholson, "a man who is striving for a purer and higher order of the social state." Nicholson had placed boxes outside his house and filled them with pacifist and abolitionist literature, including copies of the *Liberator* and Wright's antiwar tracts. Notices were nailed on posts supporting the boxes with the following inscription in large letters: "Whatever tends to injure

in the communities he visited. "We have been in session nearly four hours," he reported from New Salem, "and the people seem unwearied and indisposed to leave. War is a terribly absorbing question."[65] In addition, he was to prove once again a thorn in the flesh of many Quakers and moderate peace men, whose support for government he constantly proclaimed as tantamount to approval of the war system and of human exploitation.

Wright also toured New England and the middle states around this time. And in the former area, the heartland of the nonresistance movement, the Mexican War does seem to have led to some slight revival of activity. From around the spring of 1847 until at least the summer of 1848, we find quarterly meetings of the Society being reported in the columns of Ballou's *Practical Christian*—apparently a new development; these were held successively at various centers in Massachusetts and Rhode Island. But after the first few years, the annual reports of the Society tell the same story. Each year there is the same lament over diminishing numbers attending the conventions. True, those who came might be "the most active and efficient spirits in the various reforms of the age," as the *Liberator* reported of the 1844 meeting;[66] they might very well be persons "of the true stamp whose interest in the cause of non-resistance is deep and abiding" (it was now 1845), indeed "highly intelligent, embracing some of the best reformatory spirits of the age" (as was said of the participants in 1847).[67] Yet all this could scarcely cloak the sense of frustration at the failure of the movement, so bold only a few years back in depicting the confusion that would ensue among the forces of violence and governmental oppression at the onset of the power of nonresistance. Repeatedly, too, these annual reports tell a story of dwindling funds, finances insufficient to accomplish more than an iota of what had originally been planned. The pamphlet series outlining the principles of nonresistance, the extra agent to carry the word about the country where assuredly many must only be awaiting his arrival to become recruits in the crusade against war and violence, the expansion of the Society's program of meetings in Massachusetts and beyond, the steady appearance of a nonresistant journal to knit the membership together and provide regular am-

---

any portion of the human race should claim the attention of all mankind. Hence this effort to circulate information on the subjects of War, Slavery and Intemperance. If there are any books or papers remaining in this box, *travellers* are invited each to take one and circulate it."

[65] *Ibid.*, 28 Oct. 1848.
[66] Reprinted in *Non-Resistant*, 7 Dec. 1844.
[67] *Non-Resistant*, 9 Jan. 1847; *Non-Resistant and Practical Christian*, 22 Jan. 1848.

munition in the campaign for peace—all these hopes had to be abandoned one by one. The melancholy refrain—"the Society has not been able to carry on its operations the past year with much efficiency" (the words appear in the report for 1844)[68]—sums up the history of the nonresistance movement during these years.

If we look at accounts of the discussions at the successive annual meetings, we are struck by the repetition of the same themes year after year, a sterility of thought which could not find release in action. The affirmation of the power of nonresistance, the pros and cons of the ballot, and the iniquity of the war-supporting Constitution crop up year after year, and the same old arguments are gone over by much the same roster of speakers. Among a number of symptoms of decayed vitality was Ballou's failure to attract more than 280 subscribers for the *Non-Resistant*, which he resuscitated for a brief while in 1845 before merging it with his communitarian organ the *Practical Christian*. Admittedly, the paper under Ballou's editorship, with its highly moralistic tone, makes rather dull reading in comparison with its predecessor, which had ranged over a wide array of philosophical and political discussion: it was not likely now to make much appeal to the intellectuals of the movement. In any case, his failure to arouse sufficient interest among nonresistants and peace sympathizers was disappointing.

The last regular annual meeting of the Non-Resistance Society appears to have taken place in December 1849. According to most sources, this year also saw the final dissolution of the Society itself. However, it seems to have maintained some sort of shadowy existence at least into the middle of the next decade, for we find meetings being organized in Worcester in the name of the Society in March 1855 and again in November 1856.[69] Possibly, the organization was revived for the sole purpose of holding these meetings. At least it appears to have been completely inactive during the intervening years. Ballou and his Hopedale communitarians were mainly responsible for this short-lived renewal of activities. Some of the nonresistant "old guard" —"a precious few," Ballou had to admit[70]—including Garrison, H. C. Wright, and the Society's former Quaker president, Effingham L. Capron, participated. Prominent in the discussions was the loquacious Stephen S. Foster, who with his wife Abby (Kelley) was now living in Worcester.[71]

[68] *Non-Resistant*, N.S., 1 Jan. 1845.
[69] See the detailed reports printed in the *Practical Christian*, 7 April 1855; 21 April 1855; and 13 Dec. 1856.
[70] *Practical Christian*, 13 Jan. 1855.
[71] It was Foster who at both conventions raised the question of the relationship

At the end of 1849 Ballou had printed a letter from a rank-and-file sympathizer, one H. O. Stone from Concord (N.H.), which expressed with much feeling the dilemma that was to face the movement in the next decade. "When I consider the progress of the *Anti-Slavery* sentiment," wrote Stone, "and compare it with the progress of genuine *Peace* principles, I confess that I rejoice with fear and trembling. I rejoice unfeignedly in the appreciation of the rights of three millions of enslaved human beings. I *fear* lest those rights will be demanded or defended at the point of the bayonet, by an appeal to injurious force, through the destruction of human life." "Some," he continued, "who have agitated the anti-slavery question upon the broad basis of human brotherhood, and acknowledge the abstract truth of non-resistance have so far forgotten their brotherly love and so greatly outraged truth as to declare themselves ready to sweep slavery from the land, without regard to the requirements of absolute peace principles as soon as the people were ready to do it."[72]

Was the choice now: peace or brotherhood? Could nonresistants approve the broadening of human liberty by violent means if the mass of men stubbornly refused to follow along paths of peace? Some found themselves quite unable to resolve the question. Others, like Sam J. May, while holding on to their personal pacifism, were to abandon altogether the "no-government" views of Garrisonian nonresistance and collaborate in the not always pacific activities of the political wing of the antislavery movement.[73] A few, like Ballou, remained adamant in their refusal to countenance violent measures, even at secondhand, as it were. The passing of the Fugitive Slave Law in 1850 was to increase these difficulties immeasurably.

It had, indeed, been the issue of slavery that, first, by siphoning off the energies of many of the most capable nonresistants and, then, by challenging the validity of the nonresistant faith as an instrument for bringing about God's justice on earth had fatally weakened the movement.

The failure of the Society to develop after the first few years had, however, a second cause. Its extreme views on government, its philosophical anarchism, kept many out of its ranks whose pacifist sympathies would otherwise have brought them into the Society.[74] We have

---

between nonresistant love and the demand for social justice, as presented in the case of the slave (see chap. 7). The difficulties in reconciling the two were among the most potent causes of the dissolution of the nonresistant fellowship.
[72] *Practical Christian,* 8 Dec. 1849.
[73] See Galpin, "God's Chore Boy," chaps. VII and X.
[74] See Curti, "Non-Resistance in New England," pp. 54, 55; Galpin, *Pioneering for Peace,* p. 151.

seen this happen in the case of William Ladd and other moderate pacifists, who refused to leave the American Peace Society even after it had veered away again from absolute pacifism. Boldness of thought (at least at the outset), high intellectual quality, and unbounded enthusiasm (though mingled, it is true, with a good measure of eccentricity in some of its supporters) could not compensate for the paucity of the Society's numbers, its failure to expand beyond a very limited circle and a very confined area. In fact, after the first shock on public opinion had worn off, the Society made little impact on its environment. An intellectual elite soon became a closed coterie.

As an episode in the organizational history of reform movements in nineteenth-century America, the New England Non-Resistance Society deserves perhaps only a small niche. But as the first organized expression of radical pacifism in the country, it is certainly of much greater importance. We must now turn, therefore, to a consideration of its ideology.

Chapter 5

The Ideology of the New England Non-Resistance Society

The Declaration of Sentiments, which Garrison wrote for the new Society at the Boston Peace Convention of September 1838, had been a foundation manifesto rather than a systematic apologia for the creed of nonresistance as conceived by its New England adherents. It was, like so much that came from Garrison's pen, highly charged with emotion and written to meet the needs of the moment. Although he composed a number of articles in behalf of nonresistance, Garrison in fact added little to the development of its ideology. For this aspect of the movement we must turn to the works of several of his colleagues.

Most important from this point of view was Adin Ballou, whose treatise on *Christian Non-Resistance in all its Important Bearings* was published in Philadelphia in 1846[1] and reprinted several times subsequently. In addition, Ballou wrote two shorter pieces which deal with specific aspects of nonresistance: *Non-Resistance in Relation to Human Governments,* published in Boston in 1839 before he had formally joined the New England Non-Resistance Society, and *A Discourse on Christian Non-Resistance in Extreme Cases,* which came out twenty-one years later and was published by the community press in Hopedale. Next, we should mention the pamphlets of the less well-known theorist, Charles K. Whipple (1808-1900). In 1839 his *Evils of the Revolutionary War* was issued in Boston by the Society (and in 1846 a second edition appeared, this time a product of the Hopedale community press). Two years later, in 1841, Whipple published, again in Boston, a brief exposition of the Pauline text *The Powers that be are ordained of God* and of its relation to modern nonresistance. Then, as with Ballou, we have a long gap until 1860 when Whipple composed two further short works, the first entitled *The Non-Resistance Principle: With Particular Application to the Help of Slaves by Abolitionists*, and the second, *Non-Resistance applied to the Internal Defense of a Community*. Finally, we may mention the writings of the inordinately prolific Henry C. Wright. In his voluminous unpublished

---

[1] Lucretia Mott's son-in-law, Edmund M. Davis, suggested to Ballou that he undertake the work and shouldered the expense of publishing the first edition. See A. D. Hallowell, *James and Lucretia Mott*, p. 277. Davis, though a Quaker and former nonresistant, took part in the Civil War as an officer in the Union army. This metamorphosis he owed to his strong antislavery feelings.

journals and in the countless articles and letters he published in various papers, chiefly in the *Liberator* and the *Non-Resistant*, he dealt with various aspects of nonresistance which arose in connection with his work as chief propagandist for the nonresistance cause. In addition, he published in the forties a number of tracts on nonresistance, ranging from pamphlets of a few pages to treatises of book length. Several of these works came out in Britain, and they appear to have circulated in fairly large quantities on both sides of the Atlantic. In the 1850's the slavery issue seems to have dominated Wright's interests to the virtual exclusion of nonresistance. The polemical and propagandist element is very strong in everything that Wright wrote; yet some of it is useful in helping us to piece together a coherent picture of the ideology of the New England nonresistants.

Such a picture of their beliefs is, indeed, possible. But at this point we must set down several provisos. In the first place, even among the four writers mentioned hitherto, there were differences in emphasis and sometimes even disagreements on at least minor issues. Ballou, for instance, stressed the Christian basis of nonresistance more rigorously than the others, but he was less implacable in his opposition to government and was more ready perhaps than they were to stretch the limits of the allowable in noninjurious force. Secondly, we must not forget that nonresistant pacifism, even if we restrict its meaning to the ideology held by members of the New England Non-Resistance Society, was always a fluid doctrine and never formed a well-defined and completely rounded creed. It was constantly being argued out among members at public and private gatherings and in the press. The columns of the *Non-Resistant* (so long as it was in existence) and, to a lesser extent, Garrison's *Liberator* and Ballou's communitarian organ, *The Practical Christian*, are filled with discussions of one or another aspect of nonresistance, of its relation to current issues and to the problems of history and Biblical exegesis. Rank-and-file members of the movement wrote in to express their views, ask questions, and thresh out problems among themselves. This process of continual reexamination, of course, was kept up particularly during the first half dozen years when the nonresistance movement was still a vigorous element in the fermentation of New England's intellectual life. Later, as it became increasingly moribund and the interests and energies of its members were siphoned off into other channels, the argument grew less lively. Although little was contributed to the debate during the 1850's, there was at the beginning of the next decade a slight revival of interest in the theoretical side of nonresistance, owing perhaps to problems generated by the imminent clash between the claims of pacifism and those of the militant antislavery movement in the minds and hearts of the nonresistant abolitionists. Thus, if we bear in mind these limitations in generalizing on the subject and remember those subtler shadings in emphasis that existed between person and person and from one year to another and if we realize that a perfectly rounded philosophy of nonresistance never actually existed, we should be able to form a reasonably accurate, yet at the same time cohesive, impression of the body of doctrine held by the men and women who gave their allegiance to the New England Non-Resistance Society.

Ballou in opening his large-scale treatise on Christian nonresistance attempts to define the various types of belief on which nonresistance can be based. One category he dismisses somewhat perfunctorily: the "necessitous," that is, the adoption of nonresistance, not on principle, but simply from expediency, from the inability to resist by force of arms—a policy that might be pursued, for instance, by the subjects of an oppressive and all-powerful tyrant. The three remaining types he groups together. But, whereas "philosophical" nonresistance, based purely on rational considerations, such as the futility of war and violence and its moral impropriety as human action, and "sentimental" nonresistance, which draws its inspiration from a belief in man's higher nature progressively improving itself on the way to perfection, take no account of religion or revelation, Christian nonresistance flows directly from a desire to follow in their entirety the teachings and example of Christ as portrayed in the New Testament.[2]

Ballou thereafter concerns himself solely with the Christian variety of the nonresistant creed—and undoubtedly, with one or two exceptions,[3] the New England nonresistants, however unorthodox in some cases they may have been from the theological viewpoint,[4] were nonetheless professing Christians. Still, it is interesting to find Ballou referring here to what we would call today rationalist and humanitarian types of pacifism. This is perhaps the first mention of the possibility of the existence of an absolute pacifism not stemming from religious (that is, Christian) considerations.

The appeal of the nonresistants (as of some of the earlier exponents of pacifism) was to the spirit of Christ's teachings as much as, if not

[2] Ballou, *Christian Non-Resistance*, pp. 1, 2.
[3] For instance, nonresistant views were held by John Collins, the associationist and a Garrisonian abolitionist, who was openly a Freethinker and gained some notoriety for expression of "infidel" views.
[4] Many had become "come-outers" from the orthodox churches because of the latter's refusal to renounce war and slavery without qualification. For one of the many examples of this hostility to the churches, see H. C. Wright, *Christian Church; Anti-Slavery and Non-Resistance applied to Church Organizations* (1841), *passim*.

more than, to particular texts in the New Testament. They were convinced that this spirit spoke against war: war in fact is sin, and not only war but the whole exercise of coercion by the state. It is quite wrong, wrote Henry C. Wright, for the Christian to search through the scriptures trying to extract some justification for killing or harming, bodily or mentally, fellow creatures created, as they were, by God. "He must sit at the feet of Jesus, and ask, 'Lord, what wouldst thou have me to do?' And having learned this, he should do it without further consultation with flesh and blood." The kind of actions which would thereby be learned (in Wright's opinion) are: love to enemies as well as to friends, forgiveness of injuries, returning good for evil, readiness for sacrifice of self rather than doing the least harm to others, the full implementation of human brotherhood.[5] In one of his short tracts Wright lists thirty reasons for the incompatibility of the armed forces with such teachings of Christ and concludes: "Thus the existence of the army and navy is a *practical* abolition of Christianity and of human brotherhood—a practical dethronement of God, and the deadliest enemy of human life and human liberty."[6] As Wright explained: "The business of the army and navy is not to forgive, but to kill enemies. A soldier is merely a human butcher, hired by the month, to butcher his brethren, should he be called on to do so."[7]

Garrison, in particular, strove to liberate belief in nonresistance from

[5] Wright, *Defensive War proved to be a Denial of Christianity*, pp. 24-105. In his book of cautionary tales for small children that he published in 1843 under the title *A Kiss for a Blow: or, A Collection of Stories for Children; showing them how to prevent Quarrelling*, Wright attempted to inculcate his pupils with the nonviolent way of life, to instruct them "how much more pleasantly they could live together without fighting" (p. v). "Children fighting for a toy," he adds, "afford an illustration, in miniature, of nations contending for empire" (p. vii). The little volume, whose tone to a modern reader appears too often mawkishly sentimental, became a kind of primer of nonresistance and went through many editions in both the United States and the British Isles (including a Welsh translation printed as late as 1908). Wright was extremely fond of children, and they of him, and his own nonresistant philosophy was basically a childlike faith in the goodness of his fellow humans. "Of one thing," he wrote in 1839, "I am more and more convinced; i.e. that metaphysics and philosophy, *falsely* so called, have much less to do with non-resistance than the simple, subdued, childlike spirit of the heart" (*Non-Resistant*, 18 May 1839). Perhaps his growing vehemence during the antebellum decades against the slaveholding class in the South represented an unconscious reaction against men who had not responded as they should have done to the moral suasion of Northern abolitionists.

[6] Wright, *The Immediate Abolition of the Army and Navy* (Peace Tract, No. 3).

[7] Wright, *Forgiveness in a Bullet!* (Peace Tract, No. 2). In his antimilitarist writings, Wright (like most contemporary peace advocates) always had in mind the voluntarist principle by which the armed forces of Britain and the United States were then recruited, and not an army raised by conscription. A representative example of this view is to be found in the conclusion of his Peace Tract, No. 1: *The Heroic Boy.*

a stifling dependence on Biblical authority. Steeped in the Bible since childhood and familiar with its every page as few men have been, he came over the years to feel increasingly that it, too, could exercise a tyranny over the mind, could prevent the growth of a living religion in men's hearts, as effectually as the domination of the orthodox churches, which he so fiercely denounced for their loss of a truly Christian outlook. His Christianity remained Bible-centered but not Bible-bound. His nonresistance still rested on his interpretation of the Christian gospel to mankind; but the letter of the scriptures, even the words of Christ himself, no longer held authority with him unless confirmed by the assent of the human conscience. In 1848, for instance, we find him telling the annual meeting of the Non-Resistance Society: "We must appeal to reason, conscience, facts. Why should we go to a book to settle the character of war, when we could judge of it by its fruits? If war promoted peace, safety, and holiness, it was good; let us welcome it with joy and exultation. If, on the contrary, its fruits were evil, let it be condemned."[8] Echoing the words of scripture, he pleaded for an empirical pacifism which was justified by its consistence with reason and conscience, and not because of any divine mandate empowered to overrule these sources. Wright, too, adopted much the same view. The Bible was a record of the past spiritual experiences of the Jews and not an infallible guide to present conduct. Its precepts must be tested by the inner light within each human being; it was because they accorded with this that Christ's teachings should find acceptance.[9]

Garrison eventually went so far as to maintain that the nonresistant ethic was in no way necessarily connected with the teaching and example of Jesus, that its source was solely within each individual human soul and might be held independently of Christian belief. God could never, in his view, command any action that was contrary to morality. The act of war, like the institution of slavery, was "a *malum in se*" which no book, Jewish or Christian, could cleanse: they were both "essentially wrong." If a sacred book sought to justify them, the book must be put on one side and the promptings of conscience followed instead.[10] Garrison's pacifism, then, was basically an ethical impulse, an impulse—he would have said—that was implanted in all men and not a peculiar revelation to those within the Judaeo-Christian tradition.

[8] *Practical Christian*, vol. IX, no. 19, 20 Jan. 1849. Garrison himself attributed his emancipation from Biblical fundamentalism in large part to the influence of the liberal-minded Hicksite Quaker couple, Lucretia and James Mott, and especially to the forthright Lucretia. See Hallowell, *James and Lucretia Mott*, pp 296, 297.
[9] Wright, *Anthropology*, Letter III.
[10] *Selections from the Writings and Speeches of William Lloyd Garrison*, pp. 89, 90.

To this Ballou, indeed, took exception. "True Non-resistance," he told Garrison, "Christian Non-resistance . . . came down from Heaven." It was exemplified in the life and teaching of Christ, and to him we must look primarily for its authority.[11] And, in fact, all the leading nonresistants made plentiful appeal at least to the New Testament to buttress their arguments. Their aim was a restitution of primitive Christianity; Ballou entitles a chapter in one of his books "On the primitive Christian virtue of non-resistance."[12] The name they had taken for themselves was derived, of course, from Christ's words: "Resist not evil" (Matt. 5:39). The Sermon on the Mount was for them the center of Christian doctrine. "The term," wrote Ballou of nonresistance, "is considered more strikingly significant than any other of the principle involved, and the duty enjoined in our Saviour's precept. Hence its adoption and established use." By evil Christ had meant the infliction of personal injury by one human being on another. What deductions should we draw from this, asked Ballou, for use in everyday life? "Consider the context; consider parallel texts; . . . consider the known spirit of Christianity"; and then see how far this carries you. Briefly, Ballou's view was that a Christian nonresistant could neither kill nor maim in self-defense or in defense of others, nor willingly collaborate in any way with those engaged in such action. Further, he was precluded from any kind of participation in administration, either by voting in elections or holding office, however seemingly innocuous, since all governments as then constituted were ready to wage war and to exact the death penalty for certain offenses.[13]

In his *Christian Non-Resistance* Ballou devotes two full chapters[14] to arguing his case on scriptural grounds. He arrays his proof texts and gives his interpretation of them;[15] he then goes on to deal in considerable detail with possible objections that might be raised by non-pacifists or by pacifists who stopped short of the "no-government" position; and to this he adds further evidence for his case, culled from the writings of the apostles and from the history of the early church. On

[11] *Autobiography of Adin Ballou*, pp. 439, 447-49.
[12] *Primitive Christianity and its Corruptions*, vol. II, Discourse XIII.
[13] Ballou, *Christian Non-Resistance*, pp. 12-20.
[14] Chap. II, "Scriptural Proof," and chap. III, "Scriptural Objections Answered."
[15] For another New England nonresistant who made much of the textual argument for and against pacifism, see the *Remarks offered in a Non-Resistance Convention . . . 1841* (pp. 4ff) by the Universalist minister, the Rev. John Murray Spear. His conclusion (p. 22), so different from Garrison's more broadly ethical Christianity, was: "I am ready to engage in human butchery when God requires it by my hand," but in no other circumstances. (Spear later became a spiritualist and in the 1850's founded a community on the borders of Pennsylvania and northern New York state, which was commonly known as the "Spiritual Springs.")

the positive side, the argument was summed up in the assertion that Christ's law of love as revealed both in the letter and spirit of his teachings involves the inviolability of human life under all circumstances. As Henry C. Wright expressed it: "The position taken by *armed resistants* is, that man's right to live as man depends on his guilt or innocence. . . . Non-resistants hold that *human* government never did and never can have the right to say how much and what kind of guilt renders a man worthy of death. God alone has power to decide this."[16] On the negative side, the argument counseled a withdrawal from society, a dissociation from governments that contravened the sacredness of the human personality.

Wright defined the essence of Christian nonresistance as submission to injuries, "non-resisting and non-resenting submission to affront and wrong," along with a belief in the power of love to ultimately transform human relationships. Without the spirit of nonresistance Christianity was dead. To the question "To what extent are we required to submit?" Wright answered that there were indeed "no limitations— no exceptions in favor of extreme cases or of nations." In all instances "Christianity says—submit. Jesus suffered death without resentment or resistance; but committed himself to Him that judgeth righteously. And in this thing we are commanded to walk in his steps."[17]

In presenting the case for nonresistant pacifism, its advocates soon came upon two major stumbling blocks in the minds of the unconvinced regarding its theoretical validity. The first has been met with already in our discussion of the earlier stages of the pacifist movement in America. How could God's apparent approval of the wars waged by the Jews in the Old Testament and their repressive penal code be brought into line with Christ's prohibition of all forms of violence in the New? To this we find two different answers in the writings of the New England nonresistants. Ballou gave the conservative one pleaded by earlier pacifists: that the old dispensation has been replaced by the new, that the prophets of the Old Testament were in a sense forerunners only of the more perfect revelation given by Christ. "The New Testament," says Ballou, "supersedes the Old on all questions of divine truth and human duty."[18] This answer left pretty well unshaken the idea of the general, if not the literal, inspiration of the whole body of the scriptures and still assigned a certain relative justification to the

[16] Wright, *Man-Killing by Individuals and Nations, Wrong-Dangerous in All Cases*, p. 8. In 1850 he wrote (*Anthropology*, p. 11): "To inspire man with affectionate respect for the person of man, to rescue him from individual and governmental violence and to throw around his life and liberty the sanctions of absolute inviolability, has been the object of my life for twenty years."
[17] Wright, *Man-Killing*, p. 18.   [18] *Christian Non-Resistance*, p. 66.

wars of Old Testament times. But men like Garrison and Wright, far more radical than Ballou in their whole outlook and temperament, were prepared to cast such ideas completely aside and to brand the Jewish patriarchs as warmongers along with the military leaders of more recent times.

Listen to Garrison again at the New England Non-Resistance Society's annual meeting of 1848 presenting a resolution "that God, as a just, beneficent and unchangeable being, never did and never can authorize one portion of his children to kill and exterminate another portion, any scriptures (whether styled sacred or profane) to the contrary notwithstanding." Wright, who was present at the meeting, supported Garrison's view. Indeed, we find Wright in his public addresses up and down the country during this period occupied with this very question. For Wright, the wars of Old Testament times seemed particularly bloody, cruel, and barbaric—impossible to square with the loving Father of mankind presented in the gospels. If all use of injurious force was wrong (as the nonresistants believed), how much the less could these primitive feudings have found pleasure in God's sight? Were it true that under the so-called old dispensation Moses and Joshua had waged war at God's behest against the Canaanites and that God had inspired the Jews to enforce a penal code of exceptional harshness, then, indeed, this God acted contrary to the law of love and all morality. "The God who could sanction such an atrocity," Wright cried out, "was a demon, not the God of Love and Justice!" Or, rather, it all showed that the morality of the Old Testament books was only too fallibly human.[19]

The nonresistants not only attempted to prove their case on scriptural grounds but, in the second place, sought to answer their opponents who argued empirically that nonresistance was contrary to nature. Let it be admitted, these men said, that it is ideally the perfect Christian conduct, but in practice it goes against the natural law of self-preservation. True, Ballou replied, fighting is the usual method of self-defense among animals and men. But is there not a better way for the latter? How effective in fact has the use of injurious force been in the history of mankind? "The whole world is in arms, after nearly six thousand years' close adherence to this method of self-preservation."[20] Ballou enunciated a new law to be derived from nature, that of reciprocation: "that like must beget its like—physical, mental, moral, spiritual." According to this principle, the way of noninjury, always

[19] *Practical Christian*, 20 Jan. 1849. See also Wright, *Anthropology*, Letter IV; *Man-Killing*, pp. 9-41, 51-57.
[20] Ballou, *Christian Non-Resistance*, p. 104.

returning good for evil, will eventually evoke an answering note in an enemy, will finally bring around the evildoer from his ways. "Though the injuries we do them are done only in resistance of aggression, still they follow the same law. . . . They breed a fresh brood of injuries. If this be not strictly true in each individual case, it is true on the great whole."[21] Ballou believed that, even though the practice of nonresistance could never guarantee the security of any one individual or group from attack or even death, still it was by and large a safer, as well as a more moral, line of approach than that of using injurious force of one kind or another.[22]

In his book on *Christian Non-Resistance* he devotes a chapter entitled "The Safety of Non-Resistance" to this point, and both here and elsewhere in the book he produces a number of illustrations of the successful practice of nonresistance. "Behold," he exclaims, "robbers looked out of countenance and actually converted; ferocious banditti rendered harmless; wild savages inspired with permanent kindness; and all manner of evil overcome with good."[23] The stories tell of unarmed travelers journeying unharmed through brigand-infested lands or successfully extricating themselves from the clutches of highwaymen and robbers in more civilized countries, of Quakers and Shakers living peaceably with American Indians, of Christian missionaries preaching the gospel of peace in darkest Africa or among the cannibal-infested South Seas. "Who can contemplate such practical exemplifications of Christian non-resistance as these," Ballou writes, "and not be ravished with the excellence and loveliness of the sublime doctrine."[24] Although some of the stories do not appear to be very well authenticated, doubtless most were true.

The weakest element in the use of such illustrative material in arguing the case for pacifism (a weakness true not only of Ballou but of Henry C. Wright, whose writings are crammed with stories of this kind, as well as a host of other pacifist writers of this period) would seem to be the lack of examples of collective pacifist action. Quaker government in Pennsylvania and the experience of the Irish Quakers in the troubles of 1798 are almost the only cases cited which approximate to this kind of action. They had become, as we have seen, part of the stock-in-trade of every peace propagandist, and the New England nonresistants were able to do little to advance the argument

[21] *Ibid.*, pp. 115-21.
[22] This theme is developed at length in his *Discourse on Christian Non-Resistance in Extreme Cases*. "I might fall from my principles," he writes (p. 16), "and be driven to distraction. But I should pray that it might be otherwise."
[23] *Christian Non-Resistance*, p. 182.   [24] *Ibid.*, p. 206.

at this point. However, although it is true that they were hard put to discover instances of the adoption of nonviolence by nations or large groups, they do appear to have felt that it was personal nonresistance that was proving more of a stumbling block to the acceptance of their pacifist position rather than the adoption of pacifism on a nationwide scale. Adoption by a whole nation, it was supposed, would inspire group cohesiveness and a firmness of collective purpose, which could steel a man's will up to the point of martyrdom.

Moreover, the practical case against international war—a realization of the horrors of the battlefield, of war's economic wastefulness, and of its frequent failure to bring lasting security (an aspect of the pacifist argument, incidentally, that the New England nonresistants stressed almost as much as the religious and moral objections)—had already made some headway, in reform circles at least, if not with the public at large. The idea of unilateral disarmament—as expounded, for instance, by the American Peace Society—had even found assent in circles which were not committed to absolute pacifism. A renunciation of all forms of injurious force at the personal level, on the other hand, seemed more unfamiliar to many people at that date. This unfamiliarity, therefore, in part explains the emphasis given by Ballou and the other nonresistants to proving the efficacy of nonviolence in individual relations rather in the sphere of international politics.

The New England nonresistants were above all "immediatists," in their pacifism as much as in their abolitionism. Let us not wait to practice our Christianity until the millennium when everyone will be perfect, cries Ballou. Let us grant that nonresistance may be impractical in the present state of society, says Wright, but our object is to alter society by preaching and living out our ideals until a change comes about.[25] Let a beginning be made now. Let the vicious circle once be broken and the redeeming influence of love will eventually eradicate violence from society. For individuals as for nations, "defensive violence as surely begets offensive, as offensive violence begets defence. Nothing but the all conquering power of Christian love can subdue this spirit of resistance and attack."[26]

But what of love and justice in the relations between the members of society? It was in their attitude toward government that the New England nonresistants parted company not only with all nonpacifists but with many who shared their radical opposition to war. Those great examplars of American pacifism, the Quakers, as well as the

[25] *Ibid.*, chap. VI; Wright, *Man-Killing*, pp. 54-57. Wright (e.g., in his *Six Months at Graeffenberg*, pp. 83, 90) makes use of the well-worn analogy between teetotalism and the nonresistant pledge.
[26] Wright, *Man-Killing*, p. 46.

founding fathers of the American peace movement like Worcester and Ladd—even after they had moved over to absolute pacifism—had all found participation in the offices and activities of the state compatible with their peace principles, so long as it had no clear connection with war or the taking of life. Many of the functions of contemporary government appeared to them of positive benefit to mankind, and they felt it a duty to join with their fellow citizens in getting the best men into office. Indeed, although they differed from nonpacifists regarding the best methods to be employed in its execution, they considered civil government as essential to the very existence of a civilized, Christian society. It was hardly surprising, then, that the frontal attack made by the New England nonresistants on the very concept of "human government" in a Christian society shocked or dazed the overwhelming majority of persons who came into contact with them, and that they were subjected on all sides to virulent abuse and to ridicule for holding such opinions.

Their views on government were actually very similar to those of the pacifist sects of the Anabaptist-Mennonite tradition (though the latter probably had no direct influence on the thinking of the New England nonresistants). Both gave qualified recognition to government within God's order, while both denied that government could have any place in a Christian society. The Anabaptist-Mennonite groups were pessimistic about the possibility of achieving a nationwide, let alone a worldwide, acceptance of Christian nonresistance: the small flock of those who followed Christ's teaching would remain alone and isolated in a hostile world until the latter days. The New England nonresistants on the other hand, comprising for the most part men and women of education and culture who shared the optimistic philosophy of progress then current and were influenced, too, by the religious wave of perfectionism that had spread far and wide throughout the American populace, were not content—not even Ballou in his Hopedale community—to withdraw themselves effectively from contact with political life. One might almost say that their protest against government had to be made within government. We can see in Ballou's writings, for example, that, somewhat like his contemporary John Humphrey Noyes, he conceived of the millennium, not so much as a future event in time and space, but rather as a complete transformation of a moral and religious nature taking place within an individual. The millennium is, as it were, here already. Millennial, perfectionist rules of conduct could be carried out in the actual world as increasing numbers of individuals were caught up in the process of inner renewal. As this transformation led to the adoption of nonresistance and the unlimited acting out of the Christian gospel on an ever widening scale, the millennium within the individual soul would evolve into the coming of Christ's kingdom on earth.[27]

For all Garrison's pride in the "disorganizing" principles of his new Society, the New England nonresistants deeply resented—and with considerable justification, it should be said—the accusations of anarchy and subversion hurled against them from press and pulpit, until a curtain of silence was brought down around them that proved more effective against them than oceans of clerical and journalistic verbiage.[28] "We are no Jacobins, Revolutionists, Anarchists; though often slanderously so denominated," Ballou protested in 1839. They were not out to reform government or to purify it or to rebel against it. Theirs was a revolution of the inner man, their appeal was to the individual. Until they had succeeded in effecting an inner moral revolution in a sufficient number of such individuals so as "to supersede" human government by the laws of Christ's kingdom, laws enforced by the promptings of human conscience alone, human government would have to continue.

> So if men will not be governed by God, it is their doom to be enslaved one by another. And in this view, human government—defective as it is, bad as it is—is a *necessary evil* to those who will not be in willing subjection to the *divine*. Its *restraints* are better than *no* restraints at all—and its *evils* are preventives of greater. For thus it is that selfishness is made to thwart selfishness, pride to humble pride, revenge to check revenge, cruelty to deter cruelty, and wrath to punish wrath; that the vile lusts of men, overruled by infinite wisdom, may counterwork and destroy each other. In this way *human* government grows out of rebellious moral natures, and will *continue*, by inevitable consequence, in some form or other among men, till HE whose right it is to reign "shall be all in all."[29]

Such sentiments, indeed, would not have been out of place on the lips of a fifteenth-century Czech Brethren or a sixteenth-century German Anabaptist. Although Ballou belonged in some respects to what we might call the right wing of New England nonresistance, even the

[27] See esp. Ballou, *Non-Resistance in Relation to Human Governments*, pp. 15, 24.
[28] See—to cite just one example—the anti-nonresistant lecture entitled *A Vindication of the Right of Civil Government and Self-Defence* by a member of the Massachusetts legislature, Jeremiah Spofford. "I am for peace," wrote Spofford (p. 15), "but the way to secure it is to cause all men to do justice," even if war were the only means available.
[29] Ballou, *Non-Resistance in Relation to Human Governments*, pp. 8-11.

more thoroughgoing Garrison took essentially the same position. "The abrogation of existing laws and governmental regulations for the punishment of evil-doers," he writes, "would be calamitous, without a moral and spiritual regeneration of the people." The burden of human government was a species of punishment laid upon society for failure to live up to the full Christian ethic. For those who genuinely strove to realize this ethic in their lives, to live out the kingdom of Christ already on earth, active collaboration with government was ruled out. "Prisons, swords, muskets and soldiers are necessary to uphold governments which punish evil-doers by fines, imprisonment, and death. But these are prohibited by Christ; therefore, governments of force are prohibited to his followers."[30] Christian anarchism, not anarchy, was their ideal.

Nonresistant writers, like other exponents of Christian pacifism, were forced to give special attention to St. Paul's views on civil government in Romans 13 on account of the use made of them in the arguments of nonpacifist opponents. According to Garrison, these verses had become, as it were, "a frowning Gibraltar, inaccessible by sea and land, filled with troops and all warlike instruments, and able to vanquish every assailing force."[31] Against such a threat, "by far the most plausible and seductive objection, now urged against Christian non-resistance,"[32] the latter's defenders marshaled all their forces. The text, they declared, urged submission to, not participation in, worldly governments which have not renounced the use of the sword. Christians of St. Paul's time, while renouncing all thought of armed revolt, kept themselves apart from the powers that be, giving them only a conditional recognition within the framework of God's order. In this sense, Pharaoh and Nebuchadnezzar and Caesar were all God's instruments; yet no Christian could associate himself with the administration of such rulers.[33]

Garrison's colleague, C. K. Whipple, wrote a little tract on the subject, which he entitled simply *The Powers that be are Ordained of God*. It begins: "This proposition is fully admitted by non-resistants." But, Whipple went on, when man enacts laws and constitutions that are contrary to "God's laws," as had been the case throughout history with all rulers, whether in despotisms or democracies, then those who wish to obey God rather than man must withdraw from active collaboration in the work of government. They are forbidden the use of violence against injustice and must be submissive, meekly suffering the penalty for refusal if ordered to do wrong. Thus, as God may be said

---

[30] *Selections from . . . Garrison*, pp. 91, 92, 95, 97. [31] *Ibid.*, pp. 95, 96.
[32] Ballou, *Christian Non-Resistance*, pp. 77. [33] *Ibid.*, pp. 76-96.

to have ordained slavery, since the slave, too, along with all other men, is forbidden by the Christian gospel to use violence to right wrongs done him and must be guided in all his action by the law of love, in the same sense even the worst government may be called a divine institution.[34] In fact, in the hands of the nonresistants—as to a certain degree with some of their pacifist predecessors—St. Paul's injunctions were transformed into a proof text for the pacifist and "no-government" positions.

The New England nonresistants did, of course, recognize that man was a social being. Theirs was far from being the extreme individualistic variety of anarchism exemplified, for instance, by their contemporary in Germany, Max Stirner. If only the existing system of government with its armies and armed police force, with its capital punishment and repressive prisons, with its support of slavery and denial in practice of the brotherhood of man, and with all the pomp and panoply of power were transformed into a voluntary association of citizens living as best they could according to the ethical code of the gospels and controlling deviants from this ethic by moral suasion alone, then government would have no more enthusiastic supporters than the nonresistants. As Ballou expressed it: "If human government be understood to imply only divine government clothed in human forms and administered by human organizations, with merely incidental imperfections, non-resistance is for it *per se*. It has no necessary opposition to it whatever."

Why, then, did the nonresistants not wish to act by all legal means open to citizens in a democratic state in order to reform and remold the machinery of government according to their desires? Here all the nonresistant writers gave the same answer: the existing system was not reformable. A clear break, a clean sweep, must come before government could be christianized. The war-making power, capital punishment and a harsh penal system, slavery—these were all basic constituents of the American governmental machine; and the situation was essentially no different in other so-called Christian lands. These institutions were not merely external accretions which might be sloughed off by the judicious exercise of the franchise, leaving the system as nearly perfect as could be hoped for in this imperfect world. Instead, as Ballou maintained, "military and injurious penal power is their very life blood—the stamina of their existence." They formed a fundamental part of every constitution. To participate voluntarily in the working of government, even in the seemingly innocuous functions of voting or holding civil

[34] C. K. Whipple, *The Powers that be are ordained of God*, passim. See also H. C. Wright, *Six Months at Graeffenberg*, pp. 333-44.

office, was to be a party to an unholy compact, a betrayal of the principle of Christian nonviolence. First let us remove all those evils "with which all that is good in existing governments is inseparably interwoven," and then, perhaps, it would be proper for a nonresistant to associate himself with the world of politics.[35] Meanwhile—and here H. C. Wright was expressing the united opinion of the nonresistant movement—"It is wrong to hold an office in which we must consent to be vested with life-taking or war-making power, or to come under an obligation to use it. . . . It is wrong to VOTE for others to offices which it is wrong for us to hold. . . . Here, then, all who reject military, or man-killing power as wrong, must take their stand."[36]

The suffrage brought responsibility: the voters, in the opinion of most nonresistants, were ultimately responsible both for the total platform of the man for whom they cast their ballot and for all the functions he might possibly have to perform in the way of duty. Under the Constitution of the United States "the war-making power" was indissolubly linked with the functions of both President and Congressman, as well as with those of most other federal and state officials. The guilt of blood shed in war or law enforcement rested also on all who had elected the administration into office. "The American nation is a MURDERER. . . . The blood of murdered millions cries out against all existing national organizations."[37] President and administration in a democratic state like America are merely agents of the people. H. C. Wright, in particular, assailed voting pacifists like the Quakers or the supporters of the American Peace Society. "They say war is wrong, yet vote for it. The report of such peace-men is not believed." It was no use pleading, said Wright, that we have an obligation to elect the best man into office. We must first look to the character of the office itself and not to the candidate and the measures he proposes, however good these may be. To exercise the franchise even to effect the abolition of slavery would be wrong, would be to "vote for MURDER to prevent THEFT." "No man can love the slaves who will violate a known and acknowledged rule of right to free them," H. C. Wright explained

---

[35] Ballou, *Christian Non-Resistance*, pp. 210-17; Wright, *Anthropology*, pp. 68, 69.
[36] Wright, *Man-Killing*, pp. 50-51.
[37] Quoted from one of the Non-Resistance Society's tracts entitled "National Organizations," reprinted in the *Liberator*, 11 Jan. 1839. "Let all soldiers and all advocates of war be told," wrote H. C. Wright in 1848, "that they are murderers, and let this truth be brought home to them on all occasions, till they feel its force; and then, and not till then, will men learn and advocate war no more" (*Dick Crowninshield, the Assassin, and Zachary Taylor, the Soldier*, p. 12). See also his *The Employers of Dick Crowninshield, the Assassin, and the Employers of Zachary Taylor, the Soldier: The Difference*, for a continuation of this argument.

somewhat smugly. It was Wright, too, who gave us one of the clearest expositions of the nonresistant objection to the exercise of the franchise:

> All preparations for war, in this nation, are begun at the ballot-box. Voting is the first step; . . . a *bullet* is in every ballot; and when the ballot is cast into the box, the bullet goes in with it. They are inseparable, as the government is now constituted. Every voter, as he casts in his vote, says—"This is my will—if you resist it, I will kill you." Every ballot contains a threat of death; and he, who casts it, pledges himself to aid the government to execute it. The ballot-box is the first step—the gallows or battlefield the last; and whoever takes the first, must take the last. There is no consistent or honest stopping place between them.[38]

This uncompromising approach to the question of voting and officeholding was not matched, however, by an equally forthright stand in the matter of paying taxes to what all good nonresistants considered a warlike government. Here, at least in the past, many American Quakers had adopted a more thoroughgoing position by withholding taxes in time of war. For the nonresistants, all governments as at present constituted were in a state of perpetual warmindedness; so we might expect that they would have refused on principle to give them the financial support represented by the payment of taxes. Yet this was not the case. All the New England nonresistants, from Garrison on down, complied with Caesar's demands. They could point, of course, to Christ's words in reply to the agents sent by the chief priests and scribes. But they even went further, arguing that the submission enjoined by Christ on his followers justified a passive acceptance of the demands of government for money. "Voting is an act of government," wrote Ballou, "and assumes all the responsibility of injurious compulsion. Tax paying is submission to compulsion assumed by others. Therefore tax-paying is *non-resistance*, and *voting* is the assumption of a power to aggress and resist by deadly force."[39] Thus, a clash was avoided on this issue between the New England nonresistants—most of them law-abiders by nature and nurture, if not by conviction—and the state. On this point the movement was not called upon either to produce its Thoreaus to spend their night of lonely protest in the local jail or to endure the prolonged distraints suffered earlier by the Quakers during the Revolutionary War.

We have seen that the nonresistants' objection to civil government

[38] Wright, *Ballot Box and Battle Field*, pp. 1, 4-20.
[39] *Practical Christian*, vol. V, no. 6, 3 Aug. 1844.

was qualified by their readiness to give positive approval if all reliance on international war and internal coercion were abandoned. Was such a radical purging of the violent element in statecraft possible in this world? Was a renewal of society attainable in the foreseeable future? Or would the uncompromising followers of the peaceable kingdom always remain a minority in the kingdoms of this world? On this question the nonresistants, unlike the exponents of the Anabaptist-Mennonite tradition whose opinions on many points they shared, gave an optimistic answer. With many of their contemporaries among the purely religious revivalists, they saw the millennium at hand, when nonresistance would sweep first the American continent and then the world. "Let us all adopt it, that we may be saved," the New Hampshire editor and abolitionist, Nathaniel P. Rogers, wrote enthusiastically.[40] Ballou believed that the conversion of only two-thirds of the population to nonresistance, "with even a large share of imperfection lingering about them," would be sufficient to warrant a total abandonment of "injurious force" and the inauguration of government based on the laws of God alone. "If here and there a disorderly individual broke over the bounds of decency, the whole force of renovated public sentiment would surround and press in upon him like the waters of the ocean, and slight *uninjurious* force would prevent personal outrage in the most extreme cases." The example of the United States' conversion to nonresistance would sooner or later be emulated by the other nations of the world.[41]

Even after "the great work of revolutionizing public opinion"[42] had been completed and nonresistant pacifism was spreading to the rest of the world, its practical application would still continue to pose several difficult problems. The question of attempted conquest of a nonresistant nation by an aggressive outsider does not, however, seem to have greatly exercised the theorists of nonresistance: pacifism as a policy, they believed, would soon take root throughout the civilized world, once an example had been given. It was to the problem of maintaining public order within a nonresistant society, and of protecting it against

---

[40] *Non-Resistant*, vol. IV, no. 2, 26 Jan. 1842.

[41] Ballou, *Christian Non-Resistance*, pp. 226-29.

[42] *Practical Christian*, vol. V, no. 9, 14 Sept. 1844. The phrase is Ballou's. Toward the end of his life he appears to have become less optimistic about the chances of a speedy mass conversion to Christian nonresistance and, at the same time, more tolerant of the existing governmental system as a makeshift for the millennium. Perhaps his disappointment and dillusionment at the slow progress and setbacks inside his Hopedale community and its final dissolution made him less sanguine about any widespread appeal that nonresistant ideas might have, even within the ranks of reform. See his *Primitive Christianity and its Corruptions*, vol. II, Discourses XIII and XIV, given at the beginning of the seventies.

unprovoked attack on the part of antisocial elements, that they turned their thoughts first.

In their attitude toward the treatment of crime, the nonresistants displayed the most positive side of their faith. Here was an aspect of their creed that even friendly critics tended to ignore;[43] while, on the whole, the general public looked on the group as a bunch of wild incendiaries bent only on promoting general disorder. In fact, their views on this question were in line with the trend of modern penological theory. Ballou, for instance, saw the source of crime in bad social conditions. He castigated the self-righteous attitude of the affluent of his day, who called for the gallows and penal servitude for those who fell foul of the law. "Let them spare their maledictions against the punishable class of their fellow creatures," he wrote, and ask if they would not themselves be standing in the prisoner's dock had they been born to the poverty and material and moral misery that was the lot of the vast majority of the criminal class. What was needed was loving care and a good example, not deterrence by severity. "Therefore," he concluded, "Christian non-resistance protests against the wickedness of the *punishing* as well as the *punished* classes."[44] The principle of retaliation that underlay the existing legal and penal systems was inconsistent with the Christian spirit of love that put the redemption of the sinner in the forefront. To substitute reform for punishment as society's answer to crime: this was the stated aim of nonresistant theory.[45]

Much might be done by removing the occasion for crime. C. K. Whipple called for the "suppression" by a nonresistant community of such breeding grounds of delinquency as grog shops, gambling dens, and brothels.[46] But it was clear, of course, that this would not be sufficient to eliminate crime altogether. Here the nonresistants came up with their concept of "noninjurious physical force" (the phrase is Ballou's), a species of forceful action directed against the offender that aimed both at restraining him from doing harm to others and at helping him to become a useful member of society. Its use would also be necessary sometimes against all who were not wholly responsible for their actions, against dangerous lunatics, inebriates, the temporarily delirious as well as against minors not yet able to make moral judgments on their own. An essential condition of its remaining nonviolent was the spirit of love that must transfuse it. And, above all, the physical force used should not be so great as to risk the infliction of

[43] Whipple, *Non-Resistance applied to the Internal Defence of a Community*, p. 3.
[44] Ballou, *Christian Non-Resistance*, pp. 229-33.
[45] Whipple, *Non-Resistance applied*, pp. 5-10, 12, 13.
[46] *Ibid.*, p. 25.

injury, still less of death, on the person being restrained. Ballou, for instance, was particularly insistent on this point. "The principle of non-injury must be inviolable," he writes. "It is worth worlds and must be preserved at all hazards. What cannot be done uninjuriously must be left undone."[47]

In most instances, it was believed, the use even of such noninjurious force would be unnecessary in coping with the criminal. It would be enough just to tap him on the shoulder and lead him away—especially in view of the new principles that were to motivate the whole system of law enforcement. "Without use of deadly weapons," even the most desperate of men might be induced to submit. Perhaps, on some rare occasion, one or more policemen (who were to be recruited, Whipple suggests, from tried nonresistants and men of known humaneness, like the benevolent Quaker Isaac T. Hopper, for instance) might be killed before the criminal could finally be overwhelmed by the combined efforts—kept always within the bounds demanded by a nonviolent ethic—of the police and other members of the community whom they had called to their aid. Mob violence, too, would be dealt with by the same method. Many of the New England nonresistants, rank-and-file agitators as well as leaders like Garrison himself or Henry C. Wright, had had to face angry mobs out for their blood, especially in connection with their abolitionist activities. They had succeeded in giving personal demonstrations of the efficacy of a nonviolent stand. Although they had at times suffered severe manhandling, no life—they pointed out—had so far been lost. Their determination not to resort to arms in self-defense might, perhaps with some justification, be considered a factor in having prevented the mob in its fury from shedding blood.[48] In his discussion of the ways and means to be adopted by a society dedicated to nonviolence in dealing with mobs, Whipple, therefore, called for "a fearless and prompt interposition of the physical strength and the moral power of the police," acting without weapons but able to call upon the community for support.

Let us suppose that the lawbreaker is now in custody. What did the nonresistant writers propose to do with him next? They agreed that society had the right to impose restraints on the offender by depriving him of his liberty—with the object of training him to become a good

---

[47] Ballou, *Christian Non-Resistance*, pp. 3-12. See also, e.g., Whipple, *Non-Resistance applied*, p. 4; *Practical Christian*, vol. 5, nos. 6 and 9 (1844).

[48] This was H. C. Wright's view. "I have often been exposed to danger from mob violence," he wrote in his *Six Months at Graeffenberg* (p. 245), "and all my experience has resulted in the conviction of the safety of nonresistance."

citizen again. "This course," writes Whipple, "must not be the abandonment of patience and love, but a prolongation of them under a new form." Prisons were to be transformed into "reform schools" (or "safe moral hospitals," as Ballou called them),[49] staffed by men and women ready to work in the spirit of nonviolence. The work of reforming criminals was comparable to caring for children or the insane, persons unable to look after themselves and needing the care of loving guardians, who might sometimes have to protect them from harming either themselves or others. And, in addition, special care would be taken of the children of the criminal class, who should be brought up as wards of the state away from the demoralizing influence of their parental background.

After a suitable term, most inmates of the adult reformatories would, it was hoped, emerge cured of their social ailments and ready then to be returned to society. A handful, however, might prove less amenable to treatment. Therefore, wrote Whipple,

> A Non-Resistance government, having put under restraint a man who was dangerous to the community, . . . would keep him under restraint until he had ceased to be dangerous . . . the laws must be altered, to allow either the detention of a prisoner until he is reformed, or his discharge as soon as he is reformed . . . the convicts who remain unreformed will remain in custody, with no power any further, or in any manner, to injure the community.

Whipple contrasted these proposals with the existing state of affairs, where a genuinely penitent murderer would still be put to death while unreformed criminals (often having become even more depraved through the demoralizing atmosphere of prison life) were let loose on society at the termination of their sentences, to menace once again the security of society.[50]

From Whipple's argument, however, it was not clear what psychological criteria could be employed to ascertain when the work of reformation had been completed. We may question, too, his view that perpetual incarceration was more in line with Christian nonviolence than the employment of more obviously injurious force, the resort to which he roundly condemned. The whole atmosphere of the discussion which Whipple and the others conducted on the subject was, like so

---

[49] Ballou, *A Discourse on Christian Non-Resistance in Extreme Cases*, p. 23.

[50] Whipple, *Non-Resistance applied*, pp. 8, 13-30. Cf. H. C. Wright's reactions to his visit to the Connecticut state prison at Wethersfield (*Non-Resistant*, vol. II, no. 4, 26 Feb. 1840): "Did the spirit of Christ, of love to enemies, build this prison and supply these deadly weapons to win these erring men to God?"

much other reformist writing of the period, naively optimistic as to the immediate efficacy of the power of love in dealing with the antisocial elements in human society. The pedagogical theories of Whipple and the other nonresistants left many questions unanswered; they were, after all, amateurs, and such problems were not at the center of their social concern. Nevertheless, they pointed toward a new and more enlightened view of crime.

The moral validity of the use of violence to achieve freedom, to bring about national or social liberation, was a problem which occupied the New England nonresistants as much as, if not more than, that of its use within the community. For above all else they were crusaders, crusaders for righteousness in all its aspects—fanatics, if you will, but fanatics for the right as they conceived it. Peace was only one of the causes to which they gave their allegiance. They were universal reformers, libertarians who strove to break man's shackles to the evil past. They felt a kind of instinctive sympathy toward all who fought, even with weapons in their hand, in the name of freedom: freedom from the tyranny of absolute government, freedom from the arbitrariness of colonial rule, freedom from the worst oppression of them all—the limitless despotism of the slavemaster. Were nonresistants to condemn those who took up arms to further the causes both had at heart? Could they offer any alternative way to achieve the same goals, or was the rule of evil inevitable in this world and all efforts to better it in vain—the doctrine the German nonresistant sectaries of this continent had brought over with them from Europe?

Such complete nonconformity to the world the radical nonresistants found hard to accept. Instead, they groped for some technique, some formula which would satisfy both their pacifist impulse and their search for human freedom.

From the end of the previous century, Europe had been rocked by a series of upheavals, the result in no small part of the liberal and nationalist ferment generated by the French Revolution. By the middle of the nineteenth century, Italians and Germans, Poles and Hungarians, Serbs and Greeks, as well as Britain's Irish, had all made a bid for freedom against oppression, which usually appeared in the guise of an alien ruler. The defeat of bourgeois nationalism and liberalism had followed quickly on the heels of the premature successes of early 1848. The exiled liberals and nationalists now preached war and revolution to liberate their silenced and suppressed peoples, and their friends and sympathizers abroad underlined their pleas for support.

The New England nonresistants (along with the more conservative wing of the peace movement) welcomed the aims for which these revolutionaries were struggling. Garrison chides a critic who accused him and his friends of passivity. "Our correspondent is greatly in error," he says, "in speaking of non-resistance as a state of 'passivity.' On the contrary it is a state of activity, ever foremost to assail unjust power, ever struggling for 'liberty, equality, fraternity.'" Their disagreement with national leaders like the Magyar Kossuth, who visited the United States in the early fifties, was more one of means than of goals. True, the nonresistants deplored the European's narrow nationalism: their own definition of freedom was conceived "in no national sense, but in a world-wide sense."[51] Their chief objection, however, related of course to method. Garrison, in an article written in 1849, contrasted the "patriotism" of Kossuth with the "christianity" of Jesus and his followers.[52] The first was exclusive: Kossuth sought primarily the good of his own countrymen. Jesus's teachings, on the other hand, embraced the whole world, and he included in the orbit of his love even the oppressors of his own people. "The land of his birth was in bondage to the Roman power, but he exhibited no 'patriotic' indignation, and made no appeal to Jewish pride or revenge." He wished to overcome the enemy "by a moral regeneration, not by a physical struggle." Therefore, he refrained from inciting his oppressed fellow nationals to deeds of patriotic violence against the occupiers, while urging them at the same time to stand up to power and to refuse obedience where wrongdoing would result—"though a cruel martyrdom should be their lot."

To Garrison, Ballou, and the rest, then, nonviolent resistance seemed the only possible Christian reaction on the part of the oppressed. Garrison apostrophized the Hungarian as follows: "Oh Kossuth! not of thy abhorrence of Austrian oppression do I complain, but join with thee in execrating it. But the lessons of vengeance which thou art teaching thy countrymen are such as degrade and brutalize humanity. Tell the Hungarians, that a bloody warfare to maintain their nationality is incompatible with moral greatness and Christian love, and for an object which is low and selfish"[53]—low and selfish, however, only in comparison with the higher goal of human freedom, for Garrison gave conditional approval to the movements of national independence and meted out unqualified condemnation to their foreign oppressors.[54]

[51] *Selections . . . from Garrison*, p. 88. [52] *Ibid.*, pp. 78-86.
[53] *Ibid.*, pp. 84-85. In the early fifties Kossuth excited Garrison's wrath for having failed to condemn Southern slavery during his visit to the United States.
[54] See, e.g., *ibid.*, pp. 86-87, where Garrison writes: "We grant that every successful struggle for freedom on the part of the oppressed, even with the aid of cannon and bomb-shells, is to be hailed with rejoicing; but simply in reference to

The New England nonresistants, while registering their dissent from the methods of violence the European nationalists employed, did not attempt (perhaps they did not presume) to instruct them in the details of a nonviolent struggle. In some ways, indeed, this vagueness constitutes a serious weakness in the nonresistants' presentation of their position. But Europe at that time was still far away for the average American, and in the country's own present and past there were conflicts of principle and power more immediate to their concerns. We must turn again to that rather obscure member of the movement, Charles K. Whipple, for the best exposition of the nonresistant response to the issues presented by the War of Independence of the previous century and the long drawn out contemporary antislavery struggle, whose bloody conclusion was already beginning to shape itself in the minds of men.

The very title of Whipple's 16-page pamphlet, *Evils of the Revolutionary War* (1839), appeared almost as a challenge and was in all probability intended as such. We have seen from earlier chapters that the aura surrounding the Revolutionary legend in the minds of most Americans constituted a serious handicap in getting the pacifist message across to the public. If all war is wrong, if it is a sin, many people asked, what about our own Revolutionary struggle which made us an independent nation? It was natural, therefore, that at the outset the Non-Resistance Society should welcome a tract by one of its members which attempted to answer objections on this score.

Whipple accepts without argument the rightness of the aims of the Revolutionary leaders. His thesis is simply that "we should have attained independence as effectually, as speedily, as honorably, and under very much more favorable circumstances, if we had not resorted to arms." To have achieved this, he goes on, three things would have been necessary: a determined refusal to carry out unjustified demands, an efficient system of making the colonial case widely known, and a Quakerly readiness to endure without retaliation all violent measures taken by the home government in order to cow the colonists into submission. The boycott of imported tea and other articles arbitrarily taxed and the refusal of taxes unjustly demanded would eventually have had their effect. The patriots would, indeed, have suffered much hardship and distress, but "the evils thus endured are infinitely less than the calamities of war."[55]

We must go on the assumption, says Whipple, that "governments

---

its object, and not to the mode of its accomplishment. . . . Our correspondent burns with indignation in view of Austrian tyranny; so do we. He rejoices to see its victims rising against it; so do we."
[55] Whipple, *Evils of the Revolutionary War*, pp. 3-5.

are composed of men and not of brutes" (a proposition, incidentally, that many nonresistants, among them Whipple, found some difficulty in maintaining later in face of the enduring intransigence of the slave power). Therefore, in order that measures of passive resistance might work a moral change in the camp of the opponent, before the publicity given to the colonists' demands and their posture in support of them could win them wide support in the home country, they might have been forced to provide a clearer expression of their determination not to give in by taking the further step of declaring their independence of the mother country. Whipple continues:

> This movement excites new and more violent demonstrations of hostility on the part of the British functionaries. The signers of the Declaration of Independence, and the officers of the new government, are seized and sent to England to take their trial for high treason. . . . They are tried by the constituted authorities of England, and calmly avow and defend their revolutionary measures. They are found guilty, sentenced to death, and (for we will suppose the worst) actually executed as traitors. But their defence, their bold and clear explanation of the principles of liberty, their new view of the relative rights and duties of a government and its subjects, are in the mean time eagerly read and pondered by all the British nation.

Despite the seizure of their leaders, the American people persist in their campaign of civil disobedience, continuing to keep it within the limits of nonviolence. New leaders emerge. The prisons are filled to overflowing. The military carry out executions of selected civilians in an attempt to terrorize the rest. This only serves to strengthen the determination of the Americans to resist—"for I take it for granted that they [the British] would not attempt to put to death the great mass of the population." Meanwhile, sympathy for their cause increases throughout Europe and in Britain, too. "Can it be imagined," Whipple asks, "is it consistent with the attributes of human nature to suppose, that such a persevering and undaunted defence of principles so just would fail of working conviction in the hearts of a people like the English?" The pressure of world opinion, combined with that of domestic opposition and the resolute stand of the American people, would eventually force king and parliament ("governors and legislators are never destitute of the feelings and sympathies of men") to recognize colonial independence.[56]

[56] *Ibid.*, pp. 5-7.

Whipple saw a fourfold gain in such a substitution of nonviolent methods of gaining liberty for the arbitrament of arms. In the first place, there would have been a tremendous saving in human lives. Even if we were to calculate a loss of some ten thousand civilians, either executed by British authorities as traitors or killed by exasperated British soldiers (a figure which Whipple considered almost certainly an exaggeration), this would still have been a substantial improvement. Secondly, there was the economic argument. Material losses there would inevitably have been: losses to commerce and industry owing to the boycott, as well as those resulting from wanton destruction by the British army in its efforts to break the passive resistance campaign. But these would have been nothing compared to what the country had had to suffer in fact as a result of warlike operations. "We should have been more prosperous . . . had there been no revolutionary war." Of equal importance, on Whipple's balance sheet, with any material advantages which the nonviolent way possessed—perhaps even more important than these advantages—was the gain it would have brought to morality and religion by avoiding, at least on the American side, those inevitable concomitants of war: intemperance and Sabbath-breaking, licentiousness and profanity, and lust for killing and destruction. Finally, the nonviolent accomplishment of independence would have prevented the incorporation into the law and practice of the new state of policies inconsistent with the nonresistant creed. Thus slavery, child of war, would have had to go; the treatment of the Indian would have undergone a revolution; the spirit of revenge would have been banished from the penal system and excluded from the external relations of the country; and the death penalty, harsh prisons, and the corporal punishment of adult offenders would have become things of the past.[57]

The Gandhian strategy of nonviolent action, so influential in our century, was already foreshadowed in Whipple's pamphlet. His inspiration derived from the Christian ethic, but his presentation was almost entirely pragmatic. The moral and religious aspects, which usually predominated in contemporary expositions of pacifism, were kept in the background. Whipple's object was to show that, at least in the case under discussion, passive resistance would have *worked*. It was an attempt, and—crude as it is in parts—a not altogether unsuccessful one, to draw up a blueprint for achieving national liberation by means of this technique. For convenience' sake, the author projected the discussion into the past. Two objects were thus attained: a pillar in the

[57] *Ibid.*, pp. 8-11.

case against nonviolence—the Revolutionary legend—was shaken and, at the same time, nonresistant strategy for the future had been outlined.

The limits of the discussion, however, were of course fixed by the historical circumstances. The "enemy" was the British government, and the Whig constitutionalists who ruled eighteenth-century England were, like the parliamentary democrats of twentieth-century Britain, amenable to pressure, at least insofar as it was exerted by the political nation. The rule of law and the sovereignty of Parliament were still maintained in principle, whatever the lapses from them in practice. Gandhi and the colonial movements of our time against British imperialism used nonviolence against a power that did not prevent their case from being heard and from influencing opinion in the home country. Although democracy often looked threadbare on the peripheries, it was a real force at the center, in the places where final decisions were made. Something of this sort, *mutatis mutandis*, was implicit in Whipple's reasoning, in the importance he placed on making the colonists' case known in Britain and in his emphasis on the essential reasonableness and humanity of even the rulers—or, at least, the rulers' sensitivity to their expression in others.

The question of slavery in the American South, like that of resistance to totalitarian regimes in our own day, was in many ways less amenable to any easy solution, even on paper; it presented more agonizing dilemmas to the nonresistant than the resolution of differences between colony and mother country in the past. At first, abolitionists almost to a man eschewed all thought of the use of armed force in the task of liberating the slave—except for a half-suppressed premonition among some of inevitable violence to come, confided usually to the privacy of correspondence or diary. If not from pacifist scruples, at least from expediency and a desire to explore all ways of effecting emancipation peacefully and by due process of law, the antislavery movement—nonpacifists as much as the most convinced nonresistant— had, as we have seen in an earlier chapter, assented to the propositions incorporated by Garrison into the Declaration of Sentiments he had penned for the American Antislavery Convention of 1833. Our principles, he had written there, contrasting them with the appeal of the Revolutionary fathers to arms for the righting of wrong, "forbid the doing of evil that good may come." They relied instead on "the abolition of slavery by the spirit of repentance."[58]

But, far from repenting, the slave power had passed from almost

[58] *Selections . . . from Garrison*, pp. 66, 67.

apologetic defense to attack, presenting slavery now as a positive good and suppressing within its orbit all voices raised in protest. During the forties and fifties the antislavery crusade was slowly, but seemingly inevitably, transformed into a sectional conflict. Large portions of the abolitionist movement now looked to the ordeal of battle as the final solution. In the fifties the rising tide of violence on each side carried along some who had only just in the previous decade pledged allegiance to the nonresistant cause. The time seemed ripe, therefore, for someone among their diminishing band to review the position nonresistants should adopt in face of the increasingly bellicose stance of so many of their co-workers in the abolition movement. Again it was C. K. Whipple who undertook the task, and it was John Brown's raid in 1859 that prompted him to write his short work on *The Non-Resistance Principle: With Particular Application to the Help of Slaves by Abolitionists*, which was published in Boston in the following year.

The author praises Brown for his heroism and for the nobility of his aims; then, entering upon a discussion of the hoary old ethical problem of ends and means, he restates the nonresistant position that only the use of "noninjurious force" is consistent with Christ's teachings. All else is the casting out of Satan by Satan. By adopting a policy of nonviolence carried out in the spirit of love, we would have a good chance of winning over the adversary, for "God's arrangement for mankind is, that wrong-doing should breed self-reproach, and that this should tend to confession and amendment."[59] True, slaveowners possess no rights to their slaves' labor and are "robbers" insofar as they seize the fruits of this labor without due recompense; nonetheless, the law of love applies to them as much as to other men. In this situation the obligation of the slave, who is also a Christian, is to stand up for his rights as a human being without at the same time losing hold of the principle of love for all men. "His first duty of good-will to the slaveholder is utterly to refuse any longer to be a slave. . . . Quiet, continuous submission to enslavement is complicity with the slaveholder."

The nonresistant, whose free status precludes him from being able to take such direct action in defense of liberty, must assist in other ways. Best of all would be the achievement of emancipation legally and by general agreement. This, Whipple is forced to concede, is well nigh impossible, owing to the wicked intransigence of the slaveholders. Yet, even so, "the thing could be accomplished which John Brown sought to do, *without the resort to violent and bloody means*

---

[59] Whipple, *The Non-Resistance Principle*, pp. 3-11.

by which he proposed to maintain it against the resistance of the slaveholders." The slaves for the most part are too ignorant and downtrodden to make any effective collective resistance (a consideration that, indeed, seriously impaired the efficacy, though not the moral validity, of the nonviolence Whipple had been urging on them); therefore—and this is Whipple's main proposal—the free must help the oppressed through a vast extension of the underground railway. Hideouts must be set up in the mountains of the South where runaways could "hold themselves safely entrenched" until the loss in manpower forced the slaveowners to capitulate. If the movement failed to materialize on a large enough scale, then as many of the fugitives as possible should be helped to escape to the North.

> If also it be necessary in accomplishing such a movement, to seize and put under restraint, by uninjurious means, the persons of any slaveholders, until the departure of the slaves is safely effected, this would be perfectly right, for it is only what the government ought long since to have done. A slaveholder is a public nuisance; a person eminently dangerous to the community; and if the government does not do its duty in restraining him, any person who has the power may properly use all uninjurious means to do it.[60]

Whipple had come very near that undefined, perhaps undefinable, borderland between injurious and noninjurious force. Many of his fellow nonresistants, in fact, were having to grapple in earnest with this very problem in the course of their activities as members of the radical abolitionist camp.

Differences of opinion had existed from the beginning over the limits of nonviolence, not only between the Garrisonian nonresistants and the pacifists who remained within the American Peace Society, but also within the Non-Resistance Society itself. Some extremists, like Charles Stearns (who was to renounce his pacifism in the fifties in "bleeding Kansas"), disapproved of the employment of even noninjurious physical force in the restraint of the criminal and the antisocial; Stearns called it "a mere shame, unworthy of the name" of nonresistance, though he did not object to its application to the insane and the intoxicated, who were not in full possession of their reasoning faculties.[61] The use of physical compulsion in bringing up children was debated at length in the pages of the *Non-Resistant*. Although corporal punishment whether in school or within the family, was condemned by most,[62] nonresist-

[60] *Ibid.*, pp. 16-24.
[61] *Practical Christian*, vol. VIII, no. 16, 11 Dec. 1847; no. 18, 8 Jan. 1848.
[62] A lady freshly converted to nonresistance wrote to Maria Chapman: "But I

ants like Ballou considered it right to use some degree of force to restrain a child from hurting other children or itself, just as they approved of its use, as we have seen, in dealing with crime.

The discussion, maintained sporadically during the forties and fifties, died away as Garrisonian nonresistance finally dissolved in the fires of the Civil War. Shortly before Ballou's death at the ripe age of 87, the question reappeared in a fascinating correspondence which sprang up between the aged patriarch of nonresistance and its greatest apostle in modern times, the Russian Count Leo Tolstoy. Ballou had read a translation of Tolstoy's book *What I Believe*, which had first appeared in Russia in 1884. His feelings about it were mixed. "Found many good things in it on ethics," he confided to his journal in February 1886, "with here and there an indiscriminating extremism in the application of Christ's precepts against resisting evil with evil. . . . But on theology found him wild, crude, and mystically absurd. . . . So it seems to me in this first perusal. But I will read further and think him out more thoroughly." However, he continued to be puzzled by the extreme literalism with which Tolstoy interpreted the saying "Resist not evil," "making it inculcate complete passivity not only toward wrong-doers but toward persons rendered insane and dangerous by bad habits, inflamed passions, or unbalanced minds, to the exclusion of non-injurious and beneficent force under any and every circumstance of life."

Four years later, in June 1889, Ballou's friend and follower, the Rev. Lewis G. Wilson, who was then pastor of the Hopedale Unitarian parish, sent Tolstoy several of Ballou's writings on peace and sociopolitical problems. It was not long before the two old men struck up a lively correspondence, only to be cut short by Ballou's death in the following year. Tolstoy, who was previously unaware of the pioneering work of his American forerunner, was extremely gratified to find many of his own unorthodox opinions on these matters presented here in such compelling detail. "Two of your tracts," he wrote Ballou in March 1890, "are translated into Russian and propagated among believers and richly appreciated by them."[63] He himself agreed with much that Ballou had written; at the same time, he had to express dissent on several points, in particular with Ballou's liberal delimitation of the area of strictly nonviolent action by including within it some measure of physical force. "The Master made no concessions and we

---

must confess . . . I cannot see how our common schools could be managed by Non-Resistants. I do not say but if the children were rightly dealt with the first two years of their lives they would not need punishment but who has ever done this or will do it?" (21 Jan. 1841, Weston Papers, B.P.L. MS A.G.2, vol. 13, no. 14).
[63] *Autobiography of Adin Ballou*, pp. 508-11.

can make none," Tolstoy asserted. "A true Christian will always prefer to be killed by a madman, rather than to deprive him of his liberty."

This was a little too much for Ballou to swallow. He denied the charge that he was sanctioning a line of action that was not "dictated by the law of pure good will" and consonant with Christ's teachings, one that the person being restrained would not approve when he regained his reason. "And to construe his precept, 'Resist not evil,'" he went on, "as meaning absolute passivity to all manner of evil, because he made no specific qualifications, is to ignore the context and make him the author of self-evident absurdity." Christ never intended his injunction to mean that we must stand by and see someone out of his senses kill our nearest and dearest "rather than restrain or help restrain him by uninjurious physical force of his insane liberty."[64]

The exchange of views continued a little longer. Ballou had been perplexed by Tolstoy's earlier admission that, although we must be unyielding in upholding the theoretical absolute, compromise on an issue such as nonresistance was inevitable in practice. He suspected that the principle of nonviolence itself was being adulterated by such concessions from the man who at the same time had reproached Ballou with a lack of consistency. Tolstoy hastened to reassure him:

> What I mean is this: Man never attains perfection, but only approaches it. As it is impossible to trace in reality a mathematically straight line, and as every such line is only an approach to the latter, so is every degree of perfection attainable by man only an approach to the perfection of the Father, which Christ showed us the way to emulate. Therefore, in reality, . . . such a compromise in practice is not a sin, but a necessary condition of every Christian life. The great sin is the compromise in *theory*, is the plan to lower the ideal of Christ in view to make it attainable. And I consider the admission of force (be it even benevolent) over a madman (the great difficulty is to give a strict definition of a madman) to be such a theoretical compromise.[65]

Even if Ballou's death had not cut short the dialogue, it is doubtful whether the New Englander would ever have become a convinced Tolstoyan. The gap between theory and practice that is typical not only of Tolstoy but of much of Russian revolutionary thought was alien to the American nonresistant communalist, who, for all the utopian-

[64] Correspondence published in Lewis G. Wilson (ed.), "The Christian Doctrine of Non-Resistance," *The Arena*, III, no. 13 (Dec. 1890), 4-7.
[65] *Ibid.*, p. 10.

ism he and his fellows exhibited, had at least one foot firmly grounded on the rocky New England soil.

The New England nonresistants, both by their writings and by their example, had, as we know, helped to confirm Tolstoy in his faith in nonviolence.[66] And, ironically enough, their legacy was transmitted to twentieth-century America by way of the Russian seer (and his Hindu disciple, the mystic Gandhi) rather than through a native American line of intellectual descent. The ideological testament of these New England precursors of the contemporary nonviolent movement was only fragmentary, their reasoning often naive, and their solutions unrealistic. Yet they strove mightily in their day to win release for mankind from the wheel of violence by some other method than that of renewed conflict and governmental tyranny.[67]

[66] See *The Kingdom of God and Peace Essays*, pp. 11-22, for Tolstoy's acknowledgement of his debt to Ballou.
[67] The Society's ideology is also discussed in E. M. Schuster, *Native American Anarchism*, pp. 58-81.

Chapter 6

The Moderate Pacifists and the League of Universal Brotherhood

I

The adoption by the American Peace Society in 1837 of a pacifistic platform in respect to international war had not prevented the pacifists from dividing on the issue of the use of physical force in the domestic arena. The dissidents, who refused to recognize the validity of state and civil government so long as they had the slightest connection with coercive power, had broken away to form their New England Non-Resistance Society. This left wing within the peace movement had succeeded in attracting, as we have seen, some of the most energetic and single-minded, some of the most saintly, and some of the most intellectually gifted among the reformers of the day—as well as a generous share of the cranks and the cantankerous. By the second half of the 1840's the vigor of the nonresistant group had begun to ebb, though it was not to fade away finally until the Civil War days.

Less intellectually challenging perhaps, certainly less exotic, but no less interesting is the story of those pacifists who did not affiliate with the Non-Resistance Society, remaining—at least for the time being—within the framework of the older and more conservative organization. My purpose here is not to give a detailed account of the history of the American Peace Society but to isolate for special consideration the stream of absolute pacifism which still continued to exist within it. This element continued to be important and influential for some eight years at least after the break with the Garrisonian nonresistants; until 1846 the revised constitution of 1837 with its avowedly pacifist stand remained the official program of the Society. We have seen how men like William Ladd and Amasa Walker (not to mention that stalwart pacifist, Joshua P. Blanchard, who had withdrawn near the beginning from the Boston Peace Convention of 1838 along with George C. Beckwith and his group) had, in spite of their sympathies with some aspects of the nonresistant creed, been repelled by the "no-government" overtones of the program as shaped by Garrison and Wright. It was not merely that they were unwilling to cut their ties with the nonpacifist section of the peace movement, to end the collaboration of peace workers of various shades of opinion within one organization that had continued to exist after, as before, the changes in the American Peace Society constitution in 1837; for they disagreed as well with the basic political philosophy of the Garrisonian nonresistants. The latter, for all their disavowal of Jacobinism and their disregard of social issues, were, especially on account of their anarchistic denial of government, essentially revolutionary pacifists; while Ladd and those who thought like him were the reformists of nineteenth-century pacifism.

The two prominent members of the American Peace Society who had not withdrawn with Beckwith but remained to take part in the Boston Peace Convention, Ladd and Amasa Walker, had been impressed with the seriousness of purpose and sincerity of most of its participants. Though unwilling to join the new Non-Resistance Society, they regarded its formation—at first, at any rate—as a positive step. Ladd wrote after the convention was over that he could see no reason for antagonism between the old and the new organization—or at least, he adds, "I am determined that, so far as I am concerned, the fighting shall be all on one side."[1] At the end of the year Walker, too, was to write to Garrison that he hoped "we shall labor together *peacefully* and affectionately in the cause of universal peace."[2] But already the first shots had been fired in the battle for peace. Perhaps, as Galpin suggests,[3] fear on the part of the American Peace Society's executive committee that their policy was being confused in the public mind with that of the Non-Resistance Society was largely responsible for the pains which the American Peace Society now took to dissociate itself entirely from the new body.

In November 1838 it had issued a statement disclaiming all responsibility for the recent peace convention. Only a handful of its members had joined the new Society, whose principles and aims were "entirely foreign from the cause of peace." "It is quite another enterprise, entirely distinct from what *we* have ever taken the cause of peace to be." In fact, it really had no claim to be regarded as a distinctly peace society at all.[4] Misunderstandings concerning the American Peace Society's position continued, however, especially in view of the pacifist Article II of its existing constitution, which branded all war, including the so-called defensive war, as unchristian. In 1838 and again in 1839, therefore, the executive committee issued a detailed statement in an effort to clarify what was and was not meant by this article.

[1] *Liberator*, 18 Oct. 1838.   [2] *Ibid.*, 11 Jan. 1839.
[3] W. Freeman Galpin, *Pioneering for Peace*, p. 157.
[4] *Advocate of Peace*, II, no. 6 (Nov. 1838), 143, 144.

These "Explanatory Resolves," five in number, though declaring Article II "as designed to assert that all national wars are inconsistent with Christianity, including those supposed or alleged to be defensive," nevertheless went on to state categorically that "the article has no reference to the right of private or individual self-defence, to a denial of which the society is not committed." No pledge, "expressed or implied," was being required from members to uphold a completely pacifist, let alone a "no government," position. As in the past, so now "we invite the cooperation of all persons who seriously desire the extinction of war, whether they agree with the principle of the article as thus explained, or not."[5]

This was certainly a watering down of the pacifist witness—at least so it must have seemed to the more ardent nonresistants. They had not, from their side, shown a very conciliatory spirit toward the older organization, which they regarded, in effect, as useless in promoting true peace because of its concessions to those who had not abandoned belief in organized violence. In particular, the American Peace Society's advocacy of a congress of nations as a substitute for the war method of settling international disputes (an idea that Ladd was particularly active in promoting) was regarded as a waste of time by the nonresistants of the Garrisonian variety. Indeed, it is easy to understand why those who regarded all state organisms then existing as incarnations of violence, oppression, and the war spirit—as negations of the Christian way to a better life—should have had scant hope of founding a peaceful world order on a gathering of these very nation-states whose "overthrow," according to the Declaration of Sentiments of the Non-Resistance Society, "by a spiritual regeneration of their subjects is inevitable."[6] It was, in their view, an infinitely more useful and ultimately much surer way to work for this spiritual regeneration by means of a radical transformation of society and the elimination of all forms of violence in its midst. As Sarah Grimké had written to Henry C. Wright in the spring of 1838: "I agree entirely in your views of a Congress of Nations, it is entirely playing the fool with the public mind, fixing its attention on an igneous future which will continually flee be-

---

[5] *The Tenth Annual Report of the American Peace Society* (1838), p. 2; *Advocate of Peace*, III, no. 1, 2, quoted in Galpin, *Pioneering for Peace*, pp. 157, 158. The American Peace Society still continued to stress that it was solely with international war, and not with such matters as capital punishment and penology, the maintenance of internal order within each society, or individual defense of person and property, that the Society was concerned. "We restrict ourselves to the intercourse of states," wrote the author of the Tenth Annual Report (p. 7), who was presumably Beckwith.

[6] *Principles of the Non-Resistance Society*, p. 5.

fore it. I shall rejoice to see it exposed."[7] Garrison, too, was to denounce the scheme as a chimera: he had already launched out into a diatribe against "the moderate fighters—those who believe in blowing out a man's brains in self-defence, occasionally, or who are partial to hanging criminals, or who can think of nothing but a congress of nations."[8] After the first year the two Societies on the whole simply ignored each other, devoting most of their attention to the uphill work of winning new adherents to their cause among a sometimes hostile, or more often simply indifferent, populace.[9]

The question of the correct attitude for the peace movement to adopt toward the use of physical force within the national community was to continue to trouble the American Peace Society, however, especially so long as the moderate pacifists were to be well represented in its counsels. The latter would all have agreed (as probably not a few, like Samuel May, who were working with the Non-Resistance Society would have also) with Ladd's opinion "that a peace-man did not compromise his principles, and acknowledge the right of nations to go to war, by voting for rulers who had the power to involve the country in war."[10] Even Garrison himself did not urge a refusal to pay taxes (unless specifically for military purposes, of course). But there were further problems on which agreement was not so easily reached.

It was perhaps to help overcome the doubts of some members, as well as to clarify the American Peace Society's position for the general public, that Beckwith wrote for the Society a small tract under the title "Peace and Government."[11] What is remarkable about this production is its decided assertion of the nonresistant position in international affairs, which was, of course, the position of the Society of which Beckwith was the secretary, along with an official rejection of the principle of the inviolability of human life in domestic affairs.[12] Beckwith's views recall those of his predecessor, Noah Worcester, during his latter years.

"All war must be utterly unchristian," states Beckwith, "unless the New Testament permits it as an *exception*"; and of such permissive-

[7] Galpin, *Pioneering for Peace*, p. 121. [8] *Liberator*, 26 Sept. 1838.
[9] In a debate between Amasa Walker defending the moderate pacifist position and three advocates of the inevitability of war in the existing state of the world, which took place in the Boston Odeon on 3 January 1839 before an audience numbering some three thousand persons, the voting went heavily against pacifism. "And the audience claims to be enlightened and christianized! It manifested a tiger-spirit" was Garrison's comment in a letter to S. J. May (dated 4 Jan. 1839 in Garrison Papers, B.P.L., MS A.1.1., vol. 3, no. 26).
[10] *Advocate of Peace*, III, no. 10 (Dec. 1840), 233.
[11] Reprinted in George C. Beckwith, *The Book of Peace*, pp. 425-32.
[12] Most of the Society's pacifists, like Ladd or Walker or Blanchard, did assent to this principle, however.

ness he could find no trace in the gospels themselves. Until the defenders of the admissibility of war in certain circumstances can produce better evidence on this point, "we have no more right to kill an army of invaders in self-defence, than we have to renounce our religion." But it is quite a different matter with law enforcement within the community. "I regard civil government," writes Beckwith, "as lawful, expedient and necessary," and as in no way incompatible with the renunciation of force between nations. Civil government has been ordained by God, and as the instrument of his justice it must be endowed with the means of enforcing its will upon the refractory. It must have the power to punish the evildoer, otherwise it will be ineffective. It is permissible for it to inflict even death itself. True, capital punishment conflicts with the Biblical injunctions to love our enemies, to resist not evil, and to refrain from killing. The New Testament, however, Beckwith goes on, makes an exception here, an exception which is not to be discovered in the case of international war: "the theory of exceptions is indispensable to the vindication of civil government as an ordinance of God." "I plead, then," he says, "both for peace and for government, nor deem them at all incompatible. I believe all war contrary to the gospel, yet regard government as an institution divinely appointed for the good of mankind, and authorized at discretion to punish and coerce its subjects."

At this point Beckwith seems to have realized that his argument might not carry conviction even with his own executive committee. Had not William Ladd stated his opposition to capital punishment and Amasa Walker pleaded publicly for the inviolability of human life? And there were critics, too, from the other, the nonpacifist wing of the movement, who believed that to deprive a nation of the right to wage what it considered a defensive war on the grounds that all war was unchristian could be justified only from the standpoint of complete nonresistance. Speaking to the students of Amherst College in 1839, the Rev. John Lord (1810-1894), who had very recently resigned as agent of the American Peace Society because he could no longer agree with its new official policy, argued this view with some cogency. "When does protection begin and end," he asked, "and how many men does it take to make a mob, and where is the difference on the grand principle, between a foreign and domestic body of robbers and murderers? Do we not enforce the same principle in regard to a multitude of foreign enemies that we do of domestic ones? . . . The doctrine that *all* war is opposed to the gospel *does* run into nonresistance. It is vain and trifling to deny it."[13]

[13] John Lord, An Address . . . before the Peace Society of Amherst College, p. 9.

It was admittedly a difficult problem, the same that Pennsylvania's Quaker rulers had had to face a century or so earlier. If government in a Christian country might punish a score of pirates or half a dozen murderers with death, or, again, if it might suppress a mob or a riot or an insurrection by armed force if necessary (all which instances Beckwith had cited), why, indeed, was it wrong for it to repel by arms an invading army intent upon robbing and killing? After posing this question to himself, Beckwith answered by asserting: "*God permits the taking of life in one case, but not in the other.* He authorizes rulers to govern, but not to fight; to punish, but not to quarrel. Such acts, even if they were physically the same, would be morally different; and hence one *may* be permitted, while the other is forbidden." Even if we cannot comprehend why God has made such a distinction, still we must abide by it.[14] Moreover, civil government aimed at establishing justice among men. The outcome of war was quite different from punishment as a result of judicial process in a court of law. War was "no more than a rencounter [sic] between tigers." The soldiers who did the fighting and were killed were usually innocent of any crime; "if taken as prisoners, not one of them could be tried for murder."

Beckwith expressed his belief that there were other ways besides war whereby governments could protect their citizens from invasion from without. Although he does not state what he thought these ways were, it is probable that he was thinking of the avoidance of war by means of universal disarmament, conciliatory national policies, and the development of international arbitration for settling disputes, rather than of any form of nonviolent resistance such as had been tentatively outlined by several contemporary peace writers.

Beckwith undoubtedly believed that he did in fact adhere to what he called "the strictest principles of peace";[15] it is not hard, however, to discover in his discussion of peace and government in the early 1840's the outlines of his justification of the use of armed force against the Southern "rebellion" of the early 1860's. The fact is that Beckwith, like many peace workers of that day, was reasoning on the assumption that all wars (between civilized nations, at least) were, with a little patience and goodwill, avoidable and that, therefore, they were unnecessary in the long run. This assumption may have been largely true. But the deeper implications raised by wars of national liberation or by ideological conflict or by the will toward aggression, not

---

[14] As Beckwith wrote elsewhere: "The same God that proclaimed . . . thou shalt not kill, bade Abraham slay Isaac" (quoted in Galpin, *Pioneering for Peace*, p. 157).

[15] Quoted in *ibid*.

to speak of the economic causes of international war, were on the whole either ignored or put to one side as irrelevant to the peace issue. "We are concerned solely with the intercourse of one government with another,"[16] Beckwith writes of the American Peace Society. And it is this dichotomy in his thinking that led him into difficulties in the admittedly extremely complex and, for the pacifist, baffling problem of reconciling abandonment of the use of force in international relations with its retention in some measure in the internal affairs of the nation.

This ambivalence in the views of the secretary of the Society (which were considerably less radical, we see, than the views of his immediate predecessor Ladd or those of most of the other members of the executive committee) is not reflected on the whole in the multitude of propaganda tracts and leaflets put out by the Society during these years—understandably so, since in line with previous policy, which the new pacifist course of 1837 had not altered, the main line of attack continued to be against the institution of international war.

War was ethically wrong, economically unsound, politically ineffective in the long run, and contrary to Christian morality. Permanent and universal peace was practicable, as well as desirable, even in the world as it then existed. This, broadly, was the theme of most of the tracts which Beckwith was to gather together from the Society's publications (many of them reprints from the peace classics and from other earlier writings on the subject) and issue in book form in 1845 under the title *The Book of Peace: A Collection of Essays on War and Peace*. Out of 64 items printed, 10 condemned war *in toto*. The writings of the Quakers, Dymond and Gurney, appear here as well as Clarkson's exposition of the pacifism of the early church and Thomas Grimké's fervid plea for the adoption of nonviolent resistance by the nations. A well-known Baptist divine, Dr. Howard Malcolm (1799-1879), then president of a college in Kentucky, who was long to be a pillar of the American Peace Society and a stout upholder of the Beckwithian, conservative trend within it, contributed two pamphlets denouncing the participation of Christians in war of any sort and imploring them to withdraw from all association with military preparations. It is interesting to note that an anonymous piece entitled "Safety of Pacific Principles" argued the case for the method of love and reconciliation in dealing with evil and aggression and with the insane. The writer drew heavily for his illustrative material, as usual, on the Quaker experience in Pennsylvania and on the Irish rebellion of 1798. This method might not

---

[16] *Advocate of Peace*, II, no. 9 (Feb. 1839), 201.

work in all instances, he concluded, but it would do as well, if not better, than the "war-principle."

Propaganda by the written and the spoken word was, of course, only one weapon in the American Peace Society's armory. It also petitioned governments, especially in periods of international tension or war crisis; it organized public meetings and framed resolutions in favor of peace; it developed and strengthened ties between peace workers in America and those back in Europe; and it attempted to influence politicians toward pacific policies wherever possible.[17] But, as Curti has shown,[18] these efforts met on the whole with indifference; even the stimulus of a violently hostile reaction, such as the abolitionists met with from the public at first, was not vouchsafed America's early pacifists. They remained small in numbers, a chosen band, perhaps, and certainly of importance for the future, but a factor of little weight in the existing political and international scene.

The clergy, who should at least, one might think, have had a professional interest in peace, for the most part held themselves aloof. However, some progress could be recorded here, and we see an increasing number of ministers of religion adopting the Society's pacifist platform, though not necessarily endorsing the moderate nonresistance of a Ladd or an Amasa Walker. Evidence of this trend is to be found in the writings of contemporary peace workers. Ladd, for instance, reports from Portsmouth (N.H.) in March 1840: "A paper, pledging the signers to the principle that *all* war is contrary to the spirit of the gospel, has been signed by all the ministers in town except the Universalist, who is absent, and it is expected that the signatures of 300 male professors of religion will be obtained to it."[19] Again, in the middle of the 1840's, the Rev. A. P. Peabody, who has recorded his sense of almost complete isolation when a mere decade before he had reached unaided a full pacifist position (see chap. 2), could write of the present situation: "I am acquainted with very few clergymen, who do not think and feel as I do."[20] This was certainly an exaggeration, but it is indicative of the fact that peace propaganda had by this time succeeded in making considerable inroads within the ranks of the professional ministry.

The literature of pacifism continued to grow in the late thirties and during the forties. We have seen in the previous chapter the significant

---

[17] See Curti, *American Peace Crusade*, pp. 106ff; Christina Phelps, *The Anglo-American Peace Movement in the Mid-Nineteenth Century*, chap. II.
[18] Curti, *American Peace Crusade*, pp. 104, 105.
[19] Quoted in John Hemmenway, *The Apostle of Peace*, p. 85.
[20] Letter of A. P. Peabody, 28 Oct. 1844, in S. E. Coues's "Peace Album," Harvard University Library, MS Am.635*.

contribution to pacifist ideology made by the nonresistant group. A number of pamphlets and addresses were also produced by pacifists outside the orbit of the Non-Resistance Society, usually by clergymen and usually by persons connected more or less closely with the American Peace Society, which—aside from some small societies confined to a comparatively small locality—remained the only substantial organization devoted to the peace cause until Elihu Burritt formed his League of Universal Brotherhood in 1846.

Although the peace movement had also made some progress outside New England in the middle states and in the Midwest, it had scarcely penetrated at all into the South. Perhaps Thomas Grimké, if he had lived, would have acted as its pioneer in this area; more likely, however, he would have imitated his two sisters in migrating north. The usual combination of peace views with antislavery and strongly abolitionist opinions debarred the peace movement, from at least the 1830's on, from making any headway in the South. Indeed, the regimentation of opinion behind the proslavery ideology and the ruthless suppression of opposition views, which became more marked as the years went by, created a climate of opinion extremely hostile to the peace movement in even its more conservative guise. If we disregard the not very numerous members of the historic peace sects, pacifism after Grimké's death had, it would appear, only one vocal advocate in the deep South.

John Jacobus Flournoy (d. 1879)[21] was certainly an eccentric, both in his physical appearance and personal habits as well as in many of his views on life and politics, and he should probably be described as a fanatic, too. But he was an individualist, a man who thought independently, if inconsistently, and one who had the courage to maintain his viewpoint over the years in the face of continuous hostility from the community. An opponent of the institution of slavery (though he owned a small plantation with some dozen slaves himself) who at the same time was filled with a deep hatred of Negroes, whom he wished to see deported en masse from the country, an upholder of the Union even during the Civil War days who regarded Lincoln as a tyrant, a temperance advocate who himself was a heavy drinker, a good member of the Presbyterian church who wrote in favor of a form of polygamy which he called "trigamy" (he did, however, base his case on Biblical grounds), an outspoken pacifist who engaged in innumerable

[21] See E. Moulton Coulter, *John Jacobus Flournoy: Champion of the Common Man in the Antebellum South*. Coulter regards Flournoy as a spokesman for the grievances of the class of poor Southern whites, who hated both slavery and the Negro and resented the political and economic dominance of the planter aristocracy.

lawsuits resulting from a species of persecution mania and who did not hesitate to physically assault a man with whom he had quarrelled, this citizen of Athens, Georgia, was regarded by his neighbors—and no wonder!—as a crank, as a local joke, indeed as a man whose foibles might be tolerated because they were completely harmless. It was this seemingly harmless eccentricity, combined perhaps with the obscurity of his style which makes him almost unreadable, that gave him immunity to publish his unorthodox views on political matters freely.

Flournoy's interest in peace led him to become a member of the American Peace Society. He tried unsuccessfully to raise money for it and to find new subscribers for its publications. The same lack of success, despite his repudiation of any connection with Northern radicalism, accompanied his efforts in the late thirties to start up peace groups in the South: by these means—he tells us—he hoped to help restrain the bellicose impetuosity of young Southerners by demonstrating to them that real courage lay in the readiness, as he wrote, "to endure insults and forgive injuries." His attendance at compulsory militia musters he turned into a demonstration against militarism (though he could have gained exemption on account of his serious deafness) by supplying himself with a cotton umbrella instead of a gun. "Christ Jesus utterly, entirely prohibited warfare," he wrote to a friend. In 1838, in order to bring his peace views to the attention of the public, Flournoy published at his own expense a small pamphlet of 19 pages entitled *An Earnest Appeal for Peace to all Christians*. It sold for the modest sum of 10¢, but only one copy was bought. When its author offered to give the remainder away free, "the people of Athens," he relates, "*had the meanness to accept them.*"[22]

The booklet, which is interesting as a curiosity, if for no other reason, is a passionate plea for the renunciation of all war on religious grounds. "The single expression, 'Love thy neighbour as thyself,'" he writes, "forever precludes all admission of warlike ideas and martial feelings into any part of the human economy." War has been forbidden by "that incomparable effort of Divine benevolence, the Sermon on the Mount." He reproves the clergy for not preaching in favor of peace and holds up to his fellow Christians for imitation the example of the Quakers—"the very best and finest spirited Christians," he calls them—and of their steady refusal to fight under any circumstances. "For a forbearance of man to man—a refusal to molest for molestation, and a returning of 'good for evil,' will . . . certainly disarm the most virulent oppressors," such behavior is "an injunction from Heaven."[23] (Six

[22] *Ibid.*, pp. 67-72.
[23] *An Earnest Appeal for Peace*, pp. 3, 4, 6, 12, 17-19.

years later he was to write: "Some christian country must set an example of forbearance by enduring wrong—with long patience.")[24] A refusal to participate in wars on the part of Christians would deprive the rulers of the world, whom Flournoy held primarily responsible for stirring up conflicts between nations, of the means to wage them. With war banished from the world and the Negroes—slave and free—expelled from the country ("to have them gone is my object," he writes),[25] a new era would begin for mankind.

In the antebellum South, outside the traditional sanctuary of the uninfluential historic peace sects, pacifism might normally be preached openly only where its advocate was protected by the label of harmless crank. In the North, on the other hand, the apathy, rather than the active hostility of the public, was the main barrier to a rapid and widespread dissemination of peace doctrines, whether of conservative or radical hue. As the editor of the *Christian Mirror* (22 June 1837) wrote concerning Ladd: "He has sometimes wished that his doctrines might, at least, attract notice enough to be opposed." Yet, as we have seen, there was one issue in the peace repertoire where strong feelings were immediately aroused and the peace man who touched upon it had to be ready to face abuse and unpopularity in good measure. This issue was the justifiability of the American Revolution or—as it was usually called then—the Revolutionary War against Britain. The Revolution and the Revolutionary fathers had become part of the national mythology; to question any aspect of the myth was to risk accusations of lack of patriotism. But could an absolute pacifist accept its necessity? That he could not do so had been recognized ever since the days of Dodge (though Beckwith might, indeed, have succeeded again in reconciling the irreconcilable), and, as we have seen in previous chapters, some peace writers had spoken their opinion boldly on the subject. Others had handled it with kid gloves, and still others ignored it altogether; even Ladd felt it would be wiser to avoid the topic where possible, so as not to arouse unnecessary antagonism against the peace movement.

But now, in 1842, there came along "an interesting, earnest, devoted young clergyman of the Unitarian faith," by name the Rev. Sylvester Judd (1813-1853), who was willing, eager even, to state the full pacifist case againt the American use of arms to win freedom from their British rulers. "Mr. Judd," writes a contemporary, "had no dread of public opinion: he rather enjoyed braving it: he saw the advantage

[24] Coulter, *J. J. Flournoy*, p. 69, quoting from the *Southern Whig* (1844).
[25] *An Earnest Appeal*, p. 11.

to the peace cause of a hearty opposition."²⁶ Judd's hatred of war and militarism apparently went back to his school days. Anyhow, by the beginning of the 1840's the young pastor had become a convinced, and even militant, pacifist. On 8 November 1841 we find him writing as follows to his brother: "I am sorry you must train. The militia is a horrible system; barbarous as ten heathenisms; utterly antichristian. So I view it. Can a Christian be a fighter, a killer of his own flesh and blood? What think you of that?"²⁷ In the following year he made public his protest against war, choosing to do so in what was perhaps a somewhat provocative manner.

In a sermon preached to his own congregation of the Unitarian church in Augusta (Me.) on 13 March 1842, Judd presented "a moral review of the Revolutionary War," an address that frankly revealed "some of the evils of that event" as considered from the viewpoint of a Christian pacifist. Perhaps his sermon came as no great surprise to his listeners, for Judd had made no secret of his antiwar views, his belief "that if Christ himself were now on the earth he would never, for any pretext, reason or motive whatever engage in war." The young men of his parish he had advised to "wholly abjure *all war*"; in season and out he had urged—"not as a politician, but simply as a moralist and a Christian"—that the way of peace was ultimately a surer road to freedom and security than the war method.²⁸

As he began his sermon, however, there was as yet no reason for alarm among his listeners. First he recorded his view of the Revolution as "the holiest war on record" and then went on to pay tribute to the nobility of purpose and fine character of the Revolutionary fathers. But as he started to develop his theme, we cannot doubt that looks of apprehension and disapproval were seen creeping into the faces of some of the congregation. Briefly put, his thesis, while not questioning the necessity in the circumstances for the colonies to separate from the mother country, condemned the validity of the means used to gain independence. A policy of peace, not recourse to arms, was the course which a Christian people should have adopted to achieve what admittedly were legitimate ends. Judd's critique of the war was mainly political. In his opinion, the causes, ostensible and real, were not sufficient to justify starting a war. The violence used by the colonists provoked the British government to send over more troops, and so the war

[26] Frederick West Holland, "The History of the Peace-Cause," B.P.L., MS *5577.98, pp. 47-49.
[27] Arethusa Hall, *Life and Character of the Rev. Sylvester Judd*, pp. 28, 190.
[28] Sylvester Judd, *A Moral Review of the Revolutionary War*, pp. 3, 5, 47, 48.

spread—despite the fact that a number of influential people on each side had been opposed to the outbreak of hostilities. Judd strongly criticized the many instances of bad conduct on the part of the Revolutionary army and corruption among many civilian officials. He deplored what he called the "military dictatorship" imposed by Washington and the disastrous consequences of the French alliance. The war, he thought, could have been ended much earlier if its continuation had not been in the interests of highly placed American officials. "The separation from England," he concluded, "was unavoidable, and necessary, and certainly involved in the course of things; but . . . it might have been made peaceably, without the spilling of a drop of blood."[29]

Judd, unlike his contemporary, the nonresistant Whipple, did not put forward any nonviolent alternative to winning independence by armed rebellion. He implies that the force of events, together with the existence in England of a powerful group sympathetic to the colonists, would have sufficed to achieve this goal by peaceful means. His approach to the problem of responsibility for the war is reminiscent of the "revisionist" school of historians after the First World War: in both cases there is considerable exaggeration in the effort to redress the balance. His narrative is replete with footnote references and bibliography. His intention, however, is clearly didactic. "He looks upon war in the abstract," he writes of himself, "upon all war, as antichristian and demoralising. . . . It is war, war as practically exhibited in our own country, and among our own citizens, that he desires to exhibit in its true light."[30] If once this holiest of wars, in the eyes of the American citizen, could be shown to have been both unnecessary in its origins and, regarding the manner in which it was waged on the American side as much as on the British, scarcely consistent with Christian morality, then, indeed, one of the main obstacles in the country in the way of pacifist propaganda would be removed. This clearly was Judd's aim, and not simply the scholar's search for objective historical truth.

The sermon certainly succeeded in shocking conservative minds, and, as a result, Judd was dismissed from the honorary post of chaplain to the Maine legislature, which happened to be in session at that time. Many of its members had attended the sermon, some walking out angrily in the course of its delivery. At the next meeting of the state House of Representatives, a Mr. Otis put forward a resolution that Judd in his sermon had "evinced total disregard of the feelings of every American citizen." His dismissal was accepted by a vote of 127 to 5. On the other hand, the pacifist camp was jubilant. The Boston *Non-*

[29] *Ibid.*, pp. 3, 6ff., 42, 43.   [30] *Ibid.*, pp. 43, 47.

Resistant reprinted the sermon in installments, while "at the Anniversary of 1842, the [American] Peace Society passed a vote of sympathy with the persecuted lecturer."[31]

At this same anniversary meeting, held in Boston on 23 May, the Society heard an address from its new president, Samuel E. Coues (1787-1867). The address is revealing as an example of a certain ambiguity frequently displayed in the thinking of the American Peace Society leadership. Coues was an active exponent of the pacifist position within the Society. In the light of Christianity, he now stated, "war is either right or it is wrong. It is either permitted or forbidden" —by which he meant war under all circumstances. He took pains to prove that, in fact, armaments had never given the nations security, that they were, indeed, positively harmful, a heavy burden laid upon the peoples of the world, while, on the other hand, international disarmament would bring peace and prosperity. His ultimate appeal, however, was to the moral imperative, the Christian standard of right and wrong, which must be followed even to our material disadvantage. Come what may, we must look to principles, and not to consequences, in shaping our conduct on the national as well as the personal level. "Even if life would not be altogether safe from the abandonment of the sword, if our principles expose the nations to loss, let the loss come. If blood must flow as the price of safety to others, let it flow." At the same time, Coues was careful in his lecture to deny that his conclusions, as many critics of the American Peace Society maintained, led logically "to ultra ground, to radicalism, to nonresistance," although we know that privately he upheld the inviolability of human life as the Christian way. Why this reticence on Coues's part? It was, of course, because—to quote his own words— "we do not, as a Society, concern ourselves with the question of the right of private or personal self-defence, nor do we advocate any change of the penal code."[32]

An even more conservative stand than Coues's, but one based on somewhat similar thinking, was taken by the speaker at the Society's next anniversary meeting in 1843, the Rev. A. P. Peabody, then pastor of the Unitarian South Church in Portsmouth (N.H.). Peabody con-

---

[31] Holland, "The History of the Peace-Cause," p. 49; *Non-Resistant*, vol. IV, no. 9 (11 May 1842); Hall, *Judd*, pp. 191, 199, 211, 212, 294, 297-303. Judd was supported by his own congregation and was later reinstated as chaplain by the legislature. He continued to preach, lecture, and write on behalf of pacifism (as well as an array of other humanitarian reforms) until his death. He publicly denounced the Mexican War and around that time became a keen supporter of Burritt's League of Universal Brotherhood.

[32] S. E. Coues, *War and Christianity*, pp. 1, 5, 9-14, 16-18, 21, 22.

ceded (although what he says here is not altogether in consonance with other statements of his on the subject[33]—perhaps because he now wished to conciliate the nonpacifist element in the Society) that "violent measures in self-defence" were justified "in extreme cases,— in cases of immediate and intense danger, where the alternative is forcible resistance, or submission to severe personal injury." But he denied any parallel between such a situation and the incidence of international war. "In order to justify war on the ground of self-defence, a nation, in an unarmed condition, and in perfect quietness, must be the subject of an unprovoked attack from some other nation. Now, it is, in the very nature of things, impossible that a nation, occupying such a position, should be assailed. It is the aggressive posture—the armed truce, so to speak,—in which nations professedly at peace stand towards each other, that invites assault." Therefore, in regard to the possibility of waging defensive war, he answers: "There are no such wars." The New Testament gives war no sanction under any circumstances, and the early Christians were conscientious objectors. For a just war to exist, says Peabody (had he perhaps some acquaintance with Catholic writings on the subject?), in the first place all blame for aggression must be on one side alone—and to discover where the blame lay would necessitate the prior existence of an international court of justice to judge the case impartially, the setting up of a supranational tribunal such as the American Peace Society had, indeed, advocated for some years. Secondly, "the retribution taken must bear a just proportion to the injury received, must affect directly the authors of the injury alone, and must affect others, if at all, only indirectly and incidentally." And war, of course, could not possibly conform to these conditions.[34]

The moderate pacifists in the American Peace Society, it should be said, had considerable justification for their refusal to officially raise questions pertaining to the use of force in a country's internal government and for centering their efforts instead on international war, thereby gaining the support of peace workers who could not go quite as far as themselves in taking what they called "the high ground." They were fond of pointing out that mutual toleration existed among members on the question of civil government. But though the Society gained in numbers by this width of view, it lost in cohesiveness by the somewhat unsatisfactory compromise between the two philosophies of peace. The moderate pacifists' approval of the positive aspects of civil government, despite the continued reliance of the nations on armed

[33] E.g., his *The Triumphs of War* (1847), p. 12.
[34] Peabody, *The Nature and Influence of War*, pp. 4-7, 10.

force, made it natural that they should wish to dissociate themselves from the more extreme exponents of nonresistance. However, the moderates cannot be acquitted of the charge of failing to give an entirely consistent witness for their Christian pacifist ideal.

Some of the confusion arising from this artificial separation into entirely different categories of the issues of armed force in the international arena and in domestic policy (a confusion, be it noted, that was not present, for all its faults, in the thinking of the Non-Resistance Society) was overcome in another address given by a member of the American Peace Society. At the twenty-seventh annual meeting of the Rhode Island Peace Society on 30 June 1844, the Rev. Edward B. Hall (1800-1866), pastor of the First Congregational Church in Providence (Roger Williams's church, incidentally) spoke on the topic "Christians forbidden to fight."[35]

Like Coues, Hall bases his case primarily on a pacifist interpretation of the Sermon on the Mount. Its meaning admits of no doubt for him: "the direct word is, that we must not *return* aggression." Better "our own death" than "the violation of conscience." He believed, despite the assertions of many churchmen to the contrary, that its precepts were capable of being carried out in practice in the present. At least, he pleads, let us go as far as we humanly can in trying to do so. The early Christians and in our time the Quakers and the Moravians have made the attempt, with some measure of success, rightly believing that the same standards of Christian conduct applied in the collective affairs of the state and the nation as in personal relationships. "If it be inhuman and unchristian, in one man to kill another, it is inhuman and unchristian for one hundred men to attempt to kill a hundred men." "Christianity forbids war, without qualification."[36]

When he comes to consider the application of the teachings of the

[35] Although this local peace society was very small, Hall was not the only pacifist among the ministers of Providence. In August 1842, for instance, his colleague, the Rev. James A. M'Kenzie from the Free-will Baptists had preached a forthright *Discourse against Life-Taking*. To the question, Do the gospels ever sanction the taking of human life?, he gave a decided no. (See James A. M'Kenzie, *A Discourse, against Life-Taking*, esp. pp. 3, 9-11, 17-22.) Although M'Kenzie did not deny divine sanction for the Jewish wars of the Old Testament (pp. 3-11), he argued in favor of the efficacy of nonresistance as a defensive technique to be employed under the new dispensation (pp. 11-13). In December of the same year, M'Kenzie had inspired the members of his congregation to pass unanimously a resolution "that war, arms-bearing, learning the art of war, and the intentional taking of human life in any case or under any circumstances, are each and all contrary to the gospel" and to pledge themselves to work for peace in the spirit of the resolution they had approved. See *The Proceedings of the First General Peace Convention* . . . , London, 1843, pp. 108-12.

[36] E. B. Hall, *Christians forbidden to fight*, pp. 6-13, 23.

Sermon on the Mount to the problem of civil government, his step indeed falters; yet his argument makes a valiant attempt to grapple with some of the problems involved. It is perhaps worthwhile to illustrate this attempt by quoting Hall at some length here.

> It is objected that an argument against all war, which yet allows and defends government, defeats itself. Why? Has government never been sustained on peace principles? Did not the first Christians admit and uphold government? Were they guilty of treason and rebellion, when they refused to fight? . . . Had William Penn no government, or were seventy years no test of its strength? . . . Our government does require us to yield up a slave who flies to us for protection, and surrender him to bondage. Can you do it? I cannot, neither can I fight. I will rather suffer the consequences of refusing, whatever they may be. . . . But, it is still urged, government cannot be *sustained* without arms, nor its commands enforced. That has not been proved. It appears so in theory, I admit; and I may not see, or be able to show, in every case, how the obvious difficulties are to be overcome. But that does not destroy the principle. It does not disturb my faith in the principle. Though all theory were against it, as men reason, and all experience, as men are, I should still believe in the practicability of a thoroughly Christian government, on thorough peace principles, because I believe in the Christian religion, and in Christ's knowledge of man. But experience is not against it. Just so far as the trial has been made, the result has been favorable. Even if it could be proved, as it cannot, that a spirit of unarmed peace and uniform justice would fail to conquer an invading force, or suppress an actual insurrection, it would not follow that this spirit might not *prevent* both.

By making concessions in time, England might have avoided the American Revolution, or the French government its revolution and all the bloody consequences that ensued for all Europe.[37] Insurrections and internal disorders—he appears to be saying—are usually the results of faults in government. Effect a timely removal of abuses, and, quite in-

---

[37] *Ibid.*, pp. 21, 22. Hall's approval of certain forms of mildly injurious, but nonlethal force, if used in defense, met with stern disapproval from the nonresistant Ballou. See the controversy between the two in the *Practical Christian*, vol. V (1844), nos. 10, 12-15. Hall summed up his position on the government question as follows (*ibid.*, p. 55): "No power on earth can compel me to violate a Christian law . . . I will not fight. I will not sentence a man to death. I will do no wrong. But I will support a government which guards our rights, and, with some great evils, is an instrument of incalculable good. I will vote for the best men that are proposed to administer the government. I will do all I can to expose its errors and bring it to Christian principles."

dependently of the moral validity of using physical force within the community, need for the exercise of armed repression will also have been removed.

The approaching conflict with Mexico brought the immediate policies of the American Peace Society at least, if not the more radical nonresistants, into line with a larger segment of New England society than that which usually supported the peace cause. In that part of the country the administration's handling of the issue of Texas and its relations with Mexico were widely unpopular. Among its most vehement opponents were the "Young Whigs" (or "Conscience Whigs," as they were later known), one of whose leading spokesmen, the rising young Boston lawyer, Charles Sumner (1811-1874), had also been connected with the American Peace Society since the beginning of the decade. It was William Ellery Channing who had brought Sumner to espouse actively both peace and antislavery. (In religion Sumner inclined toward Unitarianism, though he was never a member of any church.) On both issues, however, Sumner had soon advanced further than his teacher. In regard to peace, we find Sumner early in the 1840's confiding to a friend: "I hold all wars unjust and unChristian."[38]

In 1845 the city of Boston invited Sumner to give its annual Fourth of July oration. It was a considerable honor for a man of his comparative youth: the occasion was a solemn one, with dignitaries of church and state attending the delivery of the oration, which took place in Tremont Temple. Among those present were military and naval officers. The celebration of the country's Declaration of Independence during its war with Britain was usually the opportunity for voicing patriotic and martial sentiments. Imagine, then, the surprise of Sumner's audience when, instead, they were treated to a discourse on the iniquity of war and to a lesson on universal peace as constituting, in the words of the oration's title, "the true grandeur of nations." "In our age there can be no peace that is not honorable," Sumner proclaimed, "there can be no war that is not dishonorable." Arbitration and a congress of nations must replace the old method of settling disputes through "trial by battle." Therefore, war now between civilized nations was in all circumstances no better than "organized murder: it in truth constituted civil war." Above all, international conflict is unchristian. "Christianity not only teaches the superiority of Love over Force; it positively enjoins the practice of the one, and the rejection of the other." It calls for peaceful suffering of wrong, for forgiveness and love

[38] David Donald, *Charles Sumner and the Coming of the Civil War*, p. 107. Sumner's near pacifism is discussed on pp. 106-20 of Donald's biography.

of enemies—in the case of nations as well as for individual men and women. Sumner praised Quaker defenselessness as a road to true security and urged its adoption by the Christian governments of his day. He called for the disbanding of a standing army and a regular navy and of the state militias. Let the United States dismantle all its fortifications, too, he added, for armaments tend to provoke war, even if they were not originally intended for aggression. Let a new patriotism, which sought its victories in the furthering of peace, be substituted for one that saw glory in its country's wars.[39]

The compelling eloquence of Sumner's delivery, the orator's obvious sincerity and his imposing presence, and the wealth of classical and historical learning displayed in the course of his arguments impressed, if they did not convince, all his hearers. True, his allusions are sometimes rather bookish, and there is a somewhat cloistered air about his discussion of the issues of peace and war. But it was not these defects that worried those among his auditors who objected to his line of reasoning (if we exclude the military, who could scarcely be expected to approve). It was rather the seeming transformation of the young hope of progressive Bostonian society into a peace extremist, if not quite an extreme nonresistant, that made many anxious who heard him on that Fourth of July or read his speech not long afterward.[40]

Yet their anxiety was scarcely justified. During his oration Sumner had expressed his wish to see armed naval forces preserved for the suppression of piracy or slavetrading.[41] Clearly, he was not a "no-government" man. For all his references to the Sermon on the Mount and his citing of Clarkson and others on the early Christian conscientious objectors, he can scarcely even be classified as a pacifist of the Quaker type. And for all his oblique allusions to the Christian obligation of personal nonresistance, his attacks, like the policy of the American Peace Society, were directed essentially against war as an institution, which he defines as "a public, armed, contest between na-

[39] Charles Sumner, *The True Grandeur of Nations* (1845 edn.), esp. pp. 4, 26, 27, 31-36, 46, 67, 72, 73, 78, 79. In subsequent editions Sumner toned down the asperity of his attacks on war. For the oration, see also the article on Sumner by R. Elaine Pagel and Carl Dallinger in William Norwood Brigance (ed.), *A History and Criticism of American Public Address*, II, 752, 753, 755-57, 760-63, 775.

[40] E.g., Professor Francis Bowen, of Harvard, wrote Sumner: "Hating all ultraisms, I only wished you to disclaim utter stark *non-resistance* principles in their widest latitude" (quoted in Worthington Chauncey Ford [ed.], "Sumner's Oration on the 'True Grandeur of Nations,'" *Massachusetts Historical Society Proceedings*, L [1917], 250). W. C. Ford has printed (pp. 249-307) a number of letters giving the reactions of some prominent New Englanders to the oration immediately following its delivery.

[41] Sumner, *The True Grandeur of Nations*, p. 60.

tions, in order to establish justice between them."[42] In a letter to the city administration six days later, Sumner disclaimed the notion "that force may not be employed under the sanction of justice in the conservation of the laws and of domestic quiet," even though at the time he hesitated to assert that armed coercion behind the law could easily be squared with the precepts of the gospel. "It does not seem to be in harmony with the views of Dymond," he admitted. "Still, it seems to me sufficiently clear," he went on, that a valid distinction might be drawn between the two uses of force.[43]

Sumner claimed—not without justification—that his case against war rested on arguments that were independent of religion, on arguments that were utilitarian, economic, or humanitarian in character. Still, it was the Sermon on the Mount that gave Sumner his moral inspiration and provided the prophetic fervor for many of his utterances.[44] His oration became a *cause célèbre*, for many of his critics overlooked the reservations he had inserted into his apologia for pacifism; and the fact that the occasion was a military celebration and not the gathering of a peace society highlighted the boldness of his antimilitarist views. The mid-forties, in fact, mark the peak of Sumner's enthusiasm for the peace cause.[45] In the next decade, when in 1851 he became a member of the United States Senate, his energies became increas-

---

[42] *Ibid.*, p. 7.
[43] Edward L. Pierce, *Memoir and Letters of Charles Sumner*, II, 377, 379. In the appendices to the printed version of the oration (note A, p. 90) Sumner wrote: "I think that human life may be defended at the cost of human life; in the weakness of my nature, I cannot ascend to the requirements of the gospel." These, he reiterates in the next sentence, forbid the taking of human life under any circumstances. See also note D, pp. 97-99.
[44] Sumner was well read in the literature of both the American and the British peace movement. Wayland's *Elements of Moral Science*, however, he only came upon after delivering the oration.
[45] In his anniversary address to the American Peace Society in May 1849, which he entitled *The War System of the Commonwealth of Nations*, Sumner repeated most of the arguments against international war that he had used in his 1845 oration. His repudiation of nonresistance, which was elaborated extremely hesitantly and not without some ambiguity at the earlier date, is now rather more forthright, though still tinged with a certain reluctance. "If," he writes, "sorrowfully, necessarily, cautiously—in a yet barbarous age—the sword, in the hand of an assaulted individual, may become the instrument of sincere self-defence—if, under the sanctions of a judicial tribunal, it may become the instrument of justice also—*surely it can never be the Arbiter of Justice*. Here is a distinction vital to our cause, and never to be forgotten in presenting its Christian claims. The sword of the magistrate is unlike—oh! how unlike—the flaming sword of War" (p. 24). Sumner, undoubtedly influenced in this view by the revolutionary events of the previous year, was now prepared, also, to grant the right of armed revolt in cases of terrible oppression (pp. 9-11).

ingly absorbed in the antislavery struggle. In the Civil War the Unionist war effort had no more ardent supporter than Charles Sumner.

With the outbreak of the Mexican War in April 1846, the steady trickle of pamphlets attacking war, either from the absolute pacifist standpoint[46] or on a lower ground, was joined by a stream of antiwar publications as various opponents of the war rushed into print to express their sentiments against it. As in the case of the War of 1812, the antiwar literature was mostly directed specifically against the conflict then being waged, though argument was based on moral and religious grounds as well as on purely political and economic reasoning. Opposition to the policy of "Manifest Destiny" from large sections of the North (a feeling that was by no means confined only to the so-called Conscience Whigs but was widespread, especially in New England), and their fears of an eventual domination of the whole country by the Southern sector if its schemes of expansion in the vast areas to the southwest were realized and a new life given to the hard-pressed slave system, made the war unpopular in circles unconnected hitherto with the peace movement. The American Peace Society, of course, was active in agitating against the war and the policies which led up to it, and here both the pacifist and nonpacifist wings of the movement collaborated harmoniously. Theodore Parker (1810-1860), for instance, whose opinion of war, a just war—"I hate it, I deplore it, but yet see its necessity"—epitomizes his militant crusading zeal for righteousness, opposed the Mexican War on political grounds and urged all who thought like him to refuse participation in it.[47]

Nearer to the pacifist position (though prepared to grant to governments "the right of self-protection" against actual invasion) was the

[46] Two pieces written from the complete pacifist position may be noted from 1845, the year of the annexation of Texas and near the climax of the Oregon Crisis between the United States and Britain. The first is a series of discourses by the Disciple, A. C. Comings, on *The Reign of Peace*, which was published in book form in Boston. Acknowledging his debt to the English Quaker pacifist Dymond ("His argument . . . appears to me to be incontrovertible," p. 77), Comings calls on Christians not to participate in war. The same message was contained in the sermon preached in Boston at the end of December by the Episcopalian minister, the Rev. Frederic Daniel Huntington (1819-1904), which was published early the following year under the title *Peace, the Demand of Christianity*. For Huntington, "Resist not evil" formed the core of Christ's gospel. "Indirectly, as well as directly, in a thousand ways, he forbids all violence. . . . The gospel proclaims the brotherhood of men; and whoever believes in the brotherhood of men must conclude not to believe in fighting." Although he avoided equating soldiers of the past with "murderers and highwaymen," Huntington nonetheless denied that either romance or honor could be connected with modern war. Let men, he said, substitute international arbitration and mutual negotiations for the outmoded method of war. See pp. 9-11, 21, 24.

[47] Henry Steele Commager, *Theodore Parker*, 1960 edn., pp. 192, 193.

learned Dr. Francis Wayland, whose textbook on moral philosophy has been discussed in an earlier chapter. His wartime sermons on *The Duty of Obedience to the Civil Magistrate* were preached in the chapel of Brown University. Wayland laid it down as a citizen's duty to refuse the command of the magistrate if this ran contrary to his own conscience—as in the case of fighting in an unjust war like the present one. In other words, refusal of the draft, it was implied, was the proper reaction of the conscientious American to a war of aggression.[48]

Some of the more ardent pacifists, however, felt dissatisfied with attacks on the conflict in progress which denounced it for its unchristian character but at the same time failed to condemn war as such. "I have no faith," writes one of these critics in a Thanksgiving address in November 1847, "that such opposition to war will ever accomplish much in its removal from the earth. It is no repudiation of war itself, but only of *this* war."[49]

This kind of censure of the moderate antiwar men could not fairly be leveled at the author of one of the most complete and devastating examinations published of the Mexican War and its origins, which, however, did not come out in book form until 1849. Its author, the Rev. Philip Berry, was a Southerner, an Episcopalian clergyman with a parish in Maryland, who was connected with the American Peace Society. His *Review of the Mexican War on Christian Principles*, to which he later appended "An Essay on the Means of Preventing War," was first issued in the *Southern Presbyterian Review* and then published in Columbia (S.C.) as a book. The publication in the Southern sector of a critical discussion of U.S. policy toward Mexico during and previous to the recent war, and the accusation of a lack of a conciliatory spirit on the American side, showed an independent spirit on Berry's part. Although he did not touch directly on the question of the validity of defensive wars, Berry in his examination of ways of preventing

[48] For Wayland's opposition to the annexation of Texas and the subsequent Mexican War, see Francis Wayland and H. L. Wayland, *A Memoir of Francis Wayland*, II, 54, 55. I have only been able to discover one Mexican War C.O. who was apparently unconnected previously with either a peace church or the pacifist movement. In its issue of 9 Oct. 1847 (XXI, no. 3, 24) the Orthodox Quaker *Friend* of Philadelphia reports the case of one James Thompson, a private in the second regiment of artillery, on whose behalf a clergyman and another gentleman wrote to General Winfield Scott asking for his discharge. In reply the general admitted: "It is alleged that he has imbibed conscientious scruples against performing military duty." If his refusal of service were due simply to cowardice, Scott went on, he would receive continued punishment until he agreed to fight; if, on the other hand, it was a case of insanity, the man would be discharged on a doctor's certificate. Thompson's scruples appear to have been based on religious belief rather than on an objection to a particular war.

[49] The Rev. W. P. Tilden, *All War forbidden by Christianity*, p. 4.

war goes so far as to advocate unilateral disarmament by one country, preferably the United States, as the most promising first step toward a more peaceful world.

In one passage Berry makes the very interesting suggestion of creating a kind of international peace army, a nonviolent world police force such as was to be envisaged by some pacifists in the next century, which at the threat of hostilities would interpose itself between the prospective combatants. Intervention by such a force, Berry believed, might have averted the recent war. To quote his own words, what he proposed was:

> ... that a body of peacemakers from different countries, and especially from the two recently at war on this continent, might with some effect have stood in the breach, at the commencement of the war. At the peril of their lives, if necessary (though the adventure would probably not have involved great peril) they might have shewn what it is to be soldiers of peace, whose business it is to die, if required as a testimony, equally as the soldiers of any other cause. Had this been fanaticism, then, for once, there had been good in fanaticism. The enterprise of a world-police (so to speak) however few, armed with the olive-branch alone, to arrest the collision of two armies, or to perish between them, would never have been lost on mankind, particularly the nations through whose encounter they were rendered martyrs. ... [But] why might not the parties succeed in preventing the fray and yet live? ... Why then may there not be hope, that nations professing to be *already christianised*, should be converted rapidly from mutual slaughter! The day may yet arrive, when opposed armies may adopt a new method of "conquering a peace," and, rejecting the sword, be baptized into reconciliation at the waters of strife.

Berry, it is true, puts forward these suggestions very tentatively, fearing perhaps that he would be ridiculed as a fantastic visionary, a dreamer of absurd dreams.[50] In the meantime, until a more propitious age dawned for the realization of such schemes, he fell back on the familiar American Peace Society policy of advocating the organization of peace conventions and congresses of nations, furthering free trade, etc., as the best methods of bringing universal peace nearer.[51]

In the same year that Berry's antiwar tract appeared in print, another and equally outspoken plea in favor of complete pacifism was published by a 37-year-old antislavery veteran, the Rev. Amos

[50] Berry, *A Review of the Mexican War*, pp. 53-55.
[51] *Ibid.*, pp. 55ff.

Dresser. In 1835 Dresser, while a student at Lane Seminary, had been sentenced in Nashville, Tennessee, to receive twenty lashes on his bare back for acting as a colporteur of abolitionist literature in that state. A staunch pacifist, as we have seen (p. 571), Dresser in the next decade worked for Elihu Burritt's League of Universal Brotherhood, settling in the fifties as a pastor at Farmington, Ohio. His *The Bible against War* forms a small volume—"printed for the author" in Oberlin, Ohio— of just over 250 pages. It won high praise from Amasa Walker, who described it as "one of the best works yet published, perhaps, on the religious aspects of the war question. . . . It is a work which gives evidence of great ingenuity and research, and an excellent book of reference for any one who would examine the Bible argument against war."[52]

In fact, the book does not quite equal the earlier efforts of such writers as Dodge, Worcester, or Upham: it is rambling and discursive in many places, none too well organized, and peppered with overcopious quotations from scripture, though obviously the result of a careful, and even critical, examination of both Old and New Testaments for their bearing on war. Dresser consulted the original Hebrew or Greek where he believed the Authorized Version to be inaccurate. On the question of the divine inspiration of the Jews in their Old Testament wars, he was a wholehearted modernist. "The wars which the Bible is said to sustain," he writes, "*were aggressive*. Such as no one now thinks of justifying." Echoing the sentiments of the Quaker Hannah Barnard earlier, Dresser asserts that "wars and fightings come from men's lusts as self-inflicted judgments for sin. . . . We find that even with the faint light that the Jews possessed, they had no war while they walked in that light." In modern times, the American Revolution was another example of bloodshed resulting from the sins of a people—the American people in this case having been punished for their ill-treatment of slaves and Indians. As for the problem of civil government, which had split the peace movement at the end of the previous decade, Dresser supported the moderates and refused to repudiate public office and the ballot box as essentially unchristian.[53]

The coming of the war with Mexico, if it had united all shades of opinion within the peace movement at least on the point of opposition to the war, saw the American Peace Society once again divided on the issue of its basic philosophy of peace. How deep the controversy penetrated into the rank and file of the Society it is difficult to say. At any rate, it caused a serious upheaval on the leadership level, the with-

---

[52] Amasa Walker, *Memoir of Rev. Amos Dresser*, p. 8.
[53] Amos Dresser, *The Bible against War*, pp. 59ff., 116, 137, 145-54.

drawal of the pacifist element from positions of influence within the Society, and a reorientation of its policy in a conservative direction.

In the late thirties and early forties, complete renunciation of war, international war, of every kind appeared to be firmly established as a basic tenet of the Society's program. True, the Garrisonian nonresistants on the left questioned the thoroughness of its opposition to violence, on account of its neutrality on the subject in other spheres of human activity than war. It was true, too, that the Society did not exclude from membership those peace men who could not in good conscience accept its full pacifist platform. But the controlling voice in the Society's policy was that of the moderate pacifists led by the *doyen* of the peace movement, William Ladd. Ladd's death in 1842, however, had removed the hand that was able to hold together—by the gift of conciliation rather than by the imposition of his own will—the divergent viewpoints that existed within the Society concerning its basic principles.

The confidence of the absolute pacifists that their position had now finally become the established view of the organization is shown in the words of the Rev. A. P. Peabody. In 1843 we find him writing: "When this Society was first formed, there was perhaps, out of the sect of Quakers, not an individual in the country, who stood upon the ground on which our Society now stands, namely, that of the entire and irreconcilable discrepancy between war and the gospel. Even the fathers of our Society were not then prepared to occupy this position in its full length and breadth."[54] Today, he went on, owing to the sound stand of the Society on the matter of defensive war and its quiet but not ineffective work in bringing a number of people over to this view, its position was more firmly rooted than in the past.

But Peabody was reckoning without Beckwith, who had virtually succeeded Ladd in the leadership of the movement. While giving lip service, as we have seen, to the Society's official pacifist stand, Beckwith was out of sympathy with a position which he considered an obstacle to the successful expansion of the Society's work. It tended, he believed, to scare away potential recruits from among the influential sections of society; and it gave a handle to the movement's enemies to identify it with the extremist views of the Non-Resistance Society. If the pacifist plank were removed from the Society's platform, the pacifists would not thereby be prevented from continuing to collaborate as before in the work of the Society, and, at the same time, the broader position would throw the doors wide open for the entry into

[54] Peabody, *The Nature and Influence of War*, p. 22.

the Society of all those interested in promoting peace who were yet unwilling to subscribe to an indiscriminate renunciation of all wars. Beckwith, therefore, commenced to mobilize the conservative forces in the Society in an attempt to bring about this change.

These efforts brought Beckwith up against the man on whom to some degree the mantle (though not the authority) of Ladd had fallen, Elihu Burritt (1810-1879), the "Learned Blacksmith." Burritt now came to represent those elements within the American Peace Society which strongly opposed the movement to water down its pacifist testimony.

Burritt is one of the most remarkable among those rugged self-taught individualists in which nineteenth-century Britain and America abounded.[55] Born in 1810, the son of a poverty-stricken cobbler, he was inured to poverty from his childhood on. Self-help was the only ladder available to him for climbing upward. All outward circumstances were against him. His strength of character, steady determination and native intelligence, however, proved enough to carry him to world fame in his day. Having had scarcely any formal schooling and apprenticed as a young boy to a village blacksmith, Burritt succeeded by his unaided efforts over the following years in acquiring a formidable stock of general knowledge and a prodigious mastery of foreign languages, ranging through Latin, Greek, and all the better-known European and Near Eastern tongues to such exotic items as Amharic and Breton. The exact number of languages of which he had at least a working acquaintance is disputed, but it certainly ran into several score. If knowledge of foreign languages is one of the paths to world peace, never was a peace advocate so well endowed as Burritt. His capacity for acquiring foreign languages was matched only by the enthusiasm with which he devoted himself to a large range of humanitarian causes. Abolition, temperance, the moral and material betterment of the working classes, as well as peace and internationalism, all had Burritt's ardent support. Modest and unassuming, and with a distinct dislike of publicity, he continued to work at the forge long after his learned accomplishments and his philanthropic labors had begun to win him a fair measure of local renown. Eventually, lecturing and writing in support of his good causes (Burritt, indeed, was never interested in learning for learning's sake apart from the utilitarian purposes which it could be made to serve) came to occupy all

---

[55] See Merle Curti, *The Learned Blacksmith: The Letters and Journals of Elihu Burritt*. In this volume Curti gives a brief biography of Burritt, followed by extensive extracts from the enormous bulk of his correspondence and journals.

his time and energies, but he still retained the way of life of the artisan and continued to consider himself a man of the laboring class.

The learned blacksmith first began to take an interest in the peace cause around 1843 when he was already in his early thirties. His conversion to pacifism (for he was to pledge himself to the idea of nonviolence for the remainder of his life) appears to have been a sudden one. In the course of his scientific studies, which he pursued with the same avid interest as his linguistic education, he was struck as if by a revelation with a realization of the oneness of the whole universe and all its phenomena, including man himself. Burritt's pacifism was always to be centered on this vision of the unity of all things, which expressed itself in terms of the Christian faith—for him a creed of optimism that contrasted with the New England Congregationalism to which he was nominally affiliated. His pacifism found an outlet in countless works of practical peacemaking but was essentially akin to the universal experience of the mystics of all the great religions of the world. It was, however, modern "infidel" science which had given Burritt this vision, this concept of the harmony of the universe from the smallest atom to the outermost reaches of space. That war and violence ran contrary to this "perfect symmetry" of God's work, that they contravened the law of love, "the force of gravity in the moral world" equivalent to the law of gravity in the physical world holding all the material creation in right ordering, was what had awakened Burritt to take part in the struggle for peace and for a moral nonviolent alternative to warfare.

In an essay written a few years later we can sense something of Burritt's passionate feeling for this oneness of all things gathered up in the Godhead. In lyrical and ecstatic language—too flowery, it is true, to altogether please us today—Burritt expatiated on the text, God "hath made of one blood all nations of men" [Acts 18: 26]:

> Christians, hear it! hear it in the harmonies of the universe and the voices of visionless things, that commune like whispering angels with the human soul. Hear it in the music of the birds, that never lose a note to settle any disputed territory in mid air. Hear it! the night winds sigh, that have fainted beneath the burdens they have borne from the battle-fields and scenes of human butchery. Hear it! whisper the summer breezes, that go out by moonlight a wooing the blushing flowers of every zone, and sing the same song of love over boundaries that alone make enemies of nations. Bend your ear to the lily and the rose, and hear it there.... Read it! for it is the autograph of every sunbeam, written at dawn and dewy

eve on every inch of the firmament above. Every rain-drop distilled from the ocean, that patters against your window or glitters on the rose beneath, is sent to you with this special message of love."[56]

The purple passage, for all its color, is not necessarily an indication of insincerity: Burritt's whole career was a living illustration of his dedication to the cause of peace.

Burritt spoke for the first time on the subject of peace at a meeting in Boston in June 1843. He does not appear ever to have been a very impressive speaker, but his moral earnestness and the care he took in preparing what he had to say ("Read Arabic and wrote a page on my Peace lecture" is his diary entry, a typical one, for 23 May 1843)[57] went a long way to compensate for his other inadequacies as an orator. At any rate, the leaders of the American Peace Society welcomed this new and promising recruit to their movement with open arms, and he was soon elected to its executive committee. Here he worked closely with the moderate pacifist group, supporting its policies and developing a close friendship with such men as Coues, Blanchard, and Amasa Walker. With Beckwith, Burritt never found it easy to work; "he . . . felt hampered by Mr. Beckwith's narrowness of scope and dictatorial spirit," wrote a contemporary.[58] Beckwith disliked Burritt's radical pacifist ideas, while his own conservatism was looked at askance by the latter. In particular, Burritt and his associates began to feel increasingly unhappy at the spirit in which Beckwith was editing the Society's organ, the *Advocate of Peace*. They wanted to give it a more decided slant against every kind of war and in favor of nonviolent methods of dealing with situations of conflict than Beckwith was prepared to do.

On New Year's Day 1845, Burritt had confided these thoughts to the pages of his journal: "I find my mind is setting with all its sympathies toward the subject of Peace. I am persuaded that it is reserved to crown the destiny of America, that she shall be the great peacemaker in the brotherhood of nations.[59] And I think that I cannot better employ the

---

[56] Elihu Burritt, *Thoughts and Things at Home and Abroad*, pp. 78, 79. See also pp. 114-17, 129, 130.
[57] Quoted in Curti, *The Learned Blacksmith*, p. 20.
[58] Holland, "The History of the Peace-Cause," p. 51.
[59] Another example of this identification by a radical pacifist of America's destiny with the consummation of world peace, and also a manuscript source penned only a month later, is to be found in the letter of Aaron Foster, 7 Feb. 1845, in S. E. Coues's "Peace Album." There Foster predicts that in the not too distant future "the United States will inform the civilized nations that we have resolved to make the experiment of living on principles of confidence and peace with nations, and of ceasing from military preparations, and invite the civilized

talents and time that God may give me, than to devote a year or two to this cause."⁶⁰ The opportunity for this work came in August of the same year, when the pacifists succeeded in replacing Beckwith with Burritt himself as editor of the Society's organ. As a symbol of the new and more radical policy, the paper at the end of the year became the *Advocate* not only of *Peace* but also of *Universal Brotherhood*.

Beckwith, however, was clearly unwilling to acquiesce in the new direction being given to the Society's program. He was to write a little later, rather vaguely, of efforts made "during the last two years to *radicalize* its policy, and introduce such changes as would exclude under reproach the very class of peace men who have for the most part made our Society what it is."⁶¹ At the next annual meeting, in May 1846, he succeeded in mobilizing conservative opinion within the membership behind him for an attack on the positions of the more radical peace men. First, he charged the latter with mingling in their administration of the Society "other reforms with the cause of peace," in particular with agitating against the institution of capital punishment; and, secondly, he declared his own aim to be to place "the cause of peace aright before the christian public." Beckwith failed to gain all his points,⁶² but he did succeed in carrying, by an overwhelming majority, a resolution considerably modifying the forthright stand against all war taken up by the Society since 1837. Great stress was now put upon concentrating solely on the abolition of international war, while avoiding any suspicion of dabbling with "extraneous subjects" such as capital punishment. No action was to be taken which might make it difficult for nonpacifists to collaborate in the work of the Society. This work must "be conducted in a way to render such co-operation practicable, consistent, and cordial, by not conflicting in its operations with principles, institutions or interests which the Christian community hold dear and sacred."⁶³ The resolution was passed over the protests of the pacifist members of the executive committee. True, Article II of the 1837 constitution had not been withdrawn, but the tenor of the new resolution was so clearly in contradiction with its spirit, if not its letter, that the Society had in effect been placed on a new basis. Next month, therefore, the pacifist members on the executive committee, among them such leading figures as the Society's president Coues,

---

and Christian world to cooperate in carrying these sublime principles into harmonious success."
⁶⁰ Quoted in Curti, *The Learned Blacksmith*, p. 42.
⁶¹ *Advocate of Peace*, VII, no. 2 (Feb.-March 1847), 32.
⁶² Quoted in Allen, *The Fight for Peace*, pp. 418, 419.
⁶³ *Advocate of Peace and Universal Brotherhood*, June 1846, quoted in Allen, *The Fight for Peace*, p. 415.

J. P. Blanchard, Burritt, Dr. Walter Channing (1786-1876),[64] and Amasa Walker, handed in their resignations.

Attempts were made to heal the breach. The voting had shown that the bulk of the Society's membership, though perhaps not the majority of its most active workers, were out of sympathy with the official pacifist platform and felt its elimination would further the Society's growth. The dissident members abided loyally by the decision of the majority. They remained on in the Society, but they were unwilling to withdraw their resignations, holding it incompatible with their principles to continue in office while profoundly disagreeing with the new policy. The split was only made public, however, in December. On 17 December Burritt, who had departed shortly before the annual meeting on a peace mission to the British Isles which resulted in the formation of his famous League of Universal Brotherhood, wrote in his journal: "The division of the American Peace Society is almost consummated."[65] The last number of the *Advocate* to appear under his direction had come out with the dissidents' lengthy letter of resignation published in full in its columns.[66]

This document is both an apologia for their past policies and a manifesto in favor of radical Christian pacifism. They record their dissent from the argument used by their opponents that the pacifist platform, "the fundamental principles of our society," had proved an obstacle in the struggle for peace. "It is said by those desirous of the change, that the radical position of the society narrows its influence, closes pulpits to its lectures, and prevents the hearty cooperation of 'the moderate friends of peace.'" "We believe," they go on, "that no increase of members can compensate for the loss of the high Christian principle which alone can give real and permanent strength." After all, even governments and their military advisers normally advocate war only as a last resort. What is the point of a peace society, whose standards of right and wrong are no higher than the standards of those they are trying to educate in the way of peace? They pointed to the recent success of Burritt in winning thousands of recruits within a few

---

[64] The brother of the famous Unitarian minister, William Ellery Channing, he writes of his conversion to pacifism: "I came into the service of Peace most simply and naturally. It was in the latest period of my labors after a religious life, that I became convinced that peace was its ground-principle,—the object of the coming of Christ, the leading doctrine of his religion,—the ruling practice of his life. Without the spirit of peace I felt that man could be none of His" (letter of Walter Channing, 2 Nov. 1844, in Coues's "Peace Album").

[65] Quoted in Curti, *American Peace Crusade*, p. 94.

[66] *Advocate of Peace and Universal Brotherhood*, Dec. 1846, quoted in Allen, *The Fight for Peace*, pp. 417-19. After receiving back the paper, Beckwith dropped Burritt's addition of "Universal Brotherhood" from the title.

months in both Britain and the United States to the absolutist pledge of his League of Universal Brotherhood (see below). Surely this showed that "the common sentiment of the most active friends of peace throughout the world" in fact responded more readily to the radical message than to any attempt to place the peace issue "on lower ground." "The day of doubt and fear to the friends of peace has passed away.... Our minds are clear on the subject, and we cannot in justice to our own views of duty, retain office in a society which abandons the principle that *all* war is forbidden by christianity."

What they write in their statement reveals that the division between the radical and the more conservative members of the executive committee centered ostensibly on a matter of tactics rather than on a disagreement as to the extent of their repudiation of international war, which of course remained the fundamental cause of the rift. "The question between us and our former associates of the Executive Committee," the dissidents said, "is not whether christianity, under any circumstances, tolerates international war, but whether the *Society* can be most efficient with or without asserting the radical principle." For the pacifists, this principle implicitly entailed a renunciation of violence in society as well as in international relations, an assertion of the sanctity of human life in all circumstances. To refuse to kill one's fellowmen in battle and to partake, if only indirectly, in taking life by the hand of the executioner, while not strictly contrary to the regulations of the Society, appeared a monstrous inconsistency in the eyes of Burritt and his associates. True, they had been careful to maintain (and this had been recognized at the last annual meeting) that this was a private view, the testimony of individual conscience. "But," they write, "it is still asserted, and perhaps with truth, that the position of some of us individuals, in regard to capital punishment, injures the society; that men will not separate individual acts from official conduct. By retiring from office, we remove this obstacle to the hearty cooperation in the American Peace Society of those in favor of capital punishment."

Without a clear mandate from the Society the pacifist members of the executive committee felt unable to carry on in the spirit of a commitment against all wars. "It is not a question for a majority to decide, leaving a dissatisfied minority in the executive board. The society should be organized definitely and distinctly on the one ground or on the other." The annual meeting had shown on which side the majority inclined; no other alternative remained to the minority but to withdraw from active direction of the Society, at the same time wishing the new leadership "under the more lax constitution" every success in their endeavors for peace. "We form no new organization to contend with the old," they concluded. "We . . . raise our voices against all war, against all preparations for war, and against every manifestation of the military spirit; yet we would not reject the aid of those who do not fully coincide with us in this belief; the cause of peace requires the efforts of all those who profess themselves her friends; but we have no faith in any principle or policy which tolerates for any purpose whatever that which is opposed to the spirit of christianity." Feeling that opinion in the Society was against them, nothing remained for them to do except to retire with dignity.

Burritt, in particular, was adamant in his refusal to sanction any position short of a total renunciation of war. "We could not retain any official relation to that Society for a moment after one jot or tittle of this vital principle had been abated," he wrote in December 1846 in the *Advocate*, as he prepared to place the paper back into Beckwith's hands. *"Peace advocates of defensive wars"* he derisively called his opponents, whom he criticized in the strongest terms for their readiness to attract new members "by cutting down the constitution of the society to their low level of faith." Where was the Society's distinctive testimony for peace now? "We can see no disqualifying reason why the Mexican and American soldiers who stabbed at each others' hearts in the streets of Monterey, might not alternatively subscribe to the highest article of faith remaining in the Society's creed, and that too, with the points of their bayonets newly dipped in human blood."[67]

At this point, however, Burritt had let his feelings of disappointment and frustration at the new policy of the American Peace Society overcome his sense of fairness. Although there had not yet in fact been any formal changes in the Society's constitution of 1837 (alterations were, however, being prepared by the new executive committee) and although the controversial Article II condemning all wars as incompatible with Christianity still remained, therefore, officially in force, Burritt was of course right in his view that the new interpretation given, with its implied criticism of the Society's pacifist-minded late executive, represented a repudiation of the absolute pacifist principle. But peace-minded nonpacifists, if not perhaps the soldiers of Monterey, had always been welcome to join and to participate fully in the Society's work. The Society had never required its members to take a pacifist pledge (such as Burritt had now devised for his newly formed League), and, of course, nonresistance had never constituted a part of its platform. Although before 1837 the pacifists had been a tolerated

[67] *Advocate of Peace and Universal Brotherhood*, I, no. 12 (Dec. 1846), 275.

minority, with the Society officially adopting a broad antiwar platform, from 1837 onward the situation was reversed, with pacifism the official policy and toleration given to the nonpacifists within it. The events of the summer of 1846 had simply represented, at least on the surface, a return to the pre-1837 era in the history of the Society.

The American Peace Society was now reconstructed by Beckwith on the basis of a general opposition to the institution of international war. The secretary was quick to point out that the changes were in fact aimed rather at clarifying the existing position than introducing any entirely new principles. He maintained that there had been a danger that the Society under the old management would have developed into a nonresistant society. "From these views we of course dissented," Beckwith wrote early in 1847, "but, if any article of our constitution was *liable* to such a construction, it was very naturally thought proper to let the Society have an opportunity of making such alteration in its phraseology as they might deem best." This was the reason for the new draft constitution which was being drawn up for the Society by the new executive along the lines indicated at the last annual meeting.[68] "Most of our late associates in office," wrote Beckwith a little later, "were not at home with us; and at length it became evident to themselves, as to others, that, with their views, and habits, and modes of management, they could not be comfortable as leaders in such a society as ours, and that the class of men hitherto united with us in this cause, would not work cheerfully and harmoniously under their auspices. So they wisely concluded to retire; and our best wishes go with them."[69] And so, with expressions of mutual esteem on each side, but naturally with a feeling of sadness and disappointment on the part of the ousted leaders, the division in the Society had finally been consummated.[70]

In fact, no amendments were made in the Society's constitution when the subject came up for discussion at the next annual meeting in May 1847. For this situation three reasons appear to have been responsible. In the first place, with the Mexican War still being waged, such action might have been interpreted by outsiders as intended to give the Society's support to the war. Respect, too, for the memory of the late William Ladd, who had been largely responsible for the offending Article II of the 1837 constitution, impelled the new executive to

---

[68] *Advocate of Peace*, VII, no. 1 (Jan.-Feb. 1847), 2-4.
[69] *Ibid.*, VII, no. 2 (Feb.-March 1847), 33.
[70] See Curti, *American Peace Crusade*, pp. 94, 95; Allen, *The Fight for Peace*, pp. 403, 404, 412-15; Galpin, *Pioneering for Peace*, pp. 163-67; Edson L. Whitney, *The American Peace Society*, pp. 81, 82.

use caution in the matter. And lastly, there existed a fear that too rapid a change in the Society's basic principles might cause further dissension among the radical wing, who had retained their membership though their influence was gone, and bring about new schisms. The resolutions interpreting the constitution in a latitudinarian spirit, which had been adopted the previous year, were reaffirmed as the Society's policy, and there the matter was allowed to rest. Beckwith, with the executive committee manned by his followers, mostly respectable Congregational clergy, was henceforth in complete control of the Society. Though the radicals renewed their attacks on his policies during the subsequent years, controversy degenerated after a time into a clash of personalities rather than of principles, and bitterness and heated tempers were generated on both sides. Beckwith's position within the Society remained on the whole unshaken. The reputation of the American Peace Society, however, was undoubtedly impaired as a result of these prolonged wranglings.[71]

The new era in the Society's history, which began with the withdrawal of more radical pacifists from the leadership, saw the gradual withering of its original vigor and inspiration. The process actually can already be detected earlier when the most vital peace impulse was channeled off into the Non-Resistance Society.[72] Now the organization was to become increasingly respectable in the eyes of society. It was to continue to do good work in fostering a general interest in peace, in pressing for the adoption of international arbitration, and in keeping the ideal of a congress of nations before the public. But it lacked a wider vision; it became overcautious for fear of offending public opinion and of acquiring the label of "ultraism"; creative thought on the subject of peace was banished along with the vagaries of a more radical pacifism. A hostile critic, who was a member of the moderate pacifist opposition of this period, writes of "the Jesuitical manoeuvres of Rev. George C. Beckwith, D.D."[73] Beckwith was certainly a skilled politician in organizational matters: he was in a way the *apparatchik* of the mid-nineteenth-century peace movement. But it is not fair to saddle him with conscious duplicity in furthering his own interests, as this writer goes on to imply. The latter is on firmer

[71] Curti, *American Peace Crusade*, pp. 96-102.
[72] Burritt's relations with the Garrisonian nonresistants were not always good. In particular, his support of the Liberty party riled them. In Edmund Quincy's view, Burritt was lacking in "moral courage." He had "never heard of any warrior or slaveholder, or proslavery or fighting parson that was offended by anything he has said." (Quoted in Peter Tolis, "Elihu Burritt: Crusader for Brotherhood," Ph.D. diss., Columbia U. [1965], pp. 170, 171, 187, 192, 193.)
[73] Holland, "The History of the Peace Cause," p. 45.

ground, however, when he characterizes Beckwith's activities after he had gained control of the Society in the following terms: "He, monopolizing nearly all the offices of the American [Peace] Society, wedded to a monstrous routine of money-collecting, editing the Advocate and arranging an annual meeting, with an occasional petition to Congress, seemed neither willing to move himself nor to let others move."[74] The American Peace Society soon became fossilized.

After his victory Beckwith in 1847 had published a small volume of some 250 pages, which summarized the new official Society position. Most of its pages are devoted to the indictment of the institution of war on both economic, humanitarian, moral, and religious grounds, such as is familiar to us now from our study of earlier writings of the peace movement. Remedies for war are found in a system of arbitration and the setting up of international congresses for settling disputes. Beckwith calls his book *The Peace Manual*; it would serve to counteract some dangerous notions to be found in the earlier *Manual of Peace* from the pen of Professor Thomas Upham (himself no fiery radical but an upholder during this period of the moderate pacifist position), which was still popular as propaganda in peace circles.

> The cause of peace [Beckwith wrote in the preface to his book] aims solely to do away [with] the custom of international war; and I trust there will be found in this book nothing that does not bear on this object, nor anything that interferes with the legitimate authority of government. As a friend of peace, I am of course a supporter of civil government, with all the powers requisite for the condign punishment of wrong-doers, the enforcement of law, and the preservation of social order. I deem government, in spite of its worst abuses, an ordinance of God for the good of mankind; nor can I, as a peace man, hold any doctrines incompatible in my view with its just and necessary powers over its own subjects. I condemn *only* THE GREAT DUEL OF NATIONS.

That took care of the nonresistants—and also of the absolutists within the ranks of the American Peace Society, who could scarcely uphold Beckwith in the support he gave to "*all* the powers requisite for the condign punishment of wrong-doers" (my italics), for the executioner and the application of troops to suppress mobs and rebellion were assuredly included in this array of authority, as was the use of deadly weapons in personal self-defense, too.[75] "This view of peace," con-

---

[74] *Ibid.*, p. 85.
[75] Cf. Francis Wayland, *The Duty of Obedience to the Civil Magistrate* (1847), esp. pp. 11, 19-23, 26, 30-32. Writing in the same year, Wayland was even more

tinued Beckwith later, "relieves it from a variety of extraneous questions." Let there be tolerance among members on such issues: "all these are grave questions, but come not within our province." He makes it clear, however, where his own stand, and that of the Society, lay on these issues.

In his attitude toward international war, it must be pointed out, Beckwith still seems to have maintained the pacifist stand against all war—including those claimed as purely defensive, which, we have seen from his pamphlet discussed above, was his position earlier. Beckwith's own words, however, are not altogether clear. In one place, while discussing the platform of the international peace convention held in London in 1843 ("that war is inconsistent with Christianity, and the true interests of mankind"), on which the American Peace Society had modeled itself when it adopted the controversial resolution of 1846, Beckwith says: "We grant that this language is indefinite, allowing a pretty free play of the pendulum. . . . We can *make* it express the belief of *all* war unchristian; but it *pledges* us only to a condemnation of the custom." Certainly, we know he wished to attract into the Society in greater numbers peace men who were unwilling to renounce the possibility of a nation waging a just war: that, indeed, had been one of the chief reasons for his forcing through the recent changes. But what were his personal views on the subject? And did the Society officially take a stand on the subject aside from proclaiming tolerance for divergent views?

Both Beckwith's writings and the official pronouncements issued by the American Peace Society under his direction show that the witness was still, on the whole, against all war between nations. Asks Beckwith after quoting from the Sermon on the Mount: "Now, do not such passages convey a most unequivocal condemnation of war in all its forms?" "If war is right for us," he writes a little later, "it must have been equally so for our Saviour; but can you conceive the Prince of Peace, or one of his apostles leading forth an army to their work of plunder, blood and devastation?" The moral precepts of the Bible, he says, apply as much to governments as to individuals—unless God

---

explicit than Beckwith in sanctioning the right of individuals and governments to use the sword in self-defense (provided its use was confined strictly to warding off attacks on person and liberties), while at the same time denying the legitimacy of its use in wars between the nations. "The one is a righteous and the other an unrighteous employment of force," he writes, "and to concede the necessity of one, is by no means to admit the rectitude of the other . . . the right of self-defence in no manner involves the right to wage war as it is commonly waged between nations. The objects pursued in the two cases are entirely unlike, and the means of attaining them are widely dissimilar."

specifically exempts the former from them. The alleged contradiction between the use of armed force to maintain legitimate government *within* the state and the injunctions of the gospels has, indeed, nothing in common with the Christian ban on war *between* states. "The former is the *government* question, the latter the *peace* question; points that are entirely distinct, and ought never to be confounded." Against war the early Christians, if called upon to fight, took up the stand of the conscientious objector, an attitude which was conditioned, Beckwith points out, as much by a realization of war's incompatibility with Christianity as by the fear of becoming involved in idolatry. His manual, from which these quotations have been taken,[76] was issued in the name of the American Peace Society and may properly be considered an official exposition of its position.

In fact, as we have shown, the American Peace Society had ceased to be a pacifist society despite remnants of "ultraism" in the philosophy of its director. It devoted itself henceforward almost exclusively to institutional aspects of peace and war, and the individual protest against war as the incarnation of violence, which is at the root of pacifist philosophy, was more and more relegated to the sphere of private conscience. With this the Society was no more concerned now than with, let us say, the creed of vegetarianism to which a few of its members adhered. Once the controversy over the changes accomplished in 1846 had died down, the transformation was achieved by silence and not by any overt statements repudiating formerly held positions. A body inscribing on its banners the renunciation on religious grounds of all forms of war yet composed, in fact, on both higher and lower echelons of men who regarded national wars of "defense" of the past or in the future as not inconsistent with Christianity was not likely to remain a focal point for rallying those who saw in the peace movement primarily an expression of a philosophy of nonviolence.

II

For a time, Burritt's League of Universal Brotherhood was to provide the moderate pacifists with an organization through which they could work satisfactorily for their concept of peace. As we have seen, Burritt departed for England in May 1846 on a peace mission connected with the oganization of his "Friendly International Addresses," the exchanging of which between British and American towns Burritt had arranged as a gesture of solidarity at a period of war crisis in the relations of the two countries. As Burritt was departing from the shores of

---

[76] Beckwith, *The Peace Manual*, pp. 7, 11, 147-66.

America, the two governments reached a solution of the Oregon Crisis, and tension between them relaxed. The original idea for the inter-city addresses Burritt owed to the Manchester Quaker, Joseph Crosfield, and after his arrival on British soil the American pacifist was to repay the debt by setting up in England the first international pacifist organization in the world, with a platform which pledged members to refuse participation in wars of any kind. Burritt, who had at first planned to stay in Britain for only three months, in fact remained in Europe, apart from several brief visits back home, until the middle of the next decade. Burritt's activities during these years belong, therefore, in part to the story of the British and continental peace movement. But the man himself and his approach (with all his genuine internationalism) were nineteenth-century American through and through, and the proper place for their consideration would seem to be with American pacifism, out of which, indeed, the League of Universal Brotherhood had sprung.

The idea of founding such a brotherhood had come to Burritt before he set out on his visit to England. The brotherhood, in fact, appears to have had a prototype in the little Worcester County Peace Society, which Burritt and Amasa Walker had founded in the previous February on the platform of opposition to all war and as a center of opposition, too, to the policies of Beckwith and his party within the peace movement.[77]

"We had conceived," Burritt writes, "that in travelling from village to village through England, we might find many by the wayside and fireside, especially among the poorer classes, who would be willing to subscribe their names to the pledge and principles of such an organization." Soon after his arrival in Britain, he set out on his projected missionary journey in the cause of peace. At the end of July, as he approached the village of Pershore near Worcester (England), he sat down and sketched out the wording of a pledge, which he felt should be taken by all who wished to become members of his brotherhood in order to stress the need for individual responsibility that had been lacking, in his view, in the older peace societies. Burritt would have none of the compromise with so-called defensive war so dear to the hearts of the conservative element in the American Peace Society. Instead, their exclusive concentration on the issue of international war for fear of offending someone's susceptibilities, a policy of which Burritt strongly disapproved, would be replaced by a program which de-

[77] Tolis, "Burritt," pp. 146, 171. Tolis attributes the genesis of the idea of a new international organization to Walker as much as—if not more than—to Burritt himself.

clared war on every obstacle obstructing the brotherhood of man in the belief that all humanitarian reforms were but different aspects of one cause, the welfare of all God's children.

Burritt's pledge ran as follows:

> Believing all war to be inconsistent with the spirit of Christianity, and destructive to the best interests of mankind, I do hereby pledge myself never to enlist or enter into any army or navy, or to yield any voluntary support or sanction to the preparation for or prosecution of any war, by whomsoever, for whatsoever proposed, declared, or waged. And I do hereby associate myself with all persons, of whatever country, condition, or colour, who have signed, or shall hereafter sign this pledge, in a "League of Universal Brotherhood"; whose object shall be to employ all legitimate and moral means for the abolition of all war, and all spirit, and all the manifestation of war, throughout the world; for the abolition of all restrictions upon international correspondence and friendly intercourse, and of whatever else tends to make enemies of nations, or prevents their fusion into one peaceful brotherhood; for the abolition of all institutions and customs which do not recognize the image of God and a human brother in every man of whatever clime, colour, or condition of humanity.

That very evening Burritt attended a small gathering of some twenty people, all simple folk who had come in after their day's labors in the field or at the shop counter to hear the famous American speak. Burritt lectured for some three hours on the purpose of his mission to Britain and on the implications of his peace pledge and membership in the proposed League. He produced copies of the pledge that he had written, one of which he had first signed himself, and succeeded in getting as many as nineteen further signatures from his audience. From these humble beginnings sprang an organization which was to gather in members from half a dozen countries.

After coming to England, he had found that he had, indeed, underestimated the response to his proposals and that, in addition to those in humble stations of life, many among the middle ranks of society would give them a favorable reception. In particular, the Birmingham Quaker and social reformer, Joseph Sturge (1793-1859), was active in helping the stranger to popularize the idea in England. At a soirée given on 5 August for the delegates attending the World's Temperance Convention in London, Burritt seconded Sturge in expounding the objectives of the proposed League and the nature of the pledge which its members would sign. The place chosen for announcing the idea to the public was an appropriate one, for his idea of a peace pledge—a "teetotal peace pledge," as he called it[78]—Burritt had, indeed, borrowed from the temperance movement. "We had but a few of the printed Pledges with us," Burritt relates, "but these were filled up on the spot with names that stand high in the estimation of the public, on both sides of the Atlantic." Among about sixty persons who then signed the pledge were Sturge himself, the secretary of the London Peace Society, the Rev. Joseph John Jefferson, and the well-known radical politician and reformer, James Silk Buckingham.[79]

Burritt continued to tour England, gathering in signatures for his pledge and speaking in private homes and in Quaker meetinghouses—in fact, wherever he could find a hearing. Nearly a thousand pledges came in during the first few months of the campaign. In the United States, too, Burritt's associates were busy in the work, and his weekly paper, the *Christian Citizen*, which was published in Worcester (Mass.), printed the names of the peace pledgers in both countries as they came in. Burritt's *Citizen*, together with the *Bond of Brotherhood*, a popular monthly which he had started up in the same town at the time of the Oregon Crisis and soon after transferred to England, acted as organs of the new movement.[80] The British Quakers in particular, who were less averse to action of this kind than their brethren in the United States, gave warm support to Burritt's efforts. Among them was Edmund Fry (the son of the famous prison reformer, Elizabeth Fry), who was to become one of Burritt's closest collaborators on the English side in the work of the League. "My right hand co-partners in this glorious enterprise," he calls his Quaker colleagues.[81] Many of the non-Quaker free-traders were sympathetic, too. Their economic internationalism often sprang, as in the case of John Bright, from religious roots.

How busy Burritt was at this time and how bright his hopes were for the work ahead come out in his correspondence. In October he

[78] "Lecture of Elihu Burritt" (1847), MS American Antiquarian Society, Worcester (Mass.), p. 16.

[79] Curti, *American Peace Crusade*, pp. 144-46; Burritt, *Ten-Minute Talks on All Sorts of Topics with Autobiography of the Author*, pp. 20, 21; *Christian Citizen*, vol. III, no. 38, 19 Sept. 1846.

[80] Curti, *American Peace Crusade*, pp. 146, 147, 156. The paper was edited in Burritt's absence by Thomas Drew. It campaigned for a number of causes besides peace. According to the statement of its principles (obviously Burritt's work), which was inserted in frequent numbers: "It will speak against all War in the spirit of Peace. It will speak for the Slave, as for a brother bound. It will speak for the Universal Brotherhood of mankind. The Gospel it shall preach from, will be the Gospel of the Millennium."

[81] Quoted in Curti, *The Learned Blacksmith*, p. 46.

wrote to a friend in the United States: "I have been absorbed to the whole capacity of my heart and hands in getting the 'League of Universal Brotherhood' under way. . . . I hope that 5000 in Great Britain and 5000 in the United States will have joined the covenant of peace before the close of the present year; thus constituting not only an international society for the abolition of war, but also for the abolition of slavery, restrictions on commerce and correspondence. You see that the platform of the League is large enough for all the organizations that need be formed for the elevation of mankind."[82] A couple of months later we find him writing in the same strain to a Quaker schoolmaster friend active in recruiting for the pledge: "What say you to a Peace Establishment in 1847, of 100,000 pledged *brethren* on each side of the Atlantic? Let us try for it. . . . We must try to establish a League branch in every town." Another month and he was writing: "We must say 200,000 for the year in both countries."[83]

These hopes were, of course, vastly exaggerated. Nevertheless, the new organization grew rapidly both in Britain and in the United States and even recruited a few scattered members on the continent in France, Germany, and Holland. The pledge to refuse participation in the armed forces, however, proved an obstacle in these lands, where military conscription was being enforced. The figures of signatories, fairly equally divided between Britain and the United States, went up from over 10,000 at the end of 1846 to well over 30,000 in 1847 and over 50,000 by 1850. On paper, at least, the numbers were impressive; they certainly witness to the energy and zeal of Burritt and his co-workers on both sides of the Atlantic. "A young lad of 13 years," Burritt reported, "has obtained 500 signatures to the Pledge in Worcester [England], within two months."[84] As Curti has pointed out,[85] the strength of the League on both continents lay in the simple artisans and farmers who constituted the vast majority of its membership and, encouraged by Burritt and his colleagues, made the League a flourishing concern for several years at least.[86]

[82] Letter dated 9 Oct. 1846, S.C.P.C. Archives—Elihu Burritt.
[83] Burritt to Elias Lane, letters dated 4 Dec. 1846 and 6 Jan. 1847, S.C.P.C. Archives—Burritt.
[84] *Ibid.*, 6 Jan. 1847.
[85] Curti, *The Learned Blacksmith*, p. 32.
[86] Here are two illustrations, taken from the American branch, of the way the League spoke to the condition of ordinary men and women with a concern for peace. At its first general meeting in Boston in May 1847, Thomas Haskell (see earlier) took the floor. "He was an unlearned man," he said, "and sometimes he felt glad of it when he saw men of learning and talent twisting and perverting the plainest commandments of the Almighty, to suit them to man's narrow ideas of rectitude. He had been a peace man nearly all his life; the inconsistency of

It was not until May 1847 that a formal organization was set up in both the United States and Britain; even thereafter, however, informality was its keynote, in contrast to the increasing bureaucratization of the American Peace Society under Beckwith. "Mr. Burritt's idea," writes an American colleague, "was to have as little organization as possible, employ no hired secretary, concentrate all the funds upon publications—whose sale and circulation would of course furnish fresh aid and impulse."[87]

The founding of the League had received a mixed reception from other branches of the peace movement. The London Peace Society was outwardly friendly but held itself rather aloof. In America the Garrisonian nonresistants for the most part would have nothing to do with it. "Humbug" was how Edmund Quincy dubbed it in the *Liberator*.[88] True, the Rev. Samuel J. May welcomed its appearance, but he was never too sound on the "no-government" issue anyway. Beckwith for the American Peace Society (of which, incidentally, Burritt remained a member, though he was extremely critical of its new policy) damned the League with the faintest of praise. "It is a fine conception," Beckwith wrote patronizingly, "but altogether too vague and broad for any specific purpose. It covers everything in general, but fixes necessarily on nothing in particular. . . . It is one of those vague, magnificent generalities, which for a time enrapture persons of a sanguine, excitable temperament."[89] Outside peace circles the League, where it was noticed (and it was noticed considerably more often than the older established peace organizations were now), received a not altogether unfriendly reception, although the pledge idea was usually considered too far in advance of the times.

At the meeting in Boston at the end of May 1847, when the American branch of the League was formally set up, Burritt was elected pres-

---

war and all the spirit of war with Christianity had appeared to him more than thirty years ago, as he was reading his Bible. He had always refused to do military duty, and striven to live up to the true peace principle all his life." (*Burritt's Christian Citizen*, vol. IV, no. 23 [5 June 1847].) A shoemaker from Oberlin (Ohio), where the League was particularly strong both in the college and in the town, wrote to Burritt: "I carry on a cobbler's shop here, but my mind refuses to be contained in it. It will fly away and perch itself upon the Peace Cause. I am willing to be a hewer of wood and a drawer of water to promote it. We have a few more than 700 signers of the pledge in Oberlin. I have not collected quite all, but most of them, and that in the face of the leading influences. I concluded, if I caught the sheep, the shepherds would be likely to follow" (*Bond of Brotherhood*, Dec. 1847, quoted in Allen, *The Fight for Peace*, p. 427).

[87] Holland, "The History of the Peace Cause," p. 58.
[88] Quoted in Curti, *American Peace Crusade*, p. 153.
[89] *Advocate of Peace* (May-June 1847), quoted in Allen, *The Fight for Peace*, p. 426.

ident even though lengthy absences in Europe made his office more or less nominal for the time being, and Amasa Walker became one of the corresponding secretaries. The radical pacifist group in the American Peace Society acted as the core of the new organization.

A spirited debate soon arose over the exact implications of signing the pledge. Did it savor of infidelity, as some of the clergy were alleging? At the inaugural meeting we find a Mr. Jewett, of Providence, answering such accusations. "He was," he said, "one of the most rigid of Calvinists, but he could see nothing in his faith to prevent him from signing the Pledge; and if it was incumbent upon any man on earth more than on any other to give in his adhesion to the Pledge, the true believer in the atonement, the genuine orthodox Christian was the man."[90] Did it deprive a man of the right to defend himself from attack by physical force? Was it a declaration of belief in complete nonresistance? "Many were of opinion (and some of the good peace men) that the pledge traverses the right of self defence," reports E. W. Jackson, a lay member of the Methodist Episcopal Church and one of the radical pacifists who had resigned along with Burritt from the American Peace Society leadership the previous year; "I fear that not so much good will be accomplished by the pledge in this country as would be if we had a simple pledge against the institution of war and nothing else, a simple Peace Pledge pledging ourselves never to enter any army or navy etc. etc. Such a pledge would unite nearly all." Charles Sumner, for instance, had refused to sign on this account, and some of the clergy pleaded the same reason for refusal.[91] But others were of a different opinion—the Rev. Joshua Leavitt (1794-1873), for example, who as a leader of the political anti-Garrisonian wing of abolitionism was very far from being a nonresistant. "It was a protest against war," he said of the pledge, "and every form of oppression. It was proper and necessary that those who signed it should interpret it for themselves. He signed it, as he understood it, and it was absurd to insist that he must take any other man's interpretation of it."[92] Although, it is true, "no-government" advocates were sometimes to make themselves heard at gatherings of the League, as a whole the organization—in the spirit of Burritt[93] and its other sponsors—supported the positive

[90] *Burritt's Christian Citizen*, vol. IV, no. 23, 5 June 1847.
[91] E. W. Jackson to Elias Lane, 29 May 1847, S.C.P.C. Archives—Elihu Burritt. The nonpacifist Theodore Parker, however, signed the pledge. See Tolis, "Burritt," p. 204.
[92] *Burritt's Christian Citizen*, 5 June 1847.
[93] See, e.g., Burritt's essay on "The Policeman and the Soldier" in *Thoughts and Things at Home and Abroad*, pp. 290-94. How he must have shocked Garrisonian nonresistants when he wrote, for instance (p. 290): "The State Prison has become, perhaps, the best barometer of the philanthropy of the country. It has

aspects of civil authority. Moreover, a large number of the signatories were clearly interpreting the pledge in as "broad" a fashion as the conservatives in the American Peace Society were doing in respect to the pacifist plank in its program. The New England Conference of Wesleyan Methodists, for instance, perhaps in reaction against the Mexican War which was still in progress and unpopular in some church circles, had expressed its collective approval of the pledge and advised all church members to sign it individually.[94] This was not necessarily a triumph for absolute pacifism, but more probably merely a registering of dislike for American involvement in foreign wars.

In the United States the League enjoyed an initial period of success: membership expanded rapidly, especially in the hinterland area of New England and in the Midwest; local groups sprang up; its activities received favorable publicity at first in sections of the press; the churches in many cases gave it some support. But, in comparison with its progress in England, the League failed to develop after the first few years. Undoubtedly, the increasingly tense situation inside the country from the Compromise of 1850 on, which affected the Midwest regions in particular, made peace work more difficult. Among convinced supporters of the peace movement, some, as we have seen, felt the pledge was too radical;[95] others, on the other hand, considered it too mild to be effective. But Curti points to what was the most cogent reason for the League's rapid decline in the early fifties when he writes: "Chiefly it failed in America because it possessed no outstanding leader."[96] The League, for all the dedicated service given it by men like Edmund Fry (son of the famous Elizabeth Fry) in England or Amasa Walker in the United States and by a number of devoted

---

become even now an institution of merciful and beneficent ministry to thousands —the very gate of salvation to souls arrested from the steep broad road to ruin." Of the police in contrast to the soldier he remarks (p. 291): "Their cardinal function or duty is to save life, not to destroy it; to elevate, not to degrade public morals."

[94] Allen, *The Fight for Peace*, p. 427.

[95] Burritt on a brief visit to America in the spring of 1847 devised two alternative "Declarations" to meet the requirements of some prominent peace workers in the United States who felt conscientiously unable to sign the absolutist pledge yet desired to be associated in the work of the League. The wording of the Declarations was slightly different in each case, but, while omitting the C.O. pledge, both committed signatories to a general condemnation of war, to working for its abolition, and to an assertion of the brotherhood of man. See letter from J. P. Blanchard in *Boston Daily News*, 11 April 1863. One of the Declarations is to be found printed, along with the full pledge, in a leaflet in Harvard University Library, Int.6809 (box). Here it is stated that the original suggestion to allow a looser form of association came from Charles Sumner. This may well be true.

[96] Curti, *American Peace Crusade*, pp. 155, 156.

agents working for it in both countries, was essentially a one-man organization in the sense that it was the inspiration and driving force of a single man that kept it in motion. Burritt during these years had back in Europe more work than even his hands could properly manage. Thus the League in America suffered through the prolonged absence of its founder.

At the end of 1846 Burritt had written: "Peace is a spirit, and not an intellectual abstraction; it is a life, not a theory."[97] The words are an excellent summing up of his basic philosophy of peace. But peace for Burritt was not merely a philosophy of action. We have seen that he regarded peace as but a single manifestation of the oneness of all being, of the unity of God's creation. In all the varied endeavors to improve mankind morally or spiritually he saw "a oneness or identity of spirit, aim and end, whatever may be their respective departments of labour in the great field of humanity." It would be wrong therefore —and this in particular was what riled him about Beckwith's careful paring down of the peace issue to the institution of international war alone—to isolate one reform from another, to keep each in a watertight compartment as if one issue had no close bearing on another. Burritt saw only "one broad highway of humanity" along which all who strove to help their fellowmen must go. "True philanthropy," he told his peace pledgers, "is one and the same spirit, here, now, everywhere, and forever. It comes from one source; it tends to but one end. It comes from the love of God dwelling in human hearts, and shed abroad from those human hearts upon all the immortal beings within their neighborhood; and their neighborhood is the world."[98] Thus what to some was the League's weakness, its tendency to dissipate its energies on a variety of separate causes and to divide instead of unite on a single aim, was an essential ingredient for Burritt, if not its very purpose. He was against war and all preparations for war. But a pacifist who was not also prepared to pledge himself against racial and religious prejudice, political and social injustice, and all forms of inhumanity of man against man was a pretty poor kind of pacifist in Burritt's view.

Peace was not merely negative either; it must be a leaven working in a positive fashion within society and between nations. In November 1846 he wrote in the *Bond of Brotherhood* of the objectives of the League:

> Its operations and influence will not be confined to the work of mere *abolition* [i.e., of war]; as if nothing more were requisite for the

[97] Quoted in Allen, *The Fight for Peace*, p. 420.
[98] "Lecture of Elihu Burritt" (1847), pp. 1-5, 8-11.

symmetrical development of society, or the universal growth of human happiness, than the axe to be laid to the root of existing evils. It will seek to build up, as well as to pull down. . . . It contemplates something more than a mere Peace Society, or the object of inducing nations merely to abstain from war, or to leave each other alone. It will not only aim at the mutual pacification of enemies, but at their conversion into brethren . . . being based on the whole compass of the principle, that every man is bound to be as much a brother, as God is a father, to every human being, however deep may be the moral darkness and degradation of that being; however fallen or low in the estimation of the world he may be by crime or color, or any condition of humanity within or beyond his control. Long after nations shall have been taught to war no more, long after the mere iron fetters shall have been stricken from the limbs of the last slave, and every visible yoke shall have been broken, and every formal bastille of oppression levelled with the ground, there will be a work for the League.[99]

In fact, the life of the League was cut short even before it could witness the approaching end of American slavery. The task which its founder had set for it far outstripped its capacity and outran the enthusiasm of the rank and file, even when spurred on by the indefatigable Burritt.

The decline in the activities of the League's American branch was followed within a few years by that of the British section where, as has been remarked, Quakers had formed "by far the strongest supporters of the League."[100] (On the European continent, despite Burritt's close contacts and fruitful collaboration with the leaders of the peace movement there, the League had never flourished.) The outbreak of the Crimean War in 1855 and Burritt's departure for America in the same year seriously affected its growth. Two years later its formal existence came to an end with the fusion of the British organization with the old London Peace Society and of the organization in the United States with the American Peace Society.

What had Burritt and his peace pledgers accomplished? "A work of no mean proportions" is how Curti sums up their practical achievements. For reasons we have discussed above, more was done in Britain than in the United States, but aims and methods were the same in both countries. The scheme for exchanging "Friendly Addresses" between American and British cities, which Burritt had originated at the

[99] Quoted in Allen, *The Fight for Peace*, p. 426.
[100] Tolis, "Burritt," p. 182.

time of the Oregon Crisis, was continued now in the form of interchanges between French and British towns during the periodic crises occurring during this period in the relations between the two countries. In 1849 Burritt initiated his series of "Olive Leaves," short statements on some important issue relevant to peace, which the League published and circulated in the press on both sides of the Atlantic and which evidence shows to have been read by many tens of thousands of people in various stations of life. "War must cease if Christians will not fight" and "A Word to American Christians about War"[101] were typical of the titles devised by Burritt to head such statements. Now, too, Burritt, supported by the League, began to agitate for such reforms as Ocean Penny Postage ("if the League should effect this one object alone," wrote Burritt, "it would be well worth its existence to the world")[102] and assisted emigration to America, which he believed would be a step, though an indirect one, toward a more peaceful world.[103]

Most important of all, however, was the series of international peace congresses, which were held every year in one of the great European capitals from 1848 to 1851. Here, too, the initiative and driving force behind their organization was Burritt's, though he was backed by a much larger cross section of the peace movement than his own comparatively small League and the idea itself he had derived from the earlier international peace convention held in London in 1843. The composition of the congresses reflected all shades of opinion within the peace movement, pacifist and nonpacifist, the religiously inclined and the nonreligious peace workers, with only the American nonresistants staying away. The organization of the congresses represented a visible protest against the increasing militarism and reliance on physical power that were making themselves felt, especially in Europe. Even though its immediate effect on international relations was small, it symbolized a growing unity among the forces that were working for a peaceful world order.[104]

[101] *Ibid.*, p. 160.   [102] "Lecture of Elihu Burritt," p. 26.
[103] Curti, *American Peace Crusade*, pp. 157-64.
[104] See *ibid.*, chap. VIII; A.C.F. Beales, The History of Peace, chap. IV. It is interesting to note that, after the international peace convention of 1843, Beckwith had proposed to the London Peace Society in 1844 the formation of an international peace organization to link up peace workers of all shades of opinion, from radical nonresistants to the opponents solely of aggressive war who, he realized, predominated on the European continent. "We should spread our sails," he wrote in defense of this broad platform, "for every breeze that may waft us sooner into the port of universal and permanent peace" (*A Universal Peace Society*, p. 9). For the reaction of the American peace movement to the "Springtime of the Peoples" in Europe, see Curti, "The Peace Movement and the Mid-Century Revo-

In the few years of its active existence the League, then, had been very busy. As Curti writes: "The older peace societies had never begun to carry the word of peace so effectively and on such a scale into the heart of Europe. The enthusiasm and activity of the League was comparable to that of Methodism. . . . Whereas the older peace societies sought in general to convert dignified and influential clergymen and government officials, the League aimed" at reaching the people directly.[105] For the first time a peace organization, instead of being confined to a single country or even only one limited area of a country, had flourishing sections on both continents. This was an almost unique achievement in the nineteenth century.

Although it allowed (somewhat inconsistently, perhaps) a form of associate membership for those sympathizers definitely unwilling to commit themselves to the absolutist position, the League had, as we have seen, a fully pacifist pledge. Its signatories had taken a stand against all war. Burritt was particularly firm on this point. "Until you take this ground," he had written, "claim not to be an advocate of peace. O that weak and weakening reservation in favour of *defensive* wars! So long as it is made by the Christian, of Christendom, so long will that happy epoch be deferred, when nations shall learn war no more."[106]

To sign was not difficult; but to commit oneself wholeheartedly to what one may have lightly undertaken was another matter. That old pacifist stalwart, Joshua P. Blanchard, deplored the fact that many persons attracted to the League by vaguely humanitarian sentiments had signed up without fully comprehending "the extent of its obligations" or "the sacrifices which may be required to maintain their resolution." A thoroughgoing pacifist and himself a peace pledger, he still doubted the general value of such undertakings. In the case of temperance, the pledge would steel the weakening will at the moment of temptation through fear at the breaking of a vow once taken. "But in the case of abstinence from war and military service," he argued, "the restrictive resolution is in perfect coincidence with the disposition of the mind; for such service is an object of dread, and not of desire; and a man must have come to an abhorrence of war and all preparations

---

lutions," *Advocate of Peace through Justice*, vol. 90, no. 5 (May 1928), pp. 305-10. Burritt on the whole welcomed these liberal revolutions as a step toward a peaceful world, while of course deploring the violence involved in their outbreak and maintenance (see Tolis, "Burritt," pp. 211-14). See also Curti, *American Peace Crusade*, pp. 128, 129; Galpin, *Pioneering for Peace*, pp. 196, 197.
[105] Curti, *American Peace Crusade*, p. 163.
[106] Burritt, *Voice from the Forge*, p. 44.

for it, before he will consent to give his pledge against it; and that abhorrence affords him all the resolution of abstinence he requires, to which a pledge cannot add a particle of power, for he has no opposing propensity to overcome."[107] In other words, the mere signing of a pledge to become a conscientious objector in wartime or if required to serve was no guarantee that the pledger would in fact be ready to do so when the time came; on the other hand, those who took this stand really had no need for a previously taken pledge to support the promptings of their conscience. However, this argument, though largely true, neglects the genuine influence which a mass organization of such a character might have both in guiding public opinion toward pacifism and in acting as a pressure group to counter warlike measures on the part of a government.

A second weakness of the League as an international pacifist organization lay in the difficulty of implementing the full peace pledge position on the European continent. Burritt seems to have conceived of a kind of balance in League membership among the world's leading countries, by which means the pledge would pressure the respective governments in about equal measure toward policies of peace. In this way, no one country would be exposed, as critics objected, to more than their share of potential conscientious objection. As he explained: "If the League movement were confined to one country, it might be objected with some appearance of reason, that it would be impairing the relative strength of that country, to bind a large number of its citizens by a pledge of total abstinence from all war, without reference to the attitude or disposition of other nations." This, however, was the exact opposite of the League's intention. "We intend to present the pledge to the people of every nation, whose laws will permit them to sign it, and thus to detach an equal number of persons from any participation in the custom of war, if possible, in every country. This must meet the objection of those who depend upon a balance of brute force between different nations. . . . Surely such a Peace Establishment could not endanger the safety of the countries over which it might be extended."[108]

Calculations of this sort proved quite unrealistic, of course. If membership was about equally divided between Britain and America, there were probably few on the European continent, even among the small

[107] *Christian Examiner* (May 1848), quoted in J. P. Blanchard's Scrap-book, S.C.P.C. Archives. See his *Communications on Peace* (1848) for Blanchard's views on peace and war during this period and his belief in the efficacy of "the non-resistant, non-coercive principle" (p. 10) at the national as well as the personal level.

[108] "Lecture of Elihu Burritt," pp. 14, 15.

numbers there who signed the full peace pledge and would have been willing to carry it out in practice to the extent of personally resisting their country's conscription laws. As Blanchard aptly remarked, "unhappily in despotic countries, the people dare not venture on such an opposition,"[109] while under constitutional or even revolutionary governments the situation was little better. Burritt himself was careful always to point out that on principle the League would always work through open, legal channels. "We would not seek," he writes, "to distribute any publications in France, Italy or Germany, which would not receive the approbation of the severest censorship of the press existing in these countries; nor would we desire to hold any public or private meetings which their laws would not permit and protect."[110] In fact, however, if we put on one side the fairly favorable reaction among West European peace workers to his idea of international organization for peace, the response to Burritt's basic antimilitarist and anticonscriptionist ideas was so weak in these areas that no clash with the powers that be threatened.

Ultimately indeed, as an alternative to defense by arms, Burritt was a believer in the power of nonviolence. He devoted four essays[111] written in the early fifties to different aspects of a policy of "passive resistance": its power, its dignity, its patriotism, and its economy. For all their inadequacy, these short pieces remind one of the post-Gandhian attempts to grapple with the problems associated with the adoption of nonviolence on a national scale. For Burritt, of course, there could at that date have been very little documentation of previous successful uses of nonviolent techniques in resisting oppression and invasion. The few cases he cites are not very convincingly developed: their adoption in each instance had been due to expediency, to the weakness of the force at the disposal of one side, and not to a conscious rejection of violence as such. However, of passive resistance he writes: "Necessity does not make it a virtue in any case; but . . . its inherent virtue always makes it a necessity." It was faith in its efficacy and a conviction of its moral superiority, then, rather than study of its functioning in practice that provided Burritt's impulse here. He speaks of "the irresistible power of *passive resistance*, when opposed to oppression, either from home or from abroad, by any population or people, great or small . . . [as] a force, which any community or country might employ successfully in repelling and disarming despotism, whatever amount of bayonet power it might have at its command."

[109] *Christian Examiner* as above in n. 107.
[110] "Lecture of Elihu Burritt," pp. 11-14.
[111] *Thoughts and Things at Home and Abroad*, pp. 269-86.

And of a people resolutely adopting this nonviolent way he writes: "How is this people to be subjugated? It cannot be hung, put in prison, or transported, entire, or by sections. A dozen or two, in every considerable town, might be hung, hundreds imprisoned, and hundreds exiled. Thousands might be spoiled of their goods. But all this loss of life and treasure, and calamity of another species, would not equal the bloody casualties of a single battle." Burritt, of course, is being naively optimistic, unaware apparently of the many problems involved in any nonviolent alternative to war and internal oppression. But these essays do show that he, unlike many of his contemporaries in the peace movement, was at least aware of the need for an organization like the League to develop a positive philosophy of peace action in addition to pressing the negative case against war.

For all its shortcomings, the League of Universal Brotherhood had been a grand concept, a product of vision and insight on the part of its founder. Its practical achievement, though modest, was not inconsiderable, particularly in view of the powerful forces of tradition and apathy arrayed against it. It was truly international in design and, to some extent, in practice also. It appealed to a far greater range of social classes than the older peace societies did; its propaganda campaigns, too, covered a wider variety of interests and went down deeper into the populace. Moreover, however superficial had been the assimilation in practice of his peace radicalism among the majority of those who flocked to sign the pledge in all its austerity, Burritt did not flinch from placing his organization on the "higher ground" of opposition to all war and refusal to participate therein. And on this principle he maintained the League during the eleven years of its independent existence. His efforts, indeed, represent the crowning point of the endeavors of the moderate pacifists in America over nearly two decades to combine in an effective symbiosis radical pacifism in the international field and a positive attitude toward government in the domestic arena. While upholding the need for the exercise of civil authority, they at the same time believed that this might be achieved according to principles not inconsistent with their nonviolent beliefs. Within the peace movement itself, they were assailed both by left-wing nonresistants embattled against all government and by the more conservative elements who justified armed violence under some circumstances between the nations or in their internal affairs. Nonetheless, the moderate pacifist philosophy of peace with its roots in the Christian tradition, yet more and more reaching out to grasp the modern scientific case against war, remained a positive force in the movement for the future.

Chapter 7

The Ebbing of the Pacifist Impulse

The Compromise of 1850, not the firing at Fort Sumter, finally brought down the old-time pacifist movement in the United States. Not only did the decade which followed the Compromise witness a rising tide of militancy in the North (for, if the people as a whole were very far from wishing civil war, yet feeling in the North was slowly swinging over in favor of antislavery and against the South); but the conflict which we have observed already existing within the pacifist movement itself between the demands of the abolitionist cause and the promotion of peace and conciliation also became increasingly acute. This held for both wings of the movement: the radical Garrisonian nonresistants and the moderate pacifists within and outside the American Peace Society. Garrison and his followers might preach both disunion—the peaceful separation of North and South, which, somewhat illogically, they expected would bring nearer the emancipation of the slaves—and the renunciation of a federal constitution that upheld slavery along with war and police action; Burritt, together with many Quakers, might patronize the free labor movement and advocate schemes of compensated emancipation; increasing numbers were coming to favor political action and the ballot box as the most promising path toward the desired goal. But in one way or another the apostles of nonviolence became caught up in the dynamic of the sectional struggle, which was eventually to transform itself into an irrepressible conflict between North and South and find solution on the battlefield. In their reactions to the Fugitive Slave Act of 1850, the Kansas-Nebraska Act of 1854, and John Brown's famous raid on Virginia of 1859 which ended at Harpers Ferry, we can watch the working of the pacifist dilemma, the agonizing choice which presented itself to men who prized both liberty and peace at a time when the demands of the two appeared to conflict.

We have seen, however, that the strength of pacifism had already begun to decline before mid-century and that the causes of this decline lay in certain weaknesses inherent in the movement itself. The New England Non-Resistance Society, after vegetating for half a decade, had virtually ceased to function by 1850. The American Peace Society had before this date already purged itself officially of pacifist absolutism, if not entirely of its absolute pacifist members.[1] Burritt's League of Universal Brotherhood was to wither rapidly in the course of the early fifties and to disappear altogether in 1857. Thus, by the second half of this decade (if we exclude, of course, the peace sects and such sectarian communities as Adin Ballou's Hopedale), pacifism was without organizational expression. Few new recruits were gathered in now for the cause. What we are left with is a handful of individuals, formerly active in peace organizations and now increasingly absorbed in one or other branches of the abolition movement. Aside from Burritt's League, with which we have already dealt, the history of the nonsectarian variety of pacifism in the 1850's is, therefore, fragmentary. We can, however, observe the interaction and conflict between loyalty to peace and devotion to abolition as it revealed itself in the words and actions of a number of leading individual pacifists.

The dilemma was most acute among the Garrisonian nonresistants. Their protest against all forms of violence had been an extremely emotional one, expressed in particularly dramatic form. For them, international war and civil government and Negro slavery had all three been merely different facets of one underlying evil. An army, a prison, and a slave plantation were alike crimes against God and man—crimes against God just because of their inhumanity. No wonder, then, that the passing of the Fugitive Slave Act, a measure which attempted to reinforce the recovery of runaway slaves by their former masters, in particular by making it the responsibility of the federal government, aroused the anger and dismay of the Garrisonian pacifists and filled them with as much a feeling of shame as it did the nonpacifist abolitionists. They were equally determined that this man-made law, which, they believed, directly contravened the higher law, must be resisted. That this should be done without violence was also their wish. But where was one to draw the line when it became a question of common action with the vast majority of the abolitionist faith, who entertained no such scruples concerning the use of violence, at least where it was likely to be immediately effective? Even among Garrison's followers, the nonpolitical wing of the abolitionist movement grouped in the American Anti-Slavery Society, and its New England

[1] Curti writes (*American Peace Crusade*, p. 228): "Its meetings were not always dull gatherings of up-in-the-air idealists who merely talked vague and agreeable platitudes. Who could ask for a livelier meeting than the annual one of 1851, when the radicals packed the house and tried by strategy to gain their points; when the old guard led by the faithful Beckwith tried to outwit them by an unannounced meeting; and when finally such pandemonium reigned that the gathering had to be dispersed? The secession of the nonresistance group and its activities show how high the feeling ran."

affiliate, which he still dominated, absolute pacifists were probably by now a small minority. The dilemma presented by this situation led, in effect, to a far-reaching revision in at least the tactics of New England nonresistance, if not in the theory itself.

At the end of October 1850 an English peace worker wrote one of the Weston sisters: "We are much amused at the very qualified advocacy of ultra peace principles of the non-resistant abolitionists at this political juncture. Their argument is certainly most sound and unanswerable, that all should now use whatever weapons they would themselves use in behalf of the fugitive, but the doctrine from the lips of Mr. Garrison, H. C. Wright, S. S. Foster seems very strange."[2] We may agree about the strangeness of the picture, but the position of Garrison and his friends was not without its own compelling logic, as, indeed, the above citation recognizes: in essence, it was but the application of principles long held and enunciated.

As far back even as 1831, during the *Liberator*'s first year, Garrison had maintained that those who sanctioned the use of arms against despotism and domestic oppression, all who approved of its use in the American Revolution or in the struggles of Greeks or Poles or Latin Americans for their independence, must approve too—if they were not to be guilty of inconsistency—of armed violence when directed by the Negro slaves of the American South against their white masters.[3] One of Garrison's biographers has suggested that his adoption of nonresistance stemmed in part from a desire to avoid approval of slave revolts.[4] This seems improbable, especially since his pacifism predated his interest in antislavery. Nonresistance and abolition, as we have seen, were both, with Garrison, the outcome of the humanitarian urge, the great reform impulse. Be true to your concept of the right, he told his fellow citizens, employ armed force to help the slave where necessary if you would use it in defense of yourself and what you hold dear. It is better, of course, to use nonviolent means, to eschew the way of force to promote righteousness, if such are your convictions. (Ironically, Garrison considered "Uncle Tom" as a practical exemplar of nonresistance.)[5] But do not apply a double standard to your own and the slave's interests, preaching nonviolence to the Negro where you would advocate armed resistance or assistance to the white man in a similar situation.

[2] M. A. Estlin to Caroline Weston, 30 Oct. 1850, Weston Papers, B.P.L., MS A.9.2., vol. 25, no. 35 A.
[3] *Liberator*, 9 July 1831.
[4] Ralph Korngold, *Two Friends of Man*, p. 141.
[5] Walter M. Merrill, *Against Wind and Tide*, p. 266.

Garrison's position here is strikingly similar to that of Gandhi in the twentieth century, especially to the latter's actions during the First World War. In both cases, it was misunderstood by enemies and friends alike. Essentially, it was not a compromise on principle, a concession to the way of force in human affairs, and certainly not a renunciation of a nonviolent philosophy. But it was a path fraught with difficulties when followed in practice, needing a delicate sense of the appropriate in word and action. And it must be admitted that Garrison and his nonresistant disciples were for the most part much less successful than Gandhi later in finding and maintaining a balance between outright approval of violence or incitement to violence (if perhaps with a conscience clause for oneself), on the one hand, and a doctrinaire endeavor to impose nonviolent methods in a setting where they were not acceptable, on the other.

The 1850's, especially the early part of the decade, witnessed a series of attempts at carrying out the Fugitive Slave Law. However, the return of fugitive slaves encountered throughout the North the opposition, not only of convinced abolitionists, but of many who had not before given much thought perhaps to the problem of slavery yet now resented the new law as a threat to civil liberty and a manifestation of hostility to Northern interests on the part of the Southern section. The law did much to awaken sympathy among the general population in the North for the hitherto unpopular abolitionists and was an important step in widening the breach between the sections, which eventually led to war.

Resistance to the law was rapidly organized by the abolitionists, nonpolitical Garrisonians being active in this work along with their opponents of the political wing of the movement. Vigilance committees sprang up in many places to prevent the capture and extradition of fugitives, to organize their rescue or escape where their arrest could not be prevented, and also to bring strong and even rough pressure on slaveholders and their agents seeking to recover fugitives to desist from the attempt and return back south. The abolitionists were, of course, leaders in proclaiming the need, indeed the duty, of resistance to an unjust law and obedience to the "higher law" which it contravened, although many outside the movement came more and more to sympathize and even cooperate with them in preventing the return of fugitives to their masters. Most abolitionists, including many close to Garrison himself, like his friend Wendell Phillips, were quite willing —many, indeed, were eager—to use arms in defense of the fugitive, if occasion demanded, and in resistance to what they deemed tyranny and injustice.

Where, then, did the nonresistant abolitionists stand in this situation? Let us take as our first example the case of the mild and almost saintlike Samuel J. May, whom we have met already as a close colleague of Garrison in the work of the New England Non-Resistance Society. True, May had parted company with Garrison on the issue of exercising the franchise, and his position by this time was much closer to the political abolitionists than it had been a decade earlier. Nevertheless, he remained a convinced nonresistant and was also, like Garrison, a strong disunionist, and the two men continued to be close friends. May was now Unitarian minister at Syracuse in upstate New York and a man of some influence in his local community. How did he react to the passing of the Fugitive Slave Act?

Resistance to "this diabolical law" was what he called for in the situation. In a sermon preached soon after the bill had become law, he told his congregation: "Every man and women among you is bound, as I am, to do for the protection or rescue of a fugitive from slavery what, in your hearts before God, you believe it would be right for you to do in behalf of your own life or liberty, or that of a member of your family. If you are fully persuaded that it would be right for you to maim or kill the kidnapper who had laid hands upon your wife, son, or daughter, or should be attempting to drag yourself away to be enslaved, I see not how you can excuse yourself, from helping, by the same degree of violence, to rescue the fugitive slave from the like outrage. . . ." May urged that all men of good will were "under the highest obligation to destroy this law," to prevent its execution under any circumstances. "If you know of no better way to do this than by force and arms, then are you bound to use force and arms to prevent a fellow-being from being enslaved." Their cause was just: "there cannot be, a more righteous cause for revolution than the demands made upon us by this law." Although, he went on, he had long been known as "a preacher of the doctrine of non-resistance" as an essential tenet of Christianity, "I shall go to the rescue of anyone I may hear is in danger, not intending to harm the cruel men who may be attempting to kidnap him. I shall take no weapon of violence along with me, not even the cane that I usually wear. I shall go, praying that I may say and do what will smite the hearts rather than the bodies of the impious claimants of property in human beings, pierce their consciences rather than their flesh." And he concluded his address with an impassioned appeal to action: "Fellow-citizens, fellow-men, fellow-Christians! the hour is come! A stand must be taken against the ruthless oppressors of our country. Resistants and non-resistants have now a work to do that may task to the utmost the energies of their souls."[6]

Such sentiments voiced in another climate of opinion than that of the North in the early 1850's might have brought the speaker into serious trouble with the government, whose laws he had urged be disobeyed. In fact, it was to prove extremely difficult, even hazardous, for the federal authorities to enforce the law or to bring to book those who defied it in action as well as in speech or on paper.

May's most recent biographer rightly remarks on the "modification" in May's views on nonresistance which the passage of the Fugitive Slave Law had brought about. "He had altered his concept of nonresistance in respect to the conduct of others. At Boston, Brooklyn, South Scituate, Lexington and even during the early years at Syracuse, he had faithfully taught that man under no circumstances had the moral right to use arms to protect life or property."[7] Now he seemed to falter. While reserving his own nonresistant position, he positively urged nonpacifists, "resistants" as he calls them, to take up an aggressive stand in face of the threat to liberty and human values which he saw in the new law. Only the thinnest of dividing lines separated him from fully sanctioning the employment of armed force, such as most of his abolitionist friends wanted to see used in defense of runaway slaves.

In the following year, 1851, the test came. A fugitive, Jerry McHenry, was actually arrested in Syracuse. The situation in the town was tense. Now May was faced with the decision of either holding aloof from any active attempt to save the unhappy man from return to slavery or cooperating with other antislavery people in forcible resistance to the enforcement of the law. The dilemma was a real one. His friend, Gerrit Smith, was particularly pressing; along with May himself, Smith was probably most responsible for organizing the famous "Jerry Rescue," which succeeded in delivering the man out of the hands of the law and smuggling him eventually to freedom over the Canadian border.[8] The rescue force was able to capture the police station and overpower the officers. In planning the sortie, May had insisted that no intentional injuries should be done to the policemen. "If any one is to be hurt in this fray," he said, "I hope it may be one of our own party."[9] Undoubtedly, his influence prevented the use of firearms in the affair and reduced the incidence of physical violence to

[6] S. J. May, *Some Recollections of Our Antislavery Conflict*, pp. 361, 362.
[7] W. Freeman Gilpin, "God's Chore Boy," chap. X.
[8] See R. V. Harlow, *Gerrit Smith*, pp. 297-304.
[9] *Memoir of Samuel Joseph May*, p. 220.

a minimum. The action may have been consistent with maintaining a pacifist stand at large. But it was scarcely an act of nonresistance: "When I saw poor Jerry in the hands of the official kidnappers," May confessed to Garrison, "I could not preach non-resistance very earnestly to the crowd who were clamoring for his release."[10] All this might well seem strange in a man who still continued to consider himself a nonresistant, and May's attempts at reconciling the discrepancies between his ideas and his actions are not quite convincing. Wrote May to Garrison at this time: "I have seen that it was necessary to bring the people into direct conflict with the Government—that the Government may be made to understand that it has transcended its limits—and must recede."[11] But it was not so much the act of defying authority, as the method of defiance, that seemed out of place now in May.[12]

The prosecution of May, Smith, and their accomplices for their attack on the agents of government was not in the end proceeded with, despite a full and public avowal of responsibility on the part of the accused. Similar leniency—imposed, it is true, by the state of public opinion and the weakness of the law-enforcing machinery—was shown in other cases where the existing law was set at nought by the abolitionists in obedience to what they considered the higher law of helping the fugitive slave. Eastern Massachusetts, in particular the Boston area, was the center of such civil disobedience. And this, too, was where Garrisonian nonresistance had been strongest, where its adherents were still to be found scattered among the ranks of the abolition movement. Not unexpectedly, Garrison, the leader of nonresistance and still perhaps the most formidable, if no longer the most influential, leader of nonpolitical abolitionism, did not attempt to hold back from the use of violence those who had no scruples against it. He went on stressing that the Negro slave had as much right to defend life, liberty, and property by force of arms as any other man. Implicitly, as well as explicitly, he declared the obligation of those who had not arrived at the nonviolent way for themselves to defend the rights of the slave by the best means they could.[13] Nevertheless, Garrison does not seem to have been in the confidence of those among his friends

[10] John L. Thomas, *The Liberator*, p. 381.
[11] Quoted in Harlow, *Gerrit Smith*, p. 299.
[12] The same might be said, for example, of the equally courageous participation of May's brother-in-law, the transcendentalist philosopher and quondam nonresistant, Bronson Alcott, in the Anthony Burns rescue in Boston in 1854. "To my astonishment," wrote a friend (Frederick L.H. Willis, *Alcott Memoirs*, pp. 72-76), "I saw the serene, gentle, non-resistant Alcott transformed into a warlike belligerent."
[13] See Korngold, *Two Friends of Man*, pp. 221, 224-25.

and colleagues who now organized a series of armed rescues and intimidations of prospective "kidnappers," successful and unsuccessful, over the following years. He could not very well have unreservedly approved their policies, and his presence at their counsels might have been an embarrassment.

"It was . . . not expected," wrote one of the nonresistants many years later, "that action of this sort would be taken by those abolitionists who were also nonresistants." He goes on to relate, however, how at an informal gathering of pacifists the question of the propriety of accepting an invitation to take part in such a rescue came up. Could there be some sort of aid and assistance that a believer in nonviolence could give on such an occasion (Samuel May, we have seen, believed that there was) without completely abjuring his belief in nonresistance? "A significant silence—a silence which did not imply consent—was broken by Stephen S. Foster, who said: 'I am ready to go.' 'But,' someone remonstrated, 'in expeditions of this sort active conflict is expected and is always probable, and the opponents will be armed men.' 'I have arms,' said Foster, holding them out. And the impression he made was that his share of the work in hand would be no less effective than that of any associate who put his trust in deadly weapons." Nonetheless, the writer goes on, his fellow nonresistants, who may well have doubted such claims, at any rate "agreed in thinking Foster's attitude one of doubtful propriety."[14]

The passing by Congress of the Kansas-Nebraska Act in 1854 presented no less striking, if not so direct, a challenge to American pacifists than the Fugitive Slave Act had done. The probable extension of slavery to these vast territories, which the Act had made possible, was viewed, of course, with the gravest alarm, not only by the whole abolitionist movement but by wide sections of the Northern population who feared an impending dominance of the Southern section within the Union. In addition, land speculators and the expanding railroad interests were anxious to win the area for Northern economic expansion. A struggle, therefore, ensued to forestall the South by settling the territories with Northerners wedded to a policy of free soil in such overwhelming numbers as to preclude the possibility, when the time came for granting these territories statehood, of their entering the Union as slave states. Thereby, too, they would become part of the Northern economy and political system. Kansas, the southernmost of the two territories, became the main focus of a bloody struggle, an endemic civil war between "free soilers" from the North and supporters of the

---

[14] C. K. Whipple, "An Armed Non-Resistant," in the *Boston Commonwealth*, 7 Nov. 1885.

slave interests coming in from the South. The former were reinforced morally and with money and arms from back east; and in the campaign to lend them support the abolitionists took the lead. Events in "bleeding Kansas" in the second half of the fifties became an important link in the chain leading up finally to civil war between North and South.

Some members of the peace movement, faced with the alternative (as they saw it) of peace and the extension of slavery or the maintenance of freedom by armed force, chose the latter. Among them was Gerrit Smith, who, we have seen, had been extremely sympathetic to the idea of nonresistance some fifteen years earlier (though he had never, it is true, been won over completely) and who continued active in the moderate wing of the peace movement, figuring for instance, as vice-president of the American branch of Burritt's League of Universal Brotherhood. Smith, now a member of Congress, as late as the summer of 1855 could write in answer to a request for money to buy muskets for a boy's brigade in Washington: "I am so afraid of war and patriotism, that I dare not help buy one musket—not even a boy's little musket." But a brief six months later we find him donating $250 to the New England Emigrant Aid Society, on the express understanding that it would be used to buy rifles for the free-soil settlers that the Society was helping to send out to Kansas. "Much as I abhor war," wrote Smith on this occasion, "I nevertheless believe, that there are instances in which the shedding of blood is unavoidable." He was soon to become one of the most active sponsors of the Kansas aid movement.[15]

Strangely enough, at least at first sight, at the very time he was vigorously promoting armed action on the Kansas borderland and when his faith in a peaceful solution of the slavery question was fast ebbing away, Smith delivered before the American Peace Society an eloquent plea for international pacifism and unilateral disarmament. The thesis of his address at the Society's thirteenth anniversary meeting in May 1858 was "that war can be avoided always and everywhere, and that no nation, known to refuse to engage in it, need fear it. She need not fear it at the hands of a heathen nation, nor at the hands of either a truly Christian nation or nominally Christian nation." "Such a refusal" to fight, he went on, "must be open and unambiguous. Fully and un-

---

[15] Harlow, *Gerrit Smith*, p. 345. See chap. XV: "Gerrit Smith and the Kansas Aid Movement." Cf. the reaction of the nonresistant enthusiast of the late 1830's, Mrs. Angela Weld (*née* Grimké): "We are compelled to choose between two evils, and all that we can do is to take the *least*, and baptize liberty in blood, if it must be so" (quoted in John Demos, "The Antislavery Movement and the Problem of Violent 'Means,'" *NEQ*, XXXVII, no. 4 [Dec. 1964], 522, from the *Liberator*, 7 July 1854, p. 106).

equivocally must she express her confidence that war will not be made upon her. To this end she must disband her armies, and dismantle her forts and vessels of war. Thus will she give ample proof of her trust in the power of her professed principles to protect her, as shall lead other nations to study and respect the principles which have accomplished in her effects so great and novel." A disarmed nation, therefore, "an unresisting people" disarmed not from weakness but from a principled objection to war, would not suffer from thus exposing itself to attack; rather would the other civilized, Christian nations combine (by armed intervention if necessary, Smith hints) to prevent its being molested by some predatory "heathen" invader, and sooner or later they would disarm themselves. It was useless, he told his listeners, to preach peace and prepare for war by piling up armaments; it was, in fact, as effectual "as would be a temperance lecturer who should persist in carrying a bottle in his pocket for the occasional gratification of his yet unconquered appetite."

Smith might be considered obtuse or hypocritical in uttering these words when he himself was busy at this time in arming the Kansan borderers in a situation which verged on war. But this judgment would be unjust, for he himself clarifies his position in later sections of his address.[16] He was not a nonresistant, he said. "I am slow to speak against non-resistance; for in the first place I love the pure-minded men and women who have embraced the doctrine; and in the second place I have often been deeply impressed by the ingenious and strong arguments made in its favor." But, after reflection, he had come to the conclusion that it was neither enjoined by scripture (Christ, it is true, practised it during his earthly ministry, but rather from "expediency" than as a matter of absolute principle for either himself or his followers) nor consistent with the welfare of society. Armed force was essential for effective police action, though it should, of course, be used with as much restraint as possible. Nonresistance, however, was not simply an impractical doctrine; it was, he believed, positively "pernicious." "It places on the same level the taking of life in the unnecessary and wicked strife of war, and the taking of it in the necessary and righteous work of breaking up a nest of pirates"; in this way, many who can-

[16] His plea for unilateral disarmament on the international level seems to have given rise to some misunderstanding as to his real position in regard to absolute pacifism. We find him, for instance, in 1861, after civil war had broken out in his own country, writing in reference to his proposals of 1858 that his speech, it is true, "argues that the other nations would not suffer a nation to make war upon an unresisting nation. But it does not argue that they would interpose to save a nation which refused to arm herself against traitors in her own bosom" (*Sermons and Speeches*, pp. 193, 194).

not conscientiously assent to the rejection of all force in society will feel —unnecessarily, Smith thought—that they must also reject a total repudiation of international war. In fact, after disarming unilaterally, a government would still need to keep an armed police force (let it be recruited, though, from the best, not the worst, elements in society) to maintain law and order throughout the country. (He spoke, too, of the need to suppress frontier violence, to back "the irregular but righteous government" set up on Kansas territory with arms, to deliver the slave "at whatever harm to the slaveholder," and to restrain the slaveowners "from enslaving their fellow men by whatever terrors it is necessary to hold over them.") He believed, indeed, that no nation would be persuaded to disarm unless it were at the same time permitted to maintain an armed police force within the country. "Such a police would, it is true, be a brute force; but it would be a moral force also."[17]

Smith's address surprises us, not by the content of either of the two separate arguments against external war and in favor of armed force to maintain internal order, which are presented with considerable cogency in each case, but by the juxtaposition of his advocacy of an "unresisting" nation in the international sphere alongside the militancy of his stand in the intersectional conflict within the nation. The lawabiding American Peace Society secretary, George C. Beckwith, had not approved of Smith's references to dispatching arms to Kansas and the intervention of private individuals to defend the slave where the state was remiss; yet he had had the speech printed and distributed in both a full and a condensed version in several hundred thousand copies.[18] More forcibly than any earlier utterance perhaps, Smith's address foreshadowed the dilemma that was soon to face the old peace organization: what if the use of armed force in internal law enforcement, of which the Society did not disapprove, should eventually spill over into full-fledged war, not, it is true, of nation against nation but of sectional government against sectional government—still, war which the Society had seemed officially and explicitly to repudiate?

Only slightly less militant than Gerrit Smith's stance was the attitude of some Garrisonian nonresistants, who not so very long ago had been among the most ardent proponents of nonviolence. "Even our devoted indomitable reformers, S. S. Foster and H. C. Wright," Ballou had

---

[17] Gerrit Smith, *Peace better than War*, pp. 5-10, 12-15, 18-21. Cf. his "Speech on War, Jan. 18, 1854" in *Speeches of Gerrit Smith in Congress*, pp. 45-67, where he voiced very similar ideas on peace and war without, however, directly broaching the question of unilateral disarmament.

[18] Smith, *Peace better than War*, p. 31. See also Harlow, *Gerrit Smith*, p. 401; Curti, *American Peace Crusade*, p. 221.

written in 1850, "though affirming that they themselves are Non-Resistants, declare it to be the duty of such as hold it right to fight and kill their fellow-men ... to arm and fight to the death for the poor slave."[19] Now, at the Worcester conventions in the middle of the decade, which were organized by the almost defunct New England Non-Resistance Society,[20] it was Foster ("an unequalled intellectual gladiator on any platform," as the Rev. Thomas W. Higginson, then Unitarian minister in Worcester, described him) who expressed with considerable force the perplexed views of these nonresistants hovering uneasily on the brink of commitment to the use of violence in the cause of righteousness.[21]

Foster no longer based his pacifism on the Christian imperative or a belief in the inviolability of human life, so he told his audience. "He ... advocated it because it is useful ... and renders life, liberty and property safe." It was not, then, on the authority of any man, however wise—indeed, "he did not think Christ perfect, and left at liberty to criticize him"—that he still believed in practising nonviolence in his own life. "It is no violation of principle, or of justice," he went on (in the words of the convention report), "to take life; but it is not expedient for him to do so. Nor is it expedient for all others to rely on non-resistance. Brutes cannot defend themselves by moral means; no more can brutish or uncultivated men." Should a kidnapper come to Worcester searching for some fugitive slave, "he [Foster] would call all the people to the rescue; and he would tell them to bring with them such weapons as they believe in using, and give the slave such protection as they would give to their own families." "The liberty of the slave," in his view, was far more valuable than "the life of the kidnapper." "He would rather a hundred lives should be sacrificed, than that one fugitive should be carried back to bondage." If Foster still felt impelled to refuse to use violence against a fellow man to defend his own life and thus to point to a higher road to the welfare of

---

[19] *Practical Christian*, 21 Dec. 1850.
[20] See *ibid.*, 7 April 1855; 21 April 1855; and 13 Dec. 1856. Citations from speeches at these conventions given below are taken from these numbers.
[21] Back in the mid-forties, at the time of the Samuel Hoar case, the ebullient Foster was already displaying his militant spirit. According to Anne W. Weston (letter of 23 Jan. 1845, Weston Papers, B.P.L., MS A.9.2., vol. 21, no. 7), Foster at a meeting "introduced a resolution saying it was the duty of Mass. to apply to the General Gov. for a military force to sustain our agent in the port of Charleston and if that be refused instruct the senators and representatives to come home. Dr. [Walter] Channing, Mr. May, and others opposed this on the ground of Non-Resistance." Foster, however, supported by the nonpacifist Wendell Phillips "sustained it on the ground of the propriety of holding up Mass. to her duty, to her own standard which was one of violence."

mankind, expediency, on the other hand, could equally cause a man to take up the sword. As Foster reached the final peroration of his speech at the 1855 convention, telling his audience that "he rejoiced in the death of the kidnapper, and prayed he might never go away from Worcester with his victim," he was greeted by a wave of applause.

Foster was always to be "ultra beyond ultra" (and his substitution of a broadly humanitarian and rationalist ethos as grounds for his pacifism in place of strictly religious ones was probably not shared by most nonresistants), yet his feelings were not far removed from those of Garrison or Wright during these years. Clearly, the tablets of the Mosaic law had come to replace the Sermon on the Mount in the hearts of many of the more ardent nonresistants.

As a final pendant to the story of the New England Non-Resistance Society, which may serve as a melancholy epitaph to the buried hopes and dreams of earlier years, we may cite here the letter which Charles Stearns wrote from Lawrence, Kansas, from the very center of that strife-torn territory, early in December 1855. It was published in the *Anti-Slavery Standard*. We last took leave of Stearns some fifteen years before as he sat disconsolately in a prison cell in the Hartford County jail, with the prospect of an indefinite period of incarceration for his refusal of service in the state militia before him. His fears were not, in fact, realized, and he soon returned to an active life of antislavery activities and reform journalism. His abolitionist fervor ultimately began to outpace his nonresistant enthusiasm. And now we find him addressing the editors of the *Standard* as follows:

> When I came to Kansas, little did I dream of ever becoming a soldier, but stern fate has driven me into the ranks of the Non-Resistant *corps de reserve*, who are to fight at the last extremity. Not until the war had existed for ten days did I arm myself, and then only in consequence of becoming convinced that we had not human beings to contend with. I always believed it was right to kill a tiger, and our invaders are nothing but tigers. Christ says, "If a *man* smite thee on the one cheek, turn to him the other also." These Missourians are not men. I have always considered that, bad as they were, they had in infinitesimal spark of divinity in them; but . . . our invaders were wild beasts. . . . When I live with men made in God's image, I will never shoot them; but these pro-slavery Missourians are demons from the bottomless pit, and may be shot with impunity.

Not men, but beasts. Ballou, who reprinted the letter, devoted an indignant editorial to it under the title "Diabolical Non-Resistance." After pointing out that Stearns only a decade or so earlier had argued against Ballou's advocacy of the use of uninjurious force against drunkards or the insane as incompatible with thorough nonresistance, the latter inquired why Stearns had gone out to Kansas. "That is not the place for Non-Resistants any more than New Orleans or Charleston is for Abolitionists."[22]

At the 1856 convention Abby Foster had said: "Kansas was the great argument against us." The dilemma was a reality for all nonresistants, who were both radical pacifists and at the same time radical antislavery men. Stephen Foster and Charles Stearns, however, represented extreme reactions.[23] Their views were not shared, at least as yet, by most of their fellow nonresistants. In 1856, in the columns of the *Liberator*, Garrison had roundly condemned the action of such prominent clergymen as the Unitarian Theodore Parker and the Presbyterian Henry Ward Beecher in sending "Sharp's rifles" out to the Kansas settlers. He could find nothing in Christ's life or teaching which could justify this action.[24] An article he wrote for his paper a couple of years later gives a good presentation of his position in face of the rising tide of reliance on violence, which was encompassing the whole antislavery movement. In it he told his readers: "Do not get impatient; do not become exasperated; ... do not make yourselves familiar with the idea that blood must flow. Perhaps blood will flow—God knows, I do not; but it shall not flow through any counsel of mine." "The Southern slaveholder," he went on, "is a man, sacred before me. He is a man, not to be harmed by my hand nor with my consent.... He is a sinner before God—a great sinner; yet, while I will not cease reprobating his horrible injustice, I will let him see that in my heart there is no desire to do him harm."[25]

So far, so good. But was there not some disingenuousness in the attitude of Garrison, May, and the other radical nonresistants during

[22] Letter of 9 Dec. 1855, reprinted in the *Practical Christian*, 26 Jan. 1856. See also the *Liberator*, 13 March 1863.

[23] Equally extreme was the attitude a few years later of the former nonresistant "come-outer" Parker Pillsbury, who, according to the *Liberator*, 4 Feb. 1859, p. 19 (quoted in Demos, "The Antislavery Movement and the Problem of Violent 'Means,'" p. 523), declared that, as a result of the mounting conflict in the country over slavery, he now "longed to see the time when Boston should run with blood from Beacon Hill to the foot of Broad Street."

[24] W.L.G.: *Story of His life told by His Children*, III, 437, 438. How far, one might ask, was the action of an S. J. May, who raised funds to settle immigrants from the North in Kansas, knowing presumably that these men went all ready and armed for the struggle, consistent with the Garrisonian concept of nonresistance?

[25] Quoted in *ibid.*, III, 473, 474.

this period? It was logical, indeed highly commendable, that they should urge on each loyalty to their highest principles: the "resistants" to seek justice in their fashion and the nonresistants to abide by their belief in a nonviolent way. It showed a Christian spirit when Garrison, as we have seen, called on them to see in a slaveowner a man with a personality as sacred in God's eyes as that of his slave. (Did Garrison recall perhaps that one of the founding fathers of radical nonresistance had been a South Carolina slaveowner?)[26] But when, in season and out, he and his fellow abolition pacifists preached no compromise, no concessions, no union with slaveholders, it is difficult—even after taking into consideration both the evils of slavery and the intransigence of the South, and for all the Garrisonians' theoretical advocacy of nonresistance—to acquit them altogether of responsibility for bringing war a shade nearer. Said Samuel May: "Oppressors have no right to be what they are."[27] Men of this way of thought could show little elasticity in a concrete situation; they were doctrinaires, and for this reason alone they were scarcely able to exercise a ministry of reconciliation in a situation of desperate conflict.

At the beginning of 1857, Garrison had met for the first and only time the man who, more than any other, symbolized the fanatical spirit of the antislavery struggle in the Kansas borderland. Among other topics Garrison discussed that of nonresistance with John Brown. The debate was fruitless. The two men found no common ground, with Brown quoting copiously from the Old Testament and Garrison drawing upon the New in defense of his pacifism.[28] Two years later, in October 1859, Brown led the famous raid on Harpers Ferry which ended in his capture and execution. The character and methods of Brown and those of the Garrisonian nonresistants appeared to be diametrically opposed to each other: Old Testament ruthlessness—one may almost say—over against the gospel doctrine of love in its extremist interpretation. Garrison and his nonresistant group were not told of the plans which Brown and his abolitionist sympathizers had been

---

[26] It is, of course, not at all unlikely that Thomas S. Grimké would before long have followed his two sisters into the antislavery movement, if death had not intervened. On 9 Feb. 1833 we find him writing to another sister: "With regard to . . . slavery, I should have no difficulty on the score of interest, in parting with all I own. I keep them because I have them. I do not free them, because the law will not let me, and I am not disposed to do indirectly, and by secret trusts and concealment, what I cannot do openly" (quoted in *Letters of Theodore Dwight Weld, Angelina Grimké Weld and Sarah Grimké*, II, 518). Nevertheless, their beloved brother's attitude was a source of some embarrassment afterward to his two abolitionist sisters.

[27] May, *Liberty or Slavery, the Only Question* (1856), p. 25.

[28] W.L.G., III, 487, 488.

concocting, and the raid came as a surprise to them.[29] How, in fact, did New England nonresistance react?

We cannot expect its followers to have been properly informed concerning the brutal murders Brown had carried out a few years earlier at Pottawatomie. They accepted without question the view that pictured him as a spotless and selfless fighter for liberty, and commendably, like many other Northerners who in 1859 did not necessarily approve of the adventure, they at least honored his courage and spirit of initiative. They approved of the goal for which he was sacrificing his life, and they condemned his opponents and captors for the real responsibility for blood shed. All this, within the framework of the group's thinking, is understandable. Mrs. Lydia Child, for instance, was ready to go immediately to nurse old Brown in his Virginia prison; her offer, of course, was ignored by Governor Wise. "Believing in peace principles," she wrote to Brown, "I cannot sympathize with the method you chose to advance the cause of freedom. But I honor your generous intentions—I admire your courage, moral and physical. I reverence you for the humanity which tempered your zeal. I sympathize with you in your cruel bereavement, your sufferings, and your wrongs. In brief, I love you and I bless you."[30] This statement, if somewhat highflown, has a genuine ring.

It is not easy, however, to acquit at least some of the Garrisonian nonresistants of inconsistency when we consider their reactions to the methods chosen by Brown and his party. If we compare, for instance, their present attitude in discussing the Harpers Ferry raid with that adopted by them some twenty-two years earlier in commenting on Lovejoy's resort to arms, we notice a significant change. It is not so much the outward content of their message: there is the same formal condemnation of violence. But the tone is different; the protest is so much weaker; the qualified approval of a solution by the sword (deplored by Garrison barely a year before) is so much more emphatic.

Listen to Garrison (contrary to general opinion, probably the most consistent of the nonresistant group in his pacifism) speaking at the protest meeting organized in Boston by the American Anti-Slavery Society on 2 December 1859, the day on which Brown was to be hanged. In the course of his address at this gathering, Garrison was to call, "as a non-resistant," for a revival of the spirit of Bunker Hill, Lexington, and Concord to oppose submission to the slave power.

[29] For Gerrit Smith's complicity in Brown's schemes, see Harlow, *Gerrit Smith*, chap. XVII.
[30] *Correspondence between Lydia Maria Child and Gov. Wise and Mrs. Mason, of Virginia*, p. 14.

Earlier in his speech he had clarified his position as a pacifist in the following words, which deserve to be quoted in full:

> I am a non-resistant—a believer in the inviolability of human life, under all circumstances; I, therefore, in the name of God, disarm John Brown, and every slave at the South. But I do not stop there; if I did, I should be a monster. I also disarm, in the name of God, every slaveholder and tyrant in the world. . . . How many agree with me in regard to the doctrine of the inviolability of human life? (A single voice—"I.") There is *one*! Well, then, you who are otherwise, are not the men to point the finger at John Brown and cry "traitor" —judging you by your own standard. Nevertheless, I am a non-resistant, and I not only desire, but have labored unremittingly to effect, the peaceful abolition of slavery . . . yet, as a peace man—an "ultra" peace man—I am prepared to say: "Success to every slave insurrection at the South, and in every slave country." I do not see how I compromise or stain my peace profession in making that declaration. Whenever there is a contest between the oppressed and the oppressor . . . God knows that my heart must be with the oppressed, and always against the oppressor . . . I thank God when men who believe in the right and duty of wielding carnal weapons are so far advanced that they will take those weapons out of the scale of despotism, and throw them into the scale of freedom. It is an indication of progress, and a positive moral growth; it is one way to get up to the sublime platform of non-resistance; and it is God's method of dealing retribution upon the head of the tyrant.[31]

Even more passionate were the exhortations to civil war and insurrection issuing from the pen of another leading nonresistant, Henry C. Wright, whom we have seen as the New England Non-Resistance Society's leading propagandist in the forties and one of those chiefly responsible for elaborating its intellectual platform. Again, we have with Wright the same theoretical adherence to pacifism ("as to *armed* or *military* resistance to slaveholders, or to ANY evil-doers, my soul has ever resisted it, and ever must, as inexpedient, unjust and inhuman"),[32] to the most extreme "no-government" doctrines, coupled with an attitude of extreme intransigence and inflexibility in the existing situation, a refusal to explore possibilities of a peaceful solution, ex-

---

[31] Quoted *ibid.*, III, 491, 492. For Garrison's attitude toward John Brown, see also Thomas, *The Liberator*, pp. 396, 397; Merrill, *Against Wind and Tide*, pp. 271-73.
[32] Henry C. Wright, *The Natick Resolution*, p. 27. See also p. 18.

cept on the plane of a universal conversion to complete nonresistance. We have here doctrinaire pacifism without practical peacemaking.

For Wright, at any other level except that of absolute pacifism, Brown had been correct and had shown an example to be emulated "in resolving . . . to shoot down all who should oppose him in his God-appointed work." Let Northerners who were not convinced nonresistants, he wrote Garrison, strain their utmost to arouse the slaves to rebellion. Insurrection, "the torch and sabre," were holy for such an end, a duty in those who had not already on religious principle renounced their use. "Let the North cut loose from their bloody alliance with slaveholders, imitate John Brown, and form a league of offence and defence with the slaves against their enslavers."[33] A few months after Brown's execution, in a pamphlet published in Boston, Wright gives a further exposition of his views on the impending struggle. The thesis he presents is simple. Slaves have no obligations at all to their masters, who, good or bad, deserve no more respect or consideration than a gang of pirates or kidnappers. Freedom must be won by the slaves themselves in alliance with their sympathizers among white freemen—by all and every means that the latter would feel justified in using "against burglars, incendiaries and highway robbers" who might threaten them. "It is the duty of the people and States of the North," wrote Wright, "to invade slaveholding States to free the slaves, and annihilate the power that enslaves them." This was their obligation under the existing constitution, since that document had called for armed defense against aggression, the aggression in this case being that of the Southern slaveholders. "There are but two sides in this conflict to break up those kidnapping, piratical hordes of the South, called States. . . . You must fight for liberty or slavery—for the pirates or their victims. You must be wholly for one or the other."[34] Wright, then, saw the impending conflict, which he hoped would soon become actual, in terms of unrelieved black and white. That by speech and writing he had helped, in however small a way, to make the conflict inevitable is hard to deny. Probably Wright himself would not have wished to deny it.

Garrison and Wright were the most vocal among the nonresistant remnant at the time of Harpers Ferry. The reaction of others in the group, if lacking Wright's vehemence and Garrison's grandiloquence, was essentially of the same pattern.[35] There was at least one veteran

[33] *Ibid.*, pp. 28-30.
[34] Wright, *No Rights, No Duties*, esp. pp. 17, 24.
[35] For May's reaction, see Galpin, "God's Chore Boy," chap. XIII; S. J. May, *An Address Delivered Before the American Peace Society* (1860), pp. 18, 19. For

of the old Non-Resistance Society, however, who strongly dissented. Adin Ballou from his Hopedale community had, as we have seen, been chiefly responsible for prolonging the Society's existence during the second half of the forties. Perhaps his communitarian way of life allowed him, for all his abolitionist sympathies, to stand somewhat apart from the struggle, to view it in a larger perspective, and to give deeper consideration to the issues of principle involved. The attitude of Garrison and the other nonresistants toward Brown surprised and profoundly shocked Ballou. That the nonpacifist abolitionists should rejoice in Brown's exploits seemed understandable to him, but he was pained by the degree of approval given by opponents of all violence who had been for many years his colleagues in the work of the New England Non-Resistance Society. The spectacle of nonresistants, he writes, vying "with avowed pro-war men in paying homage to one whom I could regard only as a well-meaning, misguided, unfortunate zealot," was saddening. "As for me, I remained unmoved, except by sorrow for such a deplorable exhibition of mistaken ambition to promote a good end by evil means, and pity for the sufferer who had rashly plunged into a lion's den." Ballou's criticisms, which he published in his community journal, the *Practical Christian*, had no effect, however, in moderating the standpoint of Garrison and his friends.[36] The stance they had taken up in the late fifties did not change substantially after the conflict had blown up into the storm of war.

Sarah Grimké, see Benjamin P. Thomas, *Theodore Weld*, p. 237. Stephen S. Foster, who still claimed to be a nonresistant—"but not . . . a fool" (*Autobiography of Adin Ballou*, p. 419)—considered that "Brown has shown himself *a man* in comparison with the Non-Resistants," because the latter had "never been baptized into the sufferings of the slave" (*Practical Christian*, vol. XX, no. 16, 26 Nov. 1859).

[36] *Autobiography of Adin Ballou*, pp. 416-22; *Practical Christian*, vol. XX, nos. 16, 17. "We . . . appeal from the William Lloyd Garrison of to-day, to the William Lloyd Garrison of former years," wrote Ballou.

Chapter 8

The Civil War and the Antebellum Pacifists

The outbreak of hostilities between North and South in April 1861 faced the older peace movement with a crisis of conscience of the first magnitude. The friends of peace supporting a war—this seemed to make a mockery of what they had been preaching year in, year out over the previous half century. And yet for many reasons, quite apart from the pressure of public opinion on a small minority in the direction of conformity, peace workers of varying views were drawn toward a full or at least qualified endorsement of the Unionist war effort.

In the first place, the organized peace movement was confined entirely to the North; as we have seen, its efforts to gain entry into the South had been short-lived and ineffectual. It therefore shared, however much its members might differ in their views on peace and war with the majority of the population, in the general ethos of the North, in its social attitudes, its prejudices, preconceptions, and enthusiasms. It was part of the North; the South was an alien land. Secondly, most peace workers, not only the Garrisonian nonresistants and the more moderate pacifists but the middle-of-the-road and the conservative nonpacifists among them, sympathized to a greater or less degree with the abolitionist cause. Antislavery had become for them the most important aspect of that general humanitarian urge of early nineteenth-century America, from which both abolition and pacifism had originated. Thus, even Henry C. Wright's theorem—"MAN-KILLING is the basis of MAN-STEALING"; therefore, as an abolitionist I must be a nonresistant[1]—might easily be reversed to run: man-stealing is the basis of man-killing; therefore, the destruction of slavery, by whatever means, must precede the establishment of peace.[2] By 1861 the antislavery argument would certainly act as simply and quickly in favor of war with those peace men who did not hold to the inviolability of human life as with the nonresistants—and probably more quickly. Thirdly, there was no longer—in fact, there had not really been for almost a decade—an effective focus for radical pacifism. The American Peace Society, whatever the exact wording of its constitu-

---

[1] Henry C. Wright, *The Natick Resolution*, p. 27.
[2] Cf. Gerrit Smith: "When slavery is gone from the whole world, the whole world will then be freed not only from a source of war, but from the most cruel and horrid form of war. For slavery is war as well as the source of war" (quoted in Merle E. Curti, *Peace or War*, p. 54).

tion might be, had abandoned its stand against all war, and the pacifists were by now a small and powerless minority among its members. The whole peace movement, indeed, had lost its vitality. It had ceased to attract the young and the enthusiastic (few new names appear, for instance, either on the roster of the active Garrisonian nonresistants or among the more moderate peace men during this period). It had, of course, no sympathy with the political antiwar movement, which was to spring up as a result of war weariness or from latent sympathy with the Confederate cause. On the other hand, it proved itself incapable of generating a genuine and effective protest movement of its own, directed not against the ends for which the war was ostensibly being fought but against war as such.

Although the American Peace Society had publicly deplored the use of force on the occasion of Brown's attack on Harpers Ferry[3] and had continued to plead for a peaceful solution of the crisis right up to the outbreak of hostilities in 1861, it rallied to the support of the Northern war effort as soon as fighting began.[4] One member of the small pacifist group still left within the Society, Joshua P. Blanchard, now in his eighties, has given us an eyewitness account of the debates at its annual meeting in May 1861.[5] Participants could be grouped under three headings, he says: nonmembers who came in large numbers to observe the reaction of a peace society to the coming of war; a majority (as it turned out, perhaps not surprisingly) of members who had abandoned their opposition to war; and a handful who still hoped that the Society, whatever personal differences of opinion might exist within it concerning the justifiability of the present conflict, would confirm its stand, hitherto official, against all war. "The course of the Society, on that occasion," Blanchard relates, "was a surprise to all: a stranger, unapprised of the purpose of the meeting, would have supposed it for the vindication of war, rather than that of peace." The argument of the pro-war majority was simply that the conflict, which had broken out between the government and the Southern states ("the domestic traitors and pirates who are at work to overthrow it," Gerrit Smith called their leaders),[6] did not come under the heading of war and that, therefore, it did not come under the ban of the Society. It was a rebellion, and the suppression of rebellion was a legitimate task of government

---

[3] Curti (*American Peace Crusade*, p. 222) suggests that the statement issued to this effect by the American Peace Society was the result of the temporary influence of the pacifist J. P. Blanchard during a serious illness of the secretary, George C. Beckwith.
[4] See Curti, *Peace or War*, pp. 52-55.
[5] *Liberator*, 25 Sept. 1861.
[6] *Sermons and Speeches of Gerrit Smith*, p. 192.

and should have the full backing of the Society.[7] If the use of armed force to put down the rebels were contrary to Christianity, wrote the *Advocate of Peace*,[8] "then all real, effective government is wrong, and society must be abandoned to a remediless, everlasting anarchy."

Throughout the war and on into the peace years, Beckwith and the leadership of the Society continued to maintain that it had not in fact abandoned the stand taken by Article II of the 1837 constitution against all war (that is, they added, all international war) and that absolute pacifists, along with believers in defensive war, might still find a niche in an organization which officially stood about midway between these two positions. War is war between nations: civil war is not war but police action.[9] There is, one cannot help feeling, nevertheless something sophistical in such reasoning. In such a situation, the rejection of pacifism ("the anti-war and anti-army principles of our Society," in the words of Gerrit Smith)[10] would have commanded respect: to support war and pacifism showed neither clear thinking nor intellectual integrity. The Society undoubtedly lost the esteem of many outside peace circles for its lack of consistency in the hour of crisis. It would, indeed, have been better if the Society had modified its official stand to match its actual performance. As Blanchard noted: "'All war' includes civil war as well as foreign war, and, most certainly, civil war is as inconsistent as foreign with Christianity and exerts as baleful an influence." The present fighting was, he added, "a war of regions, rather than parties, like any foreign war."[11] War fever had swamped the American Peace Society to such an extent that its leaders were no longer able to discern the occurrence of war, the social evil which it was their whole reason for existence to fight, when it finally came to the American nation.

The coming of war, indeed, witnessed a flight from the peace camp of a large number of the stalwarts of the old peace movement and hesitations and doubts on the part of others, who eventually decided, for all their sympathy for many of the Northern war aims, to maintain their pacifist witness. When, for instance, old Blanchard wrote to all surviving signatories of the declarations of associate membership of Burritt's League of Universal Brotherhood (see p. 213, n. 95), inquiring whether they considered that the pledge against war given then ap-

[7] However, calling on both sides to avoid the arbitrament of arms and its attendant miseries, the *Advocate of Peace* in its March-April 1861 issue (vol. XIII) had used the significant phrase "civil war" (p. 201). It was not to appear again in its columns—at least with the editor's endorsement.
[8] Sept.-Oct. 1861, XIII, 298.
[9] See Edson L. Whitney, *The American Peace Society*, chap. XIV.
[10] *Sermons and Speeches*, p. 194.
[11] *Liberator*, 25 Sept. 1861.

plied to the present situation, only two answered in the affirmative.[12]

The argument that the fighting was not really war, but simply police action, appears to have made the transition from pacifism to belligerency easier for many in the peace movement. Listen, for example, to the Rev. A. P. Peabody, now Professor of Christian Morals at Harvard, whose conversion as a young and unknown Unitarian minister to absolute pacifism in the mid-thirties we have described earlier. For him now, the conflict "had none of the moral characteristics of a war. It was rather a vast police-movement for the suppression and punishment of multitudinous crime, justified by the same law of self-preservation which would arm the ministers of the State against a body of brigands. It was a sad necessity." He admits that it had all the forms of war, "all its horrors and sufferings; it must bear that name in history." But it was unavoidable, and, whatever the deeper causes of conflict, "those who are forced into it are blameless."[13]

Let us take one further example, one of the most striking, in fact, but not untypical—again from the Unitarian camp. The Rev. W. H. Furness (1802-1896) was the respected minister of the First Unitarian Church in Philadelphia and, on the very eve of war, a convinced nonresistant. Preaching in Boston in March 1860, not long after Harpers Ferry and in the pulpit of John Brown's militant supporter, Theodore Parker, he took as his text, "Put up thy sword into the sheath" [John 18:11]. He compared the nonviolent way of Christ and his apostles even unto death with the method of Brown and his followers in meeting the terrible crime of slavery. True, Brown was a man of courage, and a Christian could not be neutral or wash his hands of evil. What, therefore, were Christians in the North to do in face of the wrongs done to the slave? We must rely on the effectiveness of truth alone, Furness answers; it will finally conquer. To take this path may require more courage than armed resistance. But if we take up the sword in defense of liberty, we may soon find it impossible to draw a line between defense and aggression. A surer, even if perhaps slower, method of overcoming evil was the Christian way of nonresistance carried out in a spirit of love and readiness to sacrifice even life itself in the cause of peace.[14]

The outbreak of war led seemingly to a complete transformation in Furness's thinking. "This war plays the deuce with peace principles," he confided to his fellow Unitarian, Moncure D. Conway, early in

---

[12] Letter in *Boston Daily Courier*, 11 April 1863. See Curti, *Peace or War*, pp. 59, 60.
[13] A. P. Peabody, *Lessons from Our Late Rebellion*, pp. 2, 3.
[14] W. H. Furness, *Put up Thy Sword*, passim.

May 1861.¹⁵ In a discourse given in September 1862 to console the kindred of those who had fallen in battle, he raises a paean in praise of the Northern war cause. The tone of exaltation, the chiliastic note that pervades the whole discourse, is perhaps more reminiscent of a late medieval sectary than a nineteenth-century Unitarian. "Words cannot tell," he says, "the benefits that are to accrue from these generous self-sacrifices.... The blood of these Northern freemen is the blood of a new covenant which our country is making with Liberty, with Righteousness, with God." God is binding the North together in ever closer ties of Christian love and fraternal fellowship. The war is ushering in a wonderful new age, a golden age of freedom for all mankind.[16]

As Curti has aptly said: "By its very nature a civil war is a severer test of pacifism than a foreign war, particularly when it is associated with purposes or alleged purposes demanding from idealists some measure of loyalty."[17] Maintenance of the Union and the freeing of the slave were purposes which (if we except the extreme nonresistants' advocacy of disunion) most pacifists held dear. The reaction of men like Peabody and Furness showed that, when faced—as in the present crisis—with the necessity of choosing, their pacifism took second place.

An interesting example of the other sort, where loyalty to the peace cause over three decades finally won out against devotion to abolition and the Union, is the case of Amasa Walker. We have met Walker in the forties as one of the leaders of the absolute pacifist wing of the American Peace Society and later as a close collaborator with Burritt in the American branch of the League of Universal Brotherhood.

In 1859 Walker had published an interesting little satire on war preparations as a method of national defense entitled *Le Monde; or In Time of Peace Prepare for War*, which put succinctly, in the form of an allegory, the pacifist case against armaments. In his story, the peace and harmony of a group of families shipwrecked on an uninhabited island is spoiled when one family begins to arm itself with swords "in self-defence." It is followed by the other families on the island, and from swords they proceed to rifles and then to cannon. The arms race is at last halted by the doubts of one young man who asks: "Is not

---

[15] Letter dated 7 May 1861, quoted in James M. McPherson, *The Struggle for Equality*, p. 52. This study throws considerable light on the wartime and postwar activities and attitudes not only of Garrison himself but of a number of other leading nonresistants: Maria W. Chapman, Lydia M. Child, Stephen and Abby Foster, Oliver Johnson, Samuel J. May, Parker Pillsbury, Edmund Quincy, Charles Stearns, Angelina Weld, Charles K. Whipple, and Henry C. Wright.

[16] Furness, *A Word of Consolation*, esp. pp. 5-7, 12.

[17] Curti, "Poets of Peace and the Civil War," *World Unity*, X, no. 3 (June 1932), 150.

the whole system of arming against each other an absurdity, father?" And he succeeds in persuading the islanders to throw away their weapons and to use the method of conference instead in cases of dispute: "Wonderful, truly, are the results of this abandonment of preparations for self-defence," admits in the end the man who had begun the whole process of arming.[18] The pamphlet was published in both England and America by the respective peace societies and proved an effective piece of propaganda for the peace cause.

A solid citizen, a well-to-do banker, and a prominent figure in the public life of Massachusetts, a man averse to the extremism of nonresistance, Walker at the opening of the war had been caught up in the tide of war enthusiasm and brought to doubt the validity of pacifism in the existing situation, if it meant compromise with slavery as the only alternative to war. His wavering alarmed Elihu Burritt, whose own firmly anchored peace witness apparently remained unshaken throughout the struggle. "He is my dearest friend on this side of the water," wrote Burritt on 26 May 1861 to the secretary of the London Peace Society, the Rev. Henry Richard (1812-1888). He went on to speak of "the insidious drifting that has carried nearly all our peace friends into the wake of this war. It has indeed been a sifting time here. I have been saddened and amazed at the spectacle. Men who we thought stood strong and firm upon the rock, have been washed away. I have almost trembled for dear Walker. His nature is warm and impulsive, and all his sympathies run out so exuberantly for a struggle for freedom versus Slavery. His son is an adjutant general in the army, and every influence works to wash him into the rushing current of popular sentiment."[19] Nevertheless, despite a strong emotional pull initially toward support of the war, Walker decided not to abandon his pacifism, and on several occasions during the course of hostilities he spoke out fearlessly in its behalf.

In this same letter to Henry Richard we can feel Burritt's sense of disillusionment with the orthodox peace movement and his frustration at being unable to make an effective protest against the prosecution of the war.

> The great trouble with professed friends of peace here, is the habit of working up fictitious premises, then building an argument and a policy upon them. Mr. Beckwith in the Advocate, has done a great deal to commit the Peace Society to this quicksand footing. He has assumed from the beginning that this terrible conflict, in which each party is arraying 500,000 armed men against the other, is not

---

[18] Amasa Walker, *Le Monde*, pp. 10, 23, and *passim*.
[19] Quoted in Curti, *The Learned Blacksmith*, pp. 138, 139. See also Curti, *Peace or War*, pp. 50, 51.

war but quelling a mob on the part of the Federal Government, that the Northern army of half a million is only a sheriff's *posse* called out to put down an organisation of riotous individuals. I feel that this sophistry and position have shorn the locks of the Society of all the strength of principle; and I have been saddened to silence. I fear that 49 in a hundred of all the *Quakers* in America have drifted from their moorings in this storm of passion or indignation. This is truly a *trial hour*. All the ministers of the gospel, the religious press, all classes of the community have been swept into the current. I have felt distressed at my inability to put forth a feather's weight of influence against the war spirit.... The position taken by the Advocate of Peace completely nullifies that as an exponent of our fundamental principles, and there is no possibility of getting a hearing of a public audience for views adverse to the war.... I feel I have gone as far as I could, without exposing myself to arrest, in opposing the war; I feel powerless and almost alone. Dear old Father *Blanchard* stands strong as a mountain of iron, and I hope there are a few scattered through the country who hold steadfastly to our principles.[20]

If the maintenance of the Union and the desire to back the government to the hilt in its struggle with the Southern secessionists had ranged the American Peace Society officially behind the Northern war effort and had rallied to it almost all former peace men associated with the Society in some way (apart from a few scattered individuals powerless now to express their dissent in any effective way), then what of the radical nonresistants? With all their passionate (some would say mistaken) zeal for the cause of the Southern slave, had they not called for "disunion" long before the South had seriously meant secession? Could "no-government" men, who had renounced the United States Constitution and denounced all its works, be overly concerned with upholding the authority of the state against disrupters?

On 16 July 1861 an Irish Quaker wrote to one of the original founding members of the New England Non-Resistance Society: "I own that the outbreak of this war in America has caused me many surprises. I wonder greatly at the unreserved exultation on the part of many out and out friends of nonresistance among the abolitionists at the opening of a long and bloody struggle. I don't wonder that they should be glad at the prospect of the overthrow of slavery at almost any price; but I am surprised that it is such unqualified gratification."[21] Some of the

[20] *Ibid.*, pp. 139, 140. See also Curti, *Peace or War*, p. 50.
[21] Richard D. Webb to Anne W. Weston, 16 July 1861, Weston Papers, B.P.L., MS A.9.2., vol. 30, no. 70.

New England nonresistants had by this time already abandoned their pacifism; others, though not formally abandoning nonresistance, now put it aside for the duration. This seems to have been more or less the position of Henry C. Wright, whose peregrinations we have watched from the most fervid apostleship for nonviolence to the most rabid incitement to slave revolt and civil war, while all the time he still maintained, however uneasily, his personal pacifism. The Grimké sisters went further and gave the war unlimited support without any reservations of conscience. "You see how warlike I have become," wrote Angelina (now Mrs. Theodore Weld, of course) to Gerrit Smith toward the end of 1862, "O, yes—war is better than slavery."[22] A couple of years later her sister Sarah in a letter to Garrison grew almost lyrical in describing the benefits the war would bring to both white and black: "This blessed war is working out the salvation of the Anglo-Saxon as well as of the African race. The eyes of the nation are being anointed with the eye-salve of the King of heaven. . . . This war, the holiest ever waged, is emphatically God's war."[23] The Grimké sisters' old colleague in both the abolitionist and the nonresistant causes, Mrs. Lydia M. Child, was almost as militant. "I abhor war," she wrote to the abolitionist Congressman George W. Julian in June 1862, "and

[22] Quoted in Benjamin P. Thomas, *Theodore Weld*, p. 245. However, the Welds' son, Charles Stuart Faucherand Weld (1839-1901), then a student at Harvard, chose to take the stand of a C.O.—obviously to the distress of his father, who had hoped "a sense of duty" would lead his son at least to allow him to hire a substitute to fight for freedom in Charles's place. "All I have to say on the point is this," Charles answered indignantly (letter dated 2 June 1862, Weld-Grimké Papers, William L. Clements Library, University of Michigan). "I must request you if the conscription takes place to let the law take its course. . . . I should much regret that I was even the *indirect* means of sending one more man to fight in what I regard as an unjust cause and very possibly to be thanklessly and mercilessly slaughtered." He contested his father's legal right to make payment without his own prior agreement; he stressed his unwillingness to escape arrest if that were the consequence of his refusal to fight. If his father paid, Charles went on, "I shall feel in duty bound to see the U.S. officers and tell them *how the case stands*. I should feel mean if I did not. They shall know that I am not such a coward that though supporting the war I refuse to fight or that condemning the war as I do I can for an instant consent to escape the penalty of a refusal." In the fall of the same year, when it was rumored that Harvard was to introduce compulsory drilling for the students, Charles wrote to his father (letter dated 25 Sept. 1862): "I hope on your account the whole matter may fall through so that at all events there will be no requisition about it. I confess father I am astonished that you do not regard my view respecting this matter as correct." To comply would be equivalent to approval of the war and a seeming readiness to fight if called upon to do so. "This would be a deception, a false promise, a lie, and I can have nothing to do with it." (See also Thomas, *Weld*, p. 239.) The correspondence is tantalizingly fragmentary. One would like to know the precise grounds for Charles's pacifism (seemingly a selective objection), how far it was the fruit of his mother's former nonresistant faith, and what her reactions to her son's stand were now.

[23] *Liberator*, 15 Jan. 1864.

have the greatest dread of military supremacy; yet I have become so desperate with hope—deferred, that a hurra goes up from my heart, when the army rises to carry out God's laws. . . . I am convinced that this is the great battle of Armageddon between the Angels of Freedom and the Demons of Despotism."[24] Other former nonresistants were carried along, too, like the Grimké sisters and Mrs. Child, into full approval of the war method.[25]

What of Garrison himself and his closest associates among the nonresistants? It would lead us too far afield to enter into a discussion of Garrison's attitude toward the Lincoln administration and of the increasing differences between him and his fellow radical abolitionist, Wendell Phillips—Garrison advocating restraint and understanding and trust in Lincoln's good intentions in regard to the slave and Phillips distrustful of the President's half-measures and his procrastination in proclaiming full emancipation and suspicious, also, of his earnestness in opposing the Confederate power.[26] We do, indeed, see in his late fifties a somewhat mellowed Garrison ready, unlike the young editor of the *Liberator* three decades or so earlier, at least to consider in some instances the subtle shadings in opinion, which make it difficult to divide good and bad into categories of unrelieved black and white. In his hatred of slavery and the slave power he remained inflexible. But war and government he had now ceased to see as totally evil. There was a plane on which they might be considered as the lesser evil, if not quite a positive good. The slaughter was a judgment of God on both sides for so long tolerating such a monstrous evil in its midst, for so long withstanding all attempts to abolish slavery by peaceful means. War for the maintenance of the Union certainly held little

[24] James A. Barnes (ed.), "Letters of a Massachusetts Woman Reformer to an Indiana Radical," *Indiana Magazine of History*, XXVI, no. 1 (March 1930), 53. After the war had come to an end, she was to call for life imprisonment for the former Confederate president. Explaining that she was, indeed, opposed on principle to capital punishment, she confided to Julian that otherwise she would have felt that only death was commensurate retribution for Davis's terrible crimes. In any case, she concluded, "as long as *any*body is hung, I can see no good reason why Jeff Davis should be exempted from the penalty" (p. 58).

[25] See *Liberator*, 13 March 1863, letter from Seward Mitchell of Maine, for an example of a rank-and-file nonresister who had been converted to the Garrisonian position seventeen years earlier and now, after two years of war and increasing doubts about the relevance of pacifism, had become convinced that only armed force was possible in dealing with the South. "All our appeals to tyrants, on the ground that their acts are wrong, are despised . . . I now see the use of war. I see its *absolute necessity*." See also Devere Allen, *The Fight for Peace*, pp. 449-60, for other examples of pro-war or near pro-war attitudes on the part of former pacifists.

[26] See Russel B. Nye, *William Lloyd Garrison and the Humanitarian Reformers*, pp. 169-77, 180-87.

attraction for him (had he not earlier been ready to let the recreant South go sooner than see the North linked any longer with the upholders of Negro slavery?); but he welcomed the opportunity war gave the administration to effect the liberation of the slaves (for he believed, as we see, in the reality of Lincoln's antislavery principles). So much for the lower level, the plane on which ninety-nine percent, or more, of the American nation moved. Garrison's recognition of its legitimate existence—people being what they were—did not mean, he still claimed, that in his opinion the nonviolent way was not preferable if adopted from conviction, or that, even though as yet only a handful, pacifists must abandon their belief in the higher ground of nonresistance. But he had no sympathy whatsoever with the political opposition of the "copperheads" to the Northern war effort.

Let us allow Garrison to speak for himself and show the substance of his thinking on these problems as it reveals itself in two letters he wrote to friends in the second half of April 1861, just as hostilities were beginning.

> Now that civil war has begun [he told Oliver Johnson] and a whirlwind of violence and excitement is to sweep through the country, every day increasing in intensity until its bloodiest culmination, it is . . . no time for minute criticism of Lincoln, Republicanism, or even the other parties, now that they are fusing for a death-grapple with the Southern slave oligarchy; for they are instruments in the hands of God to carry forward and help achieve the great object of emancipation, for which we have so long been striving. The war is fearfully to scourge the nation, but . . . grand results are to follow, should no dividing root of bitterness rise up at the North. All our sympathies and wishes must be with the government, as against the Southern desperadoes and buccaneers; yet, of course, without any compromise of principle on our part.[27]

A few days later, writing to another friend, he continues in the same strain concerning the struggle:

> I see the hand of God in it for judgement long withheld, but not unmixed with mercy. All my sympathies and wishes are with the government, because it is entirely in the right, and acting strictly in self-defence and for self-preservation. This I can say, without any compromise of my peace-principles. The struggle is necessarily geo-

[27] Garrison to Oliver Johnson, 19 April 1861, in *W.L.G.*, IV, 21, 22. For a good summary of Garrison's pacifist position in time of war, see Johnson, *William Lloyd Garrison and His Times*, pp. 347, 348. See also John L. Thomas, *The Liberator*, pp. 413, 422, 423, 480, 481.

graphical—between the North and the South—between freemen and a desperate slave oligarchy—and on either side of the line, a unity of purpose prevails to conquer or die, which is prophetic of one of the fiercest and bloodiest appeals to arms that the world has ever seen. The whole land is to be severely scourged—there will be desolation and death on a frightful scale, weeping, and mourning, and lamentation for the slain and wounded in thousands of families—but if it shall end in the speedy and total abolition of slavery . . . it will bring with it inconceivable blessings, and the land will have rest, and the old waste places be restored. But if it shall terminate in new compromises, whereby the traffic in human flesh shall be indefinitely prolonged, then our condition as a nation will be awful indeed, and the next outpouring of divine retribution will be for the extinction of the republic. It seems to me that the day has gone by for any compromises to be made, and that either freedom or slavery is to obtain universal supremacy. God grant it may be the former![28]

Throughout the war Garrison kept the columns of his *Liberator* open for discussion of nonresistance (it was almost the only forum left to pacifists outside the press of the peace sects), and contributions for and against are to be found scattered among its pages. Of course, the question of emancipation and the progress of the conflict occupy most of the space. The paper supported vigorous prosecution of the war and opposed concessions to the South, attacking in particular any movement for a negotiated peace before victory had completely routed the slave power and the efforts of the so-called peace democrats to terminate hostilities. The bellicosity and irreconcilable tone of the paper contrasted strangely with Garrison's theoretical pacifism. It is clear that Garrison failed to see any incompatibility between theory and practice in his conduct. "Although non-resistance holds human life in all cases inviolable," he argued with Adin Ballou and his Hopedale communitarians, who deplored what they regarded as his lapse from the spirit, if not the letter, of nonviolence, "yet it is perfectly consistent for those professing it to petition, advise, and strenuously urge a prowar government to abolish slavery solely by the war-power."[29] In fact, although his "moral line of measurement" might still be "the Golden Rule" and the Sermon on the Mount,[30] his political line differed in no essential from that of the war's most ardent supporters.

[28] Garrison to T. B. Drew, 25 April 1861, Garrison Papers, B.P.L., MS A.1.1., vol. 6, no. 7.
[29] Adin Ballou, *Autobiography*, p. 439. The exact wording of the quotation is Ballou's, but its substance is undoubtedly accurate.
[30] Garrison, *The Abolitionists and their Relations to the War*, p. 31.

Most of the Garrisonian nonresistants were already middle-aged by the time the Civil War broke out. Their heyday had been in the thirties and forties. As we have seen, by the fifties few young people could be attracted into a movement that had virtually disintegrated. The pulse had slowed down, the vital spirit had departed. The nonresistant creed, once so vigorous, had become an empty formula devoid of real meaning in the very situation it had been designed to meet. All that was left was a handful of aging men and women straining to preserve in theory a way of thinking whose spirit they had long since abandoned in practice. Militant abolitionism had almost wholly overlaid the pacifist vein in their philosophy.

The imposition of federal conscription, therefore, scarcely affected the nonresistant group in any personal way. In an editorial in the *Liberator* published anonymously in October 1862 under the title "Drafting—The Time of Trial," Garrison pleaded for equal consideration of the claims of nonresistant conscripts as conscientious objectors under the Federal Militia Act of the previous July. They had as much right, he thought, to complete exemption as members of the Society of Friends and should not be required to find a substitute or pay a fine in lieu of personal service, a way out of active military service still remaining open to all who were ready to provide the necessary money. The law had in fact confined the right to plead conscientious objection to members of the peace sects. Garrison, somewhat intolerantly, but obviously in an effort to buttress the claims of any "no-government" nonresistants who might appear, went on to suggest that the administration would be perfectly entitled to exclude from exemption as conscientious objectors all claimants who had exercised the suffrage, an act that he continued, as earlier, to consider as tantamount to approval of the state's military machine. Since they were excluded from the Act's exemption clause, Garrison foresaw that nonresistant conscientious objectors would probably have to face imprisonment for their convictions, if drafted. He ended his article, therefore, by giving some advice as to how they should conduct themselves in the hour of trial. Let them at the outset, he says, make it quite clear to the authorities that they abominate the attitude of the South. In all cases they should refuse to hire a substitute or voluntarily pay the military fine. This was not like a general tax (Garrison never pushed his "no-government" views so far as to refuse to pay taxes to Caesar); it was clearly designed to assist military operations. It was, he said, really equivalent to fighting oneself. However, if the only alternative to payment was imprisonment or worse, then he would not himself think it wrong to pay up. Anyhow, decision to pay or not must be left to the individual conscience of each objector.[31]

Later conscription acts stiffened the provisions for conscientious objection and went far to close the loopholes for those who were unwilling, for whatever reason, to serve. But the *Liberator* does not seem to have taken the matter up again. Early in 1864, however, Garrison was concerned in a personal way with the problem of conscientious objection when it seemed likely that his young son Frank, then at the Boston Latin School, would be required to undergo military drill along with the other boys in the top classes. He wrote, therefore, to the headmaster to get his son excused. "This I do," he wrote, "on the ground of conscientious scruples on my part, as well as in accordance with his own wishes."[32]

In fact, all Garrison's children, when they grew up, came to accept their father's nonresistant beliefs[33]—except the eldest son, George.[34] In the summer of 1863 George decided to volunteer for active service and received a lieutenant's commission in a newly formed Negro regiment, the 55th Massachusetts Regiment. "Though I could have wished," wrote Garrison to his son, on 11 June, shortly before his departure for the battle area with his regiment, "that you had been able understandingly and truly to adopt those principles of peace which are so sacred and divine to my own soul, yet you will bear me witness that I have not laid a straw in your way to prevent your acting up to your own highest convictions of duty; for nothing would be gained, but much lost, to have you violate these."[35]

[31] *Liberator*, 19 Sept. 1862.
[32] Garrison to Francis Gardner, 13 Jan. 1864, Garrison Papers, B.P.L., MS A.1.1., vol. 6, no. 70.
[33] Fanny Garrison Villard, *William Lloyd Garrison on Non-Resistance*, p. 19.
[34] In August 1862 Garrison wrote to Mrs. Elizabeth Buffum Chace (L.B.C. and A. C. Wyman, *Elizabeth Buffum Chace*, I, 241): "I have three sons of the requisite age—George, William and Wendell. Wendell is in principle opposed to all fighting with carnal weapons. So is William. In any case, they will not go to the tented field but will abide the consequences. George is inclined to think he shall go if drafted, as he does not claim to be a non-resistant." Garrison himself at this time hoped George and other nonpacifist abolitionists would refuse to be conscripted so long as "entire emancipation" was not proclaimed by the administration and would "take the penalties of disobedience as the friend and representative of the slave" (p. 242). Lincoln's first Emancipation Proclamation of 22 Sept. 1862 put an end to Garrison's advocacy of this type of political objection to military service.
[35] W.L.G., IV, 80. In a farewell to a young friend departing for the war, Garrison had wished him Godspeed without, however, making the slightest mention of his disapproval of war in general (see Ernest Crosby, *Garrison the Non-Resistant*, p. 85). A military camp for Negro troops was named after Garrison (see Korngold, *Two Friends of Man*, p. 333), apparently without any protest on Garrison's part. At the conclusion of the war, too, the famous nonresistant took a foremost and honored part in the victory celebrations.

We have seen how Garrison's own boys reacted to the impact of war. But what of the wider family of Garrisonian nonresistants? Did not some of them have to face the challenge of conscription and the trials which Garrison had envisaged at its introduction? We know, it is true, of a small number of individual cases during the Civil War, where men apparently unconnected with any of the peace churches took the conscientious objector stand on religious grounds when called up. But they did not emerge from the Garrisonian milieu—with the exception, seemingly, of only two instances.

There is, first, the case of the Philadelphian, Alfred H. Love, whose peace activities are dealt with in my *Pacifism in the U.S.* Love, though not a member of the Society, had been reared among Friends and was himself a lifelong attender at Quaker meeting. His pacifist inspiration, therefore, was not exclusively Garrisonian.[36] The second case is that of a young man from Quincy (Mass.) named John Wesley Pratt. Pratt at the outset of the war had for a short time wavered in his allegiance to pacifism. "The excitement consequent on the firing on Sumter," he relates, "carried me away in its almost irresistible might, until I found myself advocating the carrying on a war more cruel and relentless than any yet recorded in history." Later, however, he returned to his previous position. Therefore, when called up in the autumn of 1863, Pratt declared himself a pacifist of the Garrisonian variety, who on principle had never voted in his life and who objected as a Christian nonresistant both to bearing arms for any cause whatever and to buying his way out of service. He stood for complete exemption, though prepared to do hospital duties while under detention. The rough treatment he received at the hands of the military, which was probably aggravated by the fact that he did not belong to any church ("Non-Resistant? Nonsense!" an irate commanding officer told him on his arrival at the army depot), continued until his release came by order of higher authorities after several months spent in the army. Later, Garrison gave Pratt's experiences as a conscientious objector under military command considerable publicity in the *Liberator*.[37]

[36] *Liberator*, 12 Feb. 1864 (letter from A. H. Love). For Love's C. O. stand, see my book, *Pacifism in the United States: From the Colonial Era to the First World War*, p. 720.

[37] *Ibid.*, 12 Feb. 1864; 1 April 1863. Pratt's long letter to the editor in the latter issue is given the heading: "Experiences of a Non-Resistant Conscript." After being taken by sea to Virginia, Pratt, who now became an unwilling member of the Army of the Potomac never far from the front line, among his other trials suffered at times near starvation—along with the other military prisoners. "I picked here and there an acorn, that the squirrels had not seen," he later wrote; "I gathered the kernels of corn that the horses had left before us; I picked up bones all covered with dirt, and gnawed them, until weak with hunger and exhaustion, and sick from exposure, I reached Kelly's Ford." Pratt's release in January 1864 was

The remnant of New England nonresistance, then, contributed little to the story of conscientious objection in the Civil War. We have seen its leader, Garrison, absorbed almost completely in the struggle to make the war for the Union a war for the emancipation of the slave. What of some of the other older nonresistants who, though not liable for active service, still, like Garrison, maintained a clear, if qualified, personal pacifist faith, juxtaposed somewhat uneasily perhaps alongside their antislavery crusading zeal? Take, first, Samuel J. May at Syracuse. He had greeted Harpers Ferry, indeed, with some enthusiasm and showed a genuine regard for John Brown, though his admiration was mingled with disapproval of the method Brown had chosen to forward the cause of the oppressed. In the following year, just a year before the outbreak of civil war, while addressing the American Peace Society, May had given a very forthright criticism of the idea of defensive war and had pleaded instead for a nonviolent alternative to war. Neither the American Revolution, he said, nor the Polish uprising of 1830, whatever the provocation, had been proper ways for a Christian people to obtain redress for wrongs done or the maintenance of liberties threatened. "How wicked, how impious then, is it for any man to become a soldier. He ought to refuse to submit to the degradation, as did the primitive Christians. He ought to refuse, though it should cost him his life. Better to die at the stake as a martyr to principle, than to be a soldier."[38]

Yet, when shortly afterward May was confronted with the seeming alternatives of either sanctioning the war method and thereby bringing about the victory of the cause he had so much at heart or maintaining a consistent pacifist witness and appearing indifferent to the speedy emancipation of the Southern slave, he began to waver. "The conduct of the rebels," he wrote, "and the impending fate of our country has shaken my confidence in the *extreme* principles of the nonresistants." All the same, he added, "I cannot find it in my heart to urge men to enlist." He left this decision to the consciences of those who believed in the war method. Instead, he busied himself with the spiritual and material welfare of the troops, visiting army camps to find out where he could be of use and assisting the families of those in the service.[39]

---

the result of intervention with the authorities by several leading New England pacifists. One of those who had shared at the beginning Pratt's detention in the camp on Long Island in Boston Harbor was the Shaker C.O., Horace S. Taber (see chap. 20 of my *Pacifism in the U.S.*). The MS Letters & Documents, edited by John Whiteley, contain some interesting sidelights on Pratt's experiences at that time, as well as later with the army near the front (see pp. 50, 53, 78-87).

[38] S. J. May, An Address . . . before the A.P.S., pp. 11, 12.
[39] *Memoir of S. J. May*, pp. 226-29.

Like Garrison, he strongly urged that no compromise be reached to end the war until slavery was rooted out completely, and he was fierce in his denunciations of the Southern leaders. On news of the capture of President Davis at the end of the war he wrote: "Jeff Davis of course ought to be hanged if any man should." Even though he adds as an afterthought, "what good can it do to hang even him?" his whole attitude appears tantamount to urging the hanging of the Southern leader by those who were not conscientiously opposed to capital punishment. A sympathetic biographer writes of May's attitude in the latter years of the war: "His . . . views in 1864 and 1865 were far from being generous or humane. Indeed, it stands as the only blot upon the career of a man who always had championed truth, honor and justice."[40] May's dilemma was a real one. Even less satisfactorily perhaps than Garrison, however, had he succeeded in the difficult task of reconciling radical pacifism with militant abolitionism, when the latter cause was submitted finally to the arbitrament of war.

We can watch this curious admixture of theoretical pacifism and practical belligerence in the case of a second member of the original New England nonresistant group, who in the late fifties had become Garrison's editorial assistant on the *Liberator*. Charles K. Whipple was not one of its most outstanding members intellectually, but he was very active on its behalf and, as we have seen in an earlier chapter, had written several pamphlets in defense of nonresistance. In 1863 Whipple took issue with the English pacifist leader, Henry Richard of the London Peace Society, who had criticized in his Society's journal, the *Herald of Peace*, the bellicosity (as he considered it) of Northern abolitionists and the increasing ferocity with which the war was being waged, especially on the part of the North. Attempts by the London Peace Society at fostering negotiations between the two sides, and earlier criticisms of the belligerence of Northern peace men, had already aroused the resentment of the American Peace Society, temporarily ruffling the good relations which had hitherto existed between the peace societies of the two countries.[41]

Now Whipple entered the fray against Richard, and their correspondence was published in the columns of the *Liberator*.[42] "This is strictly a war of self-preservation," the American told Richard; "the inevitable alternative before us is to conquer or to be conquered; . . . compromise between non-slaveholders and slaveholders is precisely equivalent to a defeat of liberty; and . . . defeat for us, means the

[40] W. Freeman Galpin, "God's Chore Boy," chap. XIII; A. C. F. Beales, *The History of Peace*, pp. 106-9.
[41] See Curti, *Peace or War*, pp. 55, 56.
[42] *Liberator*, 28 Aug. 1863.

forcible establishment of the slave code North as well as South. So that there is absolutely no resource for us but to fight." He called for "extermination" of the Southern secessionists and slaveholders, if this were needed to prevent the legal reestablishment of slavery throughout the country and of the overseas slave trade, and not for any softening in the forceful prosecution of the war. Not independence but slavery was what the South was fighting for; "we can escape war with such a neighbor only by one possible means, complicity in the enforcement of slavery and suppression of anti-slavery." "Are you prepared to advise that *this* price be paid for peace?" he asked the English pacifist. And then, as if recollecting that, after all, both he and Richard still stood for the same ideal of peace and nonviolence, Whipple attempts to knit together two seemingly irreconcilable strands, an effort which soon develops into a declaration of practical impotence in making an effective peace witness. "You and I, Mr. Editor," he tells Henry Richard, "are Peace men. As we understand Christianity, it never allows fighting; and *we* propose *not* to fight, under any circumstances. But surely these ideas of ours do not prevent our recognizing the fact that most men (and some worthy and excellent men) are of the opposite persuasion; still less do our peace principles prevent us from recognizing the grounds of difference between two parties who are fighting, and distinguishing one party to be right and the other wrong in the matter about which they began to quarrel." The pacifists in America, "always an insignificant minority" of the population, had now become more impotent than ever. The abolitionist cause, on the other hand, was in the ascendant; all its advocates rejoiced that the end of slavery approached. It was slavery's Northern supporters who were raising the cry of peace with the rebels. Therefore, Whipple told Richard, "recognizing this fact . . . I, a peace man, say without hesitation that I have no desire to see an end to this contest until slavery is utterly extirpated. Call this paradoxical or self-contradictory, if you will; but I do not see the least abandonment of my principles." Can you not distinguish, he asks Richard, between the relative justice of two causes? Do you equate, for example, the Poles' cause with that of their Russian masters, the Italians' with that of their Austrian overlords? "Does no thought enter your mind but the official and technical one—'How wicked they both are to be fighting?' . . . Is Peace the *one* thing needful when it leaves one party established as tyrant and the other as slave?"

Whipple, indeed, protests too much. His remarks touching the need for pacifists to evaluate the relative merits of the contestants in any armed struggle, a point made much of by Garrison also, are certainly apt. But there is little of the healing oil of reconciliation in what Whipple has to say. It is the whole spirit of his argument that is so much in contradiction with the pacifist ethos and that makes his protestations of continued loyalty to it ring hollow.

Whipple, when pressed by Richard whether he had now abandoned the view he had held steadily since publishing some twenty years earlier his pamphlet on the *Evils of the Revolutionary War*—that passive resistance, if entered on wholeheartedly, was capable of achieving liberty and justice, the best objectives of war, but without war's bloodshed and wasted resources—gives a rather unsatisfactory answer:

> I still hold in regard to the unjustifiableness of war, precisely the ideas which I then held. But I recognize the fact that our present conflict in this country (a Revolutionary war not less than the other) is materially different from that other in regard to the attainment of its object by means other than war. Resolutely determined not to fight, myself, and continuing firm in the position of advising no one else to fight, I yet recognize the fact that, if *somebody* does not fight to prevent the success of the slaveholders, they will succeed, and will bring the whole nation under the operation of the slave system.

He still believed, he continued, as firmly as ever in "the . . . power of Christian love": that was why he would not himself fight in this war, which was being waged by the North to prevent the spread of the slave system. Love had worked with the civilized and the savage and often, too, with the criminal and the depraved. But as for its efficacy with Southern slaveholders, he was not so sure. "You speak of these people as 'our fellow-Christians.' I pray you not to do Christianity so great an unjustice. Slaveholders are *not* Christians." "God of course can, and will accomplish some good purpose with them, in some one of his days of a thousand year." But "in all *human* probability, there is not the remotest chance of succeeding with these men by the use of kindness or forbearance." That was why he could not expect American statesmen or the people of the North to adopt the personal philosophy of the nonresistants.

Whipple's arguments, growing more and more angry as the correspondence proceeded, failed to convince Richard, who was profoundly distressed by the American pacifist's belligerence. "A long plea in favour of war from the pen of an old Peace man," a "grievous apostasy among our friends" was how he described them. "It seems painfully clear," the Britisher went on, "that you are all breathing such an atmosphere of passion as to have become far too feverish to listen with any temper to what appear to you the cold-blooded counsels of unprejudiced observers." To Richard it seemed that, if Whipple were right, if pacifism and the way of Christian love had no relevance in the existing situation, then the whole crusade for peace, which their movement had been carrying on for nearly half a century, was a mistake built on false premises. The moral grandeur of the objectives which the American abolitionists hoped to see accomplished as a result of the fighting he saw as itself a source of danger to the advocate of peace. "When I see a war waged in the name of religion or of philanthropy," he wrote, "I look upon it as the worst of all wars, because it tends to consecrate an evil system, in the estimation of mankind, by associating with it a great and sacred cause, while this cause is, itself, in reality, degraded and dishonoured by the association." The two men failed completely to understand each other. To Whipple (along with almost all the other Garrisonian nonresistants at this time, as we have seen), the evil of slavery, and what appeared to be the wickedness of those who upheld it, overshadowed all other considerations. Pacifism seemed to provide no answer which could be presented to those fighting for liberty as a practical alternative to the war method.[43] It could only remain a personal philosophy for those ready themselves to endure the burden of suffering that its adoption would bring with it. For Richard, on the other hand, standing, as it were, above the battle and perhaps underestimating, because of his distance from the conflict, the strength and resilience of the slave power, the way of love and its application to each individual Southerner were all-important. Pacifism, if it were to be meaningful, must speak to the man in the slaveowner, must recognize a brother in the enemy.

If the American Peace Society leadership and the overwhelming majority of rank-and-file members had capitulated completely to the war spirit and if most of the Garrisonian nonresistants had put their pacifism into cold storage and their energies into the struggle to achieve the final victory of the abolitionist cause, a scattered handful of the pacifist old guard continued to maintain a radical peace testimony in wartime, alongside that of the peace sects. It was actually the moderate pacifists, who had opposed the "no-government" views of the Gar-

---

[43] Two decades after the conclusion of the Civil War, Whipple, then an old man, published a virtual recantation of his earlier views. The nonresistants of the antebellum era, he now wrote, had failed to realize that Christ's injunctions such as "Resist not evil," etc., were given in expectation of an imminent end of the world. They could not be applied literally in later times. See *Boston Commonwealth*, 7 Nov. 1885.

risonian nonresistants, who now in wartime proved the more consistent in their advocacy of peace views.[44]

Amasa Walker, for instance, spoke up manfully for the absolutist position at the American Peace Society's annual gatherings in 1862[45] and 1863. True, he did not contest the position we have seen the Society had taken at the outset, that the Civil War, "the rebellion," was a matter of internal order and therefore outside its cognizance; nor did he feel that, once passions had been aroused to fever pitch on each side, appeals for a just termination of the war on grounds of reason or religion would have much chance of success. But he stated his own pacifist convictions quite frankly. "I have no faith in war," he said. "I had none at the commencement of our own contest, and if it were possible, I have less now. I expect nothing good from this or any war, that might not be obtained in a better way. My confidence in the principle on which our movement is founded, and the feasibility of it, are entirely unshaken. The consummation may be further off than it seemed ten years ago, but not the less certain."[46]

Elihu Burritt, too, whom we have watched at the opening of the struggle apprehensive at signs of wavering in his old friend Amasa Walker, spoke out publicly against the war, urging as a solution what he called "a plan of adjustment, involving a partial separation of the Southern and Northern States."[47] "I have from the beginning," he wrote to Henry Richard on 27 October 1862, "been opposed to this war not only on principle but on policy. . . . I condemn it here up to almost the prison door."[48] However, it is interesting to note that his open antiwar attitude did not prevent the Northern administration

---

[44] But see, e.g., the small work by H. H. Brigham, *A Voice from Nazareth* (1865), for a New England nonresistant's wartime defense of Christian pacifism. Brigham, a lay Baptist, had withdrawn in 1841 from his church in South Abington (Mass.) because of its refusal to come out squarely in favor of abolition, but he now opposed war as a means of bringing about emancipation. (See esp. pp. 7, 19, 33.) Another little-known product of New England pacifism during the war period is the 32-page pamphlet which T. F. Tukesbury published in Boston in 1864 under the title *The Taking of Human Life Incompatible with Christianity*. There is little that is original in the work, which bases its appeal for nonparticipation in war and for the application of noninjurious methods of overcoming evils, even of the magnitude of slavery, on the injunctions of the New Testament and the gospel spirit of love. "The Word is full of proofs," Tukesbury wrote, "that the doctrine of physical . . . resistance is wrong, and that peace is right, and always right; and that it is the duty of an individual to act upon this principle whether others do or not." (See pp. 21, 27, 28, 30.) It is very unlikely that the author made an impression on more than a handful of his contemporaries.

[45] Walker, *Iron-clad War-ships*, esp. pp. 9-11.
[46] Walker, *The Suicidal Folly of the War System* (1863), pp. 5, 6, 18-20.
[47] Quoted in Curti, *Learned Blacksmith*, p. 140.
[48] Quoted *ibid.*, p. 146.

from recognizing his talents (and the importance of the contacts he had with influential circles in England) by appointing him American consul in Birmingham early in 1865—a credit, indeed, to its tolerant spirit.[49]

Most vigorous and determined in its opposition to war was the little pacifist circle that had formed around such men as the now aged Joshua P. Blanchard and the younger Ezra H. Heywood (1829-1893), who was to be active throughout his life in radical reform. The British pacifist, Henry Richard, described Heywood as "this brave man who dares to be faithful among the faithless," "the bravest man in the federal states."[50] From 1862 onward the group used to meet together privately in Boston (the times were not yet ripe, they considered, and their resources too meager for any widespread public agitation). They were in touch with a few scattered sympathizers in other parts of the country, and from time to time Garrison, although he disagreed, if not with their basic viewpoint, at least with their stand on current politics, tolerantly allowed them space to express their opinions in the columns of the *Liberator*.[51]

The group regarded the attitude of the peace movement as a whole as little less than a betrayal of the truth entrusted to it. "The American Peace Society and the nonresistants generally," wrote Heywood after the war was over, "were so recreant to their principles in 1861 and thereafter, that the faith delivered to peace saints was kept only by 'copperhead' sinners. Opposed to all wars except the present one, at the very time when their ideas were of practical importance, and should have given law and unity to distracted States, in violation of all the kindly and mutual interests of the common people North and South, they joined the reprehensible pro-slavery and anti-slavery leaders in merciless advocacy of violence and blood."[52] Heywood and Blanchard, like Burritt, believed strongly that their pacifism had practical relevance even in the context of war. It was not only right from

---

[49] Devere Allen, *The Struggle for Peace*, p. 400.

[50] Quoted in Curti, *Peace or War*, p. 58. In 1863 Heywood wrote of the Quaker absolutists: "They are quite right in refusing to bear arms or pay the fine in obedience to this despotic, wicked conscription" (Wymans, *Chace*, I, 253).

[51] Robert W. Doherty, "Alfred H. Love and the Universal Peace Union," Ph.D. diss., U. of Pennsylvania, p. 39.

[52] Letter by Heywood to the *New York World*, 3 June 1868, cutting in J. P. Blanchard's Scrapbook, the second volume of which, containing *inter alia* a number of Blanchard's pacifist articles from the Civil War period, is deposited in the S.C.P.C. The first volume is presumably lost. It is interesting to note in connection with Heywood's attitude to the "copperheads" expressed here that his associate Blanchard contributed pro-peace articles to the *Boston Daily Courier*, the leading Democratic paper in that city and one that was opposed on political grounds to the Union war effort.

the standpoint of Christian morality; it was expedient, they thought, on the political level as well.

In the early months of the war Blanchard had pleaded for a negotiated peace on the basis of an agreement between the two sides to separate. Like the prewar advocates of "disunion," he believed that the institution of slavery would wither away in the South if no longer given the tacit consent of the Northern section. He felt, too, that in the circumstances secession was the only possible solution compatible with the American tradition of democracy, of government derived from the consent of the governed. The shame of the Fugitive Slave Law would be done away with, and the impending loss in life and property in the course of a long and bloody war would be avoided. He called his plan "the speediest and most peaceable one of abolishing slavery that can be devised."[53] If the war were continued, he felt certain that it could not be carried on in a spirit of Christian charity—as some pro-war clerics maintained was possible—and that hatred would grow into a consuming fire that would destroy love in their hearts and all desire for reconciliation.[54] Even after Lincoln had announced his preliminary Emancipation Proclamation in September 1862, Blanchard continued to speak up against the war and in favor of—to use his own words at this time—"the law of benevolent persuasion in opposition to the malignant law of force."[55] A year later we find him writing in the English *Herald of Peace*: "Christianity does not permit physical force for any but benevolent purposes. Its principle is government, not by fear, but by love"; this rules out the way of war, either civil or international, since there the object is the destruction, not the reformation, of the so-called enemy.[56] The argument is a familiar one in pacifist literature but one not often heard, even from peace advocates, in those years of fratricidal struggle.

As the war went on and each side seemed determined to fight to a finish, Blanchard, having failed to make the least impact on government, came more and more to feel that a new tactic was needed, that, in fact, the technique of the peace movement itself had been at fault over the years, since governments clung as tenaciously as ever to their powers of making war. "Some other means must . . . be found for the abolition of this enormous and mischievous power," he concluded after reviewing briefly the movement's history since its beginnings in 1815. Let the peace message be brought more directly to the

[53] See J. P. Blanchard, *Plan for Terminating the War* (single-sided broadsheet); *The War of Succession*, pp. 4ff.
[54] *The War of Succession*, pp. 2-4.
[55] In the *Bond of Brotherhood*, 1 Oct. 1862, p. 156, cutting in his Scrapbook.
[56] In the *Herald of Peace*, Oct. 1863, cutting in his Scrapbook.

people and in its most radical form. "Let us cease our hopeless attempts to influence interested rulers and statesmen in favour of peace and humanity. Let us turn to the masses of the depressed and martially-enslaved with the animating and reforming doctrine of individual independence." He did not advocate resistance to properly constituted authority in all things lawful; disobedience to the law where it infringed God's commandments, however, was another matter. If large sections of the populace were to refuse to fight out of a genuine conviction of the wrongness of all war, if a mass movement of potential conscientious objection could be generated in case of war or the threat of war, then the rulers would be forced to cease from conflict.[57] Thus, finally, in his old age this solid Boston merchant, long the pillar of the conservative wing of absolute pacifism in the American peace movement, was led to advocate a form of radical antimilitarism.

While the war lasted, Blanchard and his friends remained an obscure, isolated group powerless to influence public opinion in any substantial way. They are not without importance, however, as a link between prewar pacifism and the postwar movement which was at first centered in the Universal Peace Union (see chap. 23 of my *Pacifism in the U.S.*). They alone (if, again, we exclude the activities of the peace sects) attempted to give, within however confined a compass, something more than a purely personal witness to their pacifist faith.

Pacifism in America from the mid-thirties on, especially in its most radical form of nonresistance, had been the twin of abolitionism. War and slavery, though not by any means the only scourges besetting mankind, were perhaps, to that reforming generation at least, the most glaring denials of Christian love and brotherhood then existing. Freedom from war and violence and the liberation of the slave were but facets of one struggle, one movement to bring about the kingdom of God on earth. At least so it seemed until around mid-century the possibility grew that it would not be peaceful persuasion, but force of arms, that would in fact bring an end to slavery in the South. The dilemma was posed. What a modern historian has aptly said of abolitionists in general during this period applies with even greater cogency in the case of the nonresistant abolitionists: "Abolitionists might argue," he writes, "that they believed in the methods of peace but they could not indulge in wild talk about a bloody end of slavery without arousing a reciprocal madness in the South. . . . The slave owners were men capable of losing their tempers; when the time came for them to lose their temper completely, the abolitionists would no longer have in their

[57] From an article entitled "Unresisting Disobedience" in the *Herald of Peace*, March 1864, cutting in his Scrapbook.

own hands the choice between peace and war."[58] In a way, it is not untrue to say that Garrison and Wright and the other abolitionist nonresistants, as well as some of the pacifists outside their ranks, even if they did finally renounce their pacifism as war approached, had helped to bring the war nearer by their extreme belligerence. In their zeal for moral righteousness, which sometimes, indeed, became a species of self-righteousness but at best stemmed from a very genuine hatred of oppression, and in their efforts to avoid that common failing of peace men at all times, crying "peace, peace; when there is no peace," they had forgotten that peace is a spirit and not merely a personal credo, and that, without the spirit of peace that works reconciliation, pacifism is indeed a barren faith.

There were, as we have seen, only a few scattered individuals from the remnant of the pacifist crusade of earlier decades, men like Blanchard and Heywood, Ballou and Burritt, who succeeded in maintaining a consistent peace stand throughout the war years. The pacifist witness was borne most fully at this time of stress and testing by the young men, mostly from the peace sects, who became conscientious objectors on either side of the battle lines.[59]

[58] R. V. Harlow, *Gerrit Smith*, p. 305.
[59] See my *Pacifism in the United States*, chaps. 18-20.

Epilogue

In the Civil War the Quaker peace testimony (along with that of the other peace sects) had continued to follow the traditional pattern, although in the North some Friends abandoned their pacifism, at least temporarily, to take up arms to defend the Union and to free the slaves. This testimony stressed as before not merely the duty of a Christian conscience to suffer for the faith—and the sufferings of Quaker (and other) conscientious objectors under the Confederacy were, indeed, in some cases severe—but also the rights of that conscience over against the state. The Quaker position represented in its most considered form an assertion as much of civil rights as of religious obligation. The peace sects of German origin, on the other hand, remained loyal to their concept of pacifism with its careful demarcation between the world and its ways and the community of Christ's followers. Defense of the rights of man born to be free was not their concern; they strove, rather, to preserve a way of life in conformity with the teachings of the suffering Savior of man. After the failure of the Holy Experiment and the trials of the Revolutionary War, the Quakers had partly withdrawn from the world, had drawn nearer in their outlook to the political position of the German peace sectaries. Yet the gap had not been completely bridged. Stemming from the same source in the teachings of the New Testament, the pacifism of Quakers and German peace sectaries continued to find expression in rather different forms.

If the Civil War had found even the traditional peace sects unprepared for the ordeal, pacifism outside the peace sects had, as we have seen, virtually ceased to exist as an organized movement even before the firing started. The slavery issue had finally dealt it a fatal blow; only a few scattered individuals salvaged their private consciences from the movement's wreckage. Most peace workers, radicals and conservatives alike, had been swept along—some reluctantly, others eagerly—in the wave of war enthusiasm that had engulfed the Northern states, at least for a time. The bankruptcy of pacifism, indeed of the whole peace movement, at the moment of its trial demanded a radical reorientation, a deepening of its search into the sources of conflict and into the means of eradicating violence within both the domestic and the international orders. In fact, in subsequent decades a transformation of this kind was only effected in part and rather inadequately; the process had not got very far before the outbreak of war in Europe shattered the peace, this time of the whole world.

Almost half a century had elapsed between Appomattox and the firing of the guns of August 1914. Although the war in Europe appeared to have its roots in events remote from the North American continent, it involved the United States as an active combatant within three years of its outbreak. The First World War ultimately proved to be a landmark in American history, almost as much as it did in the history of the rest of the world. Within the narrower limits of the peace movement, too, we find that 1914 marked for both its pacifist and nonpacifist wings a turning point; the war years saw the creation of a new movement which was to evolve new ideas and new techniques of action in response to a vastly changed situation.

Yet the peace movement of the post-1914 period, for all the differences between it and the earlier movement, was embedded in the past. The half-century which preceded 1914 is particularly significant because it was during these years that the changes that eventually produced these new ideas and new techniques were taking place within the whole movement. But, when we come to study in detail the development of absolute pacifism during this period, it is difficult to avoid a certain sense of frustration. Pacifism appears to have been at a standstill: older groups, like the Society of Friends or the German-speaking sects (which were becoming increasingly English-speaking), seemed for the most part relatively unconcerned with the issue of peace, while new organizations based on a pacifist platform, such as the Universal Peace Union, were singularly ineffective. No outstanding leader—or even any person of middling stature—arose to challenge the surrounding apathy of an age of materialism.

The sources for many aspects of the story are meager—or submerged in a vast sea of reports and periodical literature dealing primarily with other topics. The most important elements, we begin to feel, are perhaps to be sought elsewhere: in the social transformation that was bringing Mennonites and Dunkers and their like out of their rural isolation, in developments within the American Society of Friends that were subtly undermining Quaker pacifism in some sections of the Society and renewing its foundations in other areas, in new ideologies that had as yet little or no contact with religious pacifism, like international socialism with its ideal of the brotherhood of man or anarchism with its goal of maximum freedom for all human beings. These forces—and others—were at work beneath the surface, but their effect was not to show itself properly until the events of August 1914 engulfed the nations in war.

Nineteenth-century American pacifism, unlike the antistate ideology of the Anabaptist-Mennonite tradition, was essentially an optimistic creed which placed its faith in the eventual perfectibility of man.

Some of its adherents strove for the immediate installation of the millennium. The New England nonresistants, for instance, pleaded for the abandonment of all instruments of coercion here and now. However, for all their bitter attacks on the American republic's power apparatus and on the Constitution of the United States, these men and women implicitly—and sometimes explicitly—believed with great fervency in the role of the New World in bringing about a peaceful international order. Their faith was firmly American.

Neither the more conservative wing of the peace movement nor the radical New England Non-Resistance Society was very successful in its efforts to enlist mass support for the peace cause. At their best these groups formed a small elite, at their worst they constituted a closed coterie. Yet, despite their naivety and their many other shortcomings, they did attempt to grapple with the major problems that have faced the twentieth-century peace movement. While the conservatives among them concentrated on investigating institutional means for eradicating war from human society, the radicals explored the possibilities of individual war resistance and of the application of noninjurious force on the domestic scene, and occasionally even sketched in outline collective techniques for nonviolent action in the international sphere as well. The grand dilemma that American pacifists of this period ultimately failed to resolve was the problem of squaring the quest for international peace with the attainment of justice and freedom within the national community (represented in this instance by the slavery issue). The old peace movement in the United States never really recovered from the impact of the Civil War; it was only the problems of global warfare in the twentieth century that eventually regalvanized the scattered peace forces.

The respectable middle-class men and women who made up the bulk of members of both the radical and conservative wings of the antebellum peace movement, it is true, found it difficult—despite manipulation of the political and economic case against war in their societies' propaganda—to comprehend the degree to which war was embedded in the socioeconomic conditions of their time. But they did at least go beyond the somewhat negative antimilitarism of the pacifist sectaries, who had hitherto often failed to carry effective opposition to the use of violence beyond a personal refusal to render military service.

In the two world wars of the twentieth century it has been the apocalyptic noncombatancy of such bodies as the Seventh-Day Adventists or Jehovah's Witnesses that has produced a high numerical proportion of conscientious objectors. Again, it is true that in our century the historic peace churches in America, liberal Quakerism in particular, have begun to display new insights into the issues of war and violence and a new humanitarian outreach in their relief work for war sufferers. Yet the world pacifist movement that sprang out of the turmoil of the First World War and its aftermath, in which American pacifism has formed an integral and important sector, has been interdenominational, indeed interfaith, in character and has embraced, too, those whose pacifism stems from ethical, humanitarian, or socialist, rather than religious, considerations. And alongside the pacifists we, in the late sixties of the twentieth century, should perhaps add the selective objector to a particular war, whose objection, indeed, is not based on pacifist beliefs but whose form of protest is the traditional one of the pacifist conscientious objectors.

The vision that has inspired this variegated witness of the contemporary pacifist and antiwar movement, both in the United States and in other countries, derives in large measure from the labors of predecessors, including those on the North American continent. With varying success in their day but with considerable determination and courage (along with occasional faltering and backsliding), American pacifists of the last century pioneered for a peaceable world.

Appendix

Quakers and the Antebellum Peace Movement*

The last years of Quaker government in Pennsylvania, climaxing in the retirement of Friends from the Provincial Assembly in 1756, and then the experiences of the Revolutionary War, two decades later, had led to a more general withdrawal from active participation in the "world," which continued into the second half of the next century. This withdrawal, indeed, was not peculiar to the Society on this side of the Atlantic. A parallel evolution was in process within the British Society. The prevailing philosophy among Quakers of this period seems to me to be very well summed up in the words uttered at its outset by Samuel Fothergill, an English Friend well acquainted with the life of the Society on both sides of the ocean. Referring to the duties of Pennsylvania Friends, now that they had withdrawn from government, Fothergill wrote thus: "Placed in the midst of this world and its commotions, we shall know our situation to be as a garden enclosed."[1]

In the period from the peace of 1815 up to the 1850's the Quaker as pacifist was concerned with a number of issues, both in their direct impact on his personal life and in their theoretical implications for the religious life of the Society. What response should he make if called upon to muster with the state militia? Should taxes be paid if, wholly or in part, they were destined for military purposes? Might war veterans who had become convinced Friends go on drawing their pensions? Where should the conscience of the Quaker merchant draw the line between peaceful trade and the profits of war? And, as Friends followed the frontier and thereby came into contact with the lawlessness of such regions, how would they meet the challenges this brought to their philosophy of nonviolence? These, and others like them, were practical questions which required an individual decision. They were questions which had had to be faced in earlier periods, some of them ever since Friends had come together in England around the middle of the seventeenth century. Friends also continued

---

* This Appendix was originally published under the title "The Peace Testimony in 'a Garden Enclosed'" in *Quaker History*, vol. 54, no. 2 (Autumn 1965), pp. 67-80.

[1] Quoted in R. Hingston Fox, *Dr. John Fothergill and His Friends*, p. 244.

to concern themselves with theoretical problems of war and peace. They composed treatises or drew up shorter statements expounding Christian pacifism in general or as it related to some particular situation. Lastly, but certainly not of least importance, we may mention Friends' reaction to the new foci of pacifism which developed outside the historic peace churches from 1815 on in nondenominational peace societies of varying shades of opinion. And this relationship is probably a part of the history of the peace testimony that is not very well known. There is little or nothing about it in the standard histories—Rufus Jones or Margaret Hirst, for instance.[2]

Now by temperament and outlook Friends of that period might be expected to feel fairly close sympathy with the more conservative wing of the peace movement. The main representative of this current of peace thought was at first the Massachusetts Peace Society, founded in 1815 in the aftermath of the Napoleonic Wars by a Unitarian minister, the Rev. Noah Worcester. This society in 1828 broadened out into the American Peace Society, which is still in existence today. From the beginning, these peace workers focused their activities chiefly in counteracting the military spirit in their propaganda and in searching for institutional alternatives to the war method: congresses of nations and international arbitration and so forth. The gradualism of these peace societies had something in common with the long-term range of the Quaker objectives. The societies frankly acknowledged their debt to the peace witness which the Quakers had upheld for nearly two centuries. They quoted in their publications from Fox and Penn and from many of the Quaker journals. The Quaker experiment in the government of Pennsylvania (pictured in rather an idealized fashion, it is true) provided them with one of their most frequently used examples of the safety of peaceable principles; and they also drew for illustrative material upon the experiences of Irish Quakers during the rebellion of 1798, as described in the book by Thomas Hancock. The essay on war of the contemporary English Quaker, Jonathan Dymond, was immensely influential on the thinking of American pacifists throughout the whole nineteenth century.

True, the membership of the peace societies was never confined to absolute pacifists. This was considered by many Friends a stumbling block in the way of collaboration. Others, however, joined with non-Friends on a common platform, agreeing, despite their different approaches, to labor together in the interests of international peace. Such

---

[2] See, however, Merle Eugene Curti, *The American Peace Crusade*, pp. 9, 13-17, 23, 33, 49, 67, 86, 104, 161; W. Freeman Galpin, *Pioneering for Peace*, pp. 13, 14, 17, 21, 22, 35 ff., 62, 65, 97, 101, 143, 146, 151.

a man was the venerable Moses Brown, a leading figure among New England Quakers. Around the time of the War of 1812, Brown became a friend of the two founding fathers of the American peace movement, David Low Dodge, founder of a peace society in New York City, and the Rev. Noah Worcester; and in 1818 he was himself instrumental, along with several other local Quakers, in getting a peace society started in his native Rhode Island, which he continued to support with his time and money.[3] On the whole, however, we do not find many Quakers among the leading figures of the early American peace movement. The initiative came from without the Society, from Unitarians and Presbyterians, Congregationalists and Baptists, rather than from any of the peace churches. In some places, in the small Pennsylvania Peace Society, for instance, Friends predominated; but its influence was confined to Philadelphia and its environs. In the movement as a whole, then, Friends played a subordinate role.

This fact surprised—and disappointed—many non-Quaker peace workers. "Why it is thus, we of course do not know," remarked William Ladd, the secretary of the American Peace Society until his death in 1841, and he pointed out that in England Friends' participation in the London Peace Society was larger and more effective.[4] It is perhaps not too difficult to resolve the enigma which puzzled William Ladd. Friends in America were slower in emerging from the social isolation into which, as I have said, the Society on both continents had retreated during the previous century. For the bulk of American Quakers, then, the activities of the peace societies were worldly, creaturely. They were not, of course, actually hostile; they gave them a certain slightly condescending approval. Moreover, Friends' periodicals drew extensively on the literature of these societies, American and British, for their peace material, reprinting in their columns extracts from the British *Herald of Peace* and the American *Advocate of Peace* and other papers and drawing, too, on the declarations issued by the respective societies. But a narrowly conceived separatism prevented most Friends from throwing their energies into organized peace work (and, as a result, the whole cause of peace suffered). A representative example of the thinking of the Society in this respect is seen in an article published in the Philadelphia *Friend* in the midthirties.

> We have sometimes doubted [writes the author] whether the institution and multiplication of Peace Societies in this country and in Europe had obtained that degree of consideration in the minds of our fellow members in religious profession, which, as it appears to

[3] Mack Thompson, *Moses Brown*, p. 282.
[4] *Calumet* (New York), vol. I, no. 15 (Sept.-Oct. 1833), p. 450.

us, their importance deserves. It is true, these societies, in their collective capacity, do not fully come up to the Christian standard according to our estimate of . . . the New Testament doctrine bearing upon this subject; and it therefore may not be expedient that our members should be found in their ranks. The Society of Friends as a body, . . . has emphatically been a Peace Society from its foundation, declaring to the world . . . that war in all its forms, offensive and defensive, is utterly at variance with the glorious gospel dispensation of "peace on earth, goodwill to men." And it is safer, at least in the present state of the world, that we keep much to ourselves, and not act as a body in reference to this important testimony, lest by joining with others we should unawares be led into a compromise or evasion of any of its requisitions.[5]

If Friends tended to take up a cautious attitude toward such bodies as the American Peace Society—among other reasons on account of their falling short of an uncomprising testimony against all wars—their reaction to the New England Non-Resistance Society, which came into being in September 1838 as a result of the efforts of William Lloyd Garrison and his abolitionist disciples, was more often than not one of downright hostility. The position of the New England nonresistants was not dissimilar to that of the great Russian pacifist, Leo Tolstoy, a few decades later. The New England nonresistants, like Tolstoy (or present-day Mennonites, for that matter), believed that government—at least all existing government—was so interwoven with the spirit of war and violence that no true follower of Christ could participate in any of its works. Christians, therefore, should not merely refuse to participate in war and oppose the death penalty; they must also refrain from holding office of any kind or voting others into office, if they wished to avoid the taint of blood.

Among the New England nonresistants were to be found some of the most earnest and devoted reformers of the day: men like Garrison or the Unitarian minister, Samuel J. May, or that cultured Boston gentleman, Edmund Quincy. Unfortunately, the movement also attracted not a few cranks. At its meetings, for instance, you would probably have seen "Father Lamson," a silent, standing figure with scythe and long snowy beard, symbolically representing Time and its passing. And you would certainly have met—her name crops up in the reports of the Non-Resistance Society's annual meetings—Miss Abigail Folsom, a more formidable character, who talked interminably and usually quite irrelevantly, whatever the subject of discussion. At last, at one meeting after she had been repeatedly requested to cut

[5] *Friend*, 30 Aug. 1834.

short her remarks, patience was lost and three stout Garrisonians picked her up bodily and began to carry her out of the hall. However, as she went through the doors on the men's shoulders, Miss Folsom got in the last word. "I'm better off than Jesus," she called out; "He had one ass to carry Him, I have three!"[6]

These people and their like gave the Non-Resistance Society a certain notoriety and undoubtedly served to alarm many respectable Friends. But, to understand the bitter feelings that quickly grew up between nonresistants and official Quakerism of both the Hicksite and Orthodox divisions, we must examine more closely the Quaker attitude toward civil government, since, as we have just seen, one of the key points in the platform of the New England nonresistants was their belief in the incompatibility between Christian pacifism and participation in any of the activities of government as then constituted.

The experience of the final years of Quaker rule in Pennsylvania, reinforced by the quietist trend which was a powerful influence at that time on Friends on both continents, had—as we know—left American Quakers profoundly disillusioned with the world of politics and determined to keep themselves as far as possible separate from its corrupting influence. The strife engendered by party struggles and the lust for office were contrary, Friends argued, to the spirit of Christian love that had led them to abandon reliance on armed force. Yet the withdrawal was never complete. A few Friends continued to sit in the Pennsylvania legislature right up through the nineteenth century, to act as magistrates and hold various other offices, provided they did not conflict directly with the peace testimony. Above all, Friends went on voting in large numbers at elections, both on the provincial and the federal levels. "The peaceable exercise of the right of suffrage, Friends have always left to the private judgment of the members," states an epistle issued by the Meeting for Sufferings of the Philadelphia Yearly Meeting (Orthodox) in 1834.[7] The belief in the possibility of so organizing the protection of society that armed force would be eliminated altogether or reduced to an absolute minimum was still widely held. As an Ohio Friend wrote: "The civil power has, perhaps in ninety-nine cases out of a hundred, been sufficient to bring criminals to punishment."[8] The same thought was

[6] Lawrence Lader, *The Bold Brahmins*, p. 71.

[7] *Friend*, 13 Sept. 1834.

[8] *Remarks by a Member of the Society of Friends, on the Subject of War, in reply to A. M., who addressed the Society on that Subject*. Its author, "E. C." (probably Elijah Coffin), wrote the pamphlet in answer to a Roman Catholic, who had published a pro-war "Address to the Society of Friends on the Subject of War" in the *Eaton Register* of 3 June 1847.

developed further by the Hicksite leader, Benjamin Ferris who wrote:

> The Society never set up the doctrines of *nonresistance*. . . . They are not enjoined either by the Yearly Meeting or the practice of Society under the Discipline to submit without resistance to personal injury or violence; so that such resistance be made without design to harm or injure the aggressor—and with the sole view of repelling or preventing mischief. The wise men who formed the Discipline have never made any rules that would unfit or disqualify us for human society—while they most ardently desired that our members, by the *inoffensiveness* of their conduct, might give evidence that they were subjects of the peaceable kingdom of Christ—never imposed on them a law which would oblige them quietly to sit down, and see their wives and children butchered, while they possessed the means of their protection, without injury to the assailant.[9]

Approval of the positive aspects of government was expressed frequently in the official statements of yearly meetings, and participation very rarely led to disownment where a connection with the military was not clearly apparent.

Opinion, however, was by no means uniform within the Society as to the practical application of Quaker pacifism in the realm of government. We have seen that the majority, while as yet remaining somewhat on the fringe of political life, maintained basically the positive view of the state that had held sway throughout most of the period of the Holy Experiment. But a minority, whose exact strength it is very difficult to estimate, had veered over to a position that was not far removed from the Anabaptist-Mennonite view, rejecting participation in civil government even where questions of military force or war taxation were not involved. This antistate attitude, a kind of Christian anarchism, had been strongest perhaps in the second half of the eighteenth century, when the crisis of 1756 and the hard years of the Revolutionary War had still been fresh in the minds of Friends. But we find many individuals sharing it in the period up to and beyond the Civil War. (A good example is that of the Hicksite minister, Jesse Kersey.)

In 1847 we find the Hicksite *Friends' Weekly Intelligencer* complaining that the antipolitical current within the Society was on the

---

[9] MS in Ferris Collection (R G 5), Series 4, Box 12, in Friends Historical Library, Swarthmore College (italics in the original). Ferris had been a conscientious objector to service in the militia during the War of 1812.

increase: "The number of those who adopt this view is, we think, large and increasing; and we are informed, that in the neighboring Yearly Meeting of New York, so general is the feeling against voting, in many places, that a prominent Friend is rarely seen at the polls."[10] This was probably an exaggeration. The activities of the non-Quaker nonresistants from around 1838 on seem, however, to have made a certain impact on the Society of Friends, even though few of its members were to be found actually enrolled in the New England Non-Resistance Society.

A small number of Friends did indeed join the Non-Resistance Society and collaborated wholeheartedly in its work, thereby sometimes risking disciplinary action if their meetings (as was quite likely) were unsympathetic. The nonresistants' first president was a highly respected Quaker, Effingham L. Capron (described as a "Friend of the straitest kind"[11]), but he does not appear to have come into collision with his meeting. However, some of the lesser lights among Massachusetts Friends who were active among the nonresistant abolitionists found themselves in trouble.[12]

Since the Non-Resistance Society's activities did not reach out much beyond the Northeast, a direct clash of this kind mainly affected New England Friends. Mention, however, should be made of Lucretia Mott's interest in the work of the Non-Resistance Society. At least during the early years, she attended its annual meetings in Boston as regularly as her domestic and philanthropic duties in Philadelphia permitted and took an active part in their proceedings. The militancy of the movement, the lack of compromise on vital issues like war or slavery, attracted a rebel spirit like Lucretia Mott. A friend once told her she was "the most belligerent Non-Resistant he ever saw." She was immensely pleased. "I have no idea," she said, "because I am a Non-Resistant, of submitting tamely to injustice inflicted either on me or the slave. I will oppose it with all the moral powers with which I am endowed." And she went on to expound her interpretation of Quaker pacifism. "Quakerism, as I understand it, does not mean quietism. The early Friends were agitators; disturbers of the peace; and were more obnoxious in their day to charges which are now so freely made than we are."[13] This kind of view had long before this aroused strong resentment against Lucretia Mott inside her own Hicksite society; many of the more respectable felt she was setting a

[10] *Friends' Weekly Intelligencer*, 21 Aug. 1847.
[11] Wendell Phillips Garrison and Francis Jackson Garrison, *William Lloyd Garrison*, I (1885), 398.
[12] *Non-Resistant*, vol. II, no. 21 (11 Nov. 1840).
[13] Otelia Cromwell, *Lucretia Mott*, pp. 61-63, 170.

dangerous example and that something should be done to prevent further harm. So when in September 1842 she was passing through New York on her way back home from the Non-Resistance Society's annual meeting in Boston, attempts were made to bring her to book. "The elders and others there," she wrote, "have been quite desirous to make me an offender for joining with those not in membership with us and accepting offices in these Societies. But our Friends here [i.e., in Philadelphia, where Lucretia Mott held her membership] knew full well that such a position is neither contrary to our Discipline, to Scripture, to reason, nor sense."[14]

Behind the action attempted against Lucretia Mott stood undoubtedly the figure of George F. White, minister and elder in the Hicksite meeting in New York. White may be taken as typical of the extreme conservative and sectarian element which dominated many meetings at this period—as much in the Orthodox branch as among the Hicksites, it should be added. Only the previous year, White's meeting had disowned the saintly Quaker bookseller, Isaac T. Hopper, for his abolitionist activities. For White and his fellow conservatives, those Friends who had thrown their energies behind the various reform movements of the day, whether peace or abolition or even temperance, and were prepared to work there alongside non-Friends, were betraying the peculiar mission of the Society and by their creaturely activities helping to lay waste the fences so arduously erected around the Quaker enclosure. "Hireling lecturers," "hireling book-agents," "emissaries of Satan," White called the abolitionists. "I had a thousand times rather be a slave, and spend my days with slaveholders, than to dwell in companionship with abolitionists."[15] Despite a genuine devotion to the Quaker peace testimony, part and parcel as it was of the heritage of the Society, White and his kind from the outset took up a position of implacable hostility toward the radical nonresistant movement, tainted as it was for them with the stigma of abolitionism, and did everything they were able to counter its influence, particularly on the younger generation of Friends.

On one occasion, after White had blasted the nonresistants while on a pastoral visit to Philadelphia, a young Friend from Philadelphia Yearly Meeting's Western Quarter wrote to Lucretia Mott: "The attack upon nonresistants was most unexpected. I almost shuddered as he heaped his denunciations upon them. Instantly my mind glanced over the names of a Chapman, Garrison, May, Capron, Burleigh, and Quincy, and my spirit sank with despondency, and yet with some-

[14] *Ibid.*, p. 111.
[15] John Cox, Jr., *Quakerism in the City of New York, 1657–1930*, p. 100.

thing of indignation, when I recollected that he was an accredited Minister of the Society of Friends."[16] Another young man, Oliver Johnson, who was one of Garrison's close collaborators in his work for abolition and nonresistance, had been led by his pacifist and abolitionist sympathies not merely to change his intention of becoming a clergyman in one of the orthodox churches but to withdraw from it altogether and seriously to contemplate joining Friends. The violent attacks of White and the social conservatives on the Non-Resistance Society came as an unpleasant shock to a man like Johnson (if we may trust his account, which he obviously wrote in a state of considerable emotion). "How surprising . . . that a minister of the Society of Friends can utter the language of scorn and reproach towards an institution based upon the identical principles" of his own church.[17] Johnson finally threw in his lot with the antislavery rebel spirits who formed the Progressive Society of Friends.

White told Johnson in the lengthy correspondence they had around 1840 that the Non-Resistance Society was a body framed "in the will of man."[18] The unorthodox religious opinions of many of its members, combined with their militant opposition against "human governments," was enough, indeed, to arouse conservative Friends against it. In addition, the obstructionist tactics and strong language adopted by some of the nonresistants in their campaigning, especially in their role of abolitionists, offended Friends who had long favored quiet and unassuming methods of forwarding their aims. This emotional incompatibility made it extremely difficult for Quakers of this kind to find common ground with radical nonresistants, despite the similarity of their ultimate objectives. So we find in 1840, for instance, the Orthodox Yearly Meetings in New England and New York in official pronouncements castigating the nonresistants roundly and dissociating themselves from "the views of those who deny the necessity of human governments."[19] The Hicksite *Friends' Weekly Intelligencer* was still fulminating, some years later, against the nonresistants, "whose souls were not baptized into the Spirit of the Lamb . . . while they are preaching up forgiveness of injuries, and love towards enemies, they indulge in denunciations towards those who differ from them."[20]

[16] Anna Davis Hallowell, *James and Lucretia Mott: Life and Letters*, pp. 207, 208.
[17] *Correspondence between Oliver Johnson and George F. White, a Minister of the Society of Friends*, pp. 21, 38.
[18] *Ibid.*, p. 5. White's side of the correspondence is characterized by a rancorous and sarcastic tone.
[19] *Non-Resistant*, vol. II, no. 21 (11 Nov. 1840); vol. III, no. 4 (24 Feb. 1841).
[20] *Friends' Weekly Intelligencer*, 21 Aug. 1847.

APPENDIX

Conservatively minded Friends in both branches clearly underestimated the earnestness and sincerity of the bulk of the men and women who threw in their lot with the Non-Resistance Society. Differences as to means, the debate on civil government, were genuine sources of disagreement. But, as we have seen, they were issues which at this date divided Friends themselves. When Sarah Pugh, Philadelphia schoolteacher and close friend of Lucretia Mott and her collaborator in many reform causes, first attended an annual meeting of the Non-Resistance Society, she was agreeably surprised by what she saw there.

> How much [she wrote] are we the creatures of custom! Little faith as I have in drab cloth and broad brims, it seemed strange to me to hear grave and solemn truths uttered by one in the world's garb. . . . Here was a large body of people zealous and earnest for the right, dressed as the worldly dress. It is cheering to see great principles unconnected with sect.[21]

Sarah Pugh, of course, was something of a rebel, and in fact only a handful of Friends ever came directly in contact with the nonresistance movement.

How did the latter react to Quaker attacks? At first many nonresistants seem to have expected considerable support from Friends, and they stressed the similarities between their two viewpoints. As it soon became apparent, however, that such support was not forthcoming, that, instead, hostility was all that they could expect from the Society as a whole, a note of anger appeared; the differences in approach were now emphasized, and Friends' official stand submitted to critical analysis. Garrison wrote sarcastically: "The only difference . . . between the Society of Friends and the Non-Resistance Society, respecting the treatment of enemies, is, that the former goes for the pardon of those who come from abroad, and the latter for the pardon of all, for Christ's sake, whether they are foreign or domestic."[22] And here is that ardent nonresistant, Henry C. Wright, on this subject:

> Friends say we carry things too far, because we will not imprison evil doers. All human governments, as they are now constituted, fall back upon the lifetaking principle, in case of resistance to their laws. When a man is to be seized and imprisoned, government presents to him the alternative of submission or death. . . . Now we cannot imprison evildoers, by existing governmental means, without endangering or threatening their lives. Let us suppose a case. A

[21] *Memorial of Sarah Pugh*, pp. 30, 31.
[22] *Selections from the Writings and Speeches of William Lloyd Garrison*, p. 94.

man is to be arrested and imprisoned; what could a Quaker policeman do in such a case? The Friend seizes him; the criminal is armed and resists. What shall the policeman do? . . . The friends of the criminal come to his rescue, with arms in their hands, and set government at defiance in the person of the policeman. The Friend, when it comes to the point, finds that he is out of his sphere. He, an unarmed man, who believes it to be a sin to make war upon individuals or nations, has undertaken to administer a government, which assumes the right to enforce all its decrees at the point of the bayonet.

And Wright concludes that it is their realization that police duties under the present system are incompatible with their peace testimony that keeps Friends from entering this branch of government service.[23]

Responsibility for the use of armed force by a government, the nonresistants told their Quaker critics, rested in part on those who had voted that government into power. One could not contract out of the unpleasant aspects of government, they argued, and say that one cast his vote for the President only in a civil capacity and not as commander-in-chief as well, or that one would act as magistrate or legislator only where armed force was not involved. In all law enforcement as practised at present "the bayonets are none the less present because unseen," wrote Edmund Quincy, editor of the *Non-Resistant*, in answer to a Quaker correspondent. Granted that a country might be run on Christian, pacifist lines—but these were not the guiding principles "in *existing* government, which Friends support." Since all present-day governments, then, were based on the "life-taking principle," Quincy went on, "we pronounce the Society of Friends, as a body, false to their own principles, in taking part in such governments."[24]

After a decade of intermittent scrapping between nonresistants and radical abolitionists, on the one hand, and their conservative opponents who dominated most Quaker meetings, on the other, H. C. Wright wrote of the latter: "Their sole business now seems to be to administer their Discipline to keep their members '*out of the mixture*'."[25] And undoubtedly many Friends who might have given the radical pacifists a more sympathetic hearing were led by the denunciations of White and his sort to close their minds to an impartial consideration of nonresistant doctrines. But it is very uncertain whether at that date the

[23] Henry C. Wright, *Six Months at Graeffenberg*, pp. 164-66. See also pp. 155-57, 161, 162.
[24] *Non-Resistant*, vol. III, no. 3 (10 Feb. 1841). Italics in the original.
[25] *Non-Resistant and Practical Christian*, vol. IX, no. 12 (14 Oct. 1848). Italics in the original.

majority of Friends in either branch were ready to throw down the walls which separated them from society and, while maintaining intact their own specific peace witness, to collaborate in the work of the wider peace movement. For this reluctance, of course, the extremism and fanaticism displayed by many of the nonresistants and the interparty strife among non-Quaker peace workers were by no means without responsibility. In any case there was perhaps something inherently incompatible between the militant "immediatism" and perfectionism of the non-Quaker nonresistants and the "harmless" pacifism of nineteenth-century Friends which, in the words of one of its advocates, "carries no enmity in its bosom; and leaves the rest of the world in the quiet possession of their own principles."[26]

The story of the Society of Friends' relations with the radical nonresistants (whose movement had virtually disintegrated by the 1850's) illustrates both the strength and the weakness of the Quaker peace testimony during our period. The sober, traditional character of their witness against war prevented Quakers from swallowing the extravagancies and eccentricities associated with the Non-Resistance Society. Friends continued on their way (we cannot quite say unruffled, since some of the utterances and actions of meetings and their leading members were marked by considerable heat and acrimony), bearing a personal testimony against military service when called upon, considering carefully and prayerfully the implications of their pacifism in such matters as paying taxes and carrying on business, and occasionally demonstrating the depth of their pacifist principles in a situation of violence. Yet this witness so carefully nurtured and so rigorously guarded only too often lacked the vital spark. There was little creativity in Friends' thinking on peace during the half-century preceding the Civil War. As pacifists, Friends now had little impact on society. The organized peace movement, both its left and its right wings, while drawing immense inspiration from Friends' witness in the past, gained little assistance or backing from the Society in the present. This was, indeed, a misfortune for the cause of peace, which needed to rally all the support it could get in its uphill struggle with widespread indifference on the part of the many and actual hostility from a militarist minority of the nation.

[26] From Elisha Bates's "Letter to a Military Officer of Distinguished Rank" in the *Moral Advocate*, vol. I, no. 6 (Dec. 1821), p. 84. However, the League of Universal Brotherhood, which had been founded by "the learned blacksmith," Elihu Burritt, during a visit to England in 1846 and was active for about a decade thereafter, gained some support among American Quakers, for it stood for absolute pacifism but without the antistate slant of the New England nonresistants.

============================ *Bibliography* ============================

Note: Items marked with an asterisk came to my attention too late for consideration in the text of this book.

A. PRIMARY SOURCES

1. Archival Materials

American Antiquarian Society (Worcester, Mass.):
  MS Lecture of Elihu Burritt.
Boston Public Library:
  Garrison Papers, MSS A.1.1. and A.1.2.
  Wm. Ll. Garrison's Scrap-Book, MS *4261.64.
  Holland, Frederick West, "The History of the Peace-Cause," MS *5577.98.
  The Manchester Peace Society to the London Peace Society. Report for 1843 Spring Quarter, MS G.31.26.
  Weston Papers, MS A.9.2.
  Wright, Henry Clarke, Scrap-Books, 2 vols., *7573.15.
Harvard University Library:
  Coues, Samuel E., Peace Album, MS Am. *635.
Michigan, University of, William L. Clements Library:
  Weld-Grimké Papers.
Smith College Library (Northampton, Mass.):
  Garrison Letters in Sophia Smith Collection.
Swarthmore College, Friends Historical Library:
  Ferris Collection (R G 5).
Swarthmore College Peace Collection:
  Blanchard, J. P., Scrapbook.
  Chessman, Daniel, "An Essay on Self Defence designed to show that War is inconsistent with Scripture and Reason," MS.
  Collective document groups: Elihu Burritt.
Western Reserve Historical Society Library (Cleveland, Ohio):
  Whiteley, John (ed.), Letters & Documents respecting the Conscription, Arrest & Suffering of Horace S. Taber, A Member of the United Society, Shirley, Mass.

2. Newspapers and Journals

Advocate of Peace (Boston—later Washington, D.C.).
Advocate of Peace and Christian Patriot (Philadelphia).
Advocate of Peace and Universal Brotherhood (Worcester, Mass.).
Boston Commonwealth, 7 Nov. 1885.
Boston Daily Courier, 2 April 1863.
Calumet (New York).
Christian Citizen (Worcester, Mass.)—also known as *Burritt's Christian Citizen*.
Christian Mirror (Portland, Me.).
Friend (Philadelphia).
Friend of Peace (Cambridge, Mass.).
Friends' Weekly Intelligencer (Philadelphia).

BIBLIOGRAPHY

Genius of Universal Emancipation (Baltimore).
Harbinger of Peace (New York).
Liberator (Boston).
Moral Advocate, A Monthly Publication, on War, Duelling, Capital Punishments, and Prison Discipline (Mt. Pleasant, Ohio).
Non-Resistant (Boston).
Non-Resistant and Practical Christian, 1848 (Hopedale, Mass.).
Practical Christian (Hopedale, Mass.).
Radical Spiritualist (Hopedale, Mass.), later *Spiritual Reformer*.
Voice of Peace, 1st ser. (Philadelphia and Mystic, Conn.).

3. Books and Pamphlets: Contemporary Printings

Appeal to American Christians on the Practice of War. By Pacificus, New York, 1830.
Ballou, Adin, *A Discourse on Christian Non-Resistance in Extreme Cases*, Hopedale, 1860.
———, *Non-Resistance in Relation to Human Governments*, Boston, 1839.
Beckwith, George C., *The Book of Peace: A Collection of Essays on War and Peace*, Boston, 1845.
———, *Eulogy on William Ladd, late President of the American Peace Society*, Boston, 1841.
———, *The Peace Manual: or War and its Remedies*, Boston, 1847.
———, *A Universal Peace Society, with the Basis of Co-operation in the Cause of Peace*, Boston, 1844.
Berry, Philip, *A Review of the Mexican War on Christian Principles: and an Essay on the Means of Preventing War*, Columbia (S.C.), 1849.
Blanchard, J. P., *Address delivered at the Thirteenth Anniversary of the Massachusetts Peace Society, December 25, 1828*, Boston, 1829.
———, *Communications on Peace; Written for the Christian Citizen*, Boston, 1848.
———, *Plan for Terminating the War, by Division of the United States, without Concession of Principle or Right on the Part of the North*, n.p.p., [1861].
———, *The War of Secession*, Boston, 1861.
Brigham, H. H., *A Voice from Nazareth. A Letter addressed to the Rev. H. D. Walker, in reply to a War Sermon, preached by him in September 1864*, Plymouth (Mass.), 1865.
Burritt, Elihu, *Ten-Minute Talks on All Sorts of Topics, with Autobiography of the Author*, Boston, 1874.
———, *Thoughts and Things at Home and Abroad*, Boston, 1854.
———, *Voice From the Forge*, London, 1848.
Child, Lydia Maria, *Correspondence between Lydia Maria Child and Gov. Wise and Mrs. Mason, of Virginia*, Boston, 1860.
———, *Letters of Lydia Maria Child*, Boston, 1883.
A Circular Letter from the Massachusetts Peace Society, respectfully addressed to the Various Associations, Presbyteries, Assemblies and Meetings of the Ministers of Religion in the United States, Cambridge (Mass.), 1816.
Cleveland, Aaron, *The Life of Man Inviolable by the Laws of Christ*, Colchester (Conn.), 1815.

Cleveland, Richard C., *Abstract of an Address before the Peace Society of Windham County, at its Annual Meeting in Brooklyn, August 22, 1832*, Brooklyn (Conn.), 1832.
Comings, A. G., *The Reign of Peace. A Series of Discourses*, Boston, 1845.
Correspondence between Oliver Johnson and George F. White, a Minister of the Society of Friends, New York, 1841.
Coues, Samuel E., *War and Christianity: An Address before the American Peace Society on the Fourteenth Anniversary in Boston, Mass., May 23, 1842*, Boston, 1842.
Cox, Samuel Hanson, *Quakerism not Christianity*, New York, 1833.
A Dialogue, between Telemachus and Mentor, on the Rights of Conscience, and Military Requisitions, Boston, 1818.
Dialogues between Frank and William, illustrating the Principles of Peace, Boston, 1838.
Dodge, David Low, *Observations on the Kingdom of Peace, under the Benign Reign of Messiah*, New York, 1816.
———, *Remarks upon an Anonymous Letter, styled, "The Duty of a Christian in a Trying Situation": addressed to the Author of a Pamphlet, entitled, "The Mediator's Kingdom Not of This World,"* Etc., New York, 1810.
Dresser, Amos, *The Bible Against War*, Oberlin, 1849.
Fitch, George, *The Duty of a Christian in a Trying Situation: A Letter to the Author of a Pamphlet, entitled, "The Mediator's Kingdom not of this World, but Spiritual, Heavenly, and Divine,"* New York, 1810.
Flournoy, John J., *An Earnest Appeal for Peace, to all Christians, who, in Heart and Soul, truly love the Lord Jesus Christ, and ardently wish for his Triumph*, Athens (Ga.), 1838.
Furness, W. H., *Put up Thy Sword: A Discourse delivered before Theodore Parker's Society, at the Music Hall, Boston, Sunday, March 11, 1860*, Boston, 1860.
———, *A Word of Consolation for the Kindred of those who have fallen in Battle. A Discourse delivered September 28, 1862*, Philadelphia, 1862.
Garrison, William Lloyd, *The Abolitionists, and their Relations to War*, n.p.p., 1862.
———, *Selections from the Writings and Speeches of William Lloyd Garrison*, Boston, 1852.
Gregory, John, *Anti-War, Two Discourses, delivered at Williston and Burlington, July 1846. Likewise a Discourse, delivered at the Universalist State Convention, Montpelier, August 26, 1846*, Burlington (Vt.) and Boston, 1847.
Grew, Henry, *Address delivered before the Peace Society of Hartford and the Vicinity, Sept. 7, 1828*, Hartford, 1828.
Grimké, Thomas S., *Address on the Truth, Dignity, Power and Beauty of the Principles of Peace, and on the Unchristian Character and Influence of War and the Warrior: delivered in the Centre Church at New Haven, during the Session of the Legislature of Connecticut, at the Request of the Connecticut Peace Society. On Sunday Evening, the 6th of May, 1832*, Hartford, 1832.
———, *Correspondence on the Principles of Peace, Manual Labor Schools, &c.*, Charleston (S.C.), 1833.

―――, (ed.), J. Dymond's *Inquiry into the Accordance of War with Christianity etc....*, Philadelphia, 1834.

―――, *A Letter to the People of South-Carolina*, Charleston, 1832.

Hall, Edward B., *Christians Forbidden to Fight: An Address before the Rhode-Island Peace Society; at its Twenty-Seventh Annual Meeting, June 30, 1844*, Providence, 1844.

Haynes, Sylvanus, *A Brief Reply to the Friend of Peace, or A Concise Vindication of Defensive War*, Auburn (N.Y.), 1824.

Heaton, Adna, *War and Christianity Contrasted; with a Comparative View of their Nature and Effects. Recommended to the Serious and Impartial Consideration of the Professors of the Christian Religion*, New York, 1816.

Hickok, Laurens P., *The Sources of Military Delusion, and the Practicability of their Removal. An Address before the Connecticut Peace Society; delivered at their Second Anniversary, during the Session of the Legislature of Connecticut, Sunday Evening, May 5, 1833, in the Centre Church, Hartford*, Hartford, 1833.

Holcombe, Henry, *The First Fruits, in a Series of Letters*, Philadelphia, 1812.

―――, *The Martial Christian's Manual*, Philadelphia, 1823.

Huntington, F. D., *Peace, the Demand of Christianity. A Sermon preached in the South Congregational Church, December 28, 1845*, Boston, 1846.

Jones, Elijah, *Address delivered at the Fifth Anniversary of the Peace Society of Minot, November 5, 1828*, Portland (Me.), 1828.

Judd, Sylvester, *A Moral Review of the Revolutionary War, or Some of the Evils of that Event Considered*, Hallowell (Me.), 1842.

Kellogg, Ezra B., *War Contrary to the Gospel. A Sermon, preached before the Peace Society of Windham County, February 4, 1830*. Providence (R.I.), 1830.

Ladd, William, *The Duty of Women to Promote the Cause of Peace*, Boston, 1840 edn.

―――, "History of Peace Societies" in *Scientific Tracts, for the Diffusion of Useful Knowledge*, Boston, 1836.

―――, *Obstacles and Objections to the Cause of Permanent and Universal Peace considered by a Layman*, Boston, 1837.

Lord, Eleazar, *Thoughts on the Practical Advantages of those who hold the Doctrines of Peace, over those who vindicate War. Addressed to those who "follow Peace with All Men,"* New York, 1816.

Lord, John, *An Address delivered before the Peace Society of Amherst College, July 4, 1839*, Amherst, 1839.

Lovejoy, Joseph and Owen, *Memoir of the Rev. Elijah P. Lovejoy; who was murdered in Defence of the Liberty of the Press at Alton, Illinois, Nov. 7, 1837*, New York, 1838.

May, Samuel J., *An Address delivered before the American Peace Society, in Park Street Church, Boston, May 28, 1860*, Boston, 1860.

―――, *Liberty or Slavery, the Only Question*, Syracuse, 1856.

―――, *Some Recollections of our Antislavery Conflict*, Boston, 1869.

M'Kenzie, James A., *A Discourse, against Life-Taking, delivered by request, before the Rhode-Island Quarterly Meeting in Tiverton, August 24, 1842*, 2nd edn., Providence, 1842.

Memorial of Sarah Pugh. A Tribute of Respect from her Cousins, Philadelphia, 1888.

The Military Profession Unlawful for a Christian, Norwich (England), n.d.
Noyes, John H., *The Berean: A Manual for the Help of those who seek the Faith of the Primitive Church*, Putney (Vt.), 1847.
Peabody, Andrew P., *Lessons from Our Late Rebellion. An Address delivered at the Anniversary of the American Peace Society, May 19, 1867*, Boston, 1867.
———, *The Nature and Influence of War. An Address delivered before the American Peace Society at its Annual Meeting, May 29, 1843*, Boston, 1843.
———, *The Triumphs of War. A Sermon preached on the Day of the Annual Fast, April 15, 1847*, Portsmouth (N.H.), 1847.
Pilkington, George (ed.), *Testimonies of Ministers, of Various Denominations, shewing the Unlawfulness to Christians of All Wars, Offensive or Defensive*, London, 1837.
The Proceedings of the First General Peace Convention: held in London, June 22, 1843, and the Two Following Days, London, 1843.
Proceedings of the Peace Convention, held in Boston, in the Marlboro' Chapel, September 18, 19 & 20, 1838, Boston, 1838.
The Question of War Reviewed, New York, 1818.
Remarks by a Member of the Society of Friends on the Subject of War, in reply to A.M., who addressed the Society on that Subject, n.p.p., n.d. [1847?]
Report on the Injustice and Inequality of the Militia Law of Massachusetts, with Regard to the Rights of Conscience, Boston, 1838.
Report of the New-York Peace Society, at the Anniversary, Dec. 25, 1818, New York, 1818.
Report on the Tendency and Effects of the Pacific Principle, and also on Military Establishments in Time of Peace, Boston, 1838.
Smith, Gerrit, *Peace better than War. Address delivered before the American Peace Society, at its Thirteenth Anniversary held in the City of Boston, May 24, 1858*, Boston, 1858.
———, *Sermons and Speeches of Gerrit Smith*, New York, 1861.
———, *Speeches of Gerrit Smith in Congress*, New York, 1855.
Spear, J. A., *Remarks, offered in a Non-Resistance Convention, held in East Bethel, February 24th and 25th, 1841*, Brandon (Vt.), [1841].
Spofford, Jeremiah, *A Vindication of the Right of Civil Government and Self-Defense; A Lecture Delivered at Bradford, Ms. in reply to several Itinerant Lecturers, on Non-Resistance, &c.*, Haverhill (Mass.), n.d.
Stebbins, Rufus S., *An Address delivered before the Peace Society of Amherst College, July 4, 1838*, Amherst, 1838.
———, *Address on the Subject of Peace, delivered at the Odeon, on Sabbath Evening, February 7, 1836. On the Anniversary of the Bowdoin Street Young Men's Peace Society*, Boston, 1836.
Stone, Thomas T., *Sermons on War*, Boston, 1829.
Sumner, Charles, *The True Grandeur of Nations: An Oration delivered before the Authorities of the City of Boston, July 4, 1845*, Boston, 1845.
———, *The War System of the Commonwealth of Nations*, Boston, 1849.
The Tenth Annual Report of the American Peace Society, Boston, 1838.
Tilden, W. P., *All War Forbidden by Christianity. An Address, to the Citizens of Dover, delivered on Thanksgiving Evening Nov. 25, 1847*, Dover (N.H.), 1847.

Tukesbury, T. F., *The Taking of Human Life incompatible with Christianity: with Remarks on the "Present Crisis,"* Boston, 1864.

Upham, Thomas C., *The Manual of Peace*, New York, 1836.

Walker, Amasa, *Iron-clad War-ships: Or, the Prospective Revolution in the War System. Speech of Hon. Amasa Walker, before the American Peace Society, at its Anniversary in Boston, May 26, 1862*, Boston, 1862.

———, *Le Monde; or In Time of Peace Prepare for War*, London, 1859.

———, *The Suicidal Folly of the War System. An Address before the American Peace Society, at its Anniversary in Boston May 25, 1863*, Boston, 1863.

War Unchristian; or the Custom of War compared with the Standard of Christian Duty, Hartford, 1834.

Wayland, Francis, *The Duty of Obedience to the Civil Magistrate: Three Sermons preached in the Chapel of Brown University*, Boston, 1847.

———, *The Elements of Moral Science*, New York, 1835. Also 1963 edn., ed. Joseph L. Blau, Cambridge (Mass.).

Whelpley, Samuel, *Letters addressed to Caleb Strong, Esq. late Governor of Massachusetts: showing War to be inconsistent with the Laws of Christ, and the Good of Mankind*, 2nd edn., Philadelphia, 1817.

Whelpley, Samuel W., *An Address delivered before the Peace Society of Hartford County in the Centre Church, Hartford*, Hartford, 1830.

Whipple, Charles K., *Evils of the Revolutionary War*, Boston, 1839.

———, *Non-Resistance applied to the Internal Defence of a Community*, Boston, 1860.

———, *The Non-Resistance Principle: With Particular Application to the Help of Slaves by Abolitionists*, Boston, 1860.

———, *The Powers that be are ordained of God*, Boston, 1841.

Worcester, Leonard, *A Discourse on the Alton Outrage, delivered at Peacham, Vermont, December 17, 1837*, Concord (N.H.), 1838.

Wright, Henry C., *Anthropology; or the Science of Man: in its Bearing on War and Slavery, and on Arguments from the Bible, Marriage, God, Death, Retribution, Atonement and Government, in Support of these and other Social Wrongs: in a Series of Letters to a Friend in England*, Cincinnati, 1850.

———, *Ballot Box and Battle Field. To Voters under the United States Government*, Boston, 1842.

———, *Christian Church; Anti-Slavery and Non-Resistance applied to Church Organizations*, Boston, 1841.

———, *Defensive War proved to be a Denial of Christianity and of the Government of God: with Illustrative Facts and Anecdotes*, London, 1846.

———, *Dick Crowninshield, the Assassin, and Zachary Taylor, the Soldier: The Difference between Them*, n.p.p., 1848.

———, *The Employers of Dick Crowninshield, the Assassin, and the Employers of Zachary Taylor, the Soldier: The Difference*, Hopedale (Mass.), 1848.

———, *Henry C. Wright's Peace Tracts*, Dublin, 1843: no. 1, *The Heroic Boy*; no. 2, *Forgiveness in a Bullet!*; no. 3, *The Immediate Abolition of the Army and Navy*.

———, *A Kiss for a Blow*, Dublin, 1843.

BIBLIOGRAPHY

———, *Man-Killing, by Individuals and Nations, Wrong-Dangerous in All Cases*, Boston, 1841.
———, *The Natick Resolution; or, Resistance to Slaveholders the Right and Duty of Southern Slaves and Northern Freeman*, Boston, 1859.
———, *No Rights, No Duties: Or, Slaveholders, as Such, have no Rights; Slaves, as such, owe no Duties. An Answer to a Letter from Hon. Henry Wilson, touching Resistance to Slaveholders being the Right and Duty of the Slaves, and of the People and States of the North*, Boston, 1860.
———, *Six Months at Graeffenberg; with Conversations in the Saloon, on Nonresistance and other Subjects*, London, 1845.
Yale, Cyrus, *War Unreasonable and Unscriptural. An Address before the Hartford Peace Society; delivered on the Evening of November 11, 1832, in the Centre Church, Hartford*, Hartford, 1833.

4. Later Edited Works and Documentary Collections

Ballou, Adin, *Autobiography of Adin Ballou*, ed. William S. Heywood, Lowell (Mass.), 1896.
———, *Christian Non-Resistance in all its Important Bearings, Illustrated and Defended*, ed. W. S. Heywood, Philadelphia, 1910.
———, *History of the Hopedale Community from its Inception to its Virtual Submergence in the Hopedale Parish*, ed. W. S. Heywood, Lowell (Mass.), 1897.
———, *Primitive Christianity and its Corruptions*, ed. W. S. Heywood, vol. II, Lowell (Mass.), 1899.
Barnes, Gilbert H., and Dwight L. Dumond (eds.), *Letters of Theodore Dwight Weld, Angelina Grimké Weld and Sarah Grimké, 1822-1844*, 2 vols., New York, 1934.
Barnes, James A. (ed.), "Letters of a Massachusetts Woman Reformer to an Indiana Radical," *Indiana Magazine of History* (Bloomington, Ind.), vol. XXVI, no. 1 (March 1930).
Dodge, David Low, *Memorial of Mr. David L. Dodge*, Boston, 1854.
———, *War Inconsistent with the Religion of Jesus Christ*, ed. Edwin D. Mead, Boston, 1905 edn.
Emerson, Ralph Waldo, *English Traits*, vol. V of *The Complete Works* (Autograph Centenary Edition), Cambridge (Mass.), 1903.
———, *The Journals and Miscellaneous Notebooks of Ralph Waldo Emerson*, ed. William H. Gilman and Alfred R. Ferguson, vol. III, Cambridge (Mass.), 1963.
———, *Miscellanies*, vol. XI of *The Complete Works* (Autograph Centenary Edition), Cambridge (Mass.), 1904.
Ladd, William, *An Essay on a Congress of Nations for the Adjustment of International Disputes without Resort to Arms* (1840), ed. James Brown Scott, New York, 1916.
Lynd, Staughton (ed.), *Nonviolence in America: A Documentary History*, Indianapolis, 1966.
Mayer, Peter (ed.), *The Pacifist Conscience*, London, 1966.
Thoreau, Henry David, "Civil Disobedience" in *Miscellanies*, vol. X of *The Writings of Henry David Thoreau*, Cambridge (Mass.), 1893 edn.
Tolstoy, Leo, *The Kingdom of God and Peace Essays*, London, 1936 edn.
Weinberg, Arthur and Lila (eds.), *Instead of Violence*, Boston, 1965 edn.

Wilson, Lewis G. (ed.), "The Christian Doctrine of Non-Resistance: Unpublished Correspondence between Count Leo Tolstoi and the Rev. Adin Ballou," *Arena* (Boston), vol. III, no. XIII (Dec. 1890).
Worcester, Noah, *A Solemn Review of the Custom of War*, Boston, 1904 edn.

B. SECONDARY WORKS

Books, Articles, and Dissertations

Adams, Robert, "Nathaniel Peabody Rogers: 1794-1846," *New England Quarterly*, vol. XX, no. 3 (Sept. 1947).
Allen, Devere, "Daniel Chessman: An Unheard Voice for Peace," *Friend* (Phila.), 10 Aug. 1952.
———, *The Fight for Peace*, New York, 1930.
Bardwell, Horatio, *Memoir of Rev. Gordon Hall, A.M.*, Andover, 1834.
Barnes, Gilbert Hobbs, *The Antislavery Impulse 1830-1844*, New York, 1933.
Beales, A.C.F., *The History of Peace*, London, 1931.
Birney, Caroline M., *The Grimké Sisters: Sarah and Angelina Grimké*, Boston, 1885.
Bodo, John R., *The Protestant Clergy and Public Issues 1812-1848*, Princeton (N.J.), 1954.
Brigance, William Norwood (ed.), *A History and Criticism of American Public Address*, vol. II, New York, 1943.
Brock, Peter, *Pacifism in the United States: From the Colonial Era to the First World War*, Princeton (N.J.), 1968.
Chapman, John Jay, *William Lloyd Garrison*, Boston, 1921 edn.
Commager, Henry Steele, *Theodore Parker*, Boston, 1960 edn.
Coulter, E. Merton, *John Jacobus Flournoy: Champion of the Common Man in the Antebellum South*, Savannah (Ga.), 1942.
Cox, John, Jr., *Quakerism in the City of New York 1657-1930*, New York, 1930.
Cromwell, Otelia, *Lucretia Mott*, Cambridge (Mass.), 1958.
Crosby, Ernest, *Garrison the Non-Resistant*, Chicago, 1905.
Cross, Whitney R., *The Burned-Over District*, New York, 1965 edn.
Curti, Merle Eugene, *The American Peace Crusade, 1815-1860*, Durham, (N.C.), 1929.
———, *The Learned Blacksmith: The Letters and Journals of Elihu Burritt*, New York, 1937.
———, "Non-Resistance in New England," *New England Quarterly*, vol. II, no. 1 (Jan. 1929).
———, "The Peace Movement and the Mid-Century Revolutions," *Advocate of Peace through Justice* (Washington, D.C.), vol. 90, no. 5 (May 1928).
———, *Peace or War: The American Struggle, 1636-1936*, New York, 1936.
———, "Poets of Peace and the Civil War," *World Unity* (N.Y.), vol. X, no. 3 (June 1932).
Demos, John, "The Antislavery Movement and the Problem of Violent 'Means'," *New England Quarterly*, vol. XXXVII, no. 4 (Dec. 1964).
Dillon, Merton L., *Elijah P. Lovejoy, Abolitionist Editor*, Urbana (Ill.), 1961.

BIBLIOGRAPHY

Doherty, Robert W., "Alfred H. Love and the Universal Peace Union," Ph.D. diss., U. of Pennsylvania, 1962.
Donald, David, *Charles Sumner and the Coming of the Civil War*, New York, 1960.
Ellsworth, Clayton Sumner, "The American Churches and the Mexican War," *American Historical Review*, vol. XLV, no. 2 (Jan. 1940).
Filler, Louis, *The Crusade against Slavery, 1830-1860*, New York, 1960.
———, "Parker Pillsbury: An Anti-Slavery Apostle," *New England Quarterly*, vol. XIX, no. 3 (Sept. 1946).
Ford, Worthington Chauncey, "Sumner's Oration on the 'True Grandeur of Nations,' July 4, 1845," *Massachusetts Historical Society. Proceedings*, vol. L, Boston, 1917.
Fox, R. Hingston, *Dr. John Fothergill and His Friends*, London, 1919.
Freehling, William W., *Prelude to Civil War: The Nullification Controversy in South Carolina 1816-1836*, New York, 1966.
Galpin, W. Freeman, "God's Chore Boy: Samuel Joseph May" (typescript [1939]).
———, *Pioneering for Peace: A Study of American Peace Efforts to 1846*, Syracuse (N.Y.), 1933.
Garrison, Wendell Phillips, and Francis Jackson Garrison, *William Lloyd Garrison 1805-1879: The Story of His Life told by His Children*, New York, vols. 1-2 (1885) and vols. 3-4 (1889).
Gill, John, *Tide without Turning: Elijah P. Lovejoy and Freedom of the Press*, Boston [1958].
Hall, Arethusa, *Life and Character of the Rev. Sylvester Judd*, Boston, 1854.
Hallowell, Anna Davis, *James and Lucretia Mott. Life and Letters*, Boston, 1884.
Harlow, Ralph Volney, *Gerrit Smith: Philanthropist and Reformer*, New York, 1939.
Hemleben, Sylvester John, *Plans for World Peace through Six Centuries*, Chicago, 1943.
Hemmenway, John, *The Apostle of Peace: Memoir of William Ladd*, Boston, 1872.
Hendrick, George, "The Influence of Thoreau's 'Civil Disobedience' on Gandhi's Satyagraha," *New England Quarterly*, vol. XXIX, no. 4 (Dec. 1956).
Hershberger, Guy F., "Some Religious Pacifists of the Nineteenth Century," *Mennonite Quarterly Review* (Goshen, Ind.), vol. X, no. 1 (Jan. 1936).
Hoblitzelle, Harrison, "The War against War in the Nineteenth Century: A Study of the Western Backgrounds of Gandhian Thought," Ph.D. diss., Columbia U., 1959.
Howe, M. A. DeWolfe, "Biographer's Bait: A Reminder of Edmund Quincy," *Proceedings of the Massachusetts Historical Society*, vol. LXVIII, Boston, 1952.
Huggard, William Allen, *Emerson and the Problem of War and Peace*, Iowa City (Iowa), 1938.
Johnson, Oliver, *William Lloyd Garrison and His Times*, Boston, 1880.
Korngold, Ralph, *Two Friends of Man*, Boston, 1950.
Lader, Lawrence, *The Bold Brahmins: New England's War against Slavery, 1831-1863*, New York, 1961.

BIBLIOGRAPHY

*Lerner, Gerda, *The Grimké Sisters from South Carolina: Rebels against Slavery*, Boston, 1967.
Ludlum, David M., *Social Ferment in Vermont 1791-1850*, New York, 1939.
*Lynd, Staughton, *Intellectual Origins of American Radicalism*, New York, 1968.
McPherson, James M., *The Struggle for Equality: Abolitionists and the Negro in the Civil War and Reconstruction*, Princeton (N.J.), 1964.
May, Joseph, *Samuel Joseph May: A Memorial Study*, Boston, 1898.
Memoir of Samuel Joseph May, Boston, 1873.
Merrill, Walter M., *Against Wind and Tide: A Biography of Wm. Lloyd Garrison*, Cambridge (Mass.), 1963.
Morgan, Robert H., "John Wells and Adna Heaton: Early American Exponents of Quaker Pacifism," *Friend* (Phila.), vol. 114, no. 6 (19 Sept. 1940).
Nye, Russel B., *William Lloyd Garrison and the Humanitarian Reformers*, Boston, 1955.
*Pease, William H. and Jane H., "Freedom and Peace: A Nineteenth Century Dilemma," *Midwest Quarterly* (Pittsburg, Kan.), vol. IX, no. 1 (Oct. 1967).
Phelps, Christina, *The Anglo-American Peace Movement in the Mid-Nineteenth Century*, New York, 1930.
Pierce, Edward L., *Memoir and Letters of Charles Sumner*, vol. II, Boston, 1877.
Pillsbury, Parker, *Acts of the Anti-Slavery Apostles*, Concord (N.H.), 1883.
———, "Stephen Symonds Foster," *Granite Monthly* (Manchester, N.H.), Aug. 1882.
Quincy, Josiah Phillips, "Memoir of Edmund Quincy," *Proceedings of the Massachusetts Historical Society*, 2nd ser., vol. XVIII (1905), Boston.
Sanborn, F. B., and William T. Harris, *A. Bronson Alcott: His Life and Philosophy*, vol. I, Boston, 1893.
Schou, August, *Histoire de l'Internationalisme*, vol. III, Oslo, 1963.
Schuster, Eunice Minette, *Native American Anarchism: A Study of Left-Wing American Individualism*, Northampton (Mass.), 1932.
Shepard, Odell, *Pedlar's Progress: The Life of Bronson Alcott*, Boston, 1937.
Thistlethwaite, Frank, *America and the Atlantic Community: Anglo-American Aspects, 1790-1850*, New York, 1963 edn.
Thomas, Benjamin P., *Theodore Weld: Crusader for Freedom*, New Brunswick (N.J.), 1950.
Thompson, Mack, *Moses Brown: Reluctant Reformer*, Chapel Hill (N.C.), 1962.
Tolis, Peter, "Elihu Burritt: Crusader for Brotherhood," Ph.D. diss., Columbia U., 1965.
Tyler, Alice Felt, *Freedom's Ferment*, New York, 1962 edn.
Villard, Fanny Garrison, *William Lloyd Garrison on Non-Resistance*, New York, 1924.
Walker, Amasa, *Memoir of Rev. Amos Dresser*, n.p.p., n.d.
Ware, Henry, Jr., *Memoirs of the Rev. Noah Worcester, D.D.*, Boston, 1844.
Wayland, Francis, and H. L. Wayland, *A Memoir of the Life and Labors of Francis Wayland D.D., LL.D., late President of Brown University*, vol. II, New York, 1867.

Whitney, Edson L., *The American Peace Society: A Centennial History*, Washington (D.C.), 1928.
Willis, Frederick L. H., *Alcott Memoirs*, Boston, 1915.
Wright, Edward Needles, *Conscientious Objectors in the Civil War*, New York, 1961 edn.
Wyman, Lillie Buffum Chace, and Arthur Crawford Wyman, *Elizabeth Buffum Chace 1806-1899: Her Life and Its Environment*, vol. I, Boston, 1914.

Index

Adams, President John, 27
Adams, President John Quincy, 82
Adventists, Seventh-Day, 266
Alcott, Amos Bronson, author and communitarian, 126, 131, 134, 232
Allen, Dr. William, opponent of Thomas Grimké, 57-59, 68, 74, 78
American Anti-Slavery Society, 84-86, 90-93, 164, 222
American Civil War, *see* Civil War
American Colonization Society, 94
American Peace Society, 15, 27, 32, 78-80, 86, 87, 93-95, 106, 148, 170ff., 187-90, 205, 206, 211, 254; early years of, 36ff.; and the New England Non-Resistance Society, 95, 109-14, 132, 138, 153, 166, 170-72, 203; schism in the 1840's, 193-204, 221, 222; and the Civil War, 240-42, 246, 255, 258-60; and Quakers, 269-71. *See also* Beckwith, Rev. George C.; Blanchard, Joshua P.; Ladd, William; League of Universal Brotherhood; Wright, Rev. Henry Clarke
Amish, 28, 128
Anabaptists, tradition of, 149, 150, 155, 265
Angell, Norman, writer on peace, 7

Ballou, Adin, communitarian and nonresistant, 118, 131, 133, 135-37, 239, 250, 263; writings on nonresistance, 139, 141, 144-58, 167-69, 231, 232-34, 272. *See also* Hopedale community
Barclay, Robert, Scottish Quaker and theologian, 6
Barnard, Hannah (*née* Jenkins), Quaker, and Old Testament wars, 193
Bates, Elisha, Quaker editor, 29
Beach, Rev. Thomas P., Garrisonian militant, 123, 124
Bearse, Austin, sea captain and abolitionist, 123
Beckwith, Rev. George C., secretary of the American Peace Society, 30, 37, 74, 75, 94, 172, 180, 194, 195, 197-99, 201-4, 211, 216, 222, 231; and the New England Non-Resistance Society, 95, 110, 114, 170, 171; writings on the peace question, 173, 174-76, 204-6; and the Civil War, 241, 242, 263. *See also* American Peace Society

Beecher, Rev. Henry Ward, Congregationalist minister and reformer, 234
Beecher, Rev. Lyman, Protestant preacher and reformer, 15
Benson, George W., Quaker aboltionist and nonresistant, 97, 103, 119, 126
Berry, Rev. Philip, peace advocate, 191, 192
Blanchard, Joshua P., Boston merchant and peace advocate, 25, 27, 77, 213; as conscientious objector, 3; and the American Peace Society, 43, 44, 173, 197, 199; and the New England Non-Resistance Society, 170; and the Civil War, 241, 242, 246, 260-63
Boston Free Church Peace Society, 65, 66
Bowdoin College (Brunswick, Maine), pacifist groups at, 65, 66, 69, 74
Bowdoin Street, Young Men's Peace Society, 66
Boyle, James, ex-clergyman and eccentric, 124, 125
Bradford, Samuel, Indiana nonresistant, 127, 128
Bradley, Elisha and Joseph, Revolutionary War veterans turned pacifists, 119
Brethren, Church of the, xiii, xiv, 29
Brigham, H. H., New England nonresistant, 259
Bright, John, English Quaker and politician, 209
British West Indies, Quakers in, xii
Brown, John, antislavery militant, 121, 165, 221, 235-39, 241, 243, 254
Brown, Moses, Rhode Island Quaker, 29, 270
Brownson, Orestes, writer and social reformer, 104
Buckingham, James Silk, English radical politician and reformer, 109, 113
Bullard, Baalis, conscientious objector, 3, 4
Burritt, Elihu, peace advocate and reformer, 195-203, 221, 222, 229, 244; and League of Universal Brotherhood, 178, 199, 206-20, 279; and Garrisonian nonresistants, 203, 211, 212; and the Civil War, 245-46, 259, 260, 263

Calhoun, John C., Southern politician, 50

293

INDEX

Campbell, David, health reformer and conscientious objector, 128, 129

Canada, Mennonites and Brethren in Christ in, 28

Capron, Effingham L., Quaker abolitionist and nonresistant, 103, 125, 136, 274

Carlyle, Thomas, English historian and essayist, 80

Chace, Elizabeth Buffum, Quaker, 119, 120

Channing, Dr. Walter, peace advocate and brother of William Ellery, 199, 232

Channing, Rev. William Ellery, Unitarian minister, 30, 31, 92, 187, 199

Chapman, Mrs. Maria W. (*née* Weston), Garrisonian abolitionist and nonresistant, 96, 103, 118, 125, 167, 244

Chessman, Rev. Daniel, peace advocate, 20-22

Child, David Lee, lawyer and antislavery advocate, 85

Child, Mrs. Lydia Maria, novelist and abolitionist, 96, 114, 236, 244, 247, 248

Civil War, *see* American Peace Society; Burritt Elihu; Garrison, William Lloyd; May, Rev. Samuel Joseph; New England Non-Resistance Society; Quakers; Walker, Amasa; Weld, Charles S.F.; Whipple, Charles K.; Wright, Rev. Henry Clarke

Clarkson, Thomas, English evangelical and antislavery advocate, 7, 11, 20, 57, 176, 188

Cleveland, Rev. Aaron, peace advocate, 15-18

Clinton, Governor De Witt, 17

Coffin, Elijah, Quaker, 272

Collins, John A., Garrisonian abolitionist, communitarian, and agnostic, 120, 141

Colver, Rev. Nathaniel, abolitionist and reformer, 126

"come-outers," in the New England Non-Resistance Society, 122-24, 141

Comings, A. G., Disciple of Christ and pacifist pamphleteer, 190

Connecticut Peace Society, 47, 49, 54, 55

conscientious objectors, in the antebellum peace movement, 63, 64, 68, 69, 119, 123, 128, 129, 256, 257. See *also* New England Non-Resistance Society

Conway, Moncure Daniel, pioneer of modern humanism, 243

Coues, Samuel E., peace advocate, 183, 185, 197

Cox, Rev. Samuel H., anti-Quaker polemicist, 122

Crosfield, Joseph, English Quaker, 207

Czech Brethren, Unity of (*Unitas Fratrum*), 150

Davis, Edmund M., Quaker abolitionist and son-in-law of James and Lucretia Mott, 139

Davis, Jefferson, Confederate president, 248, 255

Dodge, David Low, peace advocate, 20-23, 25, 32-36, 77, 180, 193, 269

Dresser, Rev. Amos, abolitionist and peace advocate, 125-27, 192, 193

Drew, Thomas, colleague of Elihu Burritt, 209

Dunkers, *see* Brethren, Church of the

Dymond, Jonathan, English Quaker, writer on the peace testimony, 47, 52, 62, 64, 176, 189, 269

Emerson, Ralph Waldo, and war, 78-80

Erasmus, Desiderius, 11

Estabrook, Rev. E., pacifist views of, 22, 23

Ferris, Benjamin, Quaker leader, conscientious objector in the War of 1812, 273

Flournoy, John Jacobus, writer and eccentric, 178-80

Folsom, Abigail, loquacious eccentric, 126, 130, 271-72

Foster, Aaron, peace advocate, 197, 198

Foster, Abby (*née* Kelley), Garrisonian abolitionist and nonresistant, wife of Stephen S., 96, 107, 108, 132, 136, 234, 247

Foster, Stephen Symonds, Garrisonian militant, 123, 124, 132, 136, 223, 228, 231-34, 239, 244

Fothergill, Samuel, Quaker minister, 268

Fox, George, founder of Quakerism, xi

Friends, Society of, *see* Quakers

Fry, Edmund, English Quaker, son of Elizabeth Fry, 209

Fry, Elizabeth, English Quaker and prison reformer, 209, 213

INDEX

Furness, Rev. W. H., Unitarian minister and peace advocate, 243, 244

Gandhi, Mahatma, 99, 124, 134, 163, 169, 224
Garrison, Francis Jackson, son of William Lloyd, 252
Garrison, George, son of William Lloyd, 252
Garrison, Wendell Phillips, son of William Lloyd, 252
Garrison, William Lloyd, leading abolitionist and nonresistant, 79, 89, 140, 157, 170, 173; early career of, 81-84; genesis of nonresistant views of, 83, 87, 88; and Quakers, 83; and the antislavery movement, 84-87, 90, 92, 93; and John Humphrey Noyes, 87, 88; and founding of New England Non-Resistance Society, 94ff., 271; and development of New England Non-Resistance Society, 116-20, 126-29, 131-33, 136, 221; writings on nonresistance, 142, 143, 144, 146, 150, 151, 160, 164; on nonresistance and slavery, 223-25, 227, 233, 234-39; and the Civil War, 244, 248-54, 256, 263
Garrison, William Lloyd, Jr., son of William Lloyd, 252
Goodell, Rev. William, abolitionist editor, 115
Gregory, John, Universalist nonresistant, 122
Grew, Rev. Henry, peace advocate, 42, 44
Grimké, Angelina, abolitionist and reformer, 88, 89, 92, 95, 107, 229, 235, 244, 247, 248
Grimké, Sarah, abolitionist and reformer, 88, 89, 95, 107, 108, 110, 172, 235, 239, 247, 248
Grimké, Thomas S., peace advocate, 47-52, 54, 56-59, 64, 67, 74, 77, 86, 88, 100, 178, 235
Gurney Joseph John, English Quaker minister and evangelical writer, 176

Hall, Rev. Edward B., peace advocate, 185-87
Hall, Rev. Gordon, missionary in India and pacifist, 6, 7
Hancock, Dr. Thomas, Irish Quaker, 34, 44, 47, 269
Hartford County Peace Society, 42, 44, 53

Haskell, Thomas, nonresistant and conscientious objector, 119, 210, 211
Haynes, Rev. Sylvanus, antipacifist writer, 32
Heaton, Adna, Quaker writer on peace, 20
Heywood, Ezra H., radical reformer, 260, 263
Heywood, William S., Hopedale communitarian, 66
Hickok, Rev. Laurens P., peace advocate, 54, 55
Higginson, Rev. Thomas W., abolitionist, 232
Holcombe, Rev. Henry, peace advocate, 29, 30
Hopedale community (Mass.), 130, 133, 136, 222. See also Ballou, Adin
Hopper, Isaac T., dissident Quaker and antislavery advocate, 157, 275
Huntington, Rev. Frederic Daniel, peace advocate, 190
Huxley, Aldous, English novelist and pacifist, 61

International Bible Students, see Jehovah's Witnesses
Irish Quakers, and the rebellion of 1798, 44, 47, 147, 176, 269

Jackson, President Andrew, 50, 82
Jackson, E. W., radical pacifist and follower of Elihu Burritt, 212
Jefferson, Rev. Joseph John, secretary of the London Peace Society, 209
Jehovah's Witnesses, 266
Johnson, Oliver, Garrisonian abolitionist and nonresistant, 103, 244, 249, 276
Jones, Rev. Elijah, peace advocate, 42, 43
Judd, Rev. Sylvester, peace advocate, 180-83
Julian, George W., abolitionist and congressman, 247, 248

Kelley, Abby, see Foster
Kellogg, Rev. Ezra B., peace advocate, 44
Kersey, Jesse, Quaker nonresistant, 273
Knapp, Isaac, abolitionist publisher, 66
Kossuth, Lajos, Magyar patriot, 160

Ladd, William, peace advocate, 13, 30, 77, 82, 149, 174, 180, 195, 202; and the American Peace Society, 36-42,

46, 47, 52, 57-59, 69-75, 92-94, 138, 172, 173, 176, 177, 270; and the New England Non-Resistance Society, 109-11, 113, 130, 170, 171; death of, 194

League of Universal Brotherhood, 178, 183, 193, 222, 242, 244, 279; founding of, 199, 206-9; pledge of, 200, 208, 210-13, 217, 218; development of, 209-15; decline of, 215, 217-19; achievements of, 215-17, 220. *See also* Burritt, Elihu

Leavitt, Rev. Joshua, abolitionist, 212

Ledyard, Samuel, militarist turned pacifist, 119

Lincoln, President Abraham, 248, 249, 261

London Peace Society, 14, 26, 73, 132, 211, 215, 216, 270

Lord, Rev. John, peace advocate, 174

Love, Alfred H., nonresistant and reformer, 119; conscientious objector in the Civil War, 253

Lovejoy, Rev. Elijah P., antislavery martyr, 86, 90-93, 102, 106, 124

Lowell, James Russell, poet, 106, 134

Lundy, Benjamin, Quaker, antislavery advocate, 82-84

McHenry, Jerry, fugitive slave, 226

M'Kenzie, Rev. James A., peace advocate, 185

Maine Peace Society, 36

Malcolm, Rev. Howard, peace advocate, 176, 177

Massachusetts Anti-Slavery Society, 84, 86, 92, 111

Massachusetts Peace Society, 15, 25-28, 36, 38, 43, 56, 269. *See also* Worcester, Rev. Noah

May, Rev. Samuel Joseph, Unitarian minister and reformer, 39, 47, 52, 53, 85, 87, 92-94, 97, 100, 104-7, 122, 124, 137, 173, 211, 271; on nonresistance and slavery, 225-28, 232, 234, 235; and the Civil War, 244, 254, 255

Mennonites, xiii, xiv, 29, 63, 128

Michigan, nonresistants in, 127

military service, *see* conscientious objectors; New England Non-Resistance Society

Miller, William, founder of Adventism, 121, 122

Mitchell, Seward, Garrisonian nonresistant, 248

Moravians, xiii, 185

Mott, James, Jr., Philadelphia Quaker, 143

Mott, Lucretia, wife of James Mott, Jr., reformer, 87, 125, 139, 143, 274-77

Murray, Rev. John, nonresistant and communitarian, 144

Murray, Rev. Orson S., follower of Garrison and newspaper editor, 104

Nat Turner's slave revolt, 84

New England Anti-Slavery Society, *see* Massachusetts Anti-Slavery Society

New England Non-Resistance Society, 36ff., 76, 80, 185, 221, 266; founding of, 95-104; and women's rights, 95, 96; Declaration of Sentiments, 96-100, 104, 105, 107, 110, 112, 120, 127, 139, 172; and conscientious objection, 100, 101, 119, 128, 129; Constitution of, 102, 103, 110, 120; development of, 113ff.; annual conventions, 120, 125, 126, 131, 135, 136; and Mexican War, 133-35, 187; books and pamphlets by members of, 139ff.; decline of nonresistance in the 1850's, 223-39; Garrisonian nonresistants and the Civil War, 240, 241, 244, 246-58, 260; and Quakers, 271-79. *See also* American Peace Society; Ballou, Adin; Beckwith, Rev. George C.; Blanchard, Joshua P.; "come-outers"; conscientious objectors; Garrison, William Lloyd; Ladd, William; Michigan; Ohio; Quakers; Quincy, Edmund; Wright, Rev. Henry Clarke

New York Peace Society, 12-15, 20

Nicholson, Valentine, nonresistant, 134, 135

Non-Resistance Society, *see* New England Non-Resistance Society

Noyes, John Humphrey, founder of Oneida community, 149; influence of on William Lloyd Garrison, 87, 88

Oberlin, nonresistance society at, 127

Ohio, nonresistants in, 127

Oneida community, *see* Noyes, John Humphrey

Oneida Institute, student peace group at, 69

Paine, Tom, English deist and political pamphleteer, 97

Parker, Rev. Theodore, Unitarian minister and reformer, 190, 212, 234, 243

INDEX

Paul, Rev. Nathaniel, peace advocate in Canada, 28
Peabody, Rev. Andrew P., Unitarian minister and peace advocate, 56, 177, 183, 184, 194, 243, 244
Penn, William, English Quaker and founder of Pennsylvania, xii, 37
Pennsylvania, 44; Quakers in (pre-Revolutionary period), xii; Peace Society in, 29, 270
Phillips, Wendell, abolitionist, 96, 106, 115, 224, 248
Pilkington, Captain George, English army officer turned pacifist, 29
Pillsbury, Parker, Garrisonian militant, 123, 124, 132, 234, 244
Pratt, John Wesley, nonresistant conscientious objector in the Civil War, 253, 254
Progressive Society of Friends, *see* Quakers
Pugh, Sarah, Quaker nonresistant, 277

Quakers, 5, 62, 65, 89, 128, 147, 148, 185, 209, 215; in the pre-Revolutionary period, xi, xii; in the Revolution, xiii, impact of the Revolution on, 268; and the antebellum peace movement, 13, 18, 20, 24, 25, 28, 29, 32-34, 77, 78, 100-102, 122-25, 135, 153, 154, 175, 177, 268-79; in the antebellum period, 268-69; pro-war sentiments in the North in the Civil War, 246; in the Civil War, 264; between 1865 and 1914, 265; since the First World War, 267; Progressive Society of Friends, 276. See also American Peace Society; British West Indies; Canada; Garrison, William Lloyd; Irish Quakers; New England Non-Resistance Society; Pennsylvania; Rhode Island; Wright, Rev. Henry Clarke
Quincy, Edmund, Garrisonian nonresistant, 96, 100, 101, 103, 106, 107, 121, 124-26, 203, 211, 244, 271, 278; as editor of the *Non-Resistant*, 116-18, 133
Quincy, Josiah, president of Harvard University and father of Edmund, 106

Rhode Island, 38, 92, 135; Quakers in, xii; Peace Society in, 29, 185, 270
Richard, Rev. Henry, secretary of the London Peace Society, 245, 255-60

Robinson, Marius R., former Lane seminarist, 128
Rogers, Nathaniel Peabody, Garrisonian abolitionist and nonresistant, editor, 104, 123, 155
Rogers, Rev. R. V., peace advocate, 55

Scoble, John, English antimilitarist, 132
Scott, General Winfield, 191
Shakers, xiv, 24, 25, 128, 147
Smith, Gerrit, wealthy landowner, abolitionist and reformer, 89, 120, 121, 226, 227, 240, 241, 242; and "bleeding Kansas," 229-31
Smith, Nancy, wife of Gerrit, 120
South Carolina, 47, 50, 51, 88
Spofford, Jeremiah, Massachusetts politician, 150
Stearns, Charles, abolitionist and conscientious objector, 129, 166, 233, 234, 244
Stebbins, Rev. Rufus P., peace advocate, 66
Stirner, Max, German anarchist theoretician, 152
Stone, H. O., nonresistant, 137
Stone, Rev. Thomas T., peace advocate, 43, 44
Strong, Governor Caleb, 17
Sturge, Joseph, English Quaker and political reformer, 132, 208, 209
Sumner, Charles, politician, abolitionist, and peace advocate, 134, 212, 213; views on war, 187-90

Taber, Horace S., Shaker conscientious objector, 254
Tappan, Arthur and Lewis, antislavery advocates, 84, 85
Thompson, George, English antislavery advocate, 132
Thompson, James, conscientious objector in the Mexican War, 191
Thoreau, Henry David, essayist, 133, 134
Thurston, Rev. Stephen, peace advocate, 63
Tolstoy, Count Leo, 99, 271; and Adin Ballou, 167-69
Tukesbury, T. F., peace advocate, 259

Universal Peace Society, *see* Universal Peace Union
Universal Peace Union, 119, 262, 265. *See also* Love, Alfred H.

297

INDEX

Upham, Professor Thomas C., peace advocate, 60-66, 77, 193; and his *Manual of Peace*, 61-65, 204

Virginia, 84

Walker, Amasa, banker and peace advocate, 55, 56, 66, 77, 96, 97, 109, 170, 171, 173, 174, 177, 197, 199, 207, 212, 213; and the Civil War, 244, 245, 259
Warren County (Ohio) Peace Society, 29
Wayland, Rev. Francis, New England divine, 60, 61, 191, 204, 205
Webb, Richard D., Irish Quaker, 246
Weld, Angelina, *see* Grimké
Weld, Charles S.F., son of Angelina and Theodore, selective objector in the Civil War, 247
Weld, Theodore, antislavery advocate, 89, 107, 247
Western Peace Society, 128
West Indies, *see* British West Indies
Weston, Anne W., Garrisonian nonresistant, 103, 116, 120, 125, 232
Weston Sisters, 96, 223. *See also* Chapman, Maria W.
Whelpley, Rev. Samuel, peace advocate, 44, 45
Whipple, Charles K., Garrisonian nonresistant and abolitionist, 66, 103; writings on nonresistance, 139, 151, 152, 156-59, 161-66; and the Civil War, 244, 255-58
White, George F., Quaker minister, 275, 276

Whittier, John Greenleaf, Quaker poet and abolitionist, 115
Willard, Hon. Sidney, scholar and Massachusetts politician, 104
Wilson, Rev. Lewis G., pastor of Hopedale Unitarian parish, 167
Windham County (Conn.) Peace Society, 39, 44, 52, 53
Wood, Amos, conscientious objector, 129
Woolman, John, New Jersey Quaker and reformer, xii
Worcester County Peace Society, 207
Worcester, Rev. Leonard, brother of Noah Worcester, 92
Worcester, Rev. Noah, peace advocate, 22, 40, 41, 92, 122, 149, 173, 193, 269, 270; writings on peace, 23-26, 31, 32, 62; and leadership of Massachusetts Peace Society 27-37
Wright, Rev. Elizur, abolitionist, 115
Wright, Rev. Henry Clarke, abolitionist and nonresistant, 66, 157; and Quakers, 13, 277, 278; and American Peace Society, 70-72, 75, 86, 93, 170; early career of, 86-89; and New England Non-Resistance Society, 94-97, 103, 108, 109, 116-18, 120, 121, 126, 130-36; writings on nonresistance, 139, 140, 142, 143, 145-48, 150-54, 158; on nonresistance and slavery, 223, 231, 233, 237, 238, 240; and the Civil War, 244, 247, 263

Yale, Rev. Cyrus, peace advocate, 53, 54

Augsburg College
Lindell Library
Minneapolis, MN 55454